GENIUS OF PLACE

WRITING ABOUT BRITISH COLUMBIA

GENIUS OF PLACE

WRITING ABOUT BRITISH COLUMBIA

DAVID STOUCK and MYLER WILKINSON, editors

POLESTAR

BOOK PUBLISHERS

GENIUS OF PLACE
WRITING ABOUT BRITISH COLUMBIA

Polestar Book Publishers acknowledges the ongoing support of The Canada Council; the British Columbia Ministry of Small Business, Tourism and Culture through the BC Arts Council; and the Government of Canada through the Book Publishing Industry Development Program (BPIDP).

Cover image "The Raven and the First Men" by Bill Reid, Haida, 1980.
(Collection of the Museum of Anthropology, Vancouver, Canada.)
Photograph by Bill McLennan.
Cover design by Jim Brennan.
Map of British Columbia on pages 12 and 13 by Jim Brennan.
Printed and bound in Canada.

CANADIAN CATALOGUING IN PUBLICATION DATA
Main entry under title:
Genius of place
ISBN 1-896095-48-8
1. British Columbia. I. Stouck, David, 1940- II. Wilkinson, Myler, 1953-
FC3811.7.G46 2000   971.1   C99-911335-6
F1087.5.G46 2000

LIBRARY OF CONGRESS CATALOGUE NUMBER: 99-069294

POLESTAR BOOK PUBLISHERS
c/o Raincoast Books
8680 Cambie Street
Vancouver, British Columbia
Canada   V6P 6M9

5 4 3 2 1   00 01 02 04

To the memory of my cousins Mary Gunderson,
descendant of the first peoples,
and Nils Gunderson, pioneer to British Columbia.
— ds

And to C.S., who also loved the roads and waters of this province.
— mw

"January 10 [1811] … The view now before us was an ascent of deep snow, in all appearance the height of land between the Atlantic and Pacific oceans … My men were not at their ease, yet when night came they admired the brilliancy of the stars, and as one of them said, he thought he could almost touch them with his hand. As usual, when the fire was made, I set off to examine the country before us, and we found we had now to descend the west side of the mountains … Many reflections came on my mind; a new world was in a manner before me, and my object was to be at the Pacific Ocean before the month of August."

— David Thompson, *Journey to the Pacific*

"I have faith in this land — not in any political group … nor in any system of government — but in the land and the people on the land."

— Muriel Kitigawa, April 11, 1942

"The *genius loci* is an incalculable godling whose presence is felt by many people but certainly not by all … To some, the genius of a place is inimical; to some it is kind … My genius of place is a god of water. I have lived where two rivers flow together … and on the shore of the Pacific Ocean too — my home is there, and I shall go back."

— Ethel Wilson, *Hetty Dorval* (1947)

"You were constantly made aware of your own physical insignificance by the girth of the fir, the rearing bulk of the grizzly, the crash of the whale, the massive turmoil of the tide … Komogwa and Tsonogwa were the rightful geniuses of this place."

— Jonathan Raban, *Passage to Juneau* (1999)

GENIUS OF PLACE
WRITING ABOUT BRITISH COLUMBIA

ACKNOWLEDGEMENTS

ANTHOLOGISTS, if they are fortunate, begin as "innocent" readers. They start with their own pleasure in the text, and only later move on to concerns of historic and aesthetic judgement, questions of cultural significance. But in the back of one's mind, there is always the image of the reader, perhaps an ideal reader, who might if very fortunate join in a transparent dialogue with the writer.

Bringing together the travel writings, essays and historical documents which make up *Genius of Place* was an almost completely happy experience of reading for us. As we moved through the histories, and cultures, and imaginative landscapes of British Columbia, we were impressed by the conception and beauty of the writing and began to see this non-fiction anthology as a worthy successor to *West by Northwest,* our collection of British Columbia short stories. Many of the same principles of selection apply — the link between place and imagination, geographic conditions and cultural expression, but most importantly the quality of the writing itself.

Throughout our journey we were made aware not only of the fine writing which has grown out of an experience of place, but also of a community of readers who have made that writing possible over time. We want to thank some of those readers. To our publishers at Polestar, Michelle Benjamin and Lynn Henry, goes our sincere appreciation. The idea was Lynn's first, and Michelle and Lynn were confident enough to place it in our hands. The association has been a pleasure throughout.

Margaret Greenfield of Victoria has been one of our ideal readers. Born in England, but resident in Canada since the early 1950s, she has replicated in her life many of the journeys of this book. She read with a discerning and passionate eye much of the material we were collecting and helped us to make some final decisions for this volume. We are grateful to Janet Giltrow, University of British Columbia, and Nadeane Trowse, for drawing our attention to important texts for this collection; to Hilary Stewart who shared her knowledge of John Jewitt and Northwest Coast First Nations culture; to Gray Campbell, pioneer B.C. publisher, whose stories made the past real for us; to Wayne Elwood and Anita Mahoney for their suggestions and expertise; and to Michelle Steele and Paula McQuigan who welcomed us to "The House of All Sorts."

We also want to thank Alan Twigg for generously sharing his knowledge of B.C. writing; Don Gayton for his advice at an early stage of this project; Kim Kratky and Brian Gagnon, trusted friends who know where clouds can go and something about the people who follow them; and finally Doctors John Walton and Michael O'Brien who assured us we were on the right track.

For these readers, and others like them, this book was created.

David Stouck
Myler Wilkinson

INTRODUCTION

THE WRITINGS IN THIS VOLUME reveal a complex response to the landscapes of British Columbia — to that "genius of place" which novelist Ethel Wilson observed may be "kind" or "inimical," but nevertheless shapes how we understand ourselves in relation to where we live. From the first selection, John Jewitt's 1815 narrative of captivity among the Nootka (Nuu-chah-nulth), to the closing essay by Bill Richardson, who follows contemporary wanderers to the dark places of the self, one equation persists: landscape as a metaphor for human consciousness.

When we started reading for this companion volume to *West by Northwest*, we came to understand David Thompson as he reached height of land in the Rockies and looked down into a region which would later be named British Columbia. "A new world" lay before us, a terrain composed not so much of the land and sea which confronted early explorers and latter day travellers, but an uncharted land given complex form in the explorers' journals, narratives and experimental essays we were reading. We found, like Don Gayton, that our explorations took us to borders where the distinction between journalism, historical record, personal meditation and imaginative creation began to blur. The spectrum of our research led from travel writing, such as Simon Fraser's 1805 account of his voyage down the river which bears his name, to Paul Kane's portrayal in the late 1840s of a western landscape and people transformed by the eye of the artist. The written journey in British Columbia leads inevitably through another great artist, Emily Carr, who recorded in several different genres — travel writing, autobiography, animal stories and personal diaries — the life of the transplanted English settlers to this province and the life of its aboriginal peoples.

Beyond the earliest writers, there are others who have created a landscape of the mind that names the places we come from. We feel privileged to rediscover and bring the name of Helen Meilleur before the reading public again. Her account of life at Port Simpson's Hudson Bay trading post in the mid-nineteenth century and her own girlhood there in the early twentieth century is surely one of the most distinguished volumes of cultural history written about B.C. The genre of travel writing remains a constant in our collection, but the nature of the journey and the landscape changes with each generation. European exploration gives way to a rigorous form of tourism in the mid-nineteenth century narrative of Viscount and Cheadle, and then becomes escapist vacationing in the lyrically haunting travel sketches of Wylie Blanchet. For a contemporary traveller, it acquires an urgent social purpose in the environmental essays of a naturalist like Mark Hume.

How we should live in this province, with its still frontier possibilities, is a question posed by many of the writers in this volume — by Roderick Haig-Brown as the province's first vocal ecologist, and by Arthur Erickson as a theorist of human space within that environment. But equally urgent is the question of social justice, present from the outset in the tragedy of First Nations people, whose lands and cultures were taken away from them and in many places destroyed, and articulated in the letters of Muriel Kitigawa as she watched her Japanese-Canadian community disenfranchised during the Second World War. The lives of First Nations people are documented here by non-Native writers such as Norman Newton and Hugh Brody, but even more eloquently by First Nations speakers themselves — Chief Dan George and Ernie Crey. Travel, history and the themes of landscape and social justice all converge in the book's closing essay by Bill Richardson: "The Forest Primeval," which is both exuberant and tragic, and celebrates a quintessential figure in British Columbian history — the marginalized eccentric.

In all of these writers' works the "genius of place" has taken different forms. We might say it is first made visible in the oral literature of First Nations people — in such mythological figures as D'Sonoqua and Komogwa, who embody simultaneously what is terrifying and what is bountiful in the human response to land and sea. European explorers record these same mythologies, but frame them within their exhilaration at the abundance of a new world and also within their own anxieties of displacement. After the explorers, writer and painter Emily Carr eulogized this genius of place that she saw disappearing, but she articulated it in another way: in the voice of the lonely, dispossessed individual seeking a spiritual refuge by the sea or in the mountains and forests — a voice which later, in the cities, would become a cry for justice and belonging for all individuals. No British Columbia artist has more deeply understood the connection between inner terrain and external form.

The writings collected here then take us closer to the heart of a mystery — one of origins and intimate connections to a place we call British Columbia. Like George Vancouver — who "found" this land and, arguably, himself, in the optimistic spring of 1792 — we feel that "to describe the beauties of this region" has been "a very grateful task," and that each of the writers in this volume has taken up a small part of the collective task of discovering a "most lovely country."

REGIONS OF BRITISH COLUMBIA

See next page for map showing places of interest mentioned in this book.

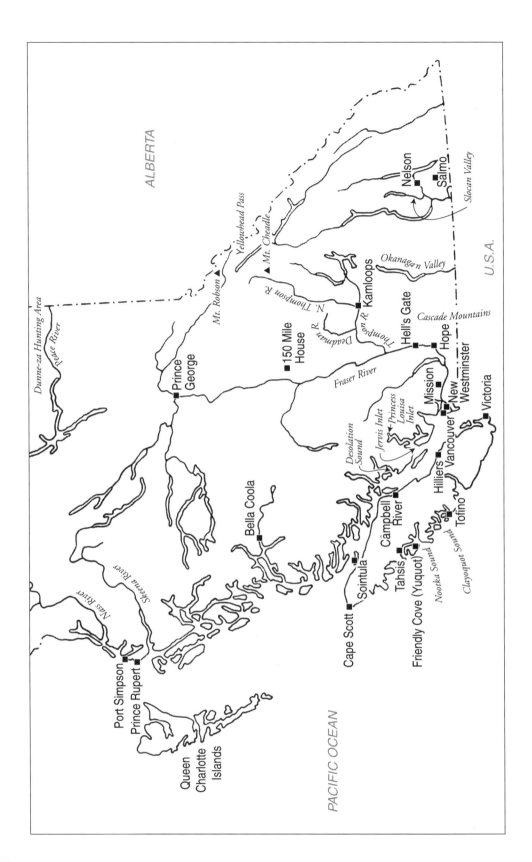

JOHN R. JEWITT (1783-1821)

The first European to record a view of any part of British Columbia was a Spanish missionary, Fray Juan Crespi, who accompanied the explorer Juan Perez on a voyage as far north as the Queen Charlotte Islands. From a British Columbia perspective his journal reads like a Genesis story: after a monotonous string of entries recording thick fogs and lowering skies, he describes the mist lifting and the sight of land in the distance on July 18, 1774. Two days later, a little farther north, a canoe comes out from shore, giving Europeans their first glimpse of the Haida people:

> While they were still some distance from the bark we heard them singing, and by the tone we knew them to be heathen, for they sang the same song as those from San Diego to Monterey. They drew near the frigate and we saw there were eight men and a boy in the canoe, seven of them rowing, while the eighth, who was painted, was standing up in the attitude of dancing, and throwing feathers on the water.

For three days the Spanish met and traded with the natives and Crespi was able to record something of their physical appearance and dress in his daybook. Then the ship turned south again. A translation of Crespi's journal for this voyage forms part of H. E. Bolton's *Fray Juan Crespi* (1927).

The first English narrative of European exploration along the coast of British Columbia is to be found in Captain James Cook's account of his third great voyage in 1778. Cook first approached the shore of western North America off the coast of Oregon, then proceeded in search of a northwest passage, arriving at a harbour he understood to be called Nootka. In a plain style he described the mountains and forests of Vancouver Island and his first sighting of the native people:

> We no sooner drew near the inlet than we found the coast to be inhabited, and three canoes came off to the ship. A person, who played the orator, wore the skin of some animal and held in each hand something which rattled as he kept shaking it. After tiring himself with his repeated exhortations, of which we did not understand a word, he was quiet, and then the others by turns said something. After the tumultuous noise had ceased, they lay at a little

distance from the ship and canoes began to come in greater number.
We had at one time thirty-two of them near the ship ... One canoe
was remarkable for a singular head, which had a bird's eye and bill,
of an enormous size, painted on it.

Cook then describes his trading with the local people, their appearance, clothing and houses, and also his interest in the sea otters, the fine skins of which were fetching such a high price by the Russians in China.

A third important record of coastal exploration is contained in *Voyage of Discovery to the North Pacific Ocean, 1790-95* (1801) written by Captain George Vancouver. Where Cook only touched at a few points along the coast from Oregon north to the Bering Strait, Vancouver methodically explored the coastline of British Columbia in detail, mapping, naming and describing water passages, islands and headlands. Vancouver's prose lacks drama, but the carefully observed details of his discoveries have provided later travellers along the coast, such as M. Wylie Blanchet and Jonathan Raban, much pleasure in following his path. The most interesting part of Vancouver's narrative describes his friendship with the Spanish explorer, Juan Francisco de la Bodega y Quadra, which has been interpreted in fictional form in George Bowering's novel, *Burning Water* (1980). It was a naturalist on board Quadra's ship, José Mariano Mozina, who wrote one of the best accounts of native life on the west coast of Vancouver Island, published in English in 1970 under the Spanish title *Noticias de Nutka*.

But the accounts of explorers and scientists cannot compare for dramatic interest to the *Narrative of Adventures and Sufferings of John R. Jewitt* (1815). Jewitt, with the editorial assistance of Richard Alsop of Connecticut, tells his story of more than two years of captivity by the "Nootka" people at Friendly Cove, beginning in March 1803. The story of his life with Maquina, the hereditary chief, is told in such a fast-paced and vigorous style that it has entertained readers for nearly two centuries, during which time the book has never been out of print. The version here has been abridged to half its original length (with Jewitt's references to "pine trees" corrected to "cedar trees"). Jewitt tells his own story and needs no introduction, but some notes on his life after the publication of his book are appended at the end of the narrative.

NARRATIVE OF ADVENTURES AND SUFFERINGS
OF JOHN R. JEWITT, CAPTIVE OF MAQUINA

I WAS BORN IN BOSTON, a considerable borough town in Lincoln-shire, in Great Britain, on the 21st of May 1783. My father, Edward Jewitt, was by trade a blacksmith and esteemed among the first in his line of business in that place. At the age of three years I had the misfortune to lose my mother, a most excellent woman. She died in child-bed, leaving an infant daughter who, with myself, and an elder brother by a former mar-riage of my father, constituted the whole of our family.

My father, who considered a good education as the greatest blessing he could bestow on his children, was very particular in paying every attention to us in that respect, always exhorting us to behave well, and endeavouring to impress on our minds the principles of virtue and morality. No expense in his power was spared to have us instructed in whatever might render us useful and respectable in society.

My brother who was four years older than myself and of a more hardy constitution, he destined for his own trade. To me he had resolved to give an education superior to that which is to be obtained in a common school, it being his intention that I should adopt one of the learned professions. Accordingly, at the age of twelve he took me from the school in which I had been taught the first rudiments of learning and placed me under the care of Mr. Moses, a celebrated teacher of an academy at Donnington about twenty miles from Boston, in order to be instructed in the Latin language and in some of the higher branches of the Mathematics. I there made considerable proficiency in writing, reading and arithmetic, and obtained a pretty good knowledge of navigation and of surveying. But my progress in Latin was slow, not only owing to the little inclination I felt for learning that language, but to a natural impediment in my speech which rendered it extremely difficult for me to pronounce it. In a short time, with my father's consent, I wholly relinquished the study.

The period of my stay at this place was the most happy of my life. My preceptor, Mr. Moses, was not only a learned but a virtuous, benevolent and amiable man, universally beloved by his pupils, who took delight in his instruction, and to whom he allowed every proper amusement that consisted with attention to their studies.

Among the scholars at this academy was one named Charles Rice, with whom I formed a particular intimacy which continued during the whole of my stay. He was my class and room mate and as the town he came from, Ashby, was more than sixty miles off, instead of returning home he used frequently during the vacation to go with me to Boston. Here he always met with a cordial welcome from my father who received me on these occasions with the greatest affection, apparently taking much pride in me. My friend in return used to take me with him to an uncle of his in Donnington, a very wealthy man who, having no children of his own, was very fond of his nephew. On his account I was always a welcome visitor at the house.

Thus passed away the two happiest years of my life. Then my father, thinking that I had received a sufficient education for the profession he intended for me, took me from school at Donnington in order to apprentice me to Doctor Mason, a surgeon of eminence at Reasby in the neighbourhood of the celebrated Sir Joseph Banks. With regret did I part from my school acquaintances, particularly my friend Rice, and returned home with my father on a short visit to my family preparatory to my intended apprenticeship. The disinclination I ever had felt for the profession my father wished me to pursue was still further increased on my return. When a child I was always fond of being in the shop among the workmen, endeavouring to imitate what I saw them do. This disposition so far increased after my leaving the academy that I could not bear to hear the least mention made of my being apprenticed to a surgeon.

I used so many entreaties with my father to persuade him to give up this plan and learn me his own trade that he at last consented. More fortunate would it probably have been for me had I gratified the wishes of this affectionate parent in adopting the profession he had chosen for me, than thus induced him to sacrifice them to mine. However it might have been, I was at length introduced into the shop. My natural turn of mind corresponding with the employment, I became in a short time uncommonly expert at the work to which I was set. I now felt myself well contented, pleased with my occupation and treated with much affection by my father and kindness by my step-mother, my father having once more entered the state of matrimony with a widow much younger than himself, who had been brought up in a superior manner, and was an amiable and sensible woman.

About a year after I had commenced this apprenticeship my father, finding that he could carry on his business to more advantage in Hull, removed thither with his family. An event of no little importance to me as it in a great measure influenced my future destiny. Hull being one of the best ports in England and a place of great trade, my father had there full employment for his numerous workmen, particularly in vessel work. This naturally leading me to an acquaintance with the sailors on board some of the ships, the many remarkable stories they told me of their voyages and adventures, and of the manners and customs of the nations they had seen, excited a strong wish in me to visit foreign countries, which was increased by my reading the voyages of Capt. Cook and some other celebrated navigators.

[After making the acquaintance of a Captain John Salter, in command of the American ship *Boston*, Jewitt persuaded his father to let him join the ship's crew as an armourer, to forge musket parts, daggers, knives and hatchets for trade with the Indians of the Northwest coast of America. He describes an emotional parting from his father, who exhorted his son to lead an honest, Christian life. From Hull the ship sailed to Brazil, then around Cape Horn.]

With a fair wind and easy weather from the 28th of December ... we pursued our voyage to the Northward until the 12th of March 1803, when we made Woody Point in Nootka Sound on the North West Coast of America. We immediately stood up the Sound for Nootka, where Captain Salter had determined to stop in order to supply the ship with wood and water before proceeding up the coast to trade. But in order to avoid the risk of any molestation or interruption to his men from the Indians while thus employed, he proceeded with the ship about five miles to the Northward of the village, which is situated on Friendly Cove, and sent out his chief mate with several of the crew in the boat to find a good place for anchoring her.

After sounding for some time they returned with information that they had discovered a secure place for anchorage on the Western side of an inlet or small bay at about half a mile from the coast, near a small island which protected it from the sea, and where there was plenty of wood and excellent water. The ship accordingly came to anchor in this place at twelve o'clock at night, in twelve fathom water, muddy bottom and so near the shore that to prevent the ship from winding we secured her by a hauser to the trees.

On the morning of the next day, the thirteenth, several of the natives came on board in a canoe from the village of Nootka with their king, called Maquina, who appeared much pleased on seeing us and, with great seeming cordiality, welcomed Capt. Salter and his officers to his country. As I had never before beheld a savage of any nation, it may readily be supposed that the novelty of their appearance, so different from any people that I had hitherto seen, excited in me strong feelings of surprise and curiosity. I was, however, particularly struck with the looks of their king who was a man of a dignified aspect, about six feet in height and extremely strait and well-proportioned.

His features were in general good and his face was rendered remarkable by a large Roman nose, a very uncommon form of feature among these people. His complexion was of a dark copper hue, though his face, legs and arms were on this occasion so covered with red paint that their natural colour could scarcely be perceived. His eyebrows were painted black in two broad stripes like a new moon, and his long black hair which shone with oil, was fastened in a bunch on the top of his head and strewed or powdered all over with white down [of birds], which gave him a most curious and extraordinary appearance.

He was dressed in a large mantle, or cloak of the black sea otter skin, which reached to his knees and was fastened around his middle by a broad belt of the cloth of the country wrought, or painted, with figures of several colours. This dress was by no means unbecoming, but on the contrary had an air of savage magnificence. His men were habited in mantles of the same cloth, which is made from the bark of the cedar tree, and has some resemblance to straw matting; these are nearly square and have two holes in the upper part large enough to admit the arms. They reach as low as the knees and are fastened around their bodies with a belt about four inches broad of the same cloth.

From his having frequently visited the English and American ships that traded to the coast, Maquina had learned the signification of a number of English words, and in general could make himself pretty well understood by us in our own language. He was always the first to go on board such ships as came to Nootka, which he was much pleased in visiting, even when he had no trade to offer, as he almost always received some small present and was in general extremely well-treated by the commanders. He remained on board of us for some time during which the Captain took him into the cabin and treated him with a glass of rum; these people being very fond of distilled spirits, and some biscuit and molasses which they prefer to any kind of food that we can offer them.

Captain Salter invited Maquina and his chiefs to dine with him, and it was curious to see how these people seat themselves with their feet under them crossed like Turks. They cannot endure the taste of salt, and the only thing they would eat with us was the ship bread which they were very fond of, especially when dipped in molasses. They had also a great liking for tea and coffee when well-sweetened.

As iron weapons and tools of almost every kind are in much request among them, whenever they came on board they were always very attentive to me, crowding around me at the forge as if to see in what manner I did my work, and in this way became quite familiar, a circumstance, as will be seen in the end, of great importance to me.

On the 20th we were nearly ready for our departure, having taken in what wood and water we were in want of. The next day Maquina came on board with nine pair of wild ducks as a present, at the same time he brought with him the gun, one of the locks of which he had broken, telling the Captain that it was *peshak*; that is, bad. Capt. Salter was very much offended at this observation, and considering it as a mark of contempt for his present, he called the king a liar, adding other opprobrious terms, and taking the gun from him tossed it indignantly into the cabin and calling me to him said, "John, this fellow has broken this beautiful fowling piece, see if you can mend it."

On examining it I told him that it could be done. As I have already observed, Maquina knew a number of English words and unfortunately understood but too well the meaning of the reproachful terms that the Captain addressed to him. He said not a word in reply but his countenance sufficiently expressed the rage he felt, though he exerted himself to suppress it. I observed him, while the Captain was speaking, repeatedly put his hand to his throat and rub it upon his bosom, which he afterwards told me was to keep down his heart which was rising into his throat and choaking him. He soon after went on shore with his men, evidently much discomposed.

On the morning of the 22nd the natives came off to us as usual with salmon, and remained on board. About noon Maquina came along side with a considerable number of his chiefs and men in their canoes who, after going through the customary examination, were admitted into the ship. He had a whistle in his hand and over his face a very ugly mask of wood representing the head of some wild beast, appeared to be remarkably good humoured and gay, and whilst his people sung and capered about the deck, entertaining us with a variety of antic tricks and gestures, he blew his whistle to a kind of tune which seemed to regulate their motions. As Capt. Salter was walking on the quarter deck amusing himself with their dancing, the king came up to him and enquired when he intended to go to sea? He answered, "tomorrow."

Maquina then said, "you love salmon — much in Friendly Cove, why not go then and catch some?"

The Captain thought that it would be very desirable to have a good supply of these fish for the voyage. On consulting with Mr. Delouisa it was agreed to send part of the crew on shore after dinner with the seine in order to procure a quantity. Maquina and his chiefs stayed and dined on board. After dinner the chief mate went off with nine men in the jolly boat and yawl to fish at Friendly Cove, having set the steward on shore at our watering place to wash the Captain's clothes. Shortly after the departure of the boats I went down to my vice-bench in the steerage, where I was employed in cleaning muskets.

I had not been there more than an hour when I heard the men hoisting in the long boat, which in a few minutes after, was succeeded by a great bustle and confusion on deck. I immediately ran up the steerage stairs, but scarcely was my head above deck when I was caught by the hair by one of the savages and lifted from my feet. Fortunately for me, my hair being short and the ribbon with which it was tied slipping, I fell from his hold into the steerage.

As I was falling he struck at me with an axe which cut a deep gash in my forehead and penetrated the skull. But in consequence of his losing his hold I luckily escaped the full force of the blow which, otherwise, would have cleft my head in two. I fell, stunned and senseless upon the floor. How long I continued in this situation I know not, but on recovering my senses the first thing that I did was to try to get up. But so weak was I from the loss of blood that I fainted and fell. I was, however, soon recalled to my recollection by three loud shouts or yells from the savages, which convinced me that they had got possession of the ship.

Having at length sufficiently recovered my senses to look around me after wiping the blood from my eyes, I saw that the hatch of the steerage was shut. This was done, as I afterwards discovered, by order of Maquina who, on seeing the savage strike at me with the axe, told him not to hurt me, for that I was the armourer, and would be useful to them in repairing their arms; while at the same time to prevent any of his men from injuring me he had the hatch closed. But to me this circumstance wore a very different appearance. I thought that these barbarians had only prolonged my life in order to deprive me of it by the most cruel tortures.

I remained in this horrid state of suspense for a very long time. At length the hatch was opened and Maquina, calling me by name, ordered me to come up. I groped my way up as well as I was able, being almost blinded with the blood that flowed from my wound, and so weak as with difficulty to walk.

The king, on perceiving my situation, ordered one of his men to bring a pot of water to wash the blood from my face, which having done, I was able to see distinctly with one of my eyes. The other was so swollen from my wounds that it was closed. But what a terrific spectacle met my eyes. Six naked savages, standing in a circle around me, covered with the blood of my murdered comrades, with their daggers uplifted in their hands, prepared to strike. I now thought my last moment had come, and recommended my soul to my Maker.

The king who, as I have already observed, knew enough of English to make himself understood, entered the circle, and placing himself before me, addressed me nearly in the following words: "John — I speak — you no say no — You say no — daggers come!"

He then asked me if I would be his slave during my life — If I would fight for him in his battles — If I would repair his muskets and make daggers and knives for him — with several other questions, to all of which I was careful to answer, yes. He then told me that he would spare my life and ordered me to kiss his hands and feet to show my submission to him, which I did. In the mean time his people were very clamorous to have me put to death so that there should be none of us left to tell our story to our countrymen and prevent them from coming to trade with them. But the king, in the most determined manner, opposed their wishes and to his favour am I wholly indebted for my being yet among the living.

As I was busy at work at the time of the attack, I was without my coat. What with the coldness of the weather, my feebleness from loss of blood, the pain of my wound and the extreme agitation and terror that I still felt, I shook like a leaf, which the king observing, went into the cabin. Bringing up a great coat that belonged to the Captain, he threw it over my shoulders, telling me to drink some rum from a bottle which he handed me at the same time, giving me to understand that it would be good for me and keep me from trembling as I did.

I took a draught of it, after which, taking me by the hand, he led me to the quarter deck where the most horrid sight presented itself that ever my eyes witnessed — the heads of our unfortunate Captain and his crew, to the number of twenty-five, were all arranged in a line. Maquina, ordering one of his people to bring a head, asked me whose it was. I answered, the Captain's.

In like manner the others were showed me. I told him the names, excepting a few that were so horribly mangled that I was not able to recognize them. I now discovered that all our unfortunate crew had been massacred. After getting possession of the ship, the savages had broke open the arm chest and magazine, and supplying themselves with ammunition and arms, sent a party on shore to attack our men who had gone thither to fish, and being joined by numbers from the village, without difficulty overpowered and murdered them, and cutting off their heads, brought them on board, after throwing their bodies into the sea.

On looking upon the deck I saw it entirely covered with the blood of my poor comrades, whose throats had been cut with their own jack-knives, the savages having seized the opportunity while they were busy in hoisting in the boat to grapple with them and overpower them by their numbers. In the scuffle the Captain was thrown overboard and despatched by those in the canoes, who immediately cut off his head. What I felt on this occasion may be more readily conceived than expressed.

After I had answered his questions, Maquina took my silk handkerchief from my neck and bound it around my head, placing over the wound a leaf of tobacco, of which we had a quantity on board. This was done at my desire, as I had often found from personal experience the benefit of this application to cuts.

Maquina then ordered me to get the ship under weigh for Friendly Cove. This I did by cutting the cables and sending some of the natives aloft to loose the sails, which they performed in a very bungling manner. But they succeeded so far in loosing the jib and topsails that, with the advantage of a fair wind, I succeeded in getting the ship into the Cove. Here, by order of the king, I ran her ashore on a sandy beach at eight o'clock at night.

We were received by the inhabitants of the village, men, women and children, with loud shouts of joy, and a most horrible drumming with sticks upon the roofs and sides of their houses, in which they had also stuck a great number of lighted torches to welcome their king's return and congratulate him on the success of his enterprize.

Maquina then took me on shore to his house, which was very large and filled with people. Here I was received with much kindness by the women, particularly those belonging to the king, who had no less than nine wives, all of whom came around me expressing much sympathy for my misfortune, gently stroking and patting my head in an encouraging and soothing manner with words expressive of condolence. How sweet is compassion even from savages? Those who have been in a similar situation can alone truly appreciate its value.

In the mean time all the warriors of the tribe, to the number of five hundred, had assembled at the king's house to rejoice for their success. They exulted greatly in having taken our ship, and each one boasted of his own particular exploits in killing our men. But they were in general much dissatisfied with my having been suffered to live, and were very urgent with Maquina to deliver me to them to be put to death. He obstinately refused, telling them that he had promised me my life and would not break his word; and that besides, I knew how to repair and to make arms and should be of great use to them.

The king then seated me by him and ordered his women to bring him something to eat. They sat before him some dried clams and train oil [rendered from whale blubber], of which he ate very heartily and encouraged me to follow his example, telling me to eat much and take a great deal of oil which would make me strong and fat. Notwithstanding his praise of this new kind of food, I felt no disposition to indulge in it, both the smell and taste being loathsome to me; and had it been otherwise, such was the pain I endured, the agitation of my mind, and the gloominess of my reflections, that I should have felt very little inclination for eating.

Not satisfied with his first refusal to deliver me up to them, the people again became clamorous that Maquina should consent to my being killed, saying that not one of us ought to be left alive to give information to others of our countrymen and prevent them from coming to trade or induce them to revenge the destruction of our ship. They at length became so boisterous that he caught up a large club in a passion and drove them all out of the house. During this scene a son of the king, of about eleven years old, attracted no doubt by the singularity of my appearance, came up to me. I caressed him. He returned my attentions with much apparent pleasure and, considering this as a fortunate opportunity to gain the good will of the father, I took the child on my knee. Cutting the metal buttons from off the coat I had on, I tied them around his neck. At this he was highly delighted and became so much attached to me that he would not quit me.

The king appeared much pleased with my attention to his son, and telling me that it was time to go to sleep, directed me to lie with his son next to him, as he was afraid lest some of his people would come while he was asleep and kill me with their daggers. I lay down as he ordered me, but neither the state of my mind nor the pain I felt would allow me to sleep.

About midnight I was greatly alarmed by the approach of one of the natives who came to give information to the king that there was one of the white men alive, who had knocked him down as he went on board the ship at night. This Maquina communicated to me, giving me to understand that as soon as the sun rose he should kill him. I endeavoured to persuade him to spare his life, but he bade me be silent and go to sleep.

As I was thinking of some plan for his preservation, it all at once came into my mind that this man was probably the sail-maker of the ship, named Thompson. I had not seen his head among those on deck, and knew that he was below at work upon the sails not long before the attack. The more I thought of it the more probable it appeared to me. As Thompson was a man nearly forty years of age and had an old look, I conceived it would be easy to make him pass for my father, and by this means prevail on Maquina to spare his life. Towards morning I fell into a doze, but was awakened with the first beams of the sun by the king, who told me that he was going to kill the man who was on board the ship, and ordered me to accompany him. I rose and followed him, leading with me the young prince his son.

On coming to the beach I found all the men of the tribe assembled. The king addressed them, saying that one of the white men had been found alive on board the ship, and requested their opinion as to saving his life or putting him to death. They were unanimously for death. This determination he made known to me. Having arranged my plan, I asked him, pointing to the boy whom I still held by the hand, if he loved his son. He answered that he did. I then asked the child if he loved his father, and on replying in the affirmative, I said and "I also love mine."

I then threw myself on my knees at Maquina's feet, and implored him with tears in my eyes to spare my father's life, if the man on board should prove to be him, telling him that if he killed my father it was my wish that he should kill me too, and that if he did not I would kill myself, and that he would thus lose my services. Whereas, by sparing my father's life he would preserve mine, which would be of great advantage to him by my repairing and making arms for him.

Maquina appeared moved by my entreaties and promised not to put the man to death if he should be my father. He then explained to his people what I had said, and ordered me to go on board and tell the man to come on shore.

[As Jewitt supposed, Thompson had hidden himself in the ship's hold; he readily agreed to Jewitt's plan that they should pass for "father" and "son," and the two presented themselves to the Nootka chief. Maquina lived up to his promise, spared Thompson's life and set him to making sails for his canoes. Shortly thereafter, Jewitt boarded the ship and brought away a blank account book in which he recorded his experiences; he also rescued a bible and prayer book. These three items provided him with great consolation. Soon afterwards, the ship was accidently set on fire and destroyed.]

After returning thanks to that merciful Being who had in so wonderful a manner softened the hearts of the savages in my favour, I had determined from the first of my capture to adopt a conciliating conduct towards them and conform myself, as far as was in my power, to their customs and mode of thinking, trusting that the same divine goodness that had rescued me from death would not always suffer me to languish in captivity among these heathen. With this view I sought to gain their good will by always endeavouring to assume a cheerfull countenance, appearing pleased with their sports and buffoon tricks, making little ornaments for the wives and children of the chiefs, by which means I became quite a favourite with them, and fish hooks, daggers etc for themselves. As a farther recommendation to their favour and what might eventually prove of the utmost importance to us, I resolved to learn their language, which in the course of a few months residence I so far succeeded in acquiring as to be able in general to make myself well understood. I likewise tried to persuade Thompson to learn it as what might prove necessary to him. But he refused, saying that he hated both them and their cursed lingo and would have nothing to do with it.

By pursuing this conciliatory plan, so far did I gain the good will of the savages, particularly the chiefs, that I scarcely ever failed experiencing kind treatment from them, and was received with a smile of welcome at their houses where I was always sure of having something given me to eat, whenever they had it. Many a good meal have I had from them when they themselves were short of provisions and suffering for the want of them. And it was a common practice with me when we had nothing to eat at home, which happened not unfrequently during my stay among them, to go around the village, and on noticing a smoke from any of the houses, which denoted that they were cooking, enter in without ceremony and ask them for something, which I was never refused. Few nations, indeed, are there, so very rude and unfeeling, whom constant mild treatment and an attention to please will not mollify and obtain from them some return of kind attention. This, the treatment I received from these people may exemplify, for not numerous, even among those calling themselves civilized, are there instances to be found of persons depriving themselves of food to give it to a stranger, whatever may be his merits.

Their mode of living is very simple — their food consisting almost wholly of fish, or fish spawn fresh or dried, the blubber of the whale, seal, or seacow, muscles, clams and berries of various kinds; all of which are eaten with a profusion of train oil for sauce, not excepting even the most delicate fruit, as strawberries and raspberries. With so little variety in their food, no great [variety] can be expected in their cookery. Of this, indeed, they may be said to know but two methods, viz. by boiling and steaming. Even the latter is not very frequently practised by them. Their mode of boiling is as follows: into one of their tubs they pour water sufficient to cook the quantity of provision wanted. A number of heated stones are then put in to make it boil. The salmon or other fish are put in without any other preparation than sometimes cutting off the heads, tails and fins, the boiling in the mean time being kept up by the application of the hot stones, after which it is left to cook until the whole is nearly reduced to one mass. It is then taken out and distributed in the trays. In a similar manner they cook their blubber and spawn, smoked or dried fish, and in fine, almost every thing they eat, nothing going down with them like broth.

When they cook their fish by steam, which are usually the heads, tails and fins of the salmon, cod and halibut, a large fire is kindled, upon which they place a bed of stones which, when the wood is burnt down, becomes perfectly heated. Layers of green leaves or boughs are then placed upon the stones, and the fish, clams etc. being laid upon them, water is poured over them and the whole closely covered with mats to keep in the steam. This is much the best mode of cooking, and clams and muscles done in this manner are really excellent. These, as I have said, may be considered as their only kinds of cookery, though I have in a very few instances known them dress the roe or spawn of the salmon and the herring, when first taken, in a different manner. This was by roasting them, the former being supported between two split pieces of cedar, and the other having a sharp stick run through it, with one end fixed in the ground. Sprats [herring] are also roasted by them in this way, a number being spitted on one stick, and this kind of food, with a little salt, would be found no contemptible eating even to a European.

At their meals they seat themselves upon the ground with their feet curled up under them, around their trays, which are generally about three feet long by one broad, and from six to eight inches deep. In eating they make use of nothing but their fingers, except for the soup or oil which they lade out with clam shells. Around one of these trays from four to six persons will seat themselves, constantly dipping in their fingers or clam shells, one after the other.

The king and chiefs alone have separate trays from which no one is permitted to eat with them, except the queen, or principal wife of the chief. Whenever the king or one of the chiefs wishes to distinguish any of his people with a special mark of favour on these occasions, he calls him and gives him some of the choice bits from his tray. The slaves eat at the same time and of the same provisions, faring in this respect as well as their masters, being seated with the family and only feeding from separate trays.

Whenever a feast is given by the king or any of the chiefs, there is a person who acts as a master of ceremonies, and whose business it is to receive the guests as they enter the house and point out to them their respective seats, which is regulated with great punctiliousness as regards rank; the king occupying the highest or the seat of honour, his son or brother sitting next him, and so on with the chiefs according to their quality; the private persons belonging to the same family being always placed together to prevent any confusion. The women are seldom invited to their feasts, and only at those times when a general invitation is given to the village.

The natives of Nootka appear to have but little inclination for the chase, though some of them were expert marksmen, and used sometimes to shoot ducks and geese, but the seal and the sea otter form the principal objects of their hunting, particularly the latter. Of this animal, so much noted for its valuable skin, the following description may not be uninteresting: The sea otter is nearly five feet in length, exclusive of the tail, which is about twelve inches, and is very thick and broad where it joins the body, but gradually tapers to the end, which is tipped with white. The colour of the rest is a shining silky black, with the exception of a broad white stripe on the top of the head. Nothing can be more beautiful than one of these animals when seen swimming, especially when on the lookout for any object. At such times it raises its head quite above the surface, and the contrast between the shining black and the white, together with its sharp ears and a long tuft of hair rising from the middle of its forehead, which look like three small horns, render it quite a novel and attractive object. They are in general very tame, and will permit a canoe or boat to approach very near before they dive. I was told, however, that they are become much more shy since they have been accustomed to shoot them with muskets, than when they used only arrows. The skin is held in great estimation in China, more especially that of the tail, the fur of which is finer and closer set than that on the body. This is always cut off and sold separately by the natives. The value of a skin is determined by its size, that being considered as a prime skin which will reach, in length, from a man's chin to his feet.

The food of the sea otter is fish, which he is very dexterous in taking, being an excellent swimmer, with feet webbed like those of a goose. They appear to be wholly confined to the sea coast, at least to the salt water. They have usually three or four young at a time, but I know not how often they breed, nor in what places they deposit their young, though I have frequently seen them swimming around the mother when no larger than rats. The flesh is eaten by the natives, cooked in their usual mode by boiling, and is far preferable to that of the seal of which they make much account.

But if not great hunters, there are few people more expert in fishing. Their lines are generally made from the sinew of the whale, and are extremely strong. For the hook, they usually make use of a straight piece of hard wood, in the lower part of which is inserted and well-secured, with thread or whale sinew, a bit of bone made very sharp at the point and bearded; but I used to make for them hooks from iron, which they preferred, not only as being less liable to break, but more certain of securing the fish. Cod, halibut and other seafish were not only caught by them with hooks, but even salmon. To take this latter fish, they practise the following method: One person seats himself in a small canoe, and baiting his hook with a sprat, which they are always careful to procure as fresh as possible, fastens his line to the handle of the paddle. This, as he plies it in the water, keeps the fish in constant motion, so as to give it the appearance of life, which the salmon seeing, leaps at it and is instantly hooked, and by a sudden and dexterous motion of the paddle, drawn on board. I have known some of the natives to take no less than eight to ten salmon of a morning in this manner, and have seen from twenty to thirty canoes at a time in Friendly Cove thus employed.

They are likewise little less skilful in taking the whale. This they kill with a kind of javelin or harpoon, thus constructed and fitted. The barbs are formed of bone which are sharpened on the outer side and hollowed within for the purpose of forming a socket for the staff. These are then secured firmly together with whale sinew, the point being fitted so as to receive a piece of muscle shell which is ground to a very sharp edge, and secured in its place by means of turpentine. To this head, or prong, is fastened a strong line of whale sinew about nine feet in length, to the end of which is tied a bark rope from fifty to sixty fathoms long, having from twenty to thirty seal skin floats, or buoys, attached to it at certain intervals in order to check the motion of the whale and obstruct his diving. In the socket of the harpoon a staff, or pole of about ten feet long, gradually tapering from the middle to each end, is placed. This the harpooner holds in his hand in order to strike the whale, and immediately detaches it as soon as the fish is struck. The whale is considered as the king's fish, and no other person, when he is present, is permitted to touch him until the royal harpoon has first drawn his blood, however near he may approach. It would be considered almost as sacrilege for any of the common people to strike a whale, before he is killed, particularly if any of the chiefs should be present. They also kill the porpoise and sea cow [sea lion] with harpoons, but this inferior game is not interdicted the lower class.

With regard to their canoes, some of the handsomest to be found on the whole coast are made at Nootka, though very fine ones are brought by the Wickanninish and the Kla-iz-zarts, who have them more highly ornamented. They are of all sizes, from such as are capable of holding only one person to their largest war canoes which will carry forty men, and are extremely light. Of these, the largest of any that I ever saw was one belonging to Maquina, which I measured and found to be forty-two feet six inches in length at the bottom, and forty-six feet from stem to stern. These are made of cedar hollowed out from a tree with their chisels solely, which are about three inches broad and six in length, and set into a handle of very hard wood. This instrument was formerly made of flint or some hard stone ground down to as sharp an edge as possible, but since they have learned the use of iron, they have almost all of them of that metal. Instead of a mallet for striking this chisel, they make use of a smooth round stone, which they hold in the palm of the hand. With this same awkward instrument they not only excavate their canoes and trays and smooth their plank, but cut down such trees as they want, either for building, fuel, or other purposes, a labour mostly done by their slaves.

The falling of trees as practised by them is a slow and most tedious process, three of them being generally from two to three days in cutting down a large one. Yet so attached were they to their own method, that notwithstanding they saw Thompson frequently with one of our axes, of which there was a number saved, fall a tree in less time than they could have gone round it with their chisels, still they could not be persuaded to make use of them.

After hollowing out their canoes, which they do very neatly, they fashion the outside, and slightly burn it for the purpose of removing any splinters or small points that might obstruct its passage through the water, after which they rub it over thoroughly, with rushes or coarse mats, in order to smooth it, which not only renders it almost as smooth as glass, but forms a better security for it from the weather. This operation of burning and rubbing down the bottoms of their canoes is practised as often as they acquire any considerable degree of roughness from use. The outside, by this means becomes quite black, and to complete their work they paint the inside a bright red with ochre or some other similar substance. The prows and sterns are almost always ornamented with figures of ducks or some other kind of bird, the former being so fashioned as to represent the head and the latter the tail. These are separate pieces from the canoe, and are fastened to it with small flexible twigs or bark cord.

Some of these canoes, particularly those employed in whaling, which will hold about ten men, are ornamented within about two inches below the gunwale with two parallel lines on each side of very small white shells running fore and aft, which has a very pretty effect. Their war canoes have no ornament of this kind but are painted on the outside with figures in white chalk representing eagles, whales, human heads etc. They are very dexterous in the use of their paddles, which are very neatly wrought, and are five feet long with a short handle and a blade seven inches broad in the middle tapering to a sharp point. With these they will make a canoe skim very swiftly on the water with scarcely any noise, while they keep time to the stroke of the paddle with their songs.

Their tunes are generally soft and plaintive, and though not possessing great variety, are not deficient in harmony. Their singing is generally accompanied with several rude kinds of instrumental music; among the most prominent of which is a kind of drum. This is nothing more than a long plank hollowed out on the under side and made quite thin, which is beat upon by a stick of about a foot long and renders a sound not unlike beating on the head of an empty cask, but much louder. But the two most favourite instruments are the rattle and the pipe, or whistle. These are, however, only used by the king, the chiefs, or some particular persons. The former is made of dried sealskin, so as to represent a fish, and is filled with a number of small smooth pebbles, has a short handle and is painted red. The whistle is made of bone, generally the leg of a deer. It is short but emits a very shrill sound. They have likewise another kind of music, which they make use of in dancing, in the manner of castanets. This is produced by a number of muscle, or cockle, shells tied together and shaken to a kind of tune, which is accompanied with the voice.

But to return to our unhappy situation. Though my comrade and myself fared as well, and even better than we could have expected among these people, considering their customs and mode of living, yet our fears lest no ship would come to our release and that we should never more behold a Christian country, were to us a source of constant pain. Our principal consolation in this gloomy state was to go on Sundays, whenever the weather would permit, to the borders of a fresh water pond, about a mile from the village. After bathing and putting on clean clothes we would seat ourselves under the shade of a beautiful cedar, while I read some chapters in the Bible, and the prayers appointed by our Church for the day, ending our devotions with a fervent prayer to the Almighty that He would deign still to watch over and preserve our lives, rescue us from the hands of the savages, and permit us once more to behold a Christian land. In this manner were the greater part of our Sundays passed at Nootka. I felt grateful to heaven, that amidst our other sufferings, we were at least allowed the pleasure of offering up our devotions unmolested, for Maquina, on my explaining to him as well as was in my power the reason of our thus retiring at this time, far from objecting, readily consented to it.

The pond was small, not more than a quarter of a mile in breadth and of no great length, the water being very clear, though not of great depth, and bordered by a beautiful forest of cedar, fir, elm and beach, free from bushes and underwood — a most delightful retreat, which was rendered still more attractive by a great number of birds that frequented it, particularly the humming bird. Thither we used to go to wash our clothes, and felt secure from any intrusion from the natives as they rarely visited it except for the purpose of cleansing themselves of their paint.

In July we at length thought that the hope of delivery we had so long anxiously indulged was on the point of being gratified. A ship appeared in the offing, but alas, our fond hopes vanished almost as soon as formed. Instead of standing in for the shore she passed to the northward and soon disappeared.

I shall not attempt to describe our disappointment — my heart sunk within me, and I felt as though it was my destiny never more to behold a Christian face. Four days after there occurred a tremendous storm of thunder and lightning, during which the natives manifest great alarm and terror, the whole tribe hurrying to Maquina's house. Here, instead of keeping within, they seated themselves on the roof amid the severest of the tempest, drumming upon the boards, and looking up to heaven, while the king beat the long hollow plank, singing, and as he afterwards told me, begging *Quahootze*, the name they gave to God, not to kill them, in which he was accompanied by the whole tribe. This singing and drumming was continued until the storm abated.

On the third of September the whole tribe quitted Nootka, according to their constant practice, in order to pass the autumn and winter at Tashees [Tahsis] and Cooptee, the latter lying about thirty miles up the Sound in a deep bay, the navigation of which is very dangerous from the great number of reefs and rocks with which it abounds. On these occasions every thing is taken with them, even the planks of their houses, in order to cover their new dwellings. To a European, such a removal exhibits a scene quite novel and strange: canoes piled up with boards and boxes, and filled with men, women and children of all ranks and sizes, making the air resound with their cries and songs. At these times, as well as when they have occasion to go some distance from their houses, the infants are usually suspended across the mother's shoulders in a kind of cradle or hammock, formed of bark, of about six inches in depth, and of the length of the child, by means of a leather band inserted through loops on its edges. This they also keep them in when at home in order to preserve them in a straight position, and prevent any distortion of the limbs, most probably a principal cause of these people being so seldom deformed or crooked.

The long boat of our ship having been repaired and furnished with a sail by Thompson, Maquina gave us the direction of it, we being better acquainted with managing it than his people. After loading her as deep as she could swim, we proceeded in company with them to the north, quitting Nootka with heavy hearts, as we could entertain no hopes of release until our return, no ships ever coming to that part of the coast. Passing Cooptee, which is situated on the southern bank, just within the mouth of a small river flowing from the east in a narrow valley at the foot of a mountain, we proceeded about fifteen miles up this stream to Tashees, between a range of lofty hills on each side, which extend a great distance inland, and are covered with the finest forest trees of the country. Immediately on our arrival we all went to work very diligently in covering the houses with the planks we had brought, the frames being ready erected, these people never pretending to remove the timber. In a very short time the work was completed, and we were established in our new residence.

Tashees is pleasantly situated and in a most secure position from the winter storms, in a small vale or hollow on the south shore, at the foot of a mountain. The spot on which it stands is level, and the soil very fine, the country in its vicinity abounding with the most romantic views, charmingly diversified, and fine streams of water falling in beautiful cascades from the mountains. The river at this place is about twenty rods in width, and in its deepest part from nine to twelve feet. This village is the extreme point of navigation as, immediately beyond, the river becomes much more shallow, and is broken into rapids and falls. The houses here are placed in a line like those at Nootka, but closer together; the situation being more confined they are also smaller, in consequence of which we were much crowded, and incommoded for room.

The principal object in coming to this place is the facility it affords these people of providing their winter stock of provisions, which consists principally of salmon, and the spawn of that fish; to which may be added herring and sprats, and herring spawn. The latter, however, is always procured by them at Nootka previous to their quitting it. At the seasons of spawning, which are early in the spring and the last of August, they collect a great quantity of hemlock branches, which they place in different parts of the Cove at the depth of about ten feet and secure them by means of heavy stones. On these the herring deposit their spawn in immense quantities. The bushes are then taken up, the spawn stripped from the branches, and after being washed and freed from the leaves by the women, is dried and put up in baskets for use. It is considered as their greatest delicacy, and eaten both cooked and raw: in the former case, being boiled and eaten with train oil, and in the latter, mixed up with cold water alone.

In many respects, our situation was less pleasant here than at Nootka. We were more incommoded for room, the houses not being so spacious, nor so well arranged, and as it was colder, we were compelled to be much more within doors. We, however, did not neglect on Sundays, when the weather would admit, to retire into the woods, and by the side of some stream, after bathing, return our thanks to God for preserving us, and offer up to him our customary devotions. I was, however, very apprehensive, soon after our arrival at this place, that I should be deprived of the satisfaction of keeping my journal. Maquina, one day observing me writing in it, enquired of me what I was doing. When I endeavoured to explain it, by telling him that I was keeping an account of the weather, he said it was not so, and that I was speaking bad about him and telling how he had taken our ship and killed the crew, so as to inform my countrymen, and that if he ever saw me writing in it again, he would throw it into the fire. I was much rejoiced that he did no more than threaten, and became very cautious afterwards not to let him see me write.

On the morning of the 13th of December commenced what appeared to us a most singular farce. Apparently without any previous notice, Maquina discharged a pistol close to his son's ear, who immediately fell down as if killed, upon which all the women of the house set up a most lamentable cry, tearing handfuls of hair from their heads and exclaiming that the prince was dead. At the same time a great number of the inhabitants rushed into the house armed with their daggers, muskets etc., enquiring the cause of their outcry. These were immediately followed by two others dressed in wolf skins, with masks over their faces representing the head of that animal. The latter came in on their hands and feet in the manner of a beast, and taking up the prince carried him off upon their backs, retiring in the same manner they entered. We saw nothing more of the ceremony, as Maquina came to us, and giving us a quantity of dried provision, ordered us to quit the house and not return to the village before the expiration of seven days. If we appeared within that period, he should kill us.

At any other season of the year such an order would by us have been considered as an indulgence, enabling us to pass our time in whatever way we wished. Even now, furnished as we were with sufficient provision for that term, it was not very unpleasant to us, more particularly Thompson who was always desirous to keep as much as possible out of the society and sight of the natives, whom he detested. Taking with us our provisions, a bundle of clothes, and our axes, we obeyed the directions of Maquina, and withdrew into the woods. Here we built ourselves a cabin to shelter us, with the branches of trees, and keeping up a good fire, secured ourselves pretty well from the cold.

Here we passed the prescribed period of our exile, with more content than much of the time while with them, employing the day in reading and praying for our release, or in rambling around and exploring the country, the soil of which we found to be very good, and the face of it, beautifully diversified with hills and valleys, refreshed with the finest streams of water, and at night enjoyed comfortable repose upon a bed of soft leaves, with our garments spread over us to protect us from the cold.

At the end of seven days we returned and found several of the people of A-i-tiz-zart with their king, or chief, at Tashees. He had been invited by Maquina to attend the close of this performance, which I now learn was a celebration, held by them annually, in honour of their God, whom they call *Quahootze*, to return him their thanks for his past, and implore his future favours. It terminated on the 21st, the day after our return, with a most extraordinary exhibition. Three men, each of whom had two bayonets run through his sides between the ribs, apparently regardless of the pain, traversed the room, backwards and forwards, singing war songs and exulting in this display of firmness.

On the arrival of the 25th we could not but call to mind, that this being Christmas, was in our country a day of the greatest festivity, when our fellow countrymen assembled in their churches, were celebrating the goodness of God, and the praises of the Saviour. What a reverse did our situation offer — captives in a savage land, and slaves to a set of ignorant beings unacquainted with religion or humanity, hardly were we permitted to offer up our devotions by ourselves in the woods, while we felt even grateful for this privilege. Thither with the king's permission we withdrew, and after reading the service appointed for the day, sung the hymn of the Nativity, fervently praying that heaven in its goodness would permit us to celebrate the next festival of this kind in some Christian land. On our return, in order to conform as much as was in our power to the custom of our country, we were desirous of having a better supper than usual. With this view we bought from one of the natives some dried clams, and oil, and a root called Kletsup, [licorice fern possibly] which we cooked by steaming, and found it very palatable. This root consists of many fibres, of about six inches long, and of the size of a crow quill. It is sweet, of an agreeable taste, not unlike the Quanoose, [possibly camas] and it is eaten with oil.

[After spending two months at Cooptee, fifteen miles from Tashees, Jewitt with Maquina's people returned to Nootka and resumed the pattern of living that had begun the year before.]

In the latter part of July, Maquina informed me that he was going to war with the A-y-charts, a tribe living at about fifty miles to the south, on account of some controversy that had arisen the preceding summer, and that I must make a number of daggers for his men, and cheetoolths for his chiefs. He wished me to make for his own use a weapon of quite a different form, in order to dispatch his enemy by one blow on the head, it being the calculation of these nations on going to war to surprize their adversaries while asleep.

When these people have finally determined on war, they make it an invariable practice for three or four weeks prior to the expedition to go into the water five or six times a day, where they wash and scrub themselves from head to foot with bushes intermixed with briars, so that their bodies and faces will often be entirely covered with blood. During this severe exercise they are continually exclaiming, "Wocash Quahootze, Teechamme ah welth, wik-etish tau-ilth — Kar-sab-matemas — Wik-sish to hauk matemas — I ya-ish kah-shittle — As-smootish warich matemas — Which signifies, Good, or great God, let me live — Not be sick — Find the enemy — Not fear him — Find him asleep, and kill a great many of him.

During the whole of this period they have no intercourse with their women, and for a week, at least, before setting out abstain from feasting or any kind of merriment, appearing thoughtful, gloomy, and morose, and for the three last days are almost constantly in the water, both day and night, scrubbing and lacerating themselves in a terrible manner. Maquina, having informed Thompson and myself that he should take us with him, was very solicitous that we should bathe and scrub ourselves in the same way with them, telling me that it would harden our skins so that the weapons of the enemy would not pierce them. But as we felt no great inclination to amuse ourselves in this manner, we declined it.

The expedition consisted of forty canoes, carrying from ten to twenty men each. Thompson and myself armed ourselves with cutlasses and pistols, but the natives, although they had a plenty of European arms, took with them only their daggers and cheetoolths, with a few bows and arrows, the latter being about a yard in length and pointed with copper, muscle shell, or bone. The bows are four feet and a half long, with strings made of whale sinew.

To go to A-y-chart, we ascended from twenty to thirty miles a river about the size of that of Tashees, the banks of which are high and covered with wood. At midnight we came in sight of the village which was situated on the west bank near the shore on a steep hill difficult of access, and well calculated for defence. It consisted of fifteen or sixteen houses, smaller than those at Nootka, and built in the same style, but compactly placed. By Maquina's directions, the attack was deferred until the first appearance of dawn, as he said that was the time when men slept the soundest.

At length, all being ready for the attack, we landed with the greatest silence, and going around so as to come upon the foe in the rear, clambered up the hill. The natives, as is their custom, entered the several huts, creeping on all fours. My comrade and myself stationed ourselves without, to intercept those who should attempt to escape, or come to the aid of their friends. I wished, if possible, not to stain my hands in the blood of any fellow creature, and though Thompson would gladly have put to death all the savages in the country, he was too brave to think of attacking a sleeping enemy.

Having entered the houses, on the war-whoop being given by Maquina, as he seized the head of the chief and gave him the fatal blow, all proceeded to the work of death. The A-y-charts, being thus surprised, were unable to make resistance and with the exception of a very few, who were so fortunate as to make their escape, were all killed or taken prisoners on condition of becoming slaves to their captors. I also had the good fortune to take four captives, whom Maquina, as a favour, permitted me to consider as mine and occasionally employ them in fishing for me. As for Thompson, who thirsted for revenge, he had no wish to take any prisoners, but with his cutlass, the only weapon he would employ against them, succeeded in killing seven stout fellows who came to attack him, an act which obtained him great credit with Maquina and the chiefs, who after this held him in much higher estimation, and gave him the appellation of *Chehiel-suma-har*, it being the name of a very celebrated warrior of their nation in ancient times, whose exploits were the constant theme of their praise.

After having put to death all the old and infirm of either sex, as is the barbarous practice of these people, and destroyed the buildings, we reembarked with our booty in our canoes for Nootka. Here we were received with great demonstrations of joy by the women and children, accompanying our war-song with a most furious drumming on the houses. The next day a great feast was given by Maquina in celebration of his victory, which was terminated as usual with a dance by Sat-sat-sak-sis.

Soon after our establishment [in Tashees again], Maquina informed me that he and his chiefs had held council both before and after quitting Nootka. They had determined that I must marry one of their women, urging as a reason to induce me to consent that as there was now no probability of a ship coming to Nootka to release me, that I must consider myself as destined to pass the remainder of my life with them, that the sooner I conformed to their customs the better, and that a wife and family would render me more contented and satisfied with their mode of living.

I remonstrated against this decision, but to no purpose. He told me that should I refuse, both Thompson and myself would be put to death, telling me, however, that if there were none of the women of his tribe that pleased me, he would go with me to some of the other tribes where he would purchase for me such an one as I should select. Reduced to this sad extremity, with death on the one side and matrimony on the other, I thought proper to choose what appeared to me the least of the two evils and consent to be married, on condition that as I did not fancy any of the Nootka women, I should be permitted to make choice of one from some other tribe.

This being settled, the next morning by day-light Maquina with about fifty men in two canoes set out with me for A-i-tiz-zart, taking with him a quantity of cloth, a number of muskets, sea otter skins etc. for the purchase of my bride. With the aid of our paddles and sails, being favoured with a fair breeze, we arrived some time before sun set at the village. Our arrival excited a general alarm and the men hastened to the shore, armed with the weapons of their country, making many warlike demonstrations and displaying much zeal and activity. We in the mean time remained quietly seated in our canoes where we remained for about half an hour, when the messenger of the chief, dressed in their best manner, came to welcome us, and invite us on shore to eat. We followed him in procession to the chief's house, Maquina at our head, taking care to leave a sufficient number in the boats to protect the property. When we came to the house we were ushered in with much ceremony, and our respective seats pointed out to us, mine being next to Maquina by his request.

After having been regaled with a feast of herring spawn and oil, Maquina asked me if I saw any among the women who were present that I liked. I immediately pointed out to him a young girl of about seventeen, the daughter of Upquesta, the chief, who was sitting near him by her mother. On this Maquina, making a sign to his men, arose and taking me by the hand, walked into the middle of the room and sent off two of his men to bring the boxes containing the presents from the canoes. In the mean time Kinneclimmets, the master of ceremonies, made himself ready for the part he was to act by powdering his hair with the white down.

When the chests were brought in, specimens of the several articles were taken out and showed by our men, one of whom held up a musket, another a skin, a third a piece of cloth etc. On this Kinneclimmets stepped forward and, addressing the chief, informed him that all these belonged to me, mentioning the number of each kind, and that they were offered him for the purchase of his daughter Eu-stoch-ee-exqua, as a wife for me. As he said this the men who held up the various articles walked up to the chief, and with a very stern and morose look, the complimentary one on these occasions, threw them at his feet. Immediately on which all the tribe, both men and women who were assembled on this occasion, set up a cry of *Klackko-Tyee*, that is, Thank ye chief.

His men, after this ceremony, having returned to their places, Maquina rose, and in a speech of more than half an hour said much in my praise to the A-i-tiz-zart chief, telling him that I was as good a man as themselves, differing from them only in being white, that I was besides acquainted with many things of which they were ignorant. I knew how to make daggers, cheetoolths and harpoons, and was a very valuable person whom he was determined to keep always with him; praising me at the same time for the goodness of my temper, and the manner in which I had conducted since I had been with them, observing that all the people of Nootka, and even the children, loved me.

While Maquina was speaking, his master of ceremonies was continually skipping about, making the most extravagant gestures and exclaiming Wocash. When he had ceased the A-i-tiz-zart chief arose amidst the acclamations of his people, and began with setting forth the many good qualities and accomplishments of his daughter; that he loved her greatly, and as she was his only one, he could not think of parting with her. He spoke in this manner for some time, but finally concluded by consenting to the proposed union, requesting that she might be well used and kindly treated by her husband. At the close of this speech, when the chief began to manifest a disposition to consent to our union, Kinneclimmets again began to call out as loud as he could bawl, Wocash, cutting a thousand capers and spinning himself around on his heel like a top.

When Upquesta had finished his speech, he directed his people to carry back the presents which Maquina had given him, to me, together with two young male slaves to assist me in fishing. These, after having been placed before me, were by Maquina's men taken on board the canoes. This ceremony being over, we were invited by one of the principal chiefs to a feast, at his house, of Klussamit, or dried herring. After the eating was over, Kinneclimmets amused the company very highly with his tricks. The evening's entertainment was closed by a new war-song from our men, and one in return from the A-i-tiz-zarts, accompanied with expressive gestures and wielding of their weapons.

After this, our company returned to lodge at Upquesta's, except a few who were left on board the canoes to watch the property. In the morning I received from the chief his daughter, with an earnest request that I would use her well, which I promised him when taking leave of her parents. She accompanied me with apparent satisfaction on board of the canoe.

The wind being ahead, the natives were obliged to have recourse to their paddles, accompanying them with their songs, interspersed with the witticisms and buffonry of Kinneclimmets, who, in his capacity of king's steersman, one of his functions which I forgot to enumerate, not only guided the course of the canoe, but regulated the singing of the boatmen. At about five in the morning we reached Tashees where we found all the inhabitants collected on the shore to receive us. We were welcomed with loud shouts of joy and exclamations of Wocash, and the women, taking my bride under their charge, conducted her to Maquina's house to be kept with them for ten days; it being a universal custom as Maquina informed me, that no intercourse should take place between the new married pair during that period. At night Maquina gave a great feast which was succeeded by a dance in which all the women joined. Thus ended the festivities of my marriage.

The term of my restriction over, Maquina assigned me as an apartment the space in the upper part of his house between him and his elder brother, whose room was opposite. Here I established myself with my family, consisting of myself and wife, Thompson and the little Sat-sat-sak-sis who had always been strongly attached to me, and now solicited his father to let him live with me, to which he consented.

This boy was handsome, extremely well-formed, amiable, and of a pleasant, sprightly disposition. I used to take a pleasure in decorating him with rings, bracelets, ear jewels etc. which I made for him of copper, and ornamented and polished them in my best manner. I was also very careful to keep him free from vermin of every kind, washing him and combing his hair every day. These marks of attention were not only very pleasing to the child, who delighted in being kept neat and clean as well as in being dressed off in his finery, but was highly gratifying both to Maquina and his queen who used to express much satisfaction at my care of him.

In making my domestic establishment, I determined, as far as possible, to live in a more comfortable and cleanly manner than the others. For this purpose I erected with planks a partition of about three feet high between mine and the adjoining rooms, and made three bedsteads of the same, which I covered with boards, for my family to sleep on, which I found much more comfortable than sleeping on the floor amidst the dirt.

Fortunately, I found my Indian princess both amiable and intelligent, for one whose limited sphere of observation must necessarily give rise to but a few ideas. She was extremely ready to agree to any thing that I proposed relative to our mode of living, was very attentive in keeping her garments and person neat and clean, and appeared in every respect solicitous to please me. She was, as I have said, about seventeen; her person was small, but well-formed, as were her features. Her complexion was, without exception, fairer than any of the women, with considerable colour in her cheeks, her hair long, black, and much softer than is usual with them, and her teeth small, even, and of a dazzling whiteness, while the expression of her countenance indicated sweetness of temper and modesty. She would, indeed, have been considered as very pretty in any country and, excepting Maquina's queen, was by far the handsomest of any of their women.

With a partner possessing so many attractions many may be apt to conclude that I must have found myself happy, at least comparatively so. But far otherwise was it with me. A compulsory marriage with the most beautiful and accomplished person in the world can never prove a source of real happiness. In my situation, I could not but view this connection as a chain that was to bind me down to this savage land, and prevent my ever again seeing a civilized country. Especially, when in a few days after Maquina informed me that there had been a meeting of his chiefs in which it was determined that as I had married one of their women, I must be considered as one of them and conform to their customs. In future, neither myself nor Thompson should wear our European clothes, but dress in Kutsaks like themselves.

On the 15th of January 1805, about midnight, I was thrown into considerable alarm in consequence of an eclipse of the moon, being awakened from my sleep by a great outcry of the inhabitants. On going to discover the cause of this tumult, I found them all out of their houses, bearing lighted torches, singing and beating upon pieces of plank. When I asked them the reason of this proceeding, they pointed to the moon and said that a great cod-fish was endeavouring to swallow her, and that they were driving him away. The origin of this superstition I could not discover.

[In] some respects my situation was rendered more comfortable since my marriage, as I lived in a more cleanly manner and had my food better and more neatly cooked. Besides, I had always a plenty, my slaves generally furnishing me, and Upquesta never failing to send me an ample supply by the canoes that came from A-i-tiz-zart. Still, from my being obliged at this season of the year to change my accustomed clothing, and to dress like the natives with only a piece of cloth of about two yards long thrown loosely around me, my European clothes having been for some time entirely worn out, I suffered more than I can express from the cold.

[Jewitt had been married in September 1804, but after being very ill the following winter, Maquina allowed him to send his Native wife, pregnant with a son, back to her people. He was also permitted to wear his badly-worn European clothing again. He grew nonetheless more despondent and despairing of rescue until in late summer of 1805 he learned that the brig *Lydia* had arrived in Nootka harbour.]

Several of our people came running into the house to inform me that a vessel under full sail was coming into the harbour. Though my heart bounded with joy, I repressed my feelings. Affecting to pay no attention to what was said, I told Thompson to be on his guard, and not betray any joy, as our release, and perhaps our lives, depended on our conducting our-selves so as to induce the natives to suppose we were not very anxious to leave them. We continued our work as if nothing had happened, when in a few minutes after Maquina came in, and seeing us at work appeared much surprised, and asked me if I did not know that a vessel had come. I answered in a careless manner that it was nothing to me. "How, John," said he, "you no glad go board." I replied that I cared very little about it, as I had become reconciled to their manner of living, and had no wish to go away. He then told me that he had called a council of his people respecting us, and that we must leave off work and be present at it.

The men having assembled at Maquina's house, he asked them what was their opinion should be done with Thompson and myself now a vessel had arrived, and whether he had not better go on board himself to make a trade and procure such articles as were wanted. Each one of the tribe who wished gave his opinion. Some were for putting us to death and pretending to the strangers that a different nation had cut off the *Boston*. Others, less barbarous, were for sending us fifteen or twenty miles back into the country until the departure of the vessel. With regard to Maquina's going on board the vessel, which he discovered a strong inclination to do, there was but one opinion. All remonstrated against it, telling him that the captain would kill him or keep him a prisoner in consequence of his having destroyed our ship. When Maquina had heard their opinions, he told them that he was afraid of being hurt from going on board the vessel, but that he would, however, in that respect be guided by John, whom he had always found true. He then turned to me, and asked me if I thought there would be any danger in his going on board. I answered that I was not surprised at the advice his people had given him, unacquainted as they were with the manner of the white men, and judging them by their own. But if they had been with them as much as I had, or even himself, they would think very different … If he wished to go on board, he might do it, in security. After reflecting a few moments he said, with much apparent satisfaction, that if I would write a letter to the captain, telling him good of him, that he had treated Thompson and myself kindly since we had been with him and to use him well, he would go. It may readily be supposed that I felt much joy at this determination; but knowing that the least incaution might annihilate all my hopes of escape, I was careful not to manifest it, and to treat his going or staying as a matter perfectly indifferent to me. I told him that if he wished me to write such a letter I had no objection, as it was the truth, otherwise I could not have done it.

I then proceeded to write the recommendatory letter, which the reader will naturally imagine was of a somewhat different tenor from the one he had required. If deception is in any case warrantable, it was certainly so in a situation like ours, where the only chance of regaining that freedom of which we had been so unjustly deprived depended upon it. I trust that few, even of the most rigid, will condemn me with severity for making use of it on an occasion which afforded me the only hope of ever beholding a Christian country and preserving myself, if not from death, at least from a life of continued suffering.

The letter which I wrote was nearly in the following terms:

To Captain —
of the Brig —
Nootka, July 19, 1805.
Sir,

THE bearer of this letter is the Indian king by the name of Maquina. He was the instigator of the capture of the ship *Boston* and of the murder of twenty-five men of her crew, the two only survivors being now on shore — Wherefore I hope you will take care to confine him according to his merits, putting in your dead lights, and keeping so good a watch over him, that he cannot escape from you. By so doing we shall be able to obtain our release in the course of a few hours.

JOHN R. JEWITT, Armourer of the Boston, *for himself and John Thompson, Sail-maker of said ship.*

I have been asked how I dared to write in this manner. My answer is that from my long residence among these people, I knew that I had little to apprehend from their anger on hearing of their king being confined. They knew his life depended upon my release, and they would sooner have given us five hundred white men than have had him injured. This will serve to explain the little apprehension I felt at their menaces afterwards, for otherwise, sweet as liberty was to me, I should hardly have ventured on so hazardous an experiment.

On my giving the letter to Maquina, he asked me to explain it to him. This I did line by line, as he pointed them out with his finger, but in a sense very different from the real, giving him to understand that I had written to the captain that as he had been kind to me since I had been taken by him, that it was my wish that the captain should treat him accordingly, and give him what molasses, biscuit and rum he wanted.

When I had finished, placing his finger in a significant manner on my name at the bottom, and eyeing me with a look that seemed to read my inmost thoughts, he said to me, "John, you no lie?"

Never did I undergo such a scrutiny, or ever experience greater apprehensions than I felt at that moment when my destiny was suspended on the slightest thread. The least mark of embarrassment on mine, or suspicion of treachery on his part, would probably have rendered my life the sacrifice. Fortunately I was able to preserve my composure, and my being painted in the Indian manner which Maquina had since my marriage required of me, prevented any change in my countenance from being noticed.

I replied with considerable promptitude, looking at him in my turn, with all the confidence I could muster, "Why do you ask me such a question, Tyee? Have you ever known me to lie?"

"No."

"Then how can you suppose I should tell you a lie now, since I have never done it."

As I was speaking, he still continued looking at me with the same piercing eye, but observing nothing to excite his suspicion, he told me that he believed what I said was true and that he would go on board, and gave orders to get ready his canoe. His chiefs again attempted to dissuade him, using every argument for that purpose, while his wives crowded around him, begging him on their knees not to trust himself with the white men. Fortunately for my companion and myself, so strong was his wish of going on board the vessel that he was deaf to their solicitations, and making no other reply to them, than, "John no lie," left the house, taking four prime skins with him as a present to the captain.

Scarcely had the canoe put off when he ordered his men to stop and, calling to me, asked me if I did not want to go on board with him. Suspecting this as a question merely intended to ensnare me, I replied that I had no wish to do it, not having any desire to leave them.

On going on board the brig, Maquina immediately gave his present of skins and my letter to the captain, who on reading it asked him into the cabin, where he gave him some biscuit and a glass of rum, at the same time privately directing his mate to go forward and return with five or six of the men armed. When they appeared, the captain told Maquina that he was his prisoner, and should continue so until the two men, whom he knew to be on shore, were released, at the same time ordering him to be put in irons and the windows secured, which was instantly done, and a couple of men placed as a guard over him.

Maquina was greatly surprised and terrified at this reception. He, however, made no attempt to resist, but requested the captain to permit one of his men to come and see him. One of them was accordingly called, and Maquina said something to him which the captain did not understand, but supposed to be an order to release us. When the man returned to the canoe, it was paddled off with the utmost expedition to the shore. As the canoe approached the inhabitants, who had all collected upon the beach, manifested some uneasiness at not seeing their king on board. When, on its arrival, they were told that the captain had made him a prisoner and that John had spoke bad about him in a letter, they all, both men and women, set up a loud howl and ran backwards and forwards upon the shore like so many lunatics, scratching their faces and tearing the hair in handfuls from their heads.

After they had beat about in this manner for some time, the men ran to their huts for their weapons, as if preparing to attack an invading enemy; while Maquina's wives and the rest of the women came around me, and throwing themselves on their knees, begged me with tears to spare his life.

Sat-sat-sak-sis, who kept constantly with me, taking me by the hand, wept bitterly, and joined his entreaties to theirs, that I would not let the white men kill his father. I told them not to afflict themselves, that Maquina's life was in no danger, nor would the least harm be done to him.

I told them that their best plan would be to send Thompson on board to desire the captain to use Maquina well till I was released, which would be soon. This they were perfectly willing to do, and I directed Thompson to go on board. But he objected, saying that he would not leave me alone with the savages. I told him not to be under any fear for me, for that if I could get him off I could manage well enough for myself, and that I wished him immediately on getting on board the brig to see the captain and request him to keep Maquina close till I was released, as I was in no danger while he had him safe.

When I saw Thompson off, I asked the natives what they intended to do with me. They said I must talk to the captain again, in another letter, and tell him to let his boat come on shore with Maquina, and that I should be ready to jump into the boat at the same time Maquina should jump on shore. I told them that the captain, who knew that they had killed my shipmates, would never trust his men so near the shore for fear they would kill them, too, as they were so much more numerous; but that if they would select any three of their number to go with me in a canoe, when we came within hail I could desire the captain to send his boat with Maquina to receive me in exchange for him.

As I was going into the canoe little Sat-sat-sak-sis, who could not bear to part with me, asked me, with an affecting simplicity, since I was going to leave him, if the white men would not let his father come on shore, and not kill him. I told him not to be concerned, for that no one should injure his father. Taking an affectionate leave of me, and again begging me not to let the white men hurt his father, he ran to comfort his mother, who was at a little distance, with the assurances I had given him.

On entering the canoe I seated myself in the prow facing the three men, having determined if it was practicable, from the moment I found Maquina was secured, to get on board the vessel before he was released, hoping by that means to be enabled to obtain the restoration of what property belonged to the *Boston* still remaining in the possession of the savages, which I thought, if it could be done, a duty that I owed to the owners.

With feelings of joy impossible to be described did I quit this savage shore, confident now that nothing could thwart my escape, or prevent the execution of the plan I had formed, as the men appointed to convey and guard me were armed with nothing but their paddles. As we came within hail of the brig they at once ceased paddling, when presenting my pistols at them, I ordered them instantly to go on, or I would shoot the whole of them. A proceeding so wholly unexpected threw them into great consternation, and resuming their paddles, in a few moments, to my inexpressible delight, I once more found myself along side of a Christian ship, a happiness which I had almost despaired of ever again enjoying.

All the crew crowded to the side to see me as the canoe came up and manifested much joy at my safety. I immediately leaped on board where I was welcomed by the Captain, Samuel Hill, of the brig *Lydia* of Boston, who congratulated me on my escape. I have no doubt, that what with my strange dress, being painted with red and black from head to foot, having a bear skin wrapped around me and my long hair, which I was not allowed to cut, fastened on the top of my head in a large bunch with a sprig of green spruce, I must have appeared more like one deranged than a rational creature. Captain Hill afterwards told me that he never saw any thing in the form of man look so wild as I did when I first came on board.

The Captain then asked me into the cabin where I found Maquina in irons, with a guard over him. He looked very melancholy, but on seeing me his countenance brightened up, and he expressed his pleasure with the welcome of "Wocash John." Taking him by the hand, I asked the Captain's permission to take off his irons, assuring him that as I was with him, there was no danger of his being in the least troublesome. He accordingly consented. I felt a sincere pleasure in freeing from fetters a man who, though he had caused the death of my poor comrades, had nevertheless always proved my friend and protector, and whom I had requested to be thus treated, only with a view of securing my liberty. Maquina smiled and appeared much pleased at this mark of attention from me.

I told him that he must content himself to remain on board with me that night. To this he agreed, on condition that I would remain with him in the cabin. I then went upon deck, and the canoe that brought me having been sent back, I hailed the inhabitants and told them that their king had agreed to stay on board till the next day when he would return, but that no canoes must attempt to come near the vessel during the night, as they would be fired upon. They answered, *Woho, woho* — very well, very well.

I then returned to Maquina, but so great were his terrors that he would not allow me to sleep, constantly disturbing me with his questions, and repeating, "John, you know when you was alone, and more than five hundred men were your enemies, I was your friend and prevented them from putting you and Thompson to death, and now I am in the power of your friends, you ought to do the same by me." I assured him that he would be detained on board no longer than the [*Boston*'s] property was released, and that as soon as it was done he would be set at liberty.

At day break I hailed the natives, and told them that it was Maquina's order that they should bring off the cannon and anchors and whatever remained with them of the cargo of the ship. This they set about doing with the utmost expedition, transporting the cannon and anchors by lashing together two of their largest canoes, and covering them with planks. In the course of two hours they delivered every thing on board that I could recollect, with Thompson's and my chest, containing the papers of the ship etc.

When every thing belonging to the ship had been restored, Maquina was permitted to return in his canoe which had been sent for him, with a present of what skins he had collected, which were about sixty, for the Captain in ackowledgment of his having spared his life and allowed him to depart unhurt. Such was also the transport he felt when Captain Hill came into the cabin and told him that he was at liberty to go, that he threw off his mantle, which consisted of four of the very best skins, and gave it to him as a mark of his gratitude. In return for which the Captain presented him with a new great coat and hat, with which he appeared much delighted. The captain then desired me to inform him that he should return to that part of the coast in November, and that he wished him to keep what skins he should get, which he would buy of him. This Maquina promised, saying to me at the same time, "John, you know I shall be then at Tashees, but when you come make *pow*, which means, fire a gun to let me know, and I will come down."

When he came to the side of the brig he shook me cordially by the hand, and told me that he hoped I would come to see him again in a big ship, and bring much plenty of blankets, biscuit, molasses and rum for him and his son who loved me a great deal, and that he would keep all the furs he got for me, observing at the same time that he should never more take a letter of recommendation from any one, or ever trust himself on board a vessel unless I was there. Then grasping both my hands with much emotion, while the tears trickled down his cheeks, he bade me farewell and stept into the canoe, which immediately paddled him on shore.

Notwithstanding my joy at my deliverance, and the pleasing anticipation I felt of once more beholding a civilized country, and again being permitted to offer up my devotions in a Christian church, I could not avoid experiencing a painful sensation on parting with this savage chief who had preserved my life and in general treated me with kindness, and considering their ideas and manners, much better than could have been expected.

As soon as Maquina had quitted us we got under weigh, and stood again to the Northward. We continued on the coast until the eleventh of August, 1806, when having completed our trade, we sailed for China, to the great joy of all our crew, and particularly so to me. With a degree of satisfaction that I can ill express, did I quit a coast to which I was resolved nothing should again tempt me to return. As the tops of the mountains sunk in the blue waves of ocean, I seemed to feel my heart lightened of an oppressive load.

[Jewitt's narrative ends when he meets a friend of his father in China. Jewitt himself returned with the *Lydia* to New England where he made his home, and in 1807 he published *A Journal Kept at Nootka Sound*, which purported to be the exact diary he had kept while living in captivity. His *Narrative of Adventures and Sufferings* was written and published in 1815 with the assistance of Richard Alsop who probably suggested Defoe's *Robinson Crusoe* as a model. Jewitt is also registered that same year as the author of a song titled "The Poor Armourer Boy." In the meantime he had married a woman by the name of Hester Jones of Boston and they had five children. But Jewitt does not seem to have been a very stable provider; it is recorded that he travelled from town to town in a wagon peddling copies of his book from a wheelbarrow. He is also known to have gone on stage in Philadelphia, playing himself in a dramatized version of his narrative titled *The Armourer's Escape* and also performing songs dressed in Nootka costume at an amusement park in the city's suburbs. A letter from his wife expresses her wish that her itinerant husband be a corpse rather than an actor. That wish, one might say, came true in January 1821 when Jewitt died at Hartford at the age of thirty-seven. The plaintive song of the armourer boy, which was sold as a broadsheet, makes clear that while Jewitt rejoiced in his deliverance from captivity, he was not subsquently a happy man; rather, in America he was "alone and a stranger ... on a far-distant shore from that which [his] childhood had known." Read as a story of fathers and sons, the *Narrative* ironically delivers its hero from filial fulfilment to domestic misery. An account of Jewitt's life can be found in an article by Dr. Edmond Meaney, Jr., first published in the July 1940 issue of *British Columbia Historical Quarterly* and reprinted in an edition of Jewitt's narrative titled *White Slaves of the Nootka*. A scholarly edition annotated and illustrated by Hilary Stewart was published in 1987.]

SIMON FRASER (1776–1862)

The first European expedition to cross British Columbia by land was led by Alexander Mackenzie in 1793. His account of that journey appeared in *Voyages from Montreal through the Continent of North America to the Frozen and Pacific Oceans in 1789 and 1793*, which was published to considerable interest in London in 1801. Mackenzie's journey was essentially a reconnaisance trip in the interests of the fur trade. The last section describes crossing the Rocky Mountains to the Pacific Ocean where near Bella Coola he wrote, "I now mixed up some vermillion in melted grease, and inscribed, in large characters, on the South-East face of the rock on which we had slept last night, this brief memorial — Alexander Mackenzie, from Canada, by land, the twenty-second of July, one thousand seven hundred and ninety-three." Unknowingly, he missed meeting George Vancouver there by about six weeks. Mackenzie's narrative is presented in journal form and written in a plain and somewhat repetitive style; nonetheless it conveys, as Victor Hopwood has observed, "a compelling vision of what single-minded ambition could achieve."

Richer in detail and broader in scope is David Thompson's *Narrative of Explorations in Western America 1784-1812*, not published until 1916. Thompson had come to North America at age fourteen and worked for both the Hudson's Bay Company and the North West Company, crossing the Rocky Mountains in 1811 and descending the Columbia River to its mouth where the Americans had established Fort Astoria. There is epic panorama to Thompson's travel narratives, as can be seen in this journal entry for January 10, 1811:

> A day of Snow and southerly Gale of wind, the afternoon fine; the view now before us was an ascent of deep snow, in all appearance to be the height of land between the Atlantic and Pacific Oceans; it was to me a most exhilarating sight, but to my uneducated men a dreadful sight, they had no scientific object in view ... on our right about one third of a mile from us lay an enormous Glacier, the eastern face of which quite steep, of about two thousand feet in height, was of a clean fine green colour ... My men were not at their ease, yet when night came they admired the brilliancy of the Stars, and as one of them said, he thought he could almost touch them with his hand.

There are also descriptions of people and events which are almost novelistic in their graphic estimate of character and their use of irony. Although his journals were not published until the twentieth century, Thompson was the first to make a detailed record of the life and customs of the Kootenae and Interior Salish of British Columbia.

But the liveliest extended account of overland travel and exploration is probably Simon Fraser's description of navigating the river that bears his name. Fraser, born in Bennington, Vermont, was the youngest son of a Loyalist officer who was imprisoned and died during the revolutionary war. His mother moved the family to Montreal where they were supported by his father's brother, John Fraser, a judge and man of means. Simon Fraser joined the North West Company in 1792 and was a company partner by 1801. His period of significant achievements began in 1805 when he was placed in charge of the Company's operations beyond the Rockies and established a series of settlements (including Prince George) in central British Columbia which he called New Caledonia, recalling his mother's description of the Highlands of Scotland. In 1808 he set out to explore the river he thought was the Columbia, entering territory that had not been seen by Europeans before. His chief hope was to establish a water route linking New Caledonia with the Pacific Ocean. The selection from his journals reprinted below describes his struggle through the hazardous stretch known as the Fraser River Canyon where at Hell's Gate, south of Lytton, the canyon walls rise more than 1,000 metres above the narrow, rushing river. The greatest single peril was that once on the river, the men could not get out. At the river's mouth, the explorer encountered aggressive hostility from the Musqueam people, and was prevented from reaching the ocean. Moreover, he took his bearings and realized he could not have been on the Columbia. With the morale of the expedition broken, it took a great deal of determination and eloquence on Fraser's part to give his men heart for the return journey to Fort George.

There is no reliable description of Fraser's character by a contemporary. On the basis of the journals he edited, W. Kaye Lamb concludes that Fraser must have had unusual physical courage and stamina and a firm, even nature, for not even the behaviour of some of his most irascible and unreliable men seems to have made him lose his temper or act unfairly. Fraser was retired from the North West Company by 1818 and living in Cornwall Township in Ontario, where in comparison to the early years he spent the rest of his long life uneventfully. He made a living for his wife and large family on extensive land holdings and from saw and grist mills on his property. Fraser had named the major eastern tributary of the river he explored after David Thompson and the latter in turn, compiling a map for the North West Company, named the Fraser River after the company associate who followed it to its mouth.

[The following text is taken from a facsimile of the original manuscript of Fraser's journey in the possession of the Toronto Public Library. Fraser's actual journal remained in the family, but by the third generation was lost. The Toronto manuscript is not in Fraser's hand, but is what is known as a "fair copy," to which deletions and revisions have been made in two distinct handwritings. Unlike Lamb's, the version printed here for the most part includes those edits.]

From JOURNALS AND LETTERS
THOMPSON RIVER TO THE STRAIT OF GEORGIA

MONDAY, June 20, 1808

About 10 a.m. we embarked. Now all our people were in canoes. Our three new guides, the great chief, a little fellow from whom we received much attention, and some others embarked to keep us company. Aided by heavy rapids and a strong current, we, in a short time, came to a portage. Here the canoes and baggage were carried up a steep hill; the ascent was dangerous — stones and fragments of rocks were continually giving way from our feet and rolling off in succession; from this cause one of our men stumbling was much hurt, and a kettle he had bounced into the river and was lost. The Indians informed us that some years since, at this place, several of their people, having lost their balance from the steps giving way, rolled down to the river in the same way and perished. We saw many graves covered with small stones all over the place.

I have, almost, forgotten to mention that on our arrival at the carrying place, one of our canoes sunk and some of our things were lost, but the crew was saved, and the canoe recovered.

On the other side of the river, Mr. Stuart, who visited the rapids, observed many kinds of trees different from those we had hitherto seen. He also observed a mineral spring, the water of which was clear and of a strong taste, but the scum was of a greenish colour. The Mountains continue to be high, and their summits covered with snow.

Two Indians from our last encampment overtook us with a piece of Iron which we had forgotten there. We considered this as an extraordinary degree of honesty and attention, particularly in this part of the world. After we had encamped, the chief with his friends went away.

Wednesday [Tuesday], June 21

Early in the morning the men made a trip with two of the canoes and part of the things which they carried more than a mile and returned for the rest. I sent Mr. Quesnel to take charge of the baggage in the absence of the men. About this time Indians appeared on the opposite bank. Our guides harangued them from our side, and all were singing and dancing.

After breakfast the men renewed their work, and Mr. Stuart and I remained in the tent writing. Soon after we were alarmed by the loud bawling of our guides whom, upon looking out, we observed running full speed towards where we were, making signs that our people were lost in the rapids. As we could not account for this misfortune we immediately ran over to the baggage where we found Mr. Quesnel all alone. We inquired of him about the men, and at the same time we discovered that three of the canoes were missing, but he had seen none of them nor did he know where they were. On casting our view across the river, we remarked one of the canoes and some of the men ashore there. From this incident we had reason to believe that the others were either ahead or, as the guide had observed, had perished. This increased our anxiety and we directed our speed to the lower end of the rapids.

At the distance of four miles or so, we found one of our men, La Chapelle, who had carried two loads of his own share of the baggage that far; he could give us no account of the others, but supposed they were following him with their proportions. We still continued; at last growing fatigued and seeing no appearance of the canoes of which we were in search, we considered it advisable to return and keep along the bank of the river.

We had not proceeded far when we observed one of our men D'Alaire walking slow with a stick in his hand from the bank, and on coming up to him we discovered that he was so wet, so weak, and so exhausted that he could scarcely speak. However after leaning a little while upon his stick and recovering his breath, he informed us that unfortunately he and the others finding the carrying place too long and the canoes too heavy, took it upon themselves to venture down by water — that the canoe, in which he was, happened to be the last in setting out.

"In the first cascade," continued he, "our canoe filled and upset. The foreman and steersman got on the outside, but I, who was in the centre, remained a long while underneath upon the bars. The canoe still drifting was thrown into smooth current, and the other two men, finding an opportunity sprang from their situation into the water and swam ashore. The impulse occasioned by their fall in leaping off raised one side of the canoe above the surface, and I having still my recollection, though I had swallowed a quantity of water, seized the critical moment to disentangle myself, and I gained but not without a struggle the top of the canoe. By this time I found myself again in the middle of the stream. Here I continued astride the canoe, humouring the tide as well as I could with my body to preserve my balance, and although I scarcely had time to look about me, I had the satisfaction to observe the other two canoes ashore near an eddy, and their crews safe among the rocks. In the second or third cascade (for I cannot remember which) the canoe from a great height plunged into the deep eddy at the foot, and striking with violence against the bottom splitted in two. Here I lost my recollection, which however, I soon recovered and was surprised to find myself on a smooth easy current with only one half of the canoe in my arms. In this condition I continued through several cascades, untill the stream fortunately conducted me into an eddy at the foot of a high and steep rock. Here my strength being exhausted I lost my hold; a large wave washed me from off the wreck among the rocks, and another still larger hoisted me clear on shore, where I remained, as you will readily believe, some time motionless; at length recovering a little of my strength I crawled up among the rocks, but still in danger, and found myself once more safe on firm ground, just as you see."

Here he finished his melancholy tale, and then pointed to the place of his landing, which we went to see, and we were lost in astonishment not only at his escape from the danger of the waves, but also at his courage and perseverence in effecting a passage up through a place which appeared to us a perfect precipice. Continuing our course along the bank we found that he had drifted three miles among rapids, cascades, whirlpools etc. all inconceivably dangerous.

Mr. Quesnel feeling extremely anxious and concerned left his charge and joined us. Two men only remained on shore carrying the baggage, and these two were equally ignorant with ourselves of the fate of the others. Some time after upon advancing towards the camp, we picked up all the men on our side of the river. The men who had been thrown ashore on the other side, joined us in the evening. They informed us that the Indians assisted to extricate them from their difficulties. Indeed the natives shewed us every possible attention during our misfortunes on this trying occasion.

Being all safe we had the happiness of encamping together as usual with our baggage. However we lost one of our canoes, and another we found too heavy to be carried such a distance. Our guides asked permission to go and sleep at the Indian Village, which was below the rapids; this was granted on condition that they should return early in the morning.

Mr. Stuart in [the] course of the day saw a snake as thick as his wrist. Small rain in the evening.

Thursday [Wednesday], June 22

Our guides returned as they had promised. Four men were employed in bringing down the canoes by water. They made several portages in course of this undertaking. The rest of the men carried the baggage by land. When this troublesome and fatiguing business was over, we crossed over to the village, where we were received with loud acclamations and generously entertained. The number of men at this place I found to be about 110. The Chief of [the Indians at] the forks and our Little Fellow came to us upon our arrival and introduced us to the others.

I sent two men to visit the rapids; but the Indians, knowing our indiscretion of the preceding day, and dreading a like attempt, voluntarily transported our canoes over land to a little river beyond the rapids. We encamped some distance from the village. The Chief went ahead to inform the Indians of the next village of our approach. He promised to accompany us until we should have passed all the dangerous places — and the Little Fellow assured us that he would not leave us before our return.

The Indians having invited us into the village, Mr. Quesnel and some of the men went and were entertained to their satisfaction with plenty of singing and dancing, besides a feast of three dogs, which were then more acceptable as at this time we depended wholly upon the natives for provisions. 'Tis true they generally furnished us with the best they could procure, but that best was commonly wretched if not disgusting.

Friday [Thursday], June 23

Rained this morning. One of the men was sick. We perceived that one way or other our people were getting out of order. They preferred walking to going by water in wooden canoes, particularly after their late sufferings in the rapids. Therefore I embarked in the bow of a canoe myself and went down several rapids.

We met some Indians and waited for the arrival of our people, who had gone by land. Walking was difficult, the country being extremely rough and uneven. Passed a carrying place; one of the men fell and broke his canoe almost to pieces. The natives from below came thus far with two canoes to assist us. They were probably sent by our friends who went ahead. In one of the rapids, Mr. Stuart's canoe filled and was nearly lost.

Soon after we came to a camp of the natives where we landed for the night. The number of the Indians here may amount to 170. They call themselves Nailgemugh [probably lower Thompson natives]. We met with a hearty welcome from them; they entertained us with singing, dancing etc.

The Nailgemugh Nation are better supplied with the necessaries of life than any of those we have hitherto seen. Their robes are made of beaver &c. We visited a tomb which was near by the camp. It was built of boards sewed together, and was about four feet square. The top was covered with Cedar bark and loaded with stones. Near it in a scaffold were suspended two canoes, and a pole from which were suspended [word indecipherable], stripes of leather, several baskets etc.

The weather is generally very hot in the day time; but at night, being in the neighbourhood of eternal snows, it is commonly cold.

Saturday [Friday], June 24

This morning traded two canoes for two calico bed gowns. Sent some men to visit the rapids, and set out at 8 a.m. After going a mile we came to a carrying place of 800 yards. Mr. Stuart had a mer[idian]. alt[itude]. 126° 57'.

Continued — passed a small camp of Indians without stopping and came to a discharge with steep hills at both ends, where we experienced some difficulty in carrying the things. Ran down the canoes; but about the middle of the rapids two of them struck against one another, by which accident one of them lost a piece of its stern, and the steersman his paddle: the canoe in consequence took in much water.

After repairing the damages we continued, and in the evening arrived at an Indian village. The Natives flocked about us, and invited us to pass the night with them. Accepting their invitation we were led to the camp which was at some distance up the hill. The Indians of this encampment were upwards [of] five hundred souls. Our friends, the Chief and the Little Fellow, with some of our acquaintances from above were here. We were well treated with fresh salmon, hazelnuts, and some other nuts of an excellent quality. The small pox was in the camp, and several of the Natives were marked with it. We fired several shots to shew the Indians the use of our guns. Some of them, through fear, dropped down at the report.

Sunday [Saturday], June 25

Fine weather. The Chief of [the] Camshins [i.e., of the Indians living in the area around the junction of the Thompson and Fraser rivers] returned this morning to his own home, but his people continued with us. This man is the greatest chief we have seen; he behaved towards us uncommonly well. I made him a present of a large silver broach which he immediately fixed on his head, and he was exceedingly well pleased with our attention.

We embarked at 5 a.m. After going a considerable distance, our Indians ordered us ashore, and we made a portage. Here we were obliged to carry up among loose stones in the face of a steep hill, over a narrow ridge between two precipices. Near the top where the ascent was perfectly perpendicular, one of the Indians climbed to the summit, and by means of a long pole drew us up, one after another. This took three hours. Then we continued our course up and down, among hills and rocks, and along the steep declivities of mountains, where hanging rocks, and projecting cliffs at the edge of the bank made the passage so small as to render it difficult even for one person to pass sideways at times.

Many of the natives from the last camp, having accompanied us, were of the greatest service to us on these intricate and dangerous occasions. In places where we were obliged to hand our guns from one to another, and where the greatest precaution was required to pass singly and free of encumbrance, the Indians went through boldly with heavy loads.

About 5 p.m. we encamped at a rapid. On our arrival I dispatched Mr. Stuart and one of the men to examine the rapids. From the place of our encampment we observed an Indian who was on the opposite side fishing Salmon with a dipping net. Our Indians had a net with which they took five Salmons, which divided among forty persons was little indeed, but better than nothing.

Monday [Sunday], June 26

This morning all hands were employed the same as yesterday. We had to pass over huge rocks, in which we were assisted by the Indians. Soon after [we] met Mr. Stuart and the man who had passed the night on the top of a mountain in sight of our smoke. They reported that the navigation was absolutely impracticable. [Fraser was now in the Hell's Gate and Black Canyon area, the most difficult and dangerous part of the journey.]

As for the road by land we scarcely could make our way in some parts even with our guns, let alone heavy loads. I have been for a long period among the Rocky Mountains, but have never seen any thing equal to this country, for I cannot find words to describe our situation at times. We had to pass where no human being should venture. Yet in those places there is a regular footpath impressed, or rather indented, by frequent travelling upon the very rocks. And besides this, steps which are formed like a ladder, or the shrouds of a ship, by poles hanging to one another and crossed at certain distances with twigs and withes [tree boughs], suspended from the top to the foot of precipices, and fastened at both ends to stones and trees, furnished a safe and convenient passage to the Natives — but we, who had not the advantages of their experience, were often in imminent danger, when obliged to follow their example.

In the evening we came in sight of a camp of the Natives, and the Chief with some others crossed the river to receive us. We were then ferried over and afterwards kindly entertained. These Indians are of the same nation with the last, but some men of a neighbouring nation called Ackinroe were with them.

The Hacamaugh promised us canoes for the next day. But their canoes being above the rapids, some of the young men went for them. It being impossible to bring them by land, or to work them down by water, they were turned adrift and left to the mercy of the current. As there were many shoals and rocks the canoes were in the greatest danger of being broken to pieces before they got to the end of the rapids.

Tuesday [Monday], June 27

This morning the Indians entertained us with a specimen of their singing and dancing. We set out at 6 a.m. accompanied as usual by many of the Natives, who assisted in carrying part of our baggage. The route we had to follow was as bad as yesterday. At 9 we came to the canoes that were sent adrift. One of them we found broken and the other much damaged. We lost some time in repairing them. Some of the men with the things embarked, and the rest continued by land.

We came to a small camp of Indians consisting [of] about sixty persons. The name of the place is Spazum [Spuzzum], and is the boundary line between the Hacamaugh and Ackinroe Nations [the Interior and Coast Salish]. Here as usual we were hospitably entertained, with fresh Salmon boiled and roasted, green and dried berries, oil and onions.

Seeing tombs of a curious construction at the forks [the mouth of Spuzzum Creek] on the opposite [west] side, I asked permission of the Chief to go and pay them a visit. This he readily granted, and he accompanied us himself. These tombs are superior to any thing of the kind I ever saw among the savages. They are about fifteen feet long and of the form of a chest of drawers. Upon the boards and posts are carved beasts and birds, in a curious but rude manner, yet pretty well proportioned. These monuments must have cost the workmen much time and labour, as they were destitute of proper tools for the execution of such a performance. Around the tombs were deposited all the property of the deceased.

Ready for our departure, our guides observed that we had better pass the night here and that they would accompany us in the morning. Sensible, from experience, that a hint from these people is equal to a command, and that they would not follow, if we Declined, we remained.

Wednesday [Tuesday], June 28

We set out at 5, our things in canoes as yesterday, and we continued by land. After much trouble both by land and water for eight miles, we came to a carrying place, where we were obliged to leave our canoes, and to proceed on foot without our baggage. Some of the Ackinroe Nation, apprised of our approach, came to meet us with roasted Salmon, and we made an excellent meal.

At this place while waiting for some of our people who were behind, I examined a net of a different construction from any I had hitherto seen. It was made of thread of the size of cod lines, the meshes were sixteen inches wide, and the net eight fathoms long. With this the natives catch Deer, and other large animals.

Continued and crossed a small river on a wooden bridge. Here the main river tumbles from rock to rock between precipices with great violence. At 11 a.m. we arrived at the first village of the Ackinroe nation, where we were received with as much kindness as if we had been their lost relations. Neat mats were spread for our reception, and plenty of Salmon served in wooden dishes was placed before us. The number of people at this place was about one hundred and forty.

This nation is different in language and manners from the other nations we had passed. They have rugs made from the wool of Aspai, or wild goat, and from dog's hair, which are equally as good as those found in Canada. We observed that the dogs were lately shorn.

We saw few or no Christian goods among them, but from their workmanship in wood they must be possessed of good tools at least for that purpose. Having been newly arrived they had not as yet constructed their shades [shelters], but had a gallery of smoked boards upon which they slept. Their bows and arrows are very neat.

At 1 p.m. we renewed our march, the natives still carrying part of our baggage. At the first point we observed a remarkable cavern in a rock which upon visiting we found to be 50 feet deep by 35 wide. A little above it is an excellent house 46 by 23 feet, and constructed like American frame houses. The planks are 3 or 4 inches thick, each passing the adjoining one a couple of inches. The posts, which are very strong, and rudely carved, receive the crossbeam. The walls are 11 feet high, and covered with a slanting roof. On the opposite side of the river, there is a considerable village with houses similar to the one upon this side.

About 4 p.m. arrived [at] a camp containing about one-hundred and fifty souls. Here we had plenty of Salmon cooked by means of hot stones in wooden vessels.

Here we understood that the river was navigable from this place to the sea. We had of course to provide canoes if possible. We saw a number of new ones, which seemed to have been hollowed with fire, and then polished.

The arms of the Indians consist of bows and arrows, spears and clubs, or horn Powmagans. We saw little or no leather, so that large animals must be scarce. Their ornaments are the same as the Hacamaugh Nation make use of; that is to say, shells of different kinds, shell beads, brass made into pipes hanging from the neck, or across the shoulders, bracelets of large brass wire, and some bracelets of horn. Their hats, which are made of wattap [roots], have broad rims and diminish gradually to the top. Some make use of cedar bark, painted in various colours, resembling ribbands which they fix around their heads. Both sexes are stoutly made, and some of the men are handsome; but I cannot say so much for the women, who seem to be their husbands' slaves, for in course of their dances, I remarked that the men were pillaging them from one another. Our Little Fellow, on one of these occasions, was presented with another man's wife as a bed fellow for the night.

There is a new tomb at this place supported on carved posts about two feet from the ground. The sculpture is rudely finished, and the posts are covered all over with bright spangled shells, which shine like mercury, but the contents of the tomb emitted an abominable stink.

At the bad rock [Lady Franklin Rock], a little distance above the village, where the rapids terminate, the natives informed us that white people like us came there from below; and they shewed us indented marks which the white people made upon the rocks, but which, by the bye, seemed to us to be nothing more than natural marks.

In the evening four men went off in canoes to inform the people below of our visit and intentions.

Thursday [Wednesday], June 29

Lost some time this morning in looking out for canoes, but could not procure any. We embarked about 9 a.m. some of us with the Indians and others without, just as best suited the Indians. The river here is wide with a strong current and some rapids — both sides adorned with fine trees. The mountains are still high and covered with snow.

About 10 passed a village, which is the residence of the last Indians. At 2 p.m. came to a camp on an Island [probably near Hope] containing about one-hundred and twenty-five souls. Here we had plenty of Salmon, oil, roots and raspberries. The natives amused us with dancing. Lost a couple of hours — went on — several of the natives followed us. At 5 we came to another camp of one-hundred and seventy souls. Here the Indians, who favoured us with the canoes thus far, left us and went home, and in consequence we were obliged to encamp. The Indians of this place promised to help us on the next morning. They were extremely civil, in so much as to force us to doubt their sincerity. They gave us plenty of sturgeon, oil and roots, but which were not of the best quality or flavour.

The Indians in this quarter are fairer than those in the interior. Their heads and faces are extremely flat; their skin and hair of a reddish cast — but this cast, I suppose, is owing to the ingredients with which they besmear their bodies. They make rugs, of dog's hair, that have stripes of different colours crossing at right angles resembling at a distance Highland plaid. Their fishing nets are of large twine, and have handles 20 feet [long]. Their spears, which are of horn, have also wooden handles of great length. Here we saw a large copper kettle shaped like a jar, and a large English hatchet stamped *Sargaret* with the figure of a crown. The river at this place is more than two miles broad, and is interspersed with Islands.

Friday [Thursday], June 30

It was 7 a.m. before we could procure canoes and take our departure. At 11 we came to a camp containing near four hundred souls. Here we saw a man from the sea, which he said we might be able to see next day. Mr. Stuart took a mer[idian]. alt[itude]. O.L.L. 127° 23'. The Indians of this place seem dirty and have an unpleasant smell; they were surprised at seeing men different from Indians come from the interior and made themselves extremely disagreeable to us through their curiosity and attention.

The Indians, who conducted us during the forenoon, returned [home] with their canoes, which took us some time to replace. It was 2 p.m. before we embarked. Continued our course with a strong current for nine miles, where the river expands into a lake. Here we saw seals, a large river coming in from the left, and a round Mountain ahead, which the natives call *shemotch* [probably Mount Baker].

After sunset we encamped upon the right side of the river. At this place the trees are remarkably large, cedars *five fathoms* in circumference, and of proportional height. Mosquitoes are in clouds, and we had little or nothing to eat. The Natives always gave us plenty of provisions in their villages, but nothing to carry away. Numbers of them followed us, but they were as destitute of provisions as ourselves. And though they were at a great distance from home, they carried no arms about them. This conduct appeared [to indicate] that they had great confidence either in our goodness, or in their own numbers.

Saturday [Friday], July 1

Foggy weather this morning. Clear at 4 and we embarked. Rugged Mountains all around. The banks of the river are low and well covered with wood; the current is slack.

At 8 a.m. we arrived at a large village. After shaking hands with many, the Chief invited us to his house, and served us with fish and berries; our Indians also were treated with fish, berries and dried oysters in large troughs. Our Hacamaugh commonly stiled Little Fellow, so often mentioned here, and who has been highly serviceable to us all along, has assumed an air of consequence from his being of our party; he ranks now with Mr. Stuart, Mr. Quesnel, and myself. The Chief made me a present of a coat of mail to make shoes. For this we may thank our little friend, who also received a present of white shells. I gave the Chief in return a calico gown, for which he was thankful and proud.

The Indians entertained us with songs and dances of various descriptions. The Chief stood in the centre of the dance or ring giving directions, while others were beating the drum against the walls of the house, and making a terrible racket — which alarmed our men who were at a distance, and who came to see what caused the noise.

The Indians, who favoured us with a passage to this place, went off with the canoes. We had to look out for others, but none could be procured for any consideration whatever. At last the Chief consented to lend us his large canoe and to accompany us himself on the morrow.

The number of Indians at this place is about two hundred, who appeared at first view to be fair, but afterwards we discovered that they made use of white paint to alter their appearance. They evinced no kind of surprise or curiosity at seeing us, nor were they afraid of our arms, so that they must have been in the habit of seeing white people.

Their houses are built of cedar planks, and in shape [are] similar to the one already described. The whole range, which is 640 feet long by 60 broad, is under one roof. The front is 18 feet high, and the covering is slanting. All the apartments, which are separated in portions, are square, excepting the Chief's which is 90 feet long. In this room the posts or pillars are nearly 3 feet [in] diameter at the base, and diminish gradually to the top. In one of these posts is an oval opening answering the purpose of a door, thro' which to crawl in and out. Above, on the outside, are carved a human figure large as life, and there are other figures in imitation of beasts and birds. These buildings have no flooring. The fires are in the centre, and the smoke goes out an opening at [the] top.

The tombs at this place are well finished. Dog's hair, which is spun with a distaff and spindle is formed into rugs. There is some red and blue cloth among them. These Indians are not so hospitable as those above, which is probably owing to scarcity of provisions.

The tide now about 2¹/₂ feet. Mr. Stuart had a mer[idian]. alt[itude]. O.L.L. 127° 13'. We cast our nets into the water, but took no fish, the current being too strong.

Sunday [Saturday], July 2

This morning we discovered that the Natives were given to thieving. They stole a smoking bag belonging to our party, and we could not prevail upon them to restore it. The dogs in course of the night dragged out and damaged many of our things.

I applied to the Chief in consequence of his promise of yesterday for his canoe, but he paid no attention to my request. I, therefore, took the canoe and had it carried to the water side. The Chief got it carried back. We again laid hold of it. He still resisted, and made us understand that he was the greatest of his nation and equal in power to the sun. However as we could not go without [the canoe] we persisted and at last gained our point. The chief and several of the tribe accompanied us. At 11 a.m. arrived at a village where we were received with the usual ceremony of shaking hands, but we were not well entertained. The houses at this place are plain and in two rows. I received two coats of mail in a present which are so good [for] shoes.

The Indians advised us not to advance any further, as the Natives of the coast or Islanders were at war with them, being very malicious, and would consequently attempt to destroy us. Upon seeing us slight their advice and going to embark, they gathered round our canoe and hauled it out of the water, and then invited us for the first time to the principal house of the village.

Leaving Mr. Quesnel with most of the men to guard the canoe and baggage, Mr. Stuart with two men and myself accepted the invitation. As soon as we were in the house, the Indians began singing and dancing, and making a terrible noise. Mr. Stuart went to see what caused this seeming disturbance; he found that one of the Natives had stolen a jacket out of the canoe, which, however, upon application to the Chief, was returned, and all was quiet again. Then we made a motion to embark accompanied by the Chief. His friends did not approve of his going, [and] flocked about him, embracing him with tenderness, as if he was never to return. Our followers seeing this scene of apparent distress between the Chief and his friends changed their minds and declined going further. Even our Little

Fellow would not embark, saying that he was also afraid of the people at the sea. Then some of them laid violent hands upon the canoe, and insisted upon taking it out of the water. We paid no attention to this violent argument, but made them desist, and without them we embarked.

We proceeded on for two miles, and came to a place where the river divides [at New Westminster] into several channels. Seeing a canoe following us we waited for its arrival. One Indian of that canoe embarked with us and conducted us into the right channel [the North Arm of the Fraser River]. In the meantime several Indians from the village were pursuing us in their canoes, armed with bows and arrows, clubs, spears etc. Singing a war song, beating time with their paddles upon the sides of the canoes, and making signs and gestures highly inimicable. The one that embarked with us became very unruly singing and dancing, and kicking up a great dust. We threatened him and he mended his manner and was quiet.

This was an alarming crisis, but we were not discouraged: confident of our superiority, at least on the water, we continued.

At last we came in sight of a gulph or bay of the sea [the Strait of Georgia]; this the Indians called *Pas-hil-roe.* It runs in a S.W. and N.E. direction. In this bay are several high and rocky Islands whose summits are covered with snow. On the right shore we noticed a village called by the Natives *Misquiame* [Musqueam]; we directed our course towards it. Our turbulent passenger conducted us up a small winding river to a small lake to the village.

Here we landed, and found but a few old men and women; the others fled into the woods upon our approach. The fort is 1500 feet in length and 90 feet in breadth. The houses, which are constructed as those mentioned in other places, are in rows; besides some that are detached. One of the Natives conducted us through all the apartments, and then desired us to go away, as otherwise the Indians would attack us.

About this time those that followed us from above arrived. Having spent one hour looking about this place we went to embark, [when] we found the tide had ebbed, and left our canoe on dry land. We had, therefore, to drag it out to the water some distance. The natives no doubt seeing our difficulty, assumed courage, and began to make their appearance from every direction, in their coats of mail, howling like so many wolves, and brandishing their war clubs. At last we got into deep water, and embarked. Our turbulent fellow, who [had] embarked in our canoe before, no sooner found himself on board than he began a repetition of his former impertinences. He asked for our daggers, for our clothes, and in fine for every thing we had. At length, fully convinced of his unfriendly disposition, we turned him out and made him and the others, who were closing in upon us, understand, that if they did not keep their distance we would fire upon them.

After this unpleasant skirmish we continued untill we came opposite the second village. Here our curiosity incited us to go ashore; but reflecting upon the reception we experienced at the first, and the character of the Natives, it was thought neither prudent nor necessary to run any risk, particularly as we had no provisions, and saw no prospect of procuring any in that hostile quarter. We, therefore, turned our course and with the intention of going back to the friendly Indians for a supply, then to return and prosecute our design. When we came opposite the hostile village [Musqueam] the same fellows, who had annoyed us before, advanced to attack us which was echoed by those on shore. In this manner they approached so near that we were obliged to adopt a threatening position, and we had to push them off with the muzzles of our guns. Perceiving our determination to be serious, their courage failed, and they gave up the pursuit and crossed to the village. The tide was now in our favour, the evening was fine, and we continued our course with great speed until 11, when we encamped within six miles of the Chief's village. The men being extremely tired, went to rest; but they were not long in bed before the tide rushed upon the beds and roused them up.

Monday [Sunday], July 3

Having been disturbed by the overflowing of the tide, we embarked early and arrived at the Chief's village at 5 a.m., where we found some of the Indians bathing — it is their custom to bathe at this early hour. The others, who were asleep, soon got up and received us at the water side. All seemed surprised to see us again.

About this time our Little Fellow, whom we left yesterday at the village below, made his appearance. He informed us that the Indians after our departure had fixed upon our destruction; that he himself was pillaged, his hands and feet tied, and that they were about to knock him on the head when the Chief of the Ackinroe appeared, released him and secured his escape to this place, where he was now detained as a slave.

This unpleasant recital served to warn us more and more of our danger. Still we were bent upon accomplishing our enterprise, to have a sight of the main [ocean] which was but a short distance from whence we had returned; but unfortunately we could not procure a morsel of provisions, and besides the Chief insisted upon having his canoe restored to him immediately. This demand we were obliged to suppress. The Chief then invited us to his house. We went, but were not above five minutes absent, before one of the men came running to inform us that the Indians had seized upon the canoe and were pillaging our people. Alarmed at this report we hastened to their assistance. We found that some of the Indians from below having arrived had encouraged the others in these violent proceedings. Sensible from our critical situation that mild measures would be improper and of no service, I pretended to be in a violent passion, spoke loud, with vehement gestures and signs exactly in their own way; and thus peace and tranquility were instantly restored.

From these specimens of the insolence and ill nature of the Natives we saw nothing but dangers and difficulties in our way. We, therefore, relinquished our design and directed our thoughts towards home — but we could not proceed without the canoe, and we had to force it away from the owner leaving a blanket in its place. Thus provided, we pushed off.

Here we missed one of our men, G.B. The fellow being afraid had fled into the woods and placed himself behind a range of tombs, where he remained during the greatest part of the time we tarried on shore and it was with difficulty we prevailed upon him to embark. At last we got under way, and had to pull hard against a strong current.

Upon doubling the first point, the Chief with a number of canoes in his suite well-manned and armed overtook us and kept in company, singing with unfriendly gestures all the while. Aware of their design we endeavoured to keep them at a proper distance for some time. At last growing outrageous at our precautions they began to surround [us] and close in, apparently with the intention of seizing upon our canoe and upsetting us. I again had recourse to threats and vehemence of speech and gestures, and which again had the desired effect. The Chief spoke to his party and they all dropped behind, but they still followed and kept us in view.

Soon after a canoe with three men in it from a river on the left shore came to examine us; these after satisfying their curiosity immediately returned. We remarked that one of the crew had a large belt suspended from his neck garnished with locks of human hair.

About dark we observed the war party [that was following us] gain the shore, but we continued all night in order to get to the next village and to secure provisions before their arrival. The night was dark and the current strong; yet we reached our destination about eight in the morning.

Here I must again acknowledge my great disappointment in not seeing the *main ocean,* having gone so near it as to be almost within view. For we wished very much to settle the situation by an observation for the longitude. The latitude is 49° nearly, while that of the entrance of the Columbia is 46° 20'. This River, therefore, is not the Columbia. If I had been convinced of this fact where I left my canoes, I would certainly have returned from thence.

Tuesday [Monday], July 4

The people of the village were greatly surprised to see us return, and enquired with impatience if we had been to the Islands, and how we had the good fortune to escape the cruelty of the Masquiamme — meaning the nations at the sea shore.

While we were endeavouring to answer these questions, our pursuers of the day before made their appearance. Still bent upon mischief, the leader at landing began to testify his hostile disposition by brandishing his horn club, and by making a violent harangue to the people of the village, who already seemed to be in his favour. He claimed his canoe; seeing a number of canoes scattered about the beach and wishing to get rid of so troublesome and persevering a persecutor, we acquiesced to his demand without much hesitation.

After fixing the baggage and placing guards over it, at the request of a chief, Mr. Stuart, Mr. Quesnel and myself accompanied him to his tent; who, as soon as we were seated, offered us Salmon to eat. We were much flattered with this token of his kindness, but had scarcely begun to partake of his bounty when one of the men came running to the door, exclaiming that the Indians were unruly and proceeding to violence. We hurried out of the tent, and at our appearance all was quiet; yet we could not feel free of alarm seeing the whole village assembled round our baggage, armed with all kinds of hostile weapons and seemingly determined upon mischief.

It was then that our situation might really be considered as critical. Placed upon a small sandy Island, few in number, without canoes, without provisions, and surrounded by upwards of seven hundred barbarians. However our resolution did not forsake us. On the contrary all hands were of one mind, ready for action, and fully determined to make our way good at all hazards.

We now applied for canoes in every direction, but could not procure any either for love or money, so that we had to regret the inadvertency committed on our arrival by parting with the one we had before. There being no alternative we had again recourse to the Chief, notwithstanding our experience of his illiberality. He asked his price — I consented — he augmented his demand — I again yielded — he still continued to increase his imposition. At length, feeling highly provoked at the impertinence of his conduct, I exclaimed violently. He then ordered the canoe to be brought.

We immediately prepared to embark, but when we began to load, the

Indians crowded about the baggage and attempted to pillage. But as they laid hold upon any of our things we pulled it from them, and had to place ourselves in a posture of defence, and to threaten them with the contents of our pieces before they desisted.

Having got ready we crossed over the river. One of the Indians, who evinced a friendly disposition, followed and gave us some fish. At the same time [we] observed several of the others embarking and steering their course parallel to us along the other bank. The canoe being leaky and some of the men being in want of paddles, we were obliged to put ashore to repair. This done we went on till 10 p.m. when we encamped upon an Island. In due time the men went to rest. Mr. Stuart and I mounted guard alternately.

Wednesday [Tuesday], July 5

Started early and at 10 a.m. arrived at *Pulagli* village. Here again we found the Chief of the big canoe, with several of his people. Their canoes being small, and consequently more easily managed than ours which was large, gave them the advantage. As we had some reason to suspect that they pressed forward on purpose to renew the quarrel and to be troublesome, and seeing the Natives more numerous here than in the last camp, we judged it advisable to avoid them by crossing over to the other side of the river. Then three men followed in a canoe, who favoured us with a paddle and with five large Salmons.

To convey an idea of the effect of our arms to these men, we fired several shots before them — then made them understand that if the Chief should pursue us any farther, he should suffer severely for his presumption. They desired us to proceed in peace, and [said] that no one would disturb us for the future.

We continued. About sunset two Indians in a canoe overtook us. We knew them; they invited us to their camp, which was at a small distance on the opposite shore; this we declined. At dark we put up for the night, all wet, the canoe was leaky, but the bank being steep it could not be repaired. We were within sight of the camp, but none of the Indians came near us.

Thursday [Wednesday], July 6

Set out early. Soon after several canoes joined [us]. In these we recognized Blondin, the Chief, that flattered us so much the 29th June — Also the two Indians of the preceeding evening who gave us fish, and who of their own accord assisted us in the rapids. Seeing them so well disposed, I gave them permission to embark in our canoe. They paddled, but were not long on board before they struck up the war song. I imposed their silence.

A moment after Blondin got Mr. Quesnel's dagger out of the scabbard, and was hiding it under his robe when he was perceived. Now convinced of their evil inclination, I had them instantly sent to shore.

Then the other Indians made us signs to follow them; doubting their sincerity we pushed from them into a different channel. Upon this they doubled their speed. By and by we discovered a large camp of Indians, whose appearance soon taught us that they were not assembled there for any good purpose. When we came opposite all were in motion — some were in canoes, others lined the shore, and all were advancing upon us. At last it was with difficulty we could prevent them with the muzzles of our guns from seizing upon the canoe. They, however, contrived to give us such a push with the intention of upsetting us, that our canoe was forced into the strong current which in spite of all our efforts carried us down the rapids. However we gained the shore at the foot of a high hill, where we tied the canoe to a tree with a line. Here I ordered Mr. Stuart with some of the men to debark in order to keep the Indians in awe. The Indians perceiving our preparations for defence retired, but still kept ahead.

I then directed the men, who were on shore, to embark, but Mr. Stuart came to inform me that several of them refused, saying that they were bent upon going by land across the Mountains to the place where we had slept the 24th June. Considering this as a desperate resolution, I debarked and endeavoured to persuade them out of their infatuation; but two of them declared in their own name and in that of others, that their plan was fixed, and that they saw no other way by which they might [save] themselves from immediate destruction, for continuing by water, said they, surrounded by hostile nations, who watched every opportunity to attack and torment them, created in their minds a state of suspicion, which was worse than death.

I remonstrated and threatened by turns. The other gentlemen joined my endeavours in exposing the folly of their undertaking, and the advantages that would accrue to us all by remaining as we had hitherto done as the only bond for our mutual safety. After much debate on both sides, our delinquents yielded and we all shook hands, resolving never to separate during the voyage; which resolution was immediately confirmed by the following oath taken on the spot by each of the party: "I solemnly swear before Almighty God that I shall sooner perish than forsake in distress any of our crew during the present voyage."

[The next morning, the "unfriendly Indians" turned back down the river; Fraser and his men eventually reached Fort George, near the modern city of Prince George, on August 6th.]

PAUL KANE (1810–1871)

Long thought a native son of Canada, Paul Kane was actually born in Mallow, County Cork, Ireland in 1810, and moved with his family to York (now Toronto) in 1818 or 1819. Regardless of place of origin, Kane is one of those seminal figures who left behind images of native life, both in painting and writing, which define our nineteenth-century image of the Canadian West as romantic wilderness. He was the first professional writer or painter not connected with either the church or the fur trade to set down his observations of the western landscape. When Kane set out to cross western Canada in 1845 he had already "determined to devote whatever talents and proficiency [he] possessed to the painting of a series of pictures illustrative of the North American Indians ... and to represent the scenery of an almost unknown country." One of his earliest supporters, Sir George Simpson, then Governor of the Hudson Bay Company, commissioned twelve paintings from Kane which would depict "buffalo hunts, Indian camps, councils, feasts, conjuring matches, dances, warlike exhibitions, or any other pieces of savage life you may consider to be most attractive or interesting." Kane explains that from the first he kept written explanations of the paintings and "jotted down in pencil" a diary of his travels. Longman's published these edited journals in 1859 under the title *Wanderings of an Artist Among the Indians of North America*. Kane traces his route west through the Great Lakes, to the Red River Settlement, the Saskatchewan Valley, and on through the Rockies, down the Columbia to the Pacific, and finally to "Vancouver's Island" and Fort Victoria in the spring and summer of 1847. Kane's perspective on Native life is coloured by his cultural prejudices, but in the incident (included here) where he does not recognise Chief Yellow-Cum, he is truly vexed by the limitations of his "seeing." His accounts of West Coast shamanism, slavery and the relations among men and women are valuable not only as history and ethnography but as the keen impressions of a gifted visual artist.

From WANDERINGS OF AN ARTIST
CHAPTERS XIV AND XV

Fort Victoria – A Chief's Inauguration – The Dead Slave – Washing the Dead – A Coasting Trip –
Indian Curiosity – Rather Violent Quacks – Catching Wild Ducks – A Great Unknown – The Fate of
"Tonquin" – Fishing for Money – Shawatun the Ugly – Caledonian Suttee

APRIL 8th: I left Nasqually this morning with six Indians in a canoe, and continued paddling on the whole day and the following night, as the tide seemed favourable, not stopping till 2 p.m., when we reached Fort Victoria on Vancouver's Island, having travelled ninety miles without stopping. Fort Victoria stands upon the banks of an inlet in the island about seven miles long and a quarter of a mile wide, forming a safe and convenient harbour, deep enough for any sized vessel. Its Indian name is the Esquimalt, or, "Place for gathering Camas," great quantities of that vegetable being found in the neighbourhood. On my arrival I was kindly welcomed by Mr. Finlayson, the gentleman in charge. He gave me a comfortable room, which I made my headquarters during the two months I was occupied in sketching excursions amongst the Indians in the neighbourhood and along the surrounding coasts.

I took a sketch of Chea-clach, the Clallum chief, of whose inauguration I heard the following account from an eyewitness. On his father becoming too old to fulfil the duties of head chief, the son was called upon by the tribe to take his place; on which occasion he left for the mountains for the ostensible purpose of fasting and dreaming for thirty days and nights; these Indians, like all other tribes, placing great confidence in dreams, and believing that it is necessary to undergo a long fast whenever they are desirous of inducing one of any importance. At the end of the period assigned, the tribe prepared a great feast. After covering himself with a thick covering of grease and goosedown, he rushed into the midst of the village, seized a small dog, and began devouring it alive, this being a customary preliminary on such occasions. The tribe collected about him singing and dancing in the wildest manner, on which he approached those whom he most regarded and bit their bare shoulders or arms, which was considered by them as a high mark of distinction, more especially those from whom he took the piece clean out and swallowed it. Of the women he took no notice.

I have seen many men on the Northwest coast of the Pacific who bore frightful marks of what they regarded as an honourable distinction; nor is this the only way in which their persons become disfigured. I have myself seen a young girl bleeding most profusely from gashes inflicted by her own hand over her arms and bosom with a sharp flint, on the occasion of losing a near relative. After some time spent in singing and dancing Chea-clach retired with his people to the feast prepared inside a large lodge, which consisted principally of whale's blubber, in their opinion the greatest of all delicacies, although they have salmon, cod, sturgeon and other excellent fish in great abundance.

Slavery in its most cruel form exists among the Indians of the whole coast, from California to Behring's Straits, the stronger tribes making slaves of all the others they can conquer. In the interior, where there is but little warfare, slavery does not exist. On the coast a custom prevails which authorizes the seizure and enslavement, unless ransomed by his friends, of every Indian met with at a distance from his tribe, although they may not be at war with each other. The master exercises the power of life and death over his slaves, whom he sacrifices at pleasure in gratification of any superstition or other whim of the moment.

One morning while I was sketching, I saw upon the rocks the dead body of a young woman, thrown out to the vultures and crows, whom I had seen a few days previously walking about in perfect health. Mr. Finlayson, the gentleman in charge of Fort Victoria, accompanied me to the lodge she belonged to, where we found an Indian woman, her mistress, who made light of her death, and was doubtless the cause of it. She told us that a slave had no right to burial, and became perfectly furious when Mr. Finlayson told her that the slave was far better than herself. "I," she exclaimed, "the daughter of a chief, no better than a dead slave!" and bridling up with all the dignity she could assume, she stalked out, and next morning she had up her lodge and was gone. I was also told by an eye-witness, of a chief, who having erected a colossal idol of wood, sacrificed five slaves to it, barbarously murdering them at its base, and asking in a boasting manner who amongst them could afford to kill so many slaves.

These Indians have a great dance, which is called "The Medicine Mask Dance"; this is performed both before and after any important action of the tribe, such as fishing, gatherine camas or going on a war party either for the purpose of gaining the goodwill of the Great Spirit in their undertaking, or else in honour of him for the success which has attended them. Six or eight of the principal men of the tribe, generally medicine men, adorn themselves with masks cut out of some soft light wood and with feathers, highly painted and ornamented, with the eyes and mouth ingeniously made to open and shut. In their hands they hold carved rattles, which are shaken in time to a monotonous song or humming noise (for there are no words to it) which is sung by the whole company as they slowly dance round and round in a circle.

Among the Clal-lums and other tribes inhabiting this region, I have never heard any traditions as to their former origin, although such traditions are common amongst those on the east side of the Rocky Mountains. They do not believe in any future state of punishment, although in this world they suppose themselves exposed to the malicious designs of the skoocoom, or evil genius, to whom they attribute all their misfortune and ill-luck.

The good spirit is called Hias-Soch-a-la-Ti-Yah, that is, the great high chief, from whom they obtain all that is good in this life, and to whose happy and peaceful hunting grounds they will all eventually go to reside forever in comfort and abundance. The medicine men of the tribe are supposed to possess a mysterious influence with these two spirits, either for good or evil. They form a secret society, the initiation into which is accompanied by great ceremony and much expense. The candidate has to prepare a feast for his friends and all who choose to partake of it, and make presents to the other medicine men. A lodge is prepared for him, which he enters, and remains alone for three days and nights without food, whilst those already initiated keep dancing and singing round the lodge the whole time. After this feast, which is supposed to endue him with wonderful skill, he is taken up apparently lifeless and plunged into the nearest cold water, where they rub and wash him until he revives: this they call "washing the dead." As soon as he revives, he runs into the woods and soon returns dressed as a medicine man, which generally consists of the light down of the goose stuck all over their bodies and heads with thick grease, and a mantle of frayed cedar bark, with the medicine rattle in his hand. He now collects all his property, blankets, shells and ornaments, and distributes the whole amongst his friends, trusting for his future support to the fees of his profession. The dancing and singing are still continued with great vigour during the division of the property, at the conclusion of which the whole party again sit down to feast, apparently with miraculous appetites, the quantity of food consumed being perfectly incredible.

As I was desirous to coast round the Straits of De Fuca and visit the tribes on its shores, I employed Chea-clach the head chief, and four of his people, to take me and the interpreter of the fort round the straits in his canoe; and on the morning of the sixth of May we started about ten o'clock, running up the east side of Vancouver's Island, and crossed the canal De

Aro to the main land. On nearing an Indian village, which contained, as I afterwards found, between five and six hundred Indians, they came rushing down to the beach in an attitude apparently hostile, and as the boats of the exploring expedition had been attacked the year before at the same place, we naturally felt some apprehension for our safety.

We had no sooner approached the shore than a dense crowd surrounded us, wading up to their middles in water, and seizing our canoe dragged us all high and dry upon the shore, and inquired what we wanted. I replied that I would explain my business to their chief, who immediately stepped forward in a friendly manner. Having told him that my business was to visit all the Indians, and to take likenesses of the head chiefs and great warriors, he took me to his lodge, where I seated myself on a mat with him in front of me and commenced my drawing. In a few minutes the place was crowded, and when it could hold no more, the people clambered to the top of the lodge and tore off the mats from the supports, to which they clung, one upon another, like a swarm of bees, peering down upon us. Look which way I could it seemed one solid mass of hideous faces, daubed with red and white mud.

I hastily finished my sketch and hurried away, first giving the chief a plug of tobacco for his civility. On coming over I found the wind so strong that I thought it advisable to risk an encampment, and pitched my tent about two hundred yards from the village. We were soon surrounded by hundreds of Indians, the chief among the rest. I gave the latter some supper, and all the news, which he eagerly inquired after, and on my telling him I was tired and wished to go to sleep, which I could not do while so many of his people were about, he instantly arose and desired them to retire, which was promptly obeyed, he going away with them.

About ten o'clock at night I strolled into the village, and on hearing a great noise in one of the lodges I entered it, and found an old woman supporting one of the handsomest Indian girls I had ever seen. She was in a state of nudity. Cross-legged and naked, in the middle of the room sat the medicine-man, with a wooden dish of water before him; twelve or fifteen other men were sitting round the lodge. The object in view was to cure the girl of a disease affecting her side. As soon as my presence was noticed a space was cleared for me to sit down. The officiating medicine-man appeared in a state of profuse perspiration from the exertions he had used, and soon took his seat among the rest as if quite exhausted; a younger medicine-man then took his place in front of the bowl, and close beside the patient. Throwing off his blanket he commenced singing and gesticulating in the most violent manner, whilst the others kept time by beating with little sticks on hollow wooden bowls and drums, singing continually. After exercising himself in this manner for about half an hour, until the perspiration ran down his body, he darted suddenly upon the young woman, catching hold of her side with his teeth and shaking her for a few minutes, while the patient seemed to suffer great agony. He then relinquished his hold, and cried out he had got it, at the same time holding his hands to his mouth; after which he plunged them in the water and pretended to hold down with great difficulty the disease which he had extracted, lest it might spring out and return to its victim.

At length, having obtained the mastery over it, he turned round to me in an exulting manner, and held something up between the finger and thumb of each hand, which had the appearance of a piece of cartilage, whereupon one of the Indians sharpened his knife, and divided it in two, leaving one end in each hand. One of the pieces he threw into the water, and the other into the fire, accompanying the action with a diabolical noise, which none but a medicine-man can make. After which he got up perfectly satisfied with himself, although the poor patient seemed to be anything but relieved by the violent treatment she had undergone …

The land to the south of us rises in one continuous range of high mountains far as the eye can reach, the peaks of many of which are covered with snow, even at this period of the year. We ascended the river about a mile to an Indian fishing station called Suck. The whole breadth of the stream is obstructed by stakes and open work of willow and other branches, with holes at intervals leading into wicker compartments, which the fish enter in their way up the river from the sea. Once in they cannot get out, as the holes are formed with wicker work inside shaped something like a funnel or a wire mouse-trap. In this preserve they are speared without trouble when required, and the village has thus a constant supply of food. They were catching great quantities at the time of my arrival, and we obtained an abundant supply for a small piece of tobacco.

These Indians also take a great many ducks by means of a fine net stretched between two posts about thirty feet high, and fifty or sixty feet apart. This is erected in a narrow valley through which the ducks fly in the evening. A smoky fire is made at the bottom of the net, which prevents the ducks from seeing it, and when they fly against it they become confused and fall down, when they are seized by the Indians.

The wind being still too strong for us to venture, we remained until May fourteenth. Chaw-u-wit, the chief's daughter, allowed me to take her likeness. Whilst she was sitting, a great many of the Indians surrounded us, causing her much annoyance, as their native bashfulness renders all squaws particularly sensitive to any public notice or ridicule. She was, perhaps, the best-looking girl I had seen in the straits …

Chea-clach, considering that our canoe was too small, succeeded in changing it for a larger one, and at eight o'clock a.m. we embarked and proceeded to make a traverse of thirty-two miles in an open sea. When we had been out for about a couple of hours the wind increased to a perfect gale, and blowing against an ebb tide caused a heavy swell. We were obliged to keep one man constantly baling to prevent our being swamped.

The Indians on board now commenced one of their wild chants, which increased to a perfect yell whenever a wave larger than the rest approached; this was accompanied with blowing and spitting against the wind as if they were in angry contention with the evil spirit of the storm. It was altogether a scene of the most wild and intense excitement: the mountainous waves roaming round our little canoe as if to engulph us every moment, the wind howling over our heads, and the yelling Indians, made it actually terrific. I was surprised at the dexterity with which they managed the canoe, all putting out their paddles on the windward side whenever a wave broke, thus breaking its force and guiding the spray over our heads to the other side of the boat.

It was with the greatest anxiety that I watched each coming wave as it came thundering down, and I must confess that I felt considerable fear as to the event. However, we arrived safely at the fort at 2 p.m, without further damage than what we suffered from intense fatigue, as might be expected, from eleven hours' hard work, thoroughly soaked and without food; but even this soon passed away before the cheerful fire and "hearty" dinner with which we were welcomed at Fort Victoria. One of the Indians told me he had no fear during the storm, except on my account, as his brethren could easily reach the shore by swimming, even should the distance have been ten miles.

A couple of days after my arrival at the fort, I was engaged in taking the likeness of an Indian. The door of my room was suddenly thrown open, and an Indian entered of a very plain and unprepossessing appearance. As I was unwilling to be disturbed, I rather unceremoniously dismissed the intruder, and closed the door on him, supposing him to be some common Indian; for were I to admit all comers, I should have been annoyed from morning till night. About half an hour afterwards, Mr. Finlayson came in, and told me that the great Yellow-cum, the head chief of the Macaws at Cape Flattery, had arrived at the fort. I had heard so much of this chief, both from his enemies, the Clallums at I-eh-nus, and the Indians at Fort

Vancouver, that I had determined to go to Cape Flattery, a distance of sixty miles, to see him. I was therefore very glad of his coming, as it would save me the journey; and I immediately went out in search of him, and was not a little astonished and vexed to find in him the visitor I had so rudely sent out of my room. I of course apologized, by stating my ignorance of who he was, and told him how anxious I had been to see him, and of my intention of going to Cape Flattery for that purpose. He said that he will-ingly acquitted me of any intentional insult; but he had felt extremely mortified at being treated so before so many Indians.

He accompanied me to my room, where I made a sketch of him, and had from him a recital of much of his private history. Yellow-cum's father was the pilot of the unfortunate *Tonquin*, the vessel sent out by John Jacob Astor to trade with the Indians north of Vancouver's Island, mentioned in Washington Irving's *Astoria*. He was the only survivor who escaped from the vessel previous to her being blown up, the rest of the unfortunate crew having been butchered on board or blown up with the ship. It was impos-sible to obtain a clear narrative of this melancholy event, as no white man lived to tell the tale.

Yellow-cum is the wealthiest man of his tribe. His property consists prin-cipally of slaves and ioquas, a small shell found at Cape Flattery, and only there, in great abundance. These shells are used as money, and a great traffic is carried on among all the tribes by means of them. They are ob-tained at the bottom of the sea, at a considerable depth, by means of a long pole stuck in a flat board about fifteen inches square. From this board a number of bone pieces project, which, when pressed down, enter the hol-low ends of the shells, which seem to be attached to the bottom by their small ends. The shells stick on the pieces, and are thus brought to the surface. They are from an inch and a half to two inches in length, and are white, slender and hollow, and tapering to a point; slightly curved, and about the size of an ordinary tobacco-pipe stem. They are valuable in pro-portion to their length, and their value increases according to a fixed ratio, forty shells being the standard number to extend a fathom's length; which number, in that case, is equal in value to a beaver skin; but if thirty-nine be found large enough to make the fathom, it would be worth two beavers' skins; if thirty-eight, three skins; and so on, increasing one beaver skin for every shell less than the standard number.

Yellow-cum presented me with a pair of ear ornaments of these shells, consisting of seventy or eighty shells in each. His wealth also partly con-sisted of sea otter skins, which are the most valuable fur found on the North American coast, their usual value in the tariff being twelve blankets;

two blankets being equal to a gun; tobacco and ammunition and other things in proportion. The blanket is the standard by which the value of all articles on the Northwest coast is calculated. Independent of his wealth, he possesses vast influence over all the tribes, and has become head chief from his own personal prowess and ability, and not from any hereditary claim to that dignity. It may be adduced, as a proof of the courage of this chief, and of his personal confidence, that I saw him at the fort surrounded by, and in cheerful conversation with, several of the chiefs of the Clallums, with whom he had often been engaged in deadly conflict. His prudence, however, led him to remain inside the fort after nightfall.

I visited the lodges of the Eus-a-nich Indians, who were on a visit. The chief was very rich, and had eight wives with him. I made him understand, by showing him some sketches, that I wished to take his likeness. This was, however, opposed so violently by his ladies that I was glad to escape out of reach of their tongues, as they were all chattering together, while he sat like a Grand Turk, evidently flattered by the interest they showed for his welfare. A few days afterwards I met the chief some distance from his camp, and alone, when he willingly consented to let me take his likeness upon my giving him a piece of tobacco.

In one of my daily excursions I was particularly struck by the ugliness of an Indian whom I met. Upon inquiry, I found he was Shawstun, the head chief of the Sinahomas. He inquired very earnestly if my sketching him would not involve the risk of his dying; and after I had finished the sketch, and given him a piece of tobacco, he held it up for some moments, and said it was a small recompense for risking his life. He followed me afterwards for two or three days, begging of me to destroy the picture; and at last, to get rid of him, I made a rough copy of it, which I tore up in his presence, pretending that it was the original.

In the interior of New Caledonia, which is east of Vancouver's Island and north of the Columbia, among the tribe called "Taw-wa-tins," who are also Babine and also among other tribes in their neighbourhood, the custom prevails of burning the bodies, with circumstances of peculiar barbarity to the widows of the deceased. The dead body of the husband is laid naked upon a large heap of resinous wood, his wife is then placed upon the body and covered over with a skin; the pile is then lighted, and the poor woman is compelled to remain until she is nearly suffocated, when she is allowed to descend as best she can through the smoke and flames. No sooner however does she reach the ground than she is expected to prevent the body from becoming distorted by the action of the fire on the muscles and sinews; and whenever such an event takes place she must, with bare hands, restore the burning corpse to its proper position; her person being the whole time exposed to the scorching effects of the intense heat. Should she fail in the due performance of this indispensable rite, from weakness or the intensity of her pain, she is held up by someone until the body is consumed. A continual singing and beating of drums is kept up throughout the ceremony, which drowns her cries. Afterwards she must collect the unconsumed pieces of bone and ashes and put them into a bag made for the purpose, which she has to carry on her back for three years, remaining for the time a slave to her husband's relations, and being neither allowed to wash nor comb herself for the whole time, so that she soon becomes a most disgusting object. At the expiration of the three years, a feast is given by her tormentors, who invite all the friends and relations of her and themselves. At the commencement they deposit, with great ceremony, the remains of the burnt dead in a box, which they affix to the top of a high pole and dance around it. The widow is then stripped naked and smeared from head to foot with fish oil, over which one of the bystanders throws a quantity of swan's down covering her entire person. She is then obliged to dance with the others. After all this is over she is free to marry again, if she have the inclination and courage enough to venture on a second risk of being roasted alive and the subsequent horrors. It has often happened that a widow who has married a second husband, in the hope perhaps of not outliving him, committed suicide in the event of her second husband's death, rather than undergo a second ordeal ...

VISCOUNT MILTON (1839–1877)
AND W. B. CHEADLE (1835–1910)

One of the most popular British travel books of the mid-nineteenth century told the story of two young Englishmen who in 1862-3 crossed North America from the Atlantic to the Pacific "for pleasure." Their narrative, published in 1865, was titled *The NorthWest Passage by Land* and carried a lengthy subtitle explaining that they travelled "*Through British Territory by one of the Northern Passes of the Rocky Mountains.*" William Fitzwilliam (Viscount Milton) and Dr. Walter Butler Cheadle were named as the book's authors, although the publication in 1931 of Cheadle's journal of the trip makes it clear that he was the author of the narrative, and that Milton, at best, may have played some part in shortening and re-arranging passages to make it more systematic and readable as narrative. When he undertook the expedition, Cheadle was a robust and enterprising twenty-seven-year-old who had excelled in both study and sports at Cambridge; when he returned from the trip he completed an M.D. at Cambridge and enjoyed a distinguished medical career in London. His companion, Lord Viscount, was four years younger and of a frailer constitution. The *Journal* creates a picture of a man less ambitious and sometimes ill-tempered and suggests that Milton might not have survived the trip except for the care of his more sturdy and sanguine Cambridge tutor.

The two travellers left Liverpool in June 1862 and reached Quebec on July 2nd. After travelling through Ontario and the upper states they reached Fort Garry by August 7th and Fort Carleton on the North Saskatchewan by the end of September. On nearby White Fish Lake they spent a long and restless winter until April 3rd, by which time they had secured guides and provisions to set out and make their way across the Rocky Mountains. By July 17th they had made the crossing by way of the Yellowhead Pass, at that time a very little-known route, but the hardest part of the trip (excerpted here) was the journey along the Thompson River to Kamloops, which they didn't reach until August 28. They abandoned rafting as being too dangerous and proceeded to cut their way with one small axe through the deadfall and underbrush of dense forest. They were assisted by an Assiniboine Métis guide, Louis Battenotte, his wife and young son, but also in their company on this leg of the journey was one Eugene Francis O'Beirne, an egotistical and destitute Irish schoolmaster and adventurer who provides the narrative with some comic relief. This expedition marks a shift in travel undertaken for exploration and furs to a viewing of the country in terms of settlement, railways and mining. In fact, the book was framed with a plea to imperial-minded Englishmen to open the Canadian West and develop transcontinental systems of transport and commerce from ocean to ocean. Although two mountains in the upper Thompson are named for Milton and Cheadle, these young men are said to be Canada's first transcontinental tourists.

From THE NORTHWEST PASSAGE BY LAND

ON THE 31ST OF JULY we left Slaughter Camp in a pouring rain, and plunged into the pathless forest before us. We were at once brought up by the steep face of a hill which came down close to the water's edge. But the steepness of the path was not the greatest difficulty. No one who has not seen a primeval forest, where trees of gigantic size have grown and fallen undisturbed for ages, can form any idea of the collection of timber, or the impenetrable character of such a region. There were pines and thujas of every size, the patriarch of three hundred feet in height standing alone, or thickly clustering groups of young ones struggling for the vacant place of some prostrate giant. The fallen trees lay piled around, forming barriers often six or eight feet high on every side: trunks of huge cedars, moss-grown and decayed, lay half-buried in the ground on which others as mighty had recently fallen; trees still green and living, recently blown down, blocking the view with the walls of earth held in their matted roots; living trunks, dead trunks, rotten trunks; dry, barkless trunks, and trunks moist and green with moss; bare trunks and trunks with branches — prostrate, reclining, horizontal, propped up at different angles; timber of every size, in every stage of growth and decay, in every possible position, entangled in every possible combination. The swampy ground was densely covered with American dogwood, and elsewhere with thickets of the aralea [devil's club], a tough-stemmed trailer, with leaves as large as those of the rhubarb plant, and growing in many places as high as our shoulders. Both stem and leaves are covered with sharp spines, which pierced our clothes as we forced our way through the tangled growth, and made the legs and hands of the pioneers scarlet from the inflammation of myriads of punctures.

The Assiniboine went first with the axe, his wife went after him leading a horse, and the rest of the party followed, driving two or three horses apiece in single file. Mr. O'B. had by this time been trained to take charge of one pack-animal, which he managed very well under favourable conditions. But although it had been hard enough to keep our caravan in order when there was a track to follow, it was ten times more difficult and troublesome now. As long as each horse could see the one in front of him, he followed with tolerable fidelity; but whenever any little delay occurred, and the leading horses disappeared amongst the trees and underwood, the rest turned aside in different directions. Then followed a rush and scramble after them, our efforts to bring them back often only causing them to plunge into a bog or entangle themselves amongst piles of logs. When involved in any predicament of this kind, the miserable animals remained stupidly passive, for they had become so spiritless and worn out, and so injured about the legs by falling amongst the timber and rocks, that they would make no effort to help themselves, except under the stimulus of repeated blows. These accidents occurring a dozen times a day caused the labour to fall very heavily; for we were so shorthanded, that each man could obtain little assistance from the rest, and was obliged to get out of his difficulties as well as he could, unaided. When this was accomplished, often only to be effected by cutting off the packs, most of the party had gone he knew not whither, and the other horses in his charge had disappeared. These had to be sought up, and a careful cast made to regain the faint trail left by the party in advance. Another similar misfortune would often occur before he joined his companions, and the same exertions again be necessary. The work was vexatious and wearisome in the extreme, and we found our stock of philosophy quite unequal to the occasion.

With a view of economising our provisions and making more rapid progress, we reduced our meals to breakfast and supper, resting only a short time at mid-day to allow the horses to feed, but not unpacking them. Our fare was what the half-breeds call "rubaboo," which we made by boiling a piece of pemmican the size of one's fist in a large quantity of water thickened with a single handful of flour. The latter commodity had now become very valuable, and was used in this way only, three or four pounds being all we had left. Occasionally we were lucky enough to kill a partridge or skunk, and this formed a welcome addition to the "rubaboo." The mess was equally divided, and two ordinary platesful formed the portion of each individual. Under these trying circumstances we had the advantage of Mr. O'B.'s advice, which he did not fail to offer at every opportunity. When we stopped for the night, and the work of unloading the horses and preparing camp was over, he would emerge from some quiet retreat, fresh from the solace of [William] Paley [Unitarian philosopher], and deliver his opinions on the prospects of the journey and his views on the course to be pursued. "Now, my lord; now, Doctor," he would say, " I don't think that we have gone on nearly so well to-day as we might have done. I don't think our route was well chosen. We may have done fifteen or twenty miles (we had probably accomplished three or four), but that's not at all satisfactory. "*Festine lente*" was wisely said by the great lyric; but he was never lost in a forest, you see. Now, what I think ought to be done is this: the Doctor and the Assiniboine are strong vigorous fellows; let them go five or six miles ahead and investigate the country, and then we shall travel much more easily to-morrow." The two "vigorous fellows" were, however, generally too much jaded by hard work during the day to adopt his advice, and declined the proposal.

The valley continued to run nearly due south, and ranges of mountains separated only by the narrowest ravines came down from the N.E. and N.W. up to it on each side at an angle of 45 degrees. These proved serious obstacles to our progress, rising almost perpendicularly from the water's edge.

On the first of August we came in sight of a fine snowy mountain which appeared to block up the valley ahead, and we hoped this might be the second of two described to us as landmarks by the old woman at The Cache, which she stated was not far from Fort Kamloops. To this Milton gave the name of Mount Cheadle, in return for the compliment previously paid him by his companion. The river also became wider and less rapid, and at one point divided into several channels, flowing round low wooded islands. Only one snowy mountain could be seen to the right, to which we gave the name of Mount St. Anne; but the road was as encumbered as ever.

After cutting a path for two days, the Assiniboine was almost disabled by thorns in his hands and legs, and as we had not accomplished more than two or three miles each day, we attempted to escape out of the narrow valley in which we were confined, in the hope of finding clearer ground above. But the mountain sides were too steep; the horses rolled down one after another, crashing amongst the fallen timber; and we were compelled to imitate the example of the King of France, and come down again. On the 3rd we reached a marsh about three hundred yards in length, scantily covered with timber, the first open space we had met with for ten days; and the change from the deep gloom of the forest to the bright sunlight made our eyes blink indeed, but produced a most cheering effect on our spirits. The horses here found plenty of pasture, although of poor quality — a great boon to them after their long course of twigs and mare's-tail.

This was altogether a brighter day than common, for we met with several patches of raspberries, as large as English garden fruit, and two species of bilberry, the size of sloes, growing on bushes two feet high. The woods were garnished with large fern, like the English male fern, a tall and slender bracken, and quantities of the oak and beech fern. We had the luck, too, to kill four partridges for supper; and although the day was showery, and we were completely soaked in pushing through the underwood, we felt rather jollier that night than we had done since the trail ended.

Before evening we came to a rocky rapid stream from the N.W. We all mounted our horses to traverse it except Mr. O'B., who had never become reconciled to riding since his dire experience along the Fraser. What was to be done? Mr. O'B. obstinately persisted that he dare not venture on horseback, and the river was too deep and rapid to be safely forded on foot. After some useless discussion with him, we plunged our horses in, the Assiniboine and his family having crossed already; but before Cheadle's horse had left the bank a yard, Mr. O'B. rushed madly after, dashed in, and grasping the flowing tail of Bucephalus with both bands, was towed over triumphantly. After this great success, his anxiety about prospective rivers was greatly alleviated.

After leaving the little marsh above-mentioned, we were again buried in the densest forest, without any opening whatever, for several days, and worked away in the old routine of cutting through timber, driving perverse horses and extricating them from difficulties, and subsisting on our scanty mess of "rubaboo." Tracks of bears were numerous, and we saw signs of beaver on all the streams, but our advance was necessarily so noisy that we had small chance of seeing game, and we could not afford to rest a day or two for the purpose of hunting.

On the 5th, the Assiniboine's single hand became so swollen and painful from the injuries caused by the thorns of the aralea, that he was unable to handle an axe, and the task of clearing a path devolved upon Cheadle. This misfortune retarded us greatly, for he was, of course, not so expert a pioneer as The Assiniboine, and his assistance could ill be spared by the horse-drivers, who were now reduced to Milton and the boy — with Mr. O'B., who began to afford more active assistance than he had done hitherto. During this day the valley appeared to open out widely a few miles ahead, and we reached a rounded hill, from which we could see some distance to the south. But we were bitterly disappointed; vast woods were still before us without a sign of open country, and in the distance the hills closed in most ominously. At the foot of this eminence we crossed a rapid stream, flowing into the main river by two channels some twenty yards in width, which Mr. O'B. crossed with great success by his improved method.

The following day we struggled on from morning to night without stopping, through difficulties greater than ever; but on the seventh of August, the eighth day of our being lost in the forest, we crossed another stream, about thirty yards wide, clear and shallow, and evidently not fed by mountain snows. We named it Elsecar River. Soon after we were greatly encouraged by entering upon a tolerably level space, about a square mile in extent, the confluence of five narrow valleys. Part of this was timbered, some of it burnt, and the rest marshy meadow, with a few stunted trees here and there. In the burnt portion we found large quantities of small bilberries, not yet ripe, on which we stayed and dined, and then forced our way to the marshy open, where we encamped.

The hopes of speedy escape which had sprung up when we first observed the retreat of the hills to the west, were quickly dispelled. The flat proved to be a mere oasis in the mountains, surrounded by steep, pine-clad hills, from which the narrow gorges between the different ranges afforded the only means of egress. On this evening we ate our last morsel of pemmican, and the only food we had left was about a quart of flour. The distance from Tete Jaune Cache to Kamloops was, according to our map, about two hundred miles; but this estimate might be very erroneous, the exact latitude of either being probably unknown when our map was made. Calculating that we had travelled ten miles a day, or seventy miles, when the road ended, and had done three miles a day, or thirty altogether, since we began to cut our way, we had still a hundred miles to travel before reaching the Fort. Nearly the whole of this distance might be country similar to what we had already encountered. At any rate, the prospect around gave us no hope of speedy change for the better. We progressed so slowly, at the best only five or six miles a day — often not one — that it must take us many days yet to get in. There seemed no chance of any assistance, for since leaving Slaughter Camp we had seen no sign that man had ever before visited this dismal region. No axe mark on a tree, no "blaze" or broken twig, no remains of an old camp fire had greeted our eyes. Animal life was scarce, and the solemn stillness, unbroken by note of bird or sound of living creature, and the deep gloom of the woods —

"*Nulli penetrabilis astro*
Lucus iners,"

as Mr. O'B. quoted — increased the sense of solitude. We had become so worn out and emaciated by the hard work and insufficient food of the last ten days, that it was clear enough we could not hold out much longer. We held a council of war after our last meal was ended, and Mr. O'B. laid down his one-eyed spectacles and his Paley, to suggest that we should immediately kill "Blackie," as he affectionately denominated the little black horse he usually took charge of on the way. The Assiniboine and Cheadle proposed to starve a few days longer, in the hope of something turning up. Against this Mr. O'B. entered a solemn protest, and eventually Milton's proposal was agreed to. This was that the Assiniboine should spend the next day in hunting: if he were successful, we were relieved; and if not, the "Petit Noir" must die. There seemed some chance for his life, for the Assiniboine had caught sight of a bear during the day, and the dog had chased another. Their tracks were tolerably numerous, and the Assiniboine we knew to be the most expert hunter of the Saskatchewan.

Early next day, the Assiniboine set out on his hunt; Cheadle and the boy went to a small lake ahead to try to get a shot at some geese which had flown over the day before; Milton gathered bilberries; and Mr. O'B. studied; whilst the woman essayed to patch together shreds of moccasins. The party was not a lively one, for there had been no breakfast that morning. Mr. O'B., wearied of his Paley, declared that he was beginning to have painful doubts concerning his faith, and would read no more. He did not keep his resolution, however, but resumed his reading the same evening, and brought out his book afterwards at every resting-place with the same regularity as ever. In the afternoon Cheadle and the boy returned empty-handed. The Assiniboine arrived about the same time, and, producing a marten, threw it down, saying drily, " J'ai trouvé rien que cela et un homme — un mort." He directed us where to find the dead body, which was only a few hundred yards from camp, and we set off with the boy to have a look at the ominous spectacle. After a long search, we discovered it at the foot of a large pine. The corpse was in a sitting posture, with the legs crossed, and the arms clasped over the knees, bending forward over the ashes of a miserable fire of small sticks. The ghastly figure was headless, and the cervical vertebrae projected dry and bare; the skin, brown and shrivelled, stretched like parchment tightly over the bony framework, so that the ribs showed through distinctly prominent; the cavity of the chest and abdomen was filled with the exuviæ of chrysales, and the arms and legs resembled those of a mummy. The clothes, consisting of woollen shirt and leggings, with a tattered blanket, still hung round the shrunken form. Near the body were a small axe, firebag, large tin kettle and two baskets made of birch-bark. In the bag were flint, steel and tinder, an old knife, and a single charge of shot carefully tied up in a piece of rag. One of the baskets contained a fishing line of cedar bark, not yet finished, and two curious hooks, made of a piece of stick and a pointed wire; the other, a few wild onions, still green and growing. A heap of broken bones at the skeleton's side — the fragments of a horse's head — told the sad story of his fate. They were chipped into the smallest pieces, showing that the unfortunate man had died of starvation, and prolonged existence as far as possible by sucking every particle of nutriment out of the broken fragments. He was probably a Rocky Mountain Shushwap, who had been, like ourselves, endeavouring to reach Kamloops, perhaps in quest of a wife. He had evidently intended to subsist by fishing, but before his tackle was completed, weakness — perchance illness — overtook him, he made a small fire, squatted down before it, and died there. But where was his head? We searched diligently everywhere, but could find no traces of it. If it had fallen off we should have found it lying near, for an animal which had dared to abstract that would have returned to attack the body. It could not have been removed by violence, as the undisturbed position of the trunk bore witness. We could not solve the problem, and left him as we found him, taking only his little axe for our necessities, and the steel, fishing line and hooks as mementoes of the strange event. We walked back to the camp silent and full of thought. Our spirits, already sufficiently low from physical weakness and the uncertainty of our position, were greatly depressed by this somewhat ominous discovery. The similarity between the attempt of the Indian to penetrate through the pathless forest — his starvation, his killing of his horse for food — and our own condition was striking. His story had been exhibited before our eyes with unmistakable clearness by the spectacle we had just left: increasing weakness; hopeless starvation; the effort to sustain the waning life by sucking the fragments of bones; the death from want at last. We also had arrived at such extremity that we should be compelled to kill a horse. The Indian had started with one advantage over us; he was in his own country — we were wanderers in a strange land. We were in the last act of the play. Would the final scene be the same?

Every one took a rather gloomy view when we discussed our prospects that evening, and "Blackie" was unanimously condemned to die at daybreak. The marten, made into a "rubaboo," with some bilberries, formed our only supper that evening, the stinking and nauseous mess being distasteful even to our ravenous appetites, and poor Mr. O'B. had not the satisfaction of retaining what it had cost him so great an effort to swallow.

Early on the 9th of August "Blackie" was led out to execution, but although all were agreed as to the necessity of the deed, every one felt compunction at putting to death an animal which had been our companion through so many difficulties. The Assiniboine, however, at last seized his gun and dispatched him with a ball behind the ear. In a few minutes steaks were roasting at the fire, and all hands were at work cutting up the meat into thin flakes for jerking. All day long we feasted to repletion on the portions we could not carry with us, whilst the rest was drying over a large fire; for although doubts had been expressed beforehand as to whether it would prove palatable, and Milton declared it tasted of the stable, none showed any deficiency of appetite. The short intervals between eating we filled up by mending our ragged clothes and moccasins, by this time barely hanging together. Before turning into our blankets we crowned the enjoyment of the feast by one last smoke. We had not had tobacco for weeks, but now obtained the flavour of it by pounding up one or two black and well-seasoned clays, and mixing the dust with "kinnikinnick." But this was killing the goose with the golden egg, and as pure "kinnikinnick" did not satisfy the craving, we laid our pipes by for a happier day. We had tea, too — not indeed the dark decoction of black Chinese indulged in by unthrifty bachelors, or the chlorotic beverage affected by careful, mature spinsters — but the "tea muskeg" used by the Indians. This is made from the leaves and flowers of a small white azalea which we found in considerable quantities growing in the boggy ground near our camp. The decoction is really a good substitute for tea, and we became very fond of it. The taste is like ordinary black tea with a dash of senna in it.

By noon on the following day the meat was dry. There was but little of it, not more than thirty or forty pounds, for the horse was small and miserably lean, and we resolved to restrict ourselves still to a small "rubaboo" twice a day. As we had now two axes, and the Assiniboine's hand was nearly well, he and Cheadle both went ahead to clear the way, and we again entered the forest, still following the Thompson Valley. The same difficulties met us as before, the same mishaps occurred, and the horses proved as perverse and obstinate as ever. The weather was fine and exceedingly hot, and the second evening after leaving "Black Horse Camp" — as we named the scene of "Blackie's" fate — the Assiniboine, worn out by the continual toll, became thoroughly disheartened, protesting it was perfectly impossible to get through such a country, and useless to attempt it. We anxiously discussed the question, as on every evening, of how many miles we had come that day, and whether it was possible that the river we had struck might not be the Thompson at all, but some unknown stream which might lead us into inextricable difficulties. We got out our imperfect map, and showed the Assiniboine that according to that the river ran due south through a narrow valley shut in by mountains up to the very Fort, in exact correspondence, so far, with the stream along the banks of which we were making our way. This encouraged him a little, and he worked away next day with his usual untiring perseverance. We found our diet of dried horsemeat, and that in exceedingly small quantity — for we still kept ourselves on half-rations — very insufficient, and we were frightfully hungry and faint all day long. We rarely killed more than two partridges in the day, and sometimes, though not often, a skunk or a marten, and these were but little amongst six people. Cheadle at this time discovered three fish-hooks amongst the wreck of our property, and made some night lines, which he set, baited with horseflesh. These produced three white trout the first night, one of which weighed at least a couple of pounds, but, although they were diligently set every night afterwards, we never had such luck again, occasionally killing a fish, but not a dozen in all during the rest of the journey. These fish were marked like a salmon-trout, but had larger heads. They were sluggish fish, lying at the bottom of the deepest holes, and would not take a fly or spinning bait, preferring, like the other barbarous fish of the country, a piece of meat to more delicate food. They had very much the flavour of ordinary trout, but their flesh was whiter and less firm.

The aspect of the country now changed, and on the 12th of August we entered a region rocky and barren, where the timber was of smaller size, but grew much more thickly, and the surface of the ground was covered only by moss and a few small lilies. The ravine suddenly narrowed, its sides became precipitous, and the river rushed over a bed of huge boulders, a roaring, mighty rapid. The fallen timber lay as thickly and entangled as the spiculæ in the children's game of spelicans; we had literally to force our way by inches. We met with a godsend, however, in the way of provisions, shooting a porcupine which had been "treed" by the dog Papillon. We found it delicious, although rather strong-flavoured, a thick layer of fat under the skin being almost equal to that of a turtle. The road at this point became so impracticable from the steep, encumbered hillsides which came down to the water's edge, that we were frequently obliged to pull up and wait for hours whilst the Assiniboine found a way by which it was possible to pass. We expected every day to come to some barrier which would completely prevent our further advance. What course could we take then? Take to a raft or abandon our horses and climb past on foot? We feared the alternative, yet were unwilling to confess the probable extremity. We had come too far to turn back, even if we had been willing to retreat.

After three days' travelling along the bank of this rapid, to which we gave the name of Murchison's Rapids, never out of hearing of its continual roar, offensive to the ears of Mr. O'B., the valley became narrower still, and we were brought to a standstill by a precipice before us. We were shut in on one side by the river, and on the other by hills so steep and embarrassed that it seemed hopeless to attempt to scale them, for we had tried that before, and miserably failed. There was nothing for it but to camp at once, and seek a way by which to pass this barrier. The horses had not tasted grass since leaving the marsh, four days ago, and for the last three had fed upon the moss and lilies growing amongst the rocks. They wandered to and fro all the night, walking in and out between us, and stepping over us as we lay on the ground. Mr. O'B., too, passed a restless night in consequence, and aroused us continually by jumping up and whacking them with his great stick. The poor animals grubbed up the moss from the rocks, and everything green within their reach had disappeared by morning. The indefatigable Assiniboine started at daybreak to search for a path, whilst the rest of us packed the horses and awaited his return. He came back in an hour or two with the news that the country ahead grew more and more difficult, but, that we could, with care, lead the horses past the present opposing bluff. This relieved us from the fear that we might be compelled to abandon our horses here, and have to make our way on foot. We had to mount the hillside by a zigzig over loose moss-grown rocks, leading the horses past one by one. The accidents which occurred, though perhaps not so numerous as on some occasions, were more extraordinary, and will serve to illustrate what occurred daily. All the horses had safely passed the dangerous precipice except one which Cheadle was leading, and Bucephalus, in charge of Mr. O'B., who brought up the rear. The length of the zigzag was about a quarter of a mile, and when the former had got nearly over, he turned to look for those behind him. They were not to be seen. Cheadle, therefore, left his horse, and going back to see what had happened, met Mr. O'B. climbing hastily up the mountain-side, but minus Bucephalus. "Where's the horse?" said Cheadle. "Oh," said Mr. O'B., " he's gone, killed, tumbled over a precipice. *Facilis descensus*, you see. He slipped and fell over — you know, Doctor, and I have not seen him since. It's not the slightest use going back, I assure you, to look for him, for he's *comminuted,* smashed to atoms, dashed to a thousand pieces ! It's a dreadful thing, isn't it?" Cheadle, however, sternly insisted that Mr. O'B. should accompany him back to the scene of the accident, and the latter reluctantly followed.

The place where the horse had slipped and struggled was easily found, for the bark torn off the recumbent trunks marked the course of his headlong decent. The place from which he fell was about 120 or 130 feet above the river, and the last 30 or 40 feet of this a perpendicular face of rock. Cheadle crept down and looked over the edge, and on a little flat space below saw Bucephalus, astride of a large tree lengthwise. The tree was propped up by others horizontally at such a height that the animal's legs hung down on each side without touching the ground. The two then descended, expecting to find him mortally injured, but, to their astonishment, he appeared quite comfortable in his novel position. The packs were taken off, and Cheadle, by a vigorous lift — Mr. O'B. declining the suggestion that he should haul at the tail, on the ground of the dangerous nature of the service — rolled the horse from his perch. He was uninjured, and Mr. O'B. led him past the most dangerous part, whilst his companion toiled after, carrying the packs up the brow to safer ground. After the horse had been re-loaded, the two pursued their way, but before many yards were passed, the other horse slipped, and rolled down the hill. He luckily brought up against some trees before reaching the bottom; but again the pack had to be cut off, again carried up, and the horse hauled on to his legs and led up the steep. Soon after they joined the rest, another horse, refusing to jump some timber in the path, bolted aside and fell into a regular pit, formed by fallen trees and rocks; every effort to extricate him was useless. We were alone, for the rest of the party had gone on, and after trying in vain for nearly an hour, Milton ran ahead, caught them up, and brought back the axe. It was another hour's work to cut him out and re-pack, but we found our companions not far before us, and indeed there was little danger of their leaving us any great distance behind.

The river still continued a grand rapid, and a short distance more brought us to a place where the ravine suddenly narrowed to about fifty feet, with high straight-cut rocks on either side, through which, for about a hundred yards, almost at a right angle, and down a swift descent, the waters raged so frightfully about huge rocks standing out in the stream, that it was instantly named by the Assiniboine the "Porte d'Enfer." No raft or canoe could have lived there for a moment, and we thankfully congratulated ourselves that we had decided to make our way by land. We camped for the night close to where we had started in the morning, and the Assiniboine, having cut his foot to the bone on the sharp rocks, amongst which we walked nearly barefoot, was completely disabled. That night he was thoroughly disheartened, declared the river we were following was not the Thompson at all, and we must make up our minds to perish miserably. Mr. O'B. of course heartily concurred, and it required all our powers of persuasion, and an explanation by the map, to restore hope.

Another day similar to the last brought us to the end of the rapid. The woman had bravely taken her husband's place ahead with an axe, and worked away like a man. The last of the dried horseflesh, boiled with the scrapings of the flour-bag, formed our supper. We had only three charges of powder left, and this we kept for special emergency. The Assiniboine, however, and his son had succeeded in "nobbling" a brace of partridges, knocking the young birds out of the trees with short sticks, missiles they used with great dexterity. We had been cheered during the day by observing the first traces of man — except the dead body of the Indian — we had seen for sixteen days. These were old stumps of trees, which bore marks of an axe, though now decayed and mossed over. The next day, however, was cold and wet, and we felt wretched enough as we forced our way for hours through a beaver swamp, where the bracken grew higher than our heads, and tangled willows of great size required cutting away at every step. Slimy, stagnant pools, treacherous and deep, continually forced us to turn aside. At last a stream, whose banks were densely clothed with underwood, barred the path, and we could not find a practicable ford. Drenched to the skin, shivering, miserable, having had no food since the previous evening, we felt almost inclined to give way to despair, for we seemed to have gained nothing by our labours. There was no sign of the end. Our journey had now lasted nearly three months; for five weeks we had not seen a human being, nor for the last three had we seen the smallest evidence of man's presence at any time in the wild forest in which we were buried.

After several futile attempts to cross the stream, the Assiniboine sat down with his wife and son, and refused to go any further. We did not attempt to argue the matter, but, merely remarking that we did not intend to give in without another struggle, took the axes and renewed the search for a crossing place. Having at length discovered a shallow place, and cut a path to it, we led the horses into the water, but the mud was so soft and deep, and the banks so beset with slippery logs, that they could not climb up, and rolled back into the water. At this juncture the Assiniboine, fairly put to shame, came to our assistance, and we unpacked the animals and hauled them out. We were quite benumbed by standing so long up to our waists in the ice-cold water, and after we had got the horses across, as the rain still poured down, we camped on a little mound in the midst of the dismal swamp. There was no chance of finding any other provision, and we therefore led out another horse and shot him at once. Another day was occupied in drying the meat, and in mending our tattered garments as before. Mr. O'B., who, it is only justice to say, had improved vastly under his severe trials, was now plunged in the depths of despair. He confided to us that he loathed Paley, whom he looked upon as a special pleader; that his faith was sapped to its foundations, and — "*curis ingentibus aeger*" — he was rapidly becoming insane, adding that he should have lost his wits long ago but for his book; and now, since he must be deprived of that consolation, there could be but one horrible result — madness. And in truth we had noticed a remarkable change during the last week. From being the most garrulous of men, he had lately become the most taciturn; and although solemn and silent in company, he muttered to himself incessantly as he walked along. Revived, however, by a plentiful meal of fresh meat, he became more cheerful, took a more orthodox view of the "Evidences," the one-eyed spectacles again stole on to his nose, Paley again came forth from the pocket of the clerical coat, and he was presently absorbed in theology once more.

The rest of us discussed our prospects, and various plans were proposed. It was certain that the horses, already mere skeletons, could not hold out many days longer, unless they found proper pasturage. For a long time past indeed we had expected some of them to lie down and die in their tracks. Their bodies mere frames of bone covered with skin, their flanks hollow, their backs raw, their legs battered, swollen and bleeding — a band for the knackers' yard — they were painful to look upon.

The project of rafting was renewed, for the river now flowed with a tempting tranquillity; but the recollection of the Grand Rapid and Porte d'Enfer decided us against it, and doubtless we thus escaped great disaster, for we afterwards met with several dangerous rapids in the river below. We agreed to stick to our horses as long as they could travel, then kill some for provisions, and make for the Fort on foot. The Assiniboine was utterly dispirited, and continued gloomy and morose, dropping from time to time hints of desertion, and reproaching us bitterly with having led him into such desperate straits. He camped apart from us, with his wife and boy, holding frequent and significant consultations with them; and it required all the forbearance we could command to prevent an open rupture with the man and his family.

On the morning of the 18th, before we started, our ears were greeted by the cry of that bird of ill omen, a crow — to us proclaiming glad tidings, for it was a sure indication of more open country being at hand. Our spirits were raised still more by observing during the day's journey signs of man's presence as recent as the preceding spring — a few branches cut with a knife, as if by some one making his way through the bushes.

A heavy thunderstorm which came on obliged us to camp very early; but the next day we struck a faint trail, which slightly improved as we advanced and towards evening we found the tracks of horses. The path disappeared, and re-appeared again, during the next two days, and was still very dubious and faint, so that we were afraid it might be a deceptive one, after all; but on the night of the 21st we came to a marsh where horse tracks were very numerous and found on the further side, where we camped, a large cedar felled, from which a canoe had been made. On a tree was an inscription which was not legible, although the words seemed to be English. To our intense delight, the next morning we hit upon a trail where the trees had been "blazed," or marked with an axe a long time ago, and old marten-traps at intervals informed us that we had at last touched the extreme end of an old trapping path from the Fort. The valley began rapidly to expand, the hills became lower, the trail continued to become more and more beaten, and at noon on the 22nd we fairly shouted for joy as we emerged from the gloom in which we had so long been imprisoned, on to a beautiful little prairie, and saw before us a free, open country, diversified with rounded hills and stretches of woodland. We stopped with one accord, and lay down on the green turf, basking in the sun, whilst we allowed our horses to feed on the rich prairie grass, such as they had not tasted since leaving Edmonton.

The day was gloriously bright and fine, and the delight with which we gazed upon the beautiful landscape before us will be appreciated, if the reader will reflect that we had travelled for more than eleven weeks without cessation, and for the last month had been lost in the forest, starving, over-worked, almost hopeless of escape. Even Mr. O'B, who had resumed the study of Paley with renewed zest, looked up from his book from time to time, and ventured to express a hope that we *might* escape, after all, and offered his advice upon the course to be pursued in the happier time at hand.

EMILY CARR (1871–1945)

Emily Carr is an artistic figure of such immense strength, sensitivity and accomplishment that she seems to cast both light and shadow on all B.C. artists who follow after her. Like the D'Sonoqua figure in one of her best known stories, Carr is both the "Wild Woman of the Woods" and "a forest creature" which no violence can "coarsen," no power "domineer" — a "graciously feminine" creative force. As a painter, Carr created a new vocabulary to represent the peoples and landscapes of the Pacific Northwest. She turned to writing after ill-health prevented her from journeying into the west coast wilderness she loved so much. From her home near Victoria's Beacon Hill Park she became known both as an eccentric and as one of the most original artists Canada has yet produced. Her book of journeys to west coast native villages, *Klee Wyck* (1941), won a Governor General's Award and has become a classic of Canadian travel writing. Carr's creativity spilled out in many other literary forms. In her collection of autobiographical sketches *The Book of Small* (1942), Carr traces a magical childhood in a small colonial outpost at the edge of the rainforest. The first essay in that book, "Sunday," is an utterly convincing portrait of Victorian family life on one eternal Sunday in Carr's life. The autobiography *Growing Pains* (1946) contains Carr's account of her return to Canada from London and the continent — "broken in health" after having "taken a rather hard whipping" — and her gradual return to health in the Cariboo country where everything is gold, and open, and free. And her journals, *Hundreds and Thousands* (1966), give the mature reflections of an artist seeking to understand the underlying forms of nature. In every genre of writing she attempted — autobiography, fiction, travel, non-fiction, journals — Carr was a Canadian original.

From THE BOOK OF SMALL
SUNDAY

ALL OUR SUNDAYS were exactly alike. They began on Saturday night after Bong the Chinaboy had washed up and gone away, after our toys, dolls and books, all but *The Peep of Day* and Bunyan's *Pilgrim's Progress*, had been stored away in drawers and boxes till Monday, and every bible and prayerbook in the house was puffing itself out, looking more important every minute.

Then the clothes-horse came galloping into the kitchen and straddled round the stove inviting our clean clothes to mount and be aired. The enormous wooden tub that looked half coffin and half baby-bath was set in the middle of the kitchen floor with a rag mat for dripping on laid close beside it. The great iron soup pot, the copper wash-boiler and several kettles covered the top of the stove, and big sister Dede filled them by working the kitchen pump-handle furiously. It was a sad old pump and always groaned several times before it poured. Dede got the brown windsor soap, heated the towels and put on a thick white apron with a bib. Mother unbuttoned us and by that time the pots and kettles were steaming.

Dede scrubbed hard. If you wriggled, the flat of the long-handled tin dipper came down spankety on your skin.

As soon as each child was bathed Dede took it pick-aback and rushed it upstairs through the cold house. We were allowed to say our prayers kneeling in bed on Saturday night, steamy, brown-windsory prayers — then we cuddled down and tumbled very comfortably into Sunday.

At seven o'clock Father stood beside our bed and said, "Rise up! Rise up! It's Sunday, children." He need not have told us; we knew Father's Sunday smell — Wright's coal-tar soap and camphor. Father had a splendid chest of camphor-wood which had come from England round the Horn in a sailing-ship with him. His clean clothes lived in it and on Sunday he was very camphory. The chest was high and very heavy. It had brass handles and wooden knobs. The top let down as a writing desk with pigeonholes; below there were little drawers for handkerchiefs and collars and long drawers for clothes. On top of the chest stood Father's locked desk for papers. The key of it was on his ring with lots of others. This desk had a secret drawer and a brass plate with R. H. CARR engraved on it.

On top of the top desk stood the little Dutchman, a china figure with a head that took off and a stomach full of little candies like coloured hailstones. If we had been very good all week we got hailstones Sunday morning.

Family prayers were uppish with big words on Sunday — reverend aweful words that only God and Father understood.

No work was done in the Carr house on Sunday. Everything had been polished frightfully on Saturday and all Sunday's food cooked too. On Sunday morning Bong milked the cow and went away from breakfast until evening milking time. Beds were made, the dinner table set, and then we got into our very starchiest and most uncomfortable clothes for church.

Our family had a big gap in the middle of it where William, John and Thomas had all been born and died in quick succession, which left a wide space between Dede and Tallie and the four younger children.

Lizzie, Alice and I were always dressed exactly alike. Father wanted my two big sisters to dress the same, but they rebelled, and Mother stood behind them. Father thought we looked like orphans if we were clothed differently. The Orphans sat in front of us at church. No two of them had anything alike. People gave them all the things their own children had grown out of — some of them were very strange in shape and colour.

When we were all dressed, we went to Mother's room to be looked over. Mother was very delicate and could not get up early or walk the two miles to church, and neither could Tallie or little Dick.

Father went to Dr. Reid's Presbyterian Church at the corner of Pandora and Blanshard streets. Father was not particularly Presbyterian, but he was a little deaf and he liked Dr. Reid because, if we sat at the top of the church, he could hear his sermons. There was just the Orphans in front of us, and the stove in front of them. The heat of the stove sent them all to sleep. But Dr. Reid was a kind preacher — he did not bang the Bible nor shout to wake them up. Sometimes I went to sleep too, but I tried not to because of what happened at home after Sunday's dinner.

If the road had not been so crooked it would have been a straight line from the gate of our lily field to the church door. We did not have to turn a single corner. Lizzie, Alice and I walked in the middle of the road and took hands. Dede was on one end of us and Father the other. Dede carried a parasol, and Father, a fat yellow stick, not a flourish stick but one to walk with. If we met anything, we dangled in a row behind Father like the tail of a kite.

We were always very early for church and could watch the Orphans march in. The Matron arranged every bad Orphan between two good ones, and put very little ones beside big ones, then she set herself down behind them where she could watch and poke any Orphan that needed it. She was glad when the stove sent them all to sleep and did not poke unless an Orphan had adenoids and snored.

The minute the church bell stopped a little door in front of the Orphans opened, and Dr. Reid came out and somebody behind him shut the door, which was rounded at the top and had a reverend shut.

Dr. Reid had very shiny eyes and very red lips. He wore a black gown with two little white tabs like the tail of a bird sticking out from under his beard. He carried a roll in his hand like Moses, and on it were all the things that he was going to say to us. He walked slowly between the Orphans and the stove and climbed into the pulpit and prayed. The S's sizzled in his mouth as if they were frying. He was a very nice minister and the only parson that Father ever asked to dinner.

The moment Dr. Reid amened, we rushed straight out of the church off home. Father said it was very bad taste for people to stand gabbing at church doors. We came down Church Hill, past the Convent Garden, up Marvin's Hill, through the wild part of Beacon Hill Park into our own gate. The only time we stopped was to gather some catnip to take home to the cats, and the only turn we made was into our own gate.

Our Sunday dinner was cold saddle of mutton. It was roasted on Saturday in a big tin oven on legs, which was pushed up to the open grate fire in the breakfast room. Father had this fireplace specially built just like the ones in England. The oven fitted right up to it. He thought everything English was much better than anything Canadian. The oven came round the Horn with him, and the big pewter hot water dishes that he ate chops and steaks off, and the heavy mahogany furniture and lots of other things that you could not buy in Canada then. The tin oven had a jack which you wound up like a clock and it turned the roast on a spit. It said 'tick, tick, tick' and turned the meat one way, and then 'tock, tock, tock' and turned it the other. The meat sizzled and sputtered. Someone was always opening the little door in the back to baste it, using a long iron spoon, with the dripping that was caught in a pan beneath the meat. Father said no roast under twenty pounds was worth eating because the juice had all run out of it, so it was lucky he had a big family.

Red currant jelly was served with the cold mutton and potato salad and pickled cabbage; afterwards was deep apple pie with lots of Devonshire cream. In the centre of the dinner table, just before the cruet stand, stood an enormous loaf of bread. Mr. Harding, the baker, cooked one for Father every Saturday. It was four loaves baked in one so that it did not get as stale as four small loaves would have. It was made cottage-loaf shape — two storeys high with a dimple in the top.

When dinner was finished, Father folded his napkin very straight, he even slipped his long fingers inside each fold again after it was in the ring, for Father always wanted everything straight and right. Then he looked up one side of the table and down the other. We all tried not to squirm because he always picked the squirmiest. When he had decided who should start, he said, "Tell me what you remember of the sermon."

If Dede was asked first, she "here and there'd" all over the sermon. If it was Lizzie, she plowed steadily through from text to amen. Alice always remembered the text. Sometimes I remembered one of Dr. Reid's jokes, that is if I was asked first — if not, I usually said, "The others have told it all, Father," and was dreadfully uncomfortable when Father said, "Very well; repeat it, then."

When we had done everything we could with Dr. Reid's sermon, Father went into the sitting room to take his Sunday nap, Mother read and Dede took hold of our religion.

She taught Sunday School in Bishop Cridge's house, to a huge family of Balls and an enormous family of Fawcetts, a smarty boy called Eddy, a few other children who came and went, and us. The Bishop's invalid sister sat in the room all the time. Her cheeks were hollow, she had sharp eyes with red rims, sat by the fire, wore a cap and coughed, not because she had to, but just to remind us that she was watching and listening.

From dinner till it was time to go to the Bishop's, we learned collects, texts and hymns. Dede was shamed because the Balls, the Fawcetts and all the others did better than I who was her own sister.

You got a little text-card when you knew your lessons. When you had six little cards you had earned a big card. I hardly ever got a little card and always lost it on the way home, so that I never earned a big one. I could sing much better than Addie Ball who just talked the hymns out very loud, but Dede only told me not to shout and let Addie groan away without any tune at all.

When Dede marched us home, Father was ready, and Mother had her hat on, to start for the Sunday walk around our place. Dede stayed home to get the tea, but first she played very loud hymns on the piano. They followed us all round the fields. Tallie was not strong enough for the walking so she lay on the horse-hair sofa in the drawing room looking very pretty, resting up for her evening visitor. Lizzie squeezed out of coming whenever she could because she had rather creep into a corner and learn more texts. She had millions of texts piled up inside her head just waiting for things to happen, then she pushed the right text over onto them. If you got mad any time after noon, the sun was going to set on your wrath. You could feel the great globe getting hotter and hotter and making your mad fiercer because of the way the text stirred it up. If you did not see things just in Lizzie's way, you were dead in your sins.

So the rest of us started for the Sunday walk. We went out the side door into the garden, through ever so many gates and the cow-yard, on into a shrubbery which ran round two sides of the cow pasture, but was railed off to keep the cows from destroying the shrubs. A twisty little path ran through the shrubbery. Father wanted his place to look exactly like England. He planted cowslips and primroses and hawthorn hedges and all the Englishy flowers. He had stiles and meadows and took away all the wild Canadian-ness and made it as meek and English as he could …

Father's stick was on the constant poke, pushing a root down or a branch up, or a stone in place, for he was very particular about everything being just right.

As we neared the top corner of our big field, that one wild place where the trees and bushes were allowed to grow thick and tangled, and where there was a deep ditch with stinging nettles about it, and a rank, muddy smell, Father began to frown and to walk faster and faster till we were crouched down in the path, running after one another like frightened quail. If there were voices on the other side of the hedge, we raced like mad.

This corner of Father's property always made him very sore. When he came from England he bought ten acres of fine land adjoining Beacon Hill Park which was owned by the City of Victoria. It took Father a lot of money to clear his land. He left every fine tree he could, because he loved trees, but he cleared away the scrub to make meadows for the cows, and a beautiful garden. Then he built what was considered in 1863 a big fine house. It was all made of California redwood. The chimneys were of California brick and the mantlepieces of black marble. Every material used in the building of Father's house was the very best, because he never bought anything cheap or shoddy. He had to send far away for most of it, and all the time his family getting bigger and more expensive, too; so, when a Mrs. Lush came and asked if he would sell her the corner acre next to the Park and farthest away from our house and as she offered a good price, he sold. But he first said, "Promise me that you will never build a Public House on the land," and Mrs. Lush said, "No, Mr. Carr, I never will." But as soon as the land was hers, Mrs. Lush broke her word, and put up one of the horridest saloons in Victoria right there. Father felt dreadful, but he could not do anything about it, except to put up a high fence and coax that part of the hawthorn hedge to grow as tall and be as prickly as it could.

Mrs. Lush's Public House was called the Park Hotel but afterwards the name was changed to the Colonist Hotel. It was just a nice drive from Esquimalt, which was then a Naval Station, and hacks filled with tipsy sailors and noisy ladies drove past our house going to the Park Hotel in the daytime and at night. It hurt Father right up till he was seventy years old, when he died.

After we had passed the Park Hotel acre we went slow again so that Father could enjoy his land. We came to the "pickets," a sort of gate without hinges; we lifted the pickets out of notches in the fence and made a hole through which we passed into the lily field.

Nothing, not even fairyland, could have been so lovely as our lily field. The wild lilies blossomed in April or May but they seemed to be always in the field, because, the very first time you saw them, they did something to the back of your eyes which kept themselves there, and something to your nose, so that you smelled them whenever you thought of them. The field was roofed by tall, thin pine trees. The ground underneath was clear and grassed. The lilies were thickly sprinkled everywhere. They were white, with gold in their hearts and brown eyes that stared back into the earth because their necks hooked down. But each lily had five sharp white petals rolling back and pointing to the tree-tops, like millions and millions of tiny quivering fingers. The smell was fresh and earthy. In all your thinkings you could picture nothing more beautiful than our lily field.

We turned back towards our house then, and climbed a stile over a snake fence. On the other side of the fence was a mass of rock, rich and soft with moss, and all round it were mock orange and spirea and oak trees.

Father and Mother sat down upon the rock. You could see the thinking in their eyes. Father's was proud thinking as he looked across the beautiful place that he had made out of wild Canadian land — he thought how splendidly English he had made it look. Mother's eyes followed our whispered Sunday playing.

When Father got up, Mother got up too. We walked round the lower hay field, going back into the garden by the black gate, on the opposite side of the house from which we had left. Then we admired the vegetables, fruit and flowers until the front door flew open and Dede jangled the big brass dinner bell for us to come in to tea.

When the meal was finished the most sober part of all Sunday came, and that was the Bible reading. Church and Sunday School had partly belonged to Dr. Reid and Dede. The Bible reading was all God's. We all came into the sitting-room with our faces very straight and our Bibles in our hands.

There was always a nice fire in the grate, because, even in summer, Victoria nights are chilly. The curtains were drawn across the windows and the table was in front of the fire. It was a round table with a red cloth, and the brass lamp sitting in the middle threw a fine light on all the Bibles when we drew our chairs in close.

Father's chair was big and stuffed, Mother's low, with a high back. They faced each other where the table began to turn away from the fire. Between their chairs where it was too hot for anyone to sit, the cats lay sprawling on the rug before the fire. We circled between Father and Mother on the other side of the table.

Father opened the big Family Bible at the place marked by the cross-stitch text Lizzie had worked. In the middle of the Bible, between the "old" and the "new," were some blank pages, and all of us were written there. Sometimes Father let us look at ourselves and at William, John and Thomas who were each written there twice, once for being born, and once for dying. That was the only time that John, Thomas and William seemed to be real and take part in the family's doings. We did little sums with their Bible dates, but could never remember if they had lived for days or years. As they were dead before we were born, and we had never known them as Johnny- or Tommy- or Willie-babies, they felt old and grown up to us.

Tallie was more interested in the marriage page. There was only one entry on it, "Richard and Emily Carr", who were Father and Mother.

Tallie said, "Father, Mother was only eighteen when she married you, wasn't she?

"Yes," said Father, "and had more sense than some girls I could name at twenty." He was always very frowny when the doorbell rang in the middle of Bible reading and Tallie went out and did not come back.

We read right straight through the Bible, begat chapters and all, though even Father stuck at some of the names.

On and on we read till the nine o'clock gun went off at Esquimalt. Father, Mother and Dede set their watches by the gun and then we went on reading again until we came to the end of the chapter. The three smallest of us had to spell out most of the words and be told how to say them. We got most dreadfully sleepy. No matter how hard you pressed your finger down on the eighth verse from the last one you had read, when the child next to you was finishing and kicked your shin you jumped and the place was lost. Then you got scolded and were furious with your finger. Mother said, "Richard, the children are tired," but Father said, "Attention! Children" and went right on to the end of the chapter. He thought it was rude to God to stop in a chapter's middle nor must we shut our Bibles up with a glad bang when at last we were through.

No matter how sleepy we had been during Bible reading, when Father got out the *Sunday at Home* we were wide awake to hear the short chapter of the serial story. Father did not believe in fairy stories for children. *At the Back of the North Wind* was as fairy as anything, but, because it was in the *Sunday at Home*, Father thought it was all right.

We kissed Mother good night. While the others were kissing Father I ran behind him (I did so hate kissing beards) and, if Father was leaning back, I could just reach his bald spot and slap the kiss there.

Dede lighted the candle and we followed her, peeping into the drawing room to say good night to Tallie and her beau. We did not like him much because he kissed us and was preachy when we cheeked pretty Tallie, who did not rule over us as Dede did; but he brought candy — chocolates for Tallie and a bag of "broken mixed" for the children, big hunky pieces that sucked you right into sleep.

Dede put Dick to bed. Lizzie had a room of her own. Alice and I shared. We undid each other and brushed our hair to long sweet suckings.

"I wish he'd come in the morning before church."

"What for?"

"Sunday'd be lots nicer if you could have a chunk of candy in your cheek all day."

"Stupid! Could you go to church with candy poking out of your cheek like another nose? Could you slobber candy over your Sunday School Lesson and the Bible reading?"

Alice was two years older than I. She stopped brushing her long red hair, jumped into bed, leaned over the chair that the candle sat on.

Pouf! ... Out went Sunday and the candle.

From GROWING PAINS
CARIBOO GOLD

JUST BEFORE I left England a letter came from Cariboo out in British Columbia. It said, "Visit us at our Cariboo Ranch on your way west." The inviters were intimate friends of my girlhood. They had married while I was in England. Much of their love-making had been in my old barn studio. The husband seconded his wife's invitation, saying in a PS., "Make it a long visit. Leave the C.P.R. train at Ashcroft. You will then travel horse-coach to the One Hundred and Fifty Mile House up the Cariboo Road, a pretty bumpy road too … I will make arrangements."

I had always wanted to see the Cariboo country. It is different from the coast, less heavily wooded, a grain and cattle-raising country. Coming as the invitation did, a break between the beating London had given me and the humiliation of going home to face the people of my own town, a failure, the Cariboo visit would be a flash of joy between two sombres. I got happier and happier every mile as we pushed west.

I loved Cariboo from the moment the C.P.R. train spat me out of its bouncy coach. It was all fresh and yet it contained the breath and westernness that was born in me, the thing I could not find in the Old World.

I will admit that I did suffer two days of violence at the mercy of the six-horse stagecoach which bumped me over the Cariboo Road and finally deposited me at the door of One Hundred and Fifty Mile House where my friend lived, her husband being manager of the Cariboo Trading Company there. It had been a strange, rough journey yet full of interest. No possible springs could endure such pitch and toss as the bumps and holes in the old Cariboo road-bed played. The coach was slung on tremendous leather straps and, for all that it was so ponderous, it swayed and bounced like a swing.

A lady schoolteacher, very unenthusiastic at being assigned a rural school in the Cariboo, shared the front top seat with the driver and me. She did not speak, only sighed. The three of us were buckled into our seats by a great leather apron. It caught driver round the middle and teacher and me under our chins. We might have both been infant triplets strapped abreast into the seat of a mammoth pram. If we had not been strapped we would have flown off the top of the stage. At the extra-worst bumps the heads of the inside passengers hit the roof of the coach. We heard them.

We changed horses every ten miles and wished we could change ourselves, holding onto yourself mile after mile got so tiresome. The horses saved all their prance for final show-off dashings as they neared the changing barns; here they galloped full pelt. Driver shouted and the whip cracked in the clear air. Fresh horses pranced out to change places with tired ones, lively and gay, full of show-off. When blinkers were adjusted on the fresh horses so as not to tell tales, the weary ones sagged into the barn, their show-off done. The whole change only took a minute, scarcely halting our journey. Sometimes the driver let us climb a short hill on foot to ease the load and to uncramp us.

It was beautiful country we passed through — open and rolling — vast cattle ranges, zig-zag snake fences and beast-dotted pasturage with little groves of cotton-poplars spread here and there. There were great wide tracts of wild grazing too.

The cotton-poplars and the grainfields were turning every shade of yellow. The foliage of the trees was threaded with the cottonwood's silverwhite stems. Long, level sweeps of rippling gold grain were made richer and more luscious by contrast with the dun, already harvested stubble fields. Men had called the land "Golden Cariboo" because of the metal they took from her soil and her crocks, but Cariboo's crust was of far more exquisite gold than the ore underneath — liquid, ethereal, living gold. Everything in Cariboo was touched with gold, even the chipmunks had golden stripes running down their brown coats. They were tiny creatures, only mouse-big. They scampered, beyond belief quick, in single file processions of twinkling hurry over the top rail of the snake fences, racing our stagecoach.

At dark we stopped at a roadhouse to eat and sleep. Cariboo provides lavishly. We ate a huge meal and were then hustled off to bed only to be torn from sleep again at two a.m. and re-mealed — a terrible spread, neither breakfast, dinner, nor supper, but a "three-in-one" meal starting with porridge, bacon and eggs, and coffee, continuing with beef-steak, roast potatoes, and boiled cabbage, culminating in pudding, pie and strong tea. The meal climaxed finally on its centre-piece, an immense, frosted jelly-cake mounted on a pedestal platter. Its gleaming frosting shimmered under a coal-oil lamp, suspended over the table's centre. At first I thought it was a wedding cake but as every meal in every roadhouse in Cariboo had just such a cake I concluded it was just Cariboo. The teacher's stomach and mine were taken aback at such a meal at such an hour. We shrank, but our hostess and the driver urged, "Eat, eat; it's a long, hard ride and no stop till noon." The bumps would digest us. We did what we could.

At three a.m. we trembled out into the cold stillness of starry not-yet-day. A slow, long hill was before us. The altitude made my head woozey. It wobbled over the edge of the leather apron buckled under our chins. Between teacher and driver I slept, cosy as jam in a "roly-poly."

The Hundred and Fifty Mile trading post consisted of a store, a roadhouse where travellers could stop or could pause between stages to get a meal, and a huge cattle barn. These wooden structures stood on a little rise and, tucked below, very primitive and beyond our seeing and hearing (because the tiny village lay under the bluff on which sat the Cariboo Trading Company) were a few little houses. These homes housed employees of the Company. On all sides, beyond the village, lay a rolling sea of land, vast cattle ranges, snake-fenced grainfields — space, space. Wild creatures, big and little, were more astonished than frightened at us; all they knew was space.

My friend met the coach.

"Same old Millie!" she laughed. Following her point and her grin, I saw at my feet a small black cat rubbing ecstatically round my shoes.

"Did you bring her all the way uncrated?"

"I did not bring her at all; does she not belong here?"

"Not a cat in the village."

Wherever she belonged, the cat claimed me. It was as if she had expected me all her life and was beyond glad to find me. She followed my every step. We combed the district later trying to discover her owner. No one had seen the creature before. At the end of my two months' visit in the Cariboo I gave her to a kind man in the store, very eager to have her. Man and cat watched the stage lumber away. The man stooped to pick up his cat, she was gone — no one ever saw her again.

I can never love Cariboo enough for all she gave to me. Mounted on a cow-pony I roamed the land, not knowing where I went — to be alive, going, that was enough. I absorbed the trackless, rolling space, its cattle, its wildlife, its shy creatures who wondered why their solitudes should be plagued by men and guns.

Up to this time I had always decorously used a sidesaddle and had ridden in a stiff hat and the long, flapping habit proper for the date. There was only one old, old horse, bony and with a rough, hard gait that would take sidesaddle in the Cariboo barns. My friend always rode this ancient beast and used an orthodox riding habit. I took my cue from a half-breed girl in the district, jumped into a Mexican cowboy saddle and rode astride, loping over the whole country, riding, riding to nowhere. Oh goodness! how happy I was! Though far from strong yet, in this freedom and fine air I was gaining every week. When tired, I threw the reins over the pommel and sat back in the saddle leaving direction to the pony, trusting him to take me home unguided. He never failed.

I tamed squirrels and chipmunks, taking them back to Victoria with me later. I helped my host round up cattle, I trailed breaks in fences when our cattle strayed. A young coyote and I met face to face in a field once. He had not seen nor winded me. We nearly collided. We sat down a few feet apart to consider each other. He was pretty, this strong young prairie-wolf.

The most thrilling sight I saw in the Cariboo was a great company of wild geese feeding in a field. Wild geese are very wary. An old gander is always posted to warn the flock of the slightest hint of danger. The flock were feeding at sundown. The field looked like an immense animated page of "pothooks" as the looped necks of the feeding birds rose and fell, rose and fell. The sentinel honked! With a whirr of wings, a straightening of necks and a tucking back of legs, the flock rose instantly — they fell into formation, a wedge cutting clean, high air, the irregular monotony of their honking tumbling back to earth, falling in a flurry through the air, helter-skelter, falling incessant as the flakes in a snow storm. Long after the sky had taken the geese into its hiding their honks came back to earth and us.

Bands of coyotes came to the creek below our windows and made night hideous by agonized howlings. No one had warned me and the first night I thought some fearfulness had overtaken the world. Their cries expressed woe, cruelty, anger, utter despair! Torn from sleep I sat up in my bed shaking, my room reeking with horror! Old miners say the coyote is a ventriloquist, that from a far ridge he can throw his voice right beside you, while from close he can make himself sound very far. I certainly thought that night my room was stuffed with coyotes.

In Cariboo I did not paint. I pushed paint away from me together with the failure and disappointment of the last five years.

There was an Indian settlement a mile or two away. I used to ride there to barter my clothing for the Indians' beautiful baskets. At last I had nothing left but the clothes I stood in but I owned some nice baskets.

My friend was puzzled and disappointed. We had known each other since early childhood. She had anticipated my companionship with pleasure — but here I was!

"Millie!" she said disgustedly, "you are as immature and unsophisticated as when you left home. You must have gone through London with your eyes shut!" and, taking her gun, she went out.

She seldom rode, preferring to walk with gun and dog. She came home in exasperated pets of disgust.

"Never saw a living creature — did you?"

"All kinds; the critters know the difference between a sketching easel and a gun," I laughed.

We never agreed on the subject of shooting. She practised on any living thing. It provoked her that creatures would not sit still to be shot.

"London has not sophisticated you at all," she complained. "I have quite outgrown you since I married."

Perhaps, but maybe London had had less to do with retarding my development than disappointment had. She was bored by this country as I had been bored by London. Quite right, we were now far apart as the poles — no one's fault. Surfacely we were very good friends, down deep we were not friends at all, not even acquaintances.

Winter began to nip Cariboo. The coast called and Vancouver Island, that one step more Western than the West. I went to her, longing yet dreading. Never had her forests looked so solemn, never her mountains so high, never her drift-laden beaches so vast. Oh, the gladness of my West again! Immense Canada! Oh, her Pacific edge, her Western limit! I blessed my luck in being born Western as I climbed the stair of my old barn studio.

During my absence my sister had lent the studio to a parson to use for a study. He had papered the walls with the *Daily Colonist,* sealed the windows. There were no cobwebs, perhaps he had concocted them into sermons. As I ran across the floor to fling the window wide everything preached at me.

Creak of rusty hinge, the clean air rushed in! The cherry tree was gone, only the memory of its glory left. Was everything gone or dead or broken? No! Hurrying to me came Peacock, my Peacock! Who had told him I was come? He had not been up on the studio roof this last five years. Glorious, exultant, he spread himself.

Victoria had driven the woods back. My sister owned a beautiful mare which she permitted me to ride. On the mare, astride as I had ridden in Cariboo, my sheepdog following, I went into the woods. No woman had ridden cross-saddle before in Victoria! Victoria was shocked! My family sighed. Carrs had always conformed; they believed in what always has been continuing always to be. Cross-saddle! Why, everyone disapproved! Too bad, instead of England gentling me into an English Miss with nice ways I was more me than ever, just pure me.

One thing England had taught me which my friends and relatives would not tolerate — smoking! Canadians thought smoking women fast, bad. There was a scene in which my eldest sister gave her ultimatum. "If smoke you must, go to the barn and smoke with the cow. Smoke in my house you shall not."

So I smoked with the cow. Neither she nor I were heavy smokers but we enjoyed each other's company.

And so I came back to British Columbia not with "know-it-all" fanfare, not a successful student prepared to carry on art in the New World, just a broken-in-health girl that had taken rather a hard whipping, and was disgruntled with the world

Of my three intimate school friends two were married and living in other places, the third was nursing in San Francisco. I made no new friends; one does not after schooldays, unless there are others who are going your way or who have interests in common. Nobody was going my way, and their way did not interest me. I took my sheepdog and rode out to the woods. There I sat, dumb as a plate, staring, absorbing tremendously, though I did not realize it at the time. Again I was struck by that vague similarity between London crowds and Canadian forests; each having its own sense of terrific power, density and intensity, but similarity ceased there. The clamorous racing of hot human blood confused, perhaps revolted me a little sometimes. The woods standing, standing, holding the cool sap of vegetation were healing, restful after seeing the boil of humanity.

It did me no harm to sit idle, still pondering in the vastness of the West where every spilled sound came tumbling back to me in echo. After the mellow sweetness of England with its perpetual undertone of humanity it was good to stand in space.

From HUNDREDS AND THOUSANDS: The Journals of Emily Carr

TUESDAY, January 20th, 1931

I have been to the woods at Esquimalt. Day was splendid — sunshine and blue, blue sky, and two arbutus with tender satin bark, smooth and lovely as naked maidens, silhouetted against the rough pine woods. Very joyous and uplifting, but surface representation does not satisfy me now. I want not "the accidentals of individual surface" but "the universals of basic form, the factor that governs the relationship of part to part, of part to whole and of the whole object to the universal environment of which it forms part."

Wednesday, January 28th

For the first time in two months the pendulum has begun to swing. I was working on a big totem with heavy woods behind. How badly I want that nameless thing! First there must be an idea, a feeling, or whatever you want to call it, the something that interested or inspired you sufficiently to make you desire to express it. Maybe it was an abstract idea that you've got to find a symbol for, or maybe it was a concrete form that you have to simplify or distort to meet your ends, but that starting point must pervade the whole. Then you must discover the pervading direction, the pervading rhythm, the dominant, recurring forms, the dominant colour, but always the *thing* must be top in your thoughts. Everything must lead up to it, clothe it, feed it, balance it, tenderly fold it, till it reveals itself in all the beauty of its idea.

Lawren Harris got the $500 award from the Baltimore show for that lovely stump thing. I am so glad he got the recognition. He so richly deserves it and doesn't get half enough. He is always so modest.

A picture does not want to be a design no matter how lovely. A picture is an expressed thought for the soul. A design is a pleasing arrangement of form and colour for the eye.

Sunday, February 1st

I worked all afternoon, first on "Koskemo Village," X. 1., and then on X. 2., "Strangled by Growth," which is also Koskemo (the cat village). It is D'Sonoqua on the housepost up in the burnt part, strangled round by undergrowth. I want the pole vague and the tangle of growth strenuous. I want the ferocious, strangled lonesomeness of that place, creepy, nervy, forsaken, dank, dirty, dilapidated, the rank smell of nettles and rotting wood, the lush greens of the rank sea grass and the overgrown bushes, and the great dense forest behind full of unseen things and great silence, and on the sea the sun beating down, and on the sand, everywhere, circling me, that army of cats, purring and rubbing, following my every footstep. That was some place! There was a power behind it all, and stark beauty.

March 19th

The earth is soaked and soggy with rain. Everything is drinking its fill and the surplus gluts the drains. The sky is full of it and lies low over the earth, heavy and dense. Even the sea is wetter than usual! I want to paint some skies so that they look roomy and moving and mysterious and to make them overhang the earth, to have a different quality in their distant horizon and their overhanging nearness. I'm still on Indian stuff as it's too wet for the woods, but, oh joy, spring is coming, growing time for the earth and all that is therein. The papers are full of horrible horrors and the earth is lovely. Money and power, how little either counts!

April 7th

Last night I went up on Beacon Hill and rose into the clouds. Everywhere was beautiful, full of colour and life. There were bulging clouds and little fussing ones, light and shadow clouds and blue, blue sky between. The broom was a wonderful green. The sea, too, was mysterious and a little hazy. There were two bright spots of gold peering through a black cloud and sending beams of light down. I thought they might have been God's eyes. Tonight it was all different, so bitterly cold, and hard, angry-looking bunches of cloud, and everything beaten about and sallow-looking and mad. One didn't want to linger but get back to the fire.

June 17th

I am always asking myself the question, What is it you are struggling for? What is that vital thing the woods contain, possess, that you want? Why do you go back and back to the woods unsatisfied, longing to express something that is there and not able to find it? This I know, I shall not find it until it comes out of my inner self, until the God quality in me is in tune with the God in it. Only by right living and a right attitude towards my fellow man, only by intense striving to get in touch, in tune with, the Infinite, shall I find that deep thing hidden there, and that will not be until my vision is clear enough to see, until I have learned and fully realize my relationship to the Infinite.

June 30th

Find the forms you desire to express your purpose. When you have succeeded in getting them as near as you can to express your idea, never leave them but push further on and on strengthening and emphasizing those forms to enclose that green idea or ideal.

September 28th

Got a new pup. He is half griffon. The other half is mistake.

November 3rd, 1932

So, the time moves on, I with it. This evening I aired the dogs and took tea on the beach. It had rained all the earlier day and the wood was too soaked to make a fire, but I sat on the rocks and ate and drank hot tea and watched the sun set, with the waves washing nearly to my feet. The dogs, Koko, Maybbe and Tantrum, were beloved, cuddly close, and all the world was sweet, peaceful, lovely. Why don't I have a try at painting the rocks and cliffs and sea? Wouldn't it be good to rest the woods? Am I one-idea'd, small, narrow? God is in them all. Now I know that is all that matters. The only thing worth striving for is to express God. Every living thing is God made manifest. All real art is the eternal seeking to express God, the one substance out of which all things are made. Search for the reality of each object, that is, its real and only beauty; recognize our relationship with all life; say to every animate and inanimate thing "brother"; be at one with all things, finding the divine in all; when one can do all this, maybe then one can paint. In the meantime one must go steadily on with open mind, courageously alert, waiting …

CONRAD KAIN (1883-1934)

Conrad Kain is a legend in Canadian mountain climbing. Perhaps no photograph in North American climbing is more famous than that of Kain — ice axe in hand, climbing ropes draped over his body, face and pose daring the elements with calm confidence — just after his first ascent of Mt. Robson in the Canadian Rockies in 1913. This was just one of many first ascents in Canada — among them Bugaboo Spire, Farnham, Mt. Louis and Saskatchewan — and major summits in Alaska, Siberia and New Zealand. Included here is Kain's stirring description of returning to the Canadian Rockies in the spring of 1913, and his account of the Mt. Robson ascent, told in a characteristically low-keyed and dignified style. Kain was born in southern Austria into wretchedly poor circumstances. His native energy and romantic temperament led him to follow a tramp's life and even engage in poaching for a time. Eventually he gained a reputation as a European mountain guide, and in his twenties Kain moved to western Canada, where he lived as a farmer and a trapper — and as his biographer says, "quickly earned a reputation as the outstanding mountaineer of his generation." *Where The Clouds Can Go* — Kain's autobiography, compiled and edited by his friend, J. Monroe Thorington — is a classic of mountaineering and wandering. First published in 1935 by The American Alpine Club, the book has been described as "timeless" in its "praise of and joy in the highest and coldest and windiest ... places that exist on earth." The title comes from an epigraph by Andreas Maurer: "Where the clouds can go, men can go; but they must be hardy men." These words are a fitting epitaph for a man whose exploits set standards for all mountaineering in Canada since his time. Kain is buried in Cranbrook, B.C.

TOPOGRAPHICAL SURVEY. GREAT DIVIDE. JULY 7, 1913

NOW I AM BACK in the mountains again. It is spring! For the first few days in camp I was cook, but now I am climbing once more. The survey is being made to map the boundary between Alberta and British Columbia.

We are old friends in the party, and I am happy to find that they are glad to have me back. They have not the eye or experience to select good routes of ascent.

I must tell you some sad news. A friend of mine at Banff, John Wilson, was held up and shot by two robbers four miles from here. Two bullets in the chest, and his neck cut. But he is alive after lying unconscious for thirty hours. One bullet has been removed at the hospital in Banff, but he is too weak for further operation. He has been working for Mr. Wheeler and the Alpine Club. He is the son of the old packer who had the Spanish prince on a bear hunt.

Life is so short, and I think one should make a good time of it if one can. The only thing I enjoy now is Nature, especially spring in the mountains, and letters from friends. Sometimes I think I have seen too much for a poor man. There are things that make a man unhappy if he sees the wrongs and can't change them. A week ago I had a letter from Mr. Hollister. I tell you, I love this fellow! He told me he might go to South America next winter collecting, and if possible would take me along.

On July 15 the Alpine Club Camp will be opened at Hector for ten days. A hundred and fifty tourists are expected. I shall not be there, but go to the Robson Camp from July 28 to August 9. I expect to have hard and possibly dangerous work there. Mt. Robson is a wicked peak. I know it very well from looking at it: I have not climbed it yet, but will surely succeed. In case it is very risky I will go only with good climbers at a high price. A guide should be well paid for such expeditions, especially by those who have enough money and often throw away $100 in a day for a couple of pleasurable hours. Many friends of mine are coming from England: Mr. Mumm, Capt. Farrar and others.

THE FIRST ASCENT OF MOUNT ROBSON
(translated for the Canadian Alpine Journal, *vi, 19, by P.A.W. Wallace)*

ON REACHING THE Robson Glacier after the ascent of Mt. Resplendent, I went down to the timber at 6700 ft. Here I met my *Herren* for Mt. Robson. Both were busy about the fire, Mr. Foster (Deputy Minister for Public Works for British Columbia) with cooking, Mr. MacCarthy with gathering wood. After a good supper, we went up, laden with firewood, to the foot of the Extinguisher. The rock bears this name on account of its form (candle extinguisher). On the moraine we made our shelter beside a wall of stones, over which we stretched a piece of canvas and crept under it like marmots into their hole.

I awoke early next morning and felt pain in my eyes, and for a long time I could not open them. It felt as if my eyes were filled with sand. My snow glasses were no good. I saw a starry sky, which was more than we had expected. I applied cold poultices for half an hour and the pain in my eyes began to abate. I lit the fire and wakened my *Herren*. Both were delighted at the sight of a cloudless sky.

At 4:30 a.m., after an early but good breakfast, we left our bivouac. We followed the route of the previous day (ascent of Mt. Resplendent), over the glacier. Before we came to the Pass, we swerved to the right. From this point began the real climb of Mt. Robson. We climbed up an avalanche trough, then under some dangerous ice bridges to the right. The snow was in bad condition. We proceeded without any difficulties towards the steep snow-slope that descends from the Dome (10,000 ft.) and reached it at seven a.m. We took a rest and deliberated over the route ahead.

Two years ago I spent hours studying this route, and did not take the bergschrund very seriously. From the Dome, one had a nearer survey of the bergschrund. We approached it over the glacier, which is here not very steep. A rib of rock comes down almost to the schrund. Over this rock I planned to ascend, but after every possible attempt we were forced to give it up, for at this place the glacier breaks off sheer. For about two hundred feet we followed along the bergschrund to the right. Here was the only possibility at hand of overcoming it. After long chopping at the ice, I stood on its 65-degree slope. Across the schrund I made more steps. Then I let both *Herren* follow.

A thin layer of snow lay on the ice, and, owing to the melting of the snow, the ice was in very bad condition for step-cutting. I made the steps in a zig-zag. Mr. Foster counted 105 steps to a ledge of rock. The rock, when seen from below, promised good climbing and a rapid advance. But it turned out otherwise. We climbed up an icy wall, and then to our disappointment had an ice-slope before us, fifty or sixty meters high. I kept as well as I could to the rocks that protruded here and there, which saved me a few steps. At the top of the slope we had another wall of rock, and above that an almost hopeless ice-slope. One could see the tracks of falling stones and avalanches. On this slope I made 110 steps. It was a relief to climb on rocks again, though they were glazed with ice. But unfortunately the satisfaction was short, and for several hundred meters we had to climb again upon a slope of ice and snow. The snow here was in danger of avalanching.

For safety, I lengthened the rope on the dangerous slope.

At last we reached the shoulder at twelve o'clock noon. I do not know whether my *Herren* contemplated with a keen Alpine eye the dangers to which we were exposed from the bergschrund. In the year 1909 this route was attempted by Mr. Mumm and Mr. Amery with the guide Inderbinen from Zermatt. The party were in danger of their lives from an avalanche. I spoke with Inderbinen: he said, "I never before saw death so near."

On the shoulder we took a mid-day rest. There came a snowy wind that wet us to the bone. We pulled out all the clothing stowed away in our rucksacks. We found the shoulder less broad than we expected. It was a snow ridge, on the northeast side of which were overhanging cornices fringed with long icicles glittering in the sun, a glorious picture.

For a few hundred meters we had to keep to the southeast side. The snow on this side was in good condition, so that we made rapid progress. There was on each side a splendid view into the depths below (*Tiefblick*). The more beautiful view was that of the Robson Glacier, Smoky Valley and Mt. Resplendent and the Lynx Range opposite.

From the shoulder to the peak, the route was no longer so dangerous, but complicated by the loose, powdery snow. It was as if we were on an entirely different climb on the southeast side. The complications arose from walls of snow. Never before on all my climbs have I seen such snow formations. The snow walls were terraced. The ledges between the walls were of different widths, and all were covered with loose snow. I often sank in to my hips. There were forms on the walls like ostrich feathers, a truly strange and beautiful winter scene. Unfortunately we had no camera with us. Some of the walls were fifteen to twenty meters high. It was difficult to find a way up from one terrace to another. At one place I worked for over half an hour without effect. We had to go back. A very narrow and steep couloir offered the only possibility. I warned my *Herren* that the piece would take considerable time to negotiate. Both had a good stand and kept moving as much as possible in order to keep warm. The wind was so bad here that I often had to stop. The steepness alone, apart from wind, made step-cutting very hard work. For a number of steps I had first to make a handhold in the ice, and swing the axe with one hand. I do not think I need to describe this method any more fully, for everyone who has ever been on the ice knows that cutting steps with one hand is a frightfully slow process. I know that in such places it is not pleasant either for those behind. As soon as I was convinced that I could make it, I called to my *Herren:* "Just be patient, the bad place will soon be conquered, and the peak is ours." Mr. MacCarthy answered: "We are all right here, we are only sorry for you. I don't understand how you can still keep on cutting steps."

When we had the difficult place behind us, the reward was a fairly steep snow-slope, with the snow in good condition so that we could all three go abreast. At the top of the snow-slope was another wall, which, however, could be outflanked without difficulty.

The last stretch to the summit was a snow-ridge. I turned to my *Herren* with the words: "Gentlemen, that's as far as I can take you."

In a few seconds both stood beside me on the peak. We shook hands with one another. I added my usual Alpine greeting in German, "Bergheil." Of course, I had to explain the word *Bergheil,* because both knew no German. There is no word in the English language which has the same meaning as *Bergheil.*

On the crest of the king of the Rockies, there was not much room to stand. We descended a few meters and stamped down a good space. It was half-past five o'clock. Our barometer showed exactly 13,000 ft.

The view was glorious in all directions. One could compare the sea of glaciers and mountains with a stormy ocean. Mt. Robson is about 2000 feet higher than all the other mountains in the neighbourhood. Indescribably beautiful was the vertical view towards Berg Lake and the camp below. Unfortunately only fifteen minutes were allowed us on the summit, ten of pure pleasure and five of teeth chattering. The rope and our damp clothes were frozen as hard as bone. And so we had to think of the long descent — 5:45 o'clock.

As far as the steep couloir, all went well. The descent over this piece was difficult. All the steps were covered with snow. Except for this, we had no difficulties till the shoulder. As it was late, I proposed to descend by the glacier on the south side, for greater safety. Besides the question of time, it seemed to me too dangerous to make our descent over the route of ascent. As a guide with two *Herren,* one has to take such dangers more into account than do amateurs, for upon one's shoulders rests the responsibility for men's lives. Also as a guide one must consider his calling and the sharp tongues that set going on all sides like clockwork when a guide with his party gets into a dangerous situation. It was clear to me that we must spend a night on the mountain. The descent was not quite clear to me. I was convinced that on this side we could get farther down than by the way we came up. My bivouac motto is: "A night out is hardly ever agreeable, and above 3000 meters always a lottery."

After the shoulder, we had a steep snow-slope to the glacier. I made about 120 steps. Once on the glacier, we went down rapidly for a few hundred meters until a sheer precipice barred the way. So far and no farther.

Vain was my search for a way down. We had to go back uphill, which was naturally no pleasure. Between rocks and glacier was a very steep icy trench which offered us the only descent. I examined the icy trench for a few minutes, and the ice cliffs overhanging us. I saw the opportunity and, of course, the dangers too. Mr. Foster asked me what my opinion was, whether we could go on or not. I answered, quite truly: "We can; it is practicable but dangerous." Captain MacCarthy said: "Conrad, if it is not too dangerous for you, cutting steps, then don't worry about us. We'll trust to you and fortune."

That made matters easier for me, as I could see that both *Herren* had no fear. I lengthened the rope and left the *Herren* in a sheltered spot. I made the steps just as carefully and quickly as I could. When I had reached a good place I let both *Herren* follow. Mr. MacCarthy went last, and I was astonished at his surefootedness. This dangerous trench took a whole hour to negotiate. The rock was frozen, but the consciousness that we had such terrible danger behind us, helped us over the rocks. In greater safety we rested beneath the rocks.

Below us was the glacier, which, seen from above, promised a good descent almost to timberline. I remembered that the glacier had still another break-off and knew that we must camp out. However, I said nothing of this to my *Herren,* but the opposite. I pointed with my axe to the woods with the words: "It will be a fine night down there in the woods beside a big fire." Both chimed in, for the word "fire" makes a very different impression when one is standing in soaking clothes upon ice and snow than the word "fire" when one is aroused by it from a sound sleep.

We did not find the glacier as good as we expected. We searched our way through ice débris in an avalanche bed. Here on the glacier the sun bade us good night. The sunset was beautiful. It would have been more beautiful to us if the sun had been delayed an hour. It was a melancholy moment when the last glow of evening faded in the west. We rested and spoke on this theme. Mr. MacCarthy said: "It is as well that the law of nature cannot be changed by men. What a panic it would raise if we succeeded in delaying the sun for an hour! It is possible that somewhere some alpinists will tomorrow morning be in the same situation as we are, and will be waiting eagerly for the friendly sun."

Despite the approach of darkness we went on. About ten o'clock in the evening we reached the rocks. It was out of the question to go any further. Our feet felt the effects of the last seventeen hours on ice and rock, and so we were easily satisfied with a resting place. A ledge of rock two meters wide offered us a good place to bivouac. We made it as comfortable as we could. We built a little sheltering wall about us. Our provision bag still had plenty of sandwiches, and Mr. MacCarthy, to our surprise, brought a large packet of chocolate from his rucksack. We took our boots off. I gave Mr. Foster my dry pair of extra mitts for socks, so we all had dry feet, which is the important thing in camping out. The *Herren* had only one rucksack between them, into which they put their feet. Both *Herren* were roped up to a rock.

I gave a few hints on bivouacking, for there are some tricks in sleeping out on cold rocks that one can only learn by experience. Fortunately the night was a warm one, threatening rain. Clouds were hanging in the sky, which, however, the west wind swept away to the east. In the valley we saw flickering the campfire of the Alpine Club and of the construction camp of the Canadian Northern and Grand Trunk Railways. I was very tired and went to sleep without any trouble. A thundering avalanche woke me from a sound sleep. I heard Mr. Foster's teeth chatter as he lay beside me. I uttered no word of sympathy, but went to sleep again.

Later I was awakened by a dream. I dreamed that we were quite close to a forest. I saw wood close at hand, and dry branches ready for kindling. In the dream I reproached myself with what the *Herren* would think of me, sleeping here in the forest with firewood, but without a fire and almost freezing. With these reproaches I awoke and sat up to convince myself whether the forest and firewood were really so near. But I saw only a few stars and in the east a few gray clouds lit up with the dawn. I could not get to sleep again, but lay quietly and listened to the thunder of the avalanches which broke the almost ghostly silence of Nature. At daybreak it became considerably warmer, so my *Herren,* who had spent a cold and sleepless night, now fell sound asleep.

At six o'clock the friendly beams of the sun reached us. I wakened my *Herren.* Both sat up and described the pain in their eyes, which they could not open. The eyes of both were greatly swollen. It was not a pleasant sight. I thought both were snow-blind. Snow-blind, at a height of 9000 feet, and in such a situation — that might have an unpleasant ending. After some cold poultices, the pain abated and both were able to keep their eyes open.

I told my dream. Both *Herren* had dreams of a similar nature, which had reference to the cold night. Mr. Foster dreamed that a number of his friends came with blankets and commiserated the barren camping ground, and no one covered him. Mr. MacCarthy, in his dream, implored his wife for more blankets, and his wife stopped him with the curt reply: "Oh no, dear, you can't have any blankets. Sleeping without any is good training if we want to go to the North Pole."

I searched for a descent over the rocks. After a quarter of an hour I came back.

"Yes, we can make it without further difficulty."

At 6:45 a.m. we left the bivouac, which will certainly remain in our memory. We did not get down so easily after all. We had to get around sheer walls. The climbing was difficult, and at some places the rock was very rotten. This was very unpleasant for my *Herren.* They could only see a few steps through their glasses and swollen eyes.

At last we had the most difficult part behind us, but not the most dangerous. We had to traverse a hanging glacier. For ten minutes we were exposed to the greatest danger. I certainly breathed freely when we lay down to rest under some overhanging rock. Our barometer showed 8200 feet, time 10:15 a.m. That eight hundred feet had taken three hours to negotiate. I said to my *Herren:* "I am happy to be able to inform you that we have all dangers behind us. We shall reach the green grass in the valley safe and sound even to our swollen eyes."

We crossed loose stones to the southwest ridge. This ridge should be the easiest way up to the peak. From here we had a beautiful view of Lake Kinney below. Without further difficulty we descended through old snow. At eleven o'clock we took a long rest and devoured everything eatable we could find left in our provision bag. Then we followed the newly-built trail to camp.

About five o'clock in the afternoon we came, hungry and tired, into camp, where we were hospitably received by our fellow campers with food and drink and congratulations.

From what Donald Phillips himself said, our ascent was really the first ascent of Mt. Robson. Phillips' words are as follows: "We reached, on our ascent (in mist and storm), an ice-dome fifty or sixty feet high, which we took for the peak. The danger was too great to ascend the dome."

Phillips and Kinney made the ascent over the west ridge. The west side is, as far as I could see, the most dangerous side that one can choose. Kinney undertook the journey from Edmonton alone with five horses. On the way he met Donald Phillips who was on a prospecting tour. Mr. Kinney persuaded Phillips to accompany him. Phillips had never before made this kind of a mountain trip and says himself that he had no suspicion of its dangers. They had between them one ice axe and a bit of ordinary rope. They deserve more credit than we, even though they did not reach the highest point, for in 1909 they had many more obstacles to overcome than we; for at that time the railway, which brought us almost to the foot of the mountain, was then no less than two hundred miles from their goal, and their way had to be made over rocks and brush, and we must not forget the dangerous river crossings. Mt. Robson is one of the most beautiful mountains in the Rockies and certainly the most difficult one. In all my mountaineering in various countries, I have climbed only a few mountains that were hemmed in with more difficulties. Mt. Robson is one of the most dangerous expeditions I have made. The dangers consist in snow and ice, stone avalanches and treacherous weather.

Ever since I came to Canada and the Rockies, it was my constant wish to climb the highest peak. My wish was fulfilled. For this ascent I could have wished for no better companions. Both *Herren* were good climbers and Nature lovers, and made me no difficulties on the way. Each had a friendly word of thanks for my guiding. In this country people are much more democratic than with us in Europe, and have less regard for titles and high officials; but still it was a satisfaction to me to have the pleasure of climbing with a Canadian statesman.

HELEN MEILLEUR (1910–)

Helen Meilleur was born and grew up in Port Simpson, B.C., near the Alaska border. In the preface to her one book, she explains that *A Pour of Rain: Stories from a West Coast Fort* (1980) was conceived during her childhood when her father, returning from a business trip to Vancouver and Victoria, described having looked through an 1839 journal for the Hudson's Bay Company at Fort Simpson (the fort was later redesignated a port). He had come home full of stories from Simpson's stockaded past and chuckled over certain historical tidbits preserved there. The idea of the journals was firmly planted in Meilleur's mind, but when in the 1930s she tried to track them down she learned they had been sent to London. It wasn't until 1973 that she discovered they were part of the Hudson's Bay Archives housed in Winnipeg. This gave her a chance at last to read the logbooks for herself and to put together one of the best histories we have of a west coast community. Port Simpson is located just south of the Nass River, an area inhabited largely by the Nisga'a people. Meilleur attended a one-room school on the Indian reservation where her father ran the general store. Later she went to the University of British Columbia, and along with careers in teaching and business she was a wife and mother of five. She didn't start writing until around 1967 when she won the Indiana University Writers' Conference scholarship for non-fiction. She was seventy years old when the book conceived in her childhood was finally written and published.

What is unique in *A Pour of Rain* is the way the author combines her personal memories of growing up in this remote northern community with a well-researched, carefully reconstructed history of the fort in the mid-nineteenth century. The events of the author's childhood are presented in the same continuum as the history of the fur-trading post with its characters and day-to-day occurences. The logbooks record lively times — Indian attacks, fighting among tribes, the appearance of gold-seekers, missionaries, even royalty on one occasion — as well as life's more mundane passages like the success or failure of the fort garden, sickness and death of fort personnel. But Meilleur's growing-up time was equally as exciting as fort history; her childhood acquaintance with Native people and her experience of going to school by steamship is continuous with the life of the port in the nineteenth century. Making a site of origins historical as well as personal makes this more than a book of nostalgic recollections — it raises the writing of local history to the level of art.

From A POUR OF RAIN
THE HUDSON'S BAY GARDEN

MOTHER HUNG small lard pails around two stiffly protesting necks. "Now," she said with satisfaction, "those are nearly as good as the baskets the Indian girls wear for berrypicking. You'll have to stand on your heads to spill your berries."

Ruth and I looked wistfully toward Finlayson Island where we had planned to row that afternoon, then turned in the opposite direction. We were only a short distance beyond the old excavation where a tangle of vegetation pushed on to the roadside when Ruth asked, "Are those raspberries?" as she poked an arm into the thicket. They were. Ruth broke through at breast height while I wiggled in along the ground. Inside the jungle, a raspberry patch was fighting and winning a territorial war against salmonberry, thimbleberry, alder, some ancient trees that might have been apple, salal, grass and weeds that grew in mats. The berries were typical, voluptuous Port Simpson raspberries. We picked in high glee; we would have our tins full in no time and then we would get out in the boat. But, while the raspberry canes emerged from their enemies only slightly twisted and bent, we fared worse. By the time our cans had begun to pull slightly on our necks, our arms and faces were scratched, Ruth's skirt was torn and one of my black stockings was without a knee.

"Perhaps we'd better stop," I called to Ruth who was charging on ahead, on the other side of the green wall that faced me.

"Not until we see how far this berry patch goes."

"My hair-ribbon's gone. My face hurts and I'm hot."

"Well, look for a place to sit down."

I had not seen a clear spot big enough to sit down upon since we left the road, but now I began to scrutinize the ground. Surprisingly, there was a mossy hummock under one of those dead apple trees. I broke off a couple of branches that snapped like spaghetti and eased myself into the resulting dark hole. I began to feel better immediately and my hands dug into the deep, damp moss with appreciation. They encountered an interesting piece of wood which I rubbed on my dress and studied. Then I looked all about my comfortable seat.

"Ruth, I think I'm sitting on a grave."

Through the bush came back the answer, "That's not nice. Get off it this minute."

Ruth was intrigued enough to come crashing back to me. I had cleared some of the weeds from my mound. It's shape and size were unmistakable. Around its perimeter, deep in the growth, were glimpses of white. When we dug for them they were revealed as whitewashed fence pickets. There was not much whitewash and not much picket left, to most of them, but they, too, were unmistakable. We attacked a stand of alder shoots growing up through the lower branches of the old apple tree and a few feet into it came upon a square whitewashed post. The alders had uprooted it and then, as though they were sorry, supported it in an almost upright position. My cleaned piece of wood fitted a notch in the post. I handed it to Ruth. Its carved letters read, "Lieut. AE Simpson, R.N."

We would have started then and there to tell Dad about our discovery, had I not tripped over an entanglement of roots and fallen headlong into a patch of salal. As I struggled out of the crushed leaves and stems, Ruth spied in the wreckage another wooden plaque. This one was smaller but had been smoothed and carved in the same manner as the first. It bore only the words, "Infant Manson." Silently Ruth and I tore at bushes and weeds until a tiny mounded grave took shape. It lay directly in line with Captain Simpson's, and hardly three feet from it. I glanced at Ruth. She was kneeling, having been pulling grass, but she was not getting up. She was just looking at that oval bit of ground. Then I realized that I, too, was kneeling.

What Ruth and I did not know that summer's day was that one of us must have been kneeling on a second baby's grave, dug on the same day as the two we saw. When Captain Simpson's remains were disinterred at Fort Simpson, Nass, so also were those of two fort babies for reburial close to their own kind. Nor did we realize that we were picking berries in a graveyard that contained at the very least a score of similar miniature graves and as many more full-sized ones. No one in the Simpson of our day seemed to know that this wild thicket concealed the plot that for thirty-one years received the fort's dead, as well as the remains of other white people who met death in that region and of chiefs and Indians of high rank and those held in special regard by the Hudson's Bay people. The men of the fort made the coffins and dug the graves. The Indians seemed to accept burial as quite fitting though they had other customs concerning disposal of the dead. One was to cremate the body and later, sometimes much later, bury the bones and ashes, or place them in boxes to be attached to trees in the woods. Another, thought to have been reserved for people of the highest rank, was to place the body in the fetal position, in a square cedar chest and consign the chest to a cave. There was such a cave on Birnie Island. Those corpses were mummified. Whether this came about by some forgotten Indian process or by the effects of the limestone cave was always a subject for dispute at Port Simpson. By the time I was old enough to be allowed to scramble to the cave mouth, the boxes and the mummies had been shamefully vandalized by white people. No Indian would ever have touched them; they were protected by a fierce Tsimshian curse.

Nobody really planned the first cemetery. It grew around Captain Simpson's grave as naturally as the garden grew in that bit of loamy ground. The new fort was only five months old when an Indian girl who had been with Dr. Kennedy's family for three years, died. That same month the young son of a French-Canadian workman died. These deaths were only the beginning of the tragedy of the fort children. All over the nineteenth-century world infant mortality was high but it seems that at Fort Simpson conditions were particularly discouraging to life after birth. The little survivors found other barriers to growing up, a major one being European childhood diseases to which they had no immunity. And so the rows of small graves in the garden grew and grew.

Two men from the Sandwich Islands were buried in the cemetery with apple trees instead of palms to wave over them. Mr. Gaskill, [an] English gentleman who had taken passage on the *Pandora*, apparently for the sake of his health, came to the end of his journey there. The half Indian wife of Captain Swanson gave birth to twins but died on Christmas Eve. Her body was not interred until nearly a month later; perhaps, since it was winter, it seemed possible to await the Captain's return on the spring trip of the supply ship. The Indian wife of a French-Canadian workman was buried there, and several women of the Indian encampment. One was called "Legaic's old wife" (chiefs often had a variety of wives, simultaneously). She had succumbed to smallpox in four days. Then there were the murdered chiefs.

Coaguele was the first. He was from a neighbouring area and was frequently a messenger for the fort people and always a friend. It was Coaguele who found [a] bitch and pups at the wreck of Fort Simpson (Nass) and delivered them by canoe to the new fort. Two years later a canoe of young Tsimshians from a Skeena tribe arrived at Fort Simpson with the news that their chief, Nashot, had died of smallpox. He was supposed to have contracted it from a member of Coaguele's tribe. That night the young men plied Coaguele and his companion with rum and then shot them. Another chief, Saloway, died with more justice but no less violence. He had killed a Stikene in a quarrel. The Stikenes, of course, would have to kill someone of equal rank in Saloway's tribe. Saloway's brother, the likeliest victim, relieved the tension and saved his own skin by shooting Saloway. Haiash, a Haida chief, died for a similar reason. He was shot by a fellow Haida chief to atone for the death they had jointly dealt out to a Tsimshian chief's brother. If this sounds complicated and gruesome today, you can be sure it was even more complicated and gruesome in 1856. Out of their turbulence, all these people came to rest in the comparative calm of the Company vegetable garden.

The three disinterred bodies that began the Fort Simpson cemetery were not the only ones to enter it. Actually, it was a disinterred body that closed it. By 1864 the [fort] Journal no longer spoke of burying the dead in the garden but now spoke of "sowing seeds in the graveyard" and there was barely room for seeds. In April 1865, a message came from Father Duncan at Metlakatla, requesting the interment of a body at Fort Simpson. After laying one of his flock to rest with solemn Anglican rites, he had been shocked to find that the burial had come undone. Mourning friends had sought consolation in rum and had become so consoled that they wished to share the source of their good feelings with their deceased fellow. They did. But Mr. Duncan, who seemed like stone against the savagery he had challenged, was shaken by this incident and dispatched the corpse to Fort Simpson. There was another death at this time, and those two coffins were the last to be squeezed into the pleasant little apple-tree cemetery.

Over the years, Alexis and Antoine had made many coffins and dug many graves. By 1865 these two survivors of the old voyageur days formed a little unit among the men, usually working together on their jobs. On a day in May, Alexis died. His grave had the distinction of being the first in the new burial ground adjoining the garden but outside it. Antoine built a small picket fence around it.

Whether or not it was a mark of progress, sometime in the latter 1800's Port Simpson's white population ceased to commit its dead to the plot next to the vegetable garden and began to lay them away in a churchyard. The Anglican church was built on a bluff well behind the fort. It was a typical English village church in a typical British Columbia north coast setting. The two styles blended admirably; long after the walls of the church had lost their alignment it gazed out of its bower of second growth, like the English gentlewoman of literature, composed and serene. But the churchyard — in my mind ancient savagery lurked there.

The Anglican funerals followed a pattern: the church bell tolled; the procession mounted the wide steps that led to the top of the bluff; the service was read in the church and then, on the leeward side of the hill among scattered tombstones, another grave was covered. There was a surprising number of graves for the size of our town. Much of the population of the white village was descended from the mixed blood of the early fort days and these people were apt to retain the Indian susceptibility to tuberculosis.

Sometime in the 1860s the slow swirl of Hudson's Bay servants from fort to fort brought a Norwegian blacksmith to Fort Simpson. In his latter years there he had a great distinction — he was the only man who won outright praise in the Fort Simpson journals. Beside his trade he could handle any job in the fort and do it well. He was apparently a man of intelligence and integrity. His Indian wife bore him several children and most of them lived. Hans must have chosen his wife as well as he did everything else, for his children grew into dependable people, respected by both the Indian and white communities. One son married a girl from an Interior fort, also of mixed blood. Once again the family discernment was infallible. This was a woman of gentle and refined character. She chose to favour the Indian half of her heritage, a fact she proclaimed by wearing the black silk head handkerchief and shawl, the costume of Indian women, well into the 1920s. Hans' son worked at the post until the Company left Port Simpson. On the highest hill overlooking the town and harbour, he built a home (we used to speculate on whether his house really did have twenty rooms) and he and his wife filled it with happy, healthy children. But when the oldest boy was in his teens he died a lingering, consumptive death and was laid in the Anglican churchyard. As the attractive daughters reached womanhood, they followed. It was the fourth of these funerals I attended, for Lizzie had been a schoolmate of mine, though a senior while I was still in the primary class. It was Lizzie who chose me for her team in the game, Run Sheep Run, though I was obviously a detriment.

The funeral service did not disturb me; it was almost a year since I had seen Lizzie and in no way could I associate her with the grey-covered casket. At the graveside the coffin was lowered out of my sight. Chilling as a loon's call, a cry out of the Indian past cut through the Anglican words and fell among us. On the edge of the grave there were struggling figures. They were holding Lizzie's mother who was straining toward the open grave.

Afterwards Mother tried to reassure me: it was the old Indian way, a sort of play-acting which relieved grief, something like the paid wailing that we understood. But I saw that mother's face and her eyes. She would have jumped.

Port Simpson was well segregated in death. The Indians had their own graveyard at the extreme opposite edge of town, on the seaward end of Rose Island. Evergreens encircled it and isolated it completely from the village. The paths between all but the newest graves were white with crushed clamshells, and, standing companionably about were upright, granite tombstones in all shades of grey and one dark shade of pink. The older ones were not quite upright and their inscriptions were difficult to read through the moss and discolouration. The others made interesting reading since the custom of inscribing last words prevailed. Apparently no one had been allowed to die in silence and even the stone for a six-month-old infant bore such a pious message as, "I go to be with God."

We saw only the cemetery where a Methodist missionary conducted a Christian burial, but, when we lived on the Reserve, we knew that after dark that same cemetery became the place where Tsimshian spirits were sent on their way with what they would require. Sometimes lights flickered here and there and a lantern burned all night on the new grave, while a fire flared on the beach, turning the deceased's possessions into smoke which could accompany his spirit. One night, from our house near the bandstand, we listened to wheelbarrows trundling toward such a fire and watched the silhouettes that moved in and out of its glow. A visiting mission lady sighed and said, "Such a dreadful pagan custom."

"Such an excellent custom for TB ridden people," said my mother.

Not all possessions were burned. Sometimes special tools or trinkets or toys were placed inside the coffin. And sometimes a saucepan, or a cup, a teddy bear, or a jackknife would be seen beside a new grave. No one, white or Indian, has even been able to make me understand the inconsistencies of the Tsimshian beliefs concerning death; but then, no one has been able to make me understand the inconsistencies of the Christian beliefs concerning death.

Though the Indian graveyard was always of shuddering interest to me, it was the drama in the tall dark trees enclosing it, that drew me to the window each day as the afternoon sun headed for the horizon. Elsie, Mother's Tsimshian helper, explained it to Ruth and me. Mother was working at the store. Elsie had just given us a snack of bread and jam and stood looking out the bay window.

"Why do you always look out the window at this time, Elsie?" Ruth asked.

"I watch the dead people," said Elsie.

Ruth and I, bread in hand, were at the window before Elsie had time to turn her head.

"Where?"

"The trees around the graveyard. The crows are the dead people. Look at them all. They're mad today. Somebody in the village has done a bad thing and they're mad."

Hundreds of crows filled the circle of tree tops. And they *were* angry. They rasped out their fury and beat their wings and darted back and forth. Next day Ruth and I were at the window ahead of Elsie.

"They have a meeting today," said Elsie.

The meeting was quiet and orderly. One by one crows spoke and the others swayed silently on top branches.

"They say what Tsimshian people should do," Elsie said.

Some days the crows broke up into small discussion groups and some days they seemed to be devoting themselves to merrymaking. "The dead people are very happy with us," was Elsie's comment on such a day.

"Where do the dead people go when they aren't at the graveyard?" Ruth asked.

"You see crows all over."

"But they aren't dead people, are they?"

"Sure. My cousin was getting wood down near Lacoo. A crow came to him and told him, 'Go home. Go home.' He jumped in his boat and rowed home as fast as he could. And when he got there his mother was dying. He just had time to speak to her. That crow was his uncle that died long time ago."

About 1930 the crows' graveyard was entirely filled. Then the Tsimshians cleared an area on Finlayson Island and made new clamshell paths. Instead of crossing the bridge, the funeral processions crossed the channel and, as the gasboats chugged away in a sweeping curve, there was a feeling of harmony about the seaborne farewell to a seaborne life.

On its route from church to embarkation, the long funeral cortege undulated noticeably as it neared the wharf approach. Here each person was forced to step over a protrusion in the road. It was the nub of a three-foot kingpost that had once marked the northwest corner of the stockade. Cross-grained and rounded, its edges worn level with the road, it had defied whatever force took down its section of posts, and the fire, and it continued to defy the weather and Simpson's foot traffic. In my day it was the only reminder of the stockades and of their posts which Hudson's Bay men called pickets.

THE PORT I KNEW

PORT SIMPSON people led salty lives. Since the town was built on a peninsula we were almost surrounded by water. The Tsimshians were as much of the sea as of the land and the rest of us were only slightly more shore-bound. The sea was our highway and our usual communications system; it was our larder; it was our heavy-duty equipment for moving large loads, the extreme high tides of the solstices, especially, being put to use in floating machinery into place or beaching boats high and dry. And the sea was our playground.

All over Port Simpson mothers called after departing children, "And don't get your feet wet." They might as well have called these words to the crabs that scuttled under the tideline rocks, for we were all on our way to join them. First we toddled to the beach behind older brothers and sisters, where we commanded the derelicts half buried in the sand, or slithered up and down the remains of the Hudson's Bay ships' ways, and fell in the water and were hauled out. When we had been properly initiated we were allowed to sit motionless on the bottoms of the small craft the older children rowed or paddled about the shoreline. These ranged through rowboats, dingys, flat-bottomed skiffs, dugouts, right down to rafts and logs. There was no status and only one requirement for a craft to enter this fleet, it had to float at least some of the time. Our next promotion allowed us to row our boats alone — to the length of the bow-line which was tied to wharf approach piling or to a beach log. Those were the days of scrounging bits of rope to lengthen the painter. Eventually we won or seized the right to inshore paddling. The tide rose and fell while we raced and reversed and made landings, complete with vocalized ships' bells, whistles and engines, or practised Chinese rowing and the fisherman's push. We learned to read tide tables about the same time we learned to read *The Tale of Peter Rabbit*; where twenty-foot tides are normal it is just as well to know what they are doing.

The first day that I rowed around The Point, out of sight of home and completely beyond parental control, I became an exultant explorer. Our coastline was lavishly set with islands, coves, creeks, reefs and narrow channels. Before I had hauled up on more than a sampling of them, with a sputter and a roar the outboard motor burst into our lives. I promptly shipped my oars and found my seaways lengthened by miles. My seamanship was stretched noticeably, too. Oars could never have won me the enmity of the entire Prince Rupert Yacht Club.

It was as a concession to my newly achieved teens that Ruth and I made our first trip to Prince Rupert on our own, by rowboat and outboard. The boat was a sixteen-foot clinker-built; we called her the *Blue Streak* and discussed her lines as though we were admiring a China clipper. Outboard motors of the early 1920s were not the behemoths that adorn the transoms of modern craft. Our motor was one of the breed that had a knob on the flywheel rather than a starting cord and was advertised to start on a quarter turn. The advertisements did not specify the *first* quarter turn and it was more likely to be a fifty-sixth that brought the thing to life. For one whole summer I wore adhesive tape on the knuckles of my right hand. When the motor developed a bad cough, as well, my father agreed that the marine engine works in Prince Rupert should look into the case. We left Dad on the boat float shouting into the wind, "The shearing pins are in the tool box."

Prince Rupert was a three-hour run south. Dad had improvised a high seat in the bow and rigged tiller lines to it so the steersman could have a clear view in all directions. We had no steering wheel — we simply clutched a line in each hand and tugged on the appropriate one. Ruth, by seniority, was skipper so it fell to my lot to keep the outboard kicking. I accomplished this through will power, cajolery and a leaner-than-specified mixture of gasoline and oil.

Ruth and I tied up diffidently at the engine works' float in Prince Rupert harbour. The *Blue Streak* looked frivolous alongside the tugboats, halibut boats and trollers docked there. We arranged to pick up our outfit the next morning and then we set off up town — in Prince Rupert the town is very literally up. We followed our usual day-on-the-town ritual which included banana splits, the newest gramaphone record, a movie and the night at the hotel. Next morning we were back at the float by ten o'clock. It was a Sunday so there was no one around the repair shop. We filled the gas tank, loaded our bags aboard and gave the flywheel an enquiring flip. When the motor stuttered into action we shouted in unison our amazement and joy and were headed into the harbour before we had even buttoned our sweaters.

A fresh breeze swept the harbour into choppy little waves and dancing upon them, in a long, ragged line, were pleasure craft of every description, from luxury cruisers to dinghys with home-built cabins. While Prince Rupert possessed more of the amenities of life than did Port Simpson, there was still no road leading off Kaien Island and the people turned to the water for their recreation, even as we. Almost every family had some sort of boat and this was their day.

"It's the Yacht Club sailpast," Ruth bellowed above the noise of our motor and the harbourful of engines.

"Let's give them a wide berth," I bellowed back and thereupon the *Blue Streak* hit the wake of a heavy, old launch. The motor leapt off the transom into my scrawny arms, never missing a stroke though its roar was like artillery fire because part of the propeller was above water. There was I, held fast on my knees in the stern, my chest supporting the heavy motor, my arms locked about its gas tank, my ribs pinning the steering arm hard over, the corner of one eye intent on the whirring flywheel half an inch below my chin and my cries for help being whipped astern by the wind. And there was Ruth in the bow, pulling frantically on first one unresponsive tiller line and then the other while the boat began to describe a circle of majestic proportions.

Prince Rupert is famous for its spacious harbour, but the harbour was not spacious enough that morning for a sailpast and a sixteen-footer gone berserk. At first the circumference of our circle did not intersect the line of boats. From wheelhouses and decks, yachters waved jauntily at us. Ruth, always conscious of social niceties, dropped a tiller line to wave back, even as she flattened herself on the seat, for we were speeding toward the hull of a thirty-foot cruiser. By some miracle of navigation it turned aside to allow us to skim under the bow and our circle, in a long sweep, headed back to the line of yachts. They were scattering like apples out of a burst bag. Once again hands were raised in salute but this time they were clenched and shaking at us. The commodore's yacht, all hand rubbed teak and brassoed brass, was looming before us when there was a thud against our keel and a scraping along the bottom. Everything in the boat jumped. The motor shoved me backwards as a chunk of driftwood knocked the propeller right out of water. The vocal fury of the engine was increased but, mercifully, we were drifting. Ruth picked herself off the floorboards, came aft, and reached under my right armpit for the shut-off button. Together we eased the motor onto the transom and began turning thumbscrews.

Dad was waiting for us on the float as we pulled in. The moment I turned off the motor, he called, "Have any trouble?"

Waves slurped and glugged around the float while I rubbed on the engine with a piece of waste. Ruth finally rallied with, "The mechanic didn't fasten the engine on but we got it screwed down."

The Union Steamship Company supplied the ships that gave life to the small settlements of the British Columbia coast. They were known as logging boats and cannery boats and ore boats. They were called freight boats and mail boats and passenger boats. They were also referred to as cruise ships and excursion boats and daddy boats. The last two classifications belonged wholly to the southern runs but in the north we expected any one Union ship to fill all the other roles and simultaneously, if necessary. In the out-of-the-way settlements we expected and received more.

In the first fifteen or so years of the century, while Simpson was still something of a centre, the Canadian Pacific's princesses and the Grand Trunk Pacific's princes called at our port. They abandoned us as Prince Rupert grew into a town and we never missed them for, by then, we had given our allegiance to the *Camosun,* the *Chelohsin* and the *Venture,* and the Union Steamship Company had become an extension of our lives.

Every fall, from remote harbours and inlets, children who had passed their entrance examinations went away to school. Our educations were the product of northern homes, southern high schools and the Union Steamship Company. By the time I was making two round trips a year, "our boat" was either the *Cardena* or the *Catala.*

Captain Andy Johnstone, hero of a hundred coastal legends, commanded the *Cardena.* His ship was like a dancing partner as he docked her: slide, pivot, swing; glide, reverse and stop. The stop was always on her toes, dramatic, and to generous applause. If he had ever decided to command a barrel going over Niagara Falls any north coaster would have accompanied him without a second thought. It was Andy Johnstone who taught us, with much hilarity, how to splice rope and make turks' heads for our oars. He taught us such assorted essentials as where to watch for blackfish, etiquette of the bridge, and coast history — he seemed to know a good story for every rock and point along the Inside Passage. He also taught us where to place our shuffleboard shots and never to pass up the Union Steamships' crab cocktails at dinner. Andy Johnstone still had a boyish look and laugh when he went out of our lives to join the Pilotage Service after twenty-three years with the company.

Captain Dickson, commodore of the fleet, was master of the *Catala.* His style was a black-and-white contrast to Andy Johnstone's. He had no Christian name as far as we knew — we always used his title in full. He must have been young during the early years of the forty he spent with the Union Steamship Company but northerners could not picture him without white hair and moustache, and dignity. We never heard his mirth in guffaws; we saw it in his eyes which were mariners' eyes protected by lines and creases and were of compelling blueness. To him I gave my first love bestowed outside of the family circle, as did all the other youngsters who made those September and June trips, and sometimes stormy December ones.

Captain Dickson taught us, too, although we did not immediately recognize the incidents as lessons. If, for fifty years, I have been able to refrain from gushing, it is probably due to an embarkation night aboard the S.S. *Catala*. The *Catala*'s Friday night sailing from Vancouver always generated action and noise and excitement. One particular departure on a summer night was late and attended by a full moon which intensified the passengers' ebullience and kept them on deck until long after the city lights disappeared behind Point Atkinson. Captain Dickson found me alone at the rail and since he felt personally responsible for every shy, northern schoolgirl who travelled on the *Catala*, led me off to the delights of midnight supper in the dining saloon. We were headed for the nearest companionway when a group of women tourists spied the three rows of gold braid on Captain Dickson's sleeve and, like a settling flock of crows, encircled him. They all talked at once.

"We think your boat is just lovely, Captain."

"Ship," said Captain Dickson.

"Now, are we on the port or starboard side? We can never remember."

"Port," said Captain Dickson.

"Those lights way off there, are they other boats? I mean ships."

"Those are the lights of Nanaimo," said the Captain.

"Nanaimo? Way over there? Imagine seeing lights on Vancouver Island."

"How far away would they be?"

"But we didn't see the lights of Victoria."

"If you are interested in seeing lights," said Captain Dickson, "look just slightly above the Nanaimo lights. Do you see those three bright lights?"

"Oh yes, I can see them."

"Tell us what they are, Captain."

"Those, Madam, are stars," and with that Captain Dickson hustled me into the companionway.

Captain Dickson had a Victorian sense of propriety. Once when he was taking me ashore at Anyox to show me the smelter, I met him at the top of the gangplank in my usual windblown state. He said, "You'd better wear your hat."

"I don't have a hat," I said, abashed.

The next year when I made the trip north, I owned, and conspicuously wore, hat and gloves. I never even slightly resented being nudged toward ladyhood by the captain until the year I turned eighteen and graduated from Normal School.

That summer it was quite obvious to me that I had become a woman of the world. The *Catala* took Port Simpson passengers north to Kincolith, Stewart and Anyox before calling in at our harbour on her southbound trip. At Kincolith a survey party boarded the *Catala*. These men had spent three months in the wilds of the Nass Valley and were exuberant as they returned to civilization as represented by the *Catala*. They were headed by a young engineer, distinctly shaggy in appearance, but, as I recognized instantly, of superior intelligence. As always north of Prince Rupert, the passenger list had dwindled drastically. I was the only female under forty aboard the ship. It was no great wonder, therefore, that when the stewards rolled up the rugs in the saloon and opened the big Victrola, the young engineer and I became dancing partners. There were only two records that were not scratched beyond use, but we found them quite adequate. We waltzed and foxtrotted alternately to them as the *Catala* glided up Portland Canal through the half-light of the summer night. The other passengers, no doubt desperate to escape those two records, drifted away from the saloon but we waltzed on alone, having made the daring decision to dance into Stewart and then go uptown to view the night scene. (Stewart was a mining town and enjoyed a gaudy reputation.) The height of romance as depicted by the movies of those days was a couple dancing the night away. Jean Arthur and Charles Boyer did it, why not I? The engineer did not look quite like Charles Boyer but it was not his fault that there were no barber shops on the upper Nass.

At 1:30 a.m. Captain Dickson took a turn around the saloon as he seemed to do at intervals all day. He hardly glanced at our best twirl. At 2:15 he made another turn, this one much slower. At 2:45 he was back and this time he stopped and we stopped. "We're going into Stewart and Hyder to see what's going on," I told him by way of explanation.

Addressing himself to the engineer, Captain Dickson said in that low-pitched voice that had been smartly obeyed for forty years, "I think Stewart's too rough for Helen at 3:30 a.m. We're going down for a bit of supper before she turns in. Goodnight, Mr. Kendrick," and he held out the crook of his arm to me with the almost imperceptible bow that always accompanied that gesture. I placed my hand in it without any more question than I would have accorded the ten commandments. As we turned down the stairs to the dining room I glanced back to see my friend standing where we had left him, his chin and lower lip seemingly detached from the rest of his face.

I found my coffee bitter that night, and refused the cold cuts, the McLaren's cheese in its white glass jar, and even the famous Union Steamship poundcake that came from Scotland, though they were all pressed upon me by the night steward whom Captain Dickson had roused from a nap at the end table. But the captain, who usually ate sparingly, had an amazing appetite that night. He drank two cups of coffee and sampled everything the steward brought forth, maintaining a pleasant, one-sided conversation all the while. When at last we ascended from the dining room, the Victrola was closed, the saloon empty. Captain Dickson escorted me to my stateroom door and bade me goodnight. Obviously, Jean Arthur had not been protected by Captain Dickson.

The next morning the passengers clustered about the forward deck to watch the landing at Port Simpson. Slightly detached from the rest, in animated conversation, stood the engineer and a little redhead from Stewart. I craned my neck to look accusingly up to the bridge, and Captain Dickson, in the middle of a docking manoeuvre, caught my eye. He fixed it in his unwavering gaze as he issued an order in a voice more like a trumpet blast than the usual low growl that he used on the bridge. "Hold her hard astern," he called.

Once, on a visit to the bridge, I watched as the first officer studied a lighthouse through binoculars. "There she is," he said, as he reached up to pull the whistle. I could make out a figure and a white object that moved. When the officer handed me the binoculars I saw that it was an elderly woman waving something. With each wave she bent nearly double. "What is she waving?" I asked.

"A bed sheet. She won't have another conversation with the outside world until our next trip."

At a logging camp at the head of a long, lonely reach, the camp tender met the steamer. From the gas boat a woman yelled, "Did you get my corset?" and on the freight deck the purser held aloft a long, slim box.

Tall stories were a specialty of the officers, and one chief engineer, Andrew Beatty, was famous the entire length of British Columbia for his. He told them in such an honest Scottish accent and with such earnestness that even old-timers were sometimes caught by them, though tourists were his favourite game. Once when the *Catala* was loading salmon at Alert Bay, a group of officers and passengers went ashore to explore the town and converged on the store. The door bore a notice, "Seal noses bought here." At that time there was a bounty on hair seals, the salmon's natural enemy, and it was collectible when a seal's nose was produced. Only the larger centres had bounty depots so storekeepers all over the coast paid the Indians the bounty, salted down the grisly proof in casks, and shipped them once or twice a season.

"Seal noses," said a female tourist. "Why do they buy seal noses?"

"There's a great demand for seal noses," said Andrew Beatty. "They're shipped straight to New York. Restaurant trade, you know. Of course they give them a French name and no one knows they are eating seal noses. Delicious sautéed."

"Well, fancy that. But the poor little seals — it must be hard for them to manage without noses."

The *Cardena's* hull is one unit in a log-pond breakwater at Powell River; the *Catala* ended her life as a floating restaurant on the California coast, and the last Union sailing was in 1959. The white village of Port Simpson is gone and so are all but a few of the ports of call of the Company ships. All those deaths were related. Port Simpson's harbour, however, lives on.

SURVIVAL

DEATH LURKED in every Indian camp. It pounced on the feeble, the hungry and the near-naked when winter assailed the lodges. At Fort Simpson, in the harsh weather of 1852, fifteen Indians had died of exposure before the middle of December. European diseases such as influenza, that sent the fort people to bed, killed the Indians outright and smallpox tore whole families and clans and sometimes whole communities right out of existence.

While there were always many women in the camps whose long hair had been cut to form a veil over their faces to signify mourning, cures were wrought, also. The medicine man used legerdemain, prescriptions, dances, rattles and chants with some success and the Indians had their household remedies, as commonplace as the bottles of Aspirin in today's medicine cabinets. Instead of the mustard plaster they used cedar bark from the fire. For a healing application they used warm, roasted frog which had been cleaned and pounded and spread with fir pitch. The skin of the frog was considered even more efficacious and was reserved for serious illnesses.

Death came from the sea, for the Indians respected their canoes more than the elements and seldom allowed violent weather to interrupt their trips to potlatches in other villages, to the seal hunting grounds far northward, to the sea otter waters to the west, to their fishing grounds or their favourite sites for drying seaweed, hunting, trapping or pursuing any of a dozen other occupations. No other deaths desolated the entire village as drownings did and the people made desperate attempts, in the same weather that had taken the lives, to recover the bodies. Apparently a lost body to them meant a soul lost forever and was an almost unbearable thought.

The natives' other element, the forest, could also bring death. Their usual method of obtaining cedar for a canoe, a totem pole or the wide boards of a lodge, was to bring the giant tree down by setting a fire at its base. They had small tools but their logging was accomplished more by ingenuity than force and the trees sometimes took revenge upon them.

At the very time nineteenth-century Indians were fighting off death by disease and accident, they were embracing death by warfare. (Twentieth-century populations all over the world seem to have suffered from the same inconsistency.) Conflict between the tribes was a state rather than an event. It was like a fire, lit in ancient times and kept smoldering through the ages by the heaping of fresh grievances upon it. At unpredictable times it blazed up, hot and red, in skirmishes and raids and massacres. The factors wrote hundreds of observations, as pointed and clear as icicles, concerning the fighting that popped and sputtered outside their stockade. They leave us with the feeling that although some enmities were deeper than others, there were no two tribes on the coast who would not shoot at one another at the drop of an insult or less. An account of the hostilities is like a roll call of the tribes. During 1836 and 1837 alone, the Tongass, a band of Tlingits, were embroiled in turn with the Tsimshians, the Stikines, the Skidegates and the Chilkats — casualties: twenty-four killed, an uncounted number wounded. In those same years the Tsimshians took on, beside the Tongass, the Skidegates, the Kygamics (both bands of Haidas) and the Stikines. Meanwhile all the other tribes were equally active.

Intertribal battles did not account for all the bloodshed; division of the tribes into clans and bands and totems and extended family units made for internal warfare and it seems that the natives were not too fussy about the tribal relationships of those receiving their musket balls; for example:

May 11, 1839: Kygarnies came to the fort to trade ammunition and reported "that the Kygarnie Indians who left this place some time ago quarreled among themselves and that the great woman Scutsay[,] her brother and three of her slaves were killed."

A month later some Tongass arrived with the news, "that Cape Fox Indians have been fighting among themselves, and that Jack the chief and four women have been killed."

And at the end of that summer, "One of the Canoes of Tongass people who arrived yesterday after trading their meat went off. As they were going off they got into a quarrel with some of their own Tribe who were ashore, they fired upon each other and kept up the fire from both sides till the canoe was out of reach."

Then there was the rather confusing affair of September 1841, that began as a Tsimshian-Haida engagement and ended as a Tsimshian-Tsimshian shoot-out. It started when the Espokelots, the Tsimshians whose home territory was the country around the mouth of the Skeena River, and a band of Haidas quarreled, to no one's surprise, over a trading transaction and "had recourse to firearms and exchanged several Shots on both Sides — and are still hard at action at this moment (11 o'clock p.m.) whether any are killed or not, cannot learn, but had occular proof of 2 or 3 getting broken arms & legs." There was little sleep at Fort Simpson that night for trade guns peppered the camps until noon the next day. By this time the Tongass had joined the fray because a Haida ball, intended for a Tsimshian, had wounded a Tongass man. This complicated the factor's attempt to negotiate a ceasefire but by noon he had arranged an acceptable three-cornered peace and the combatants threw themselves, as vigorously as they had fought, into the ritual of the blowing of down and feathers upon each others' heads and the making of long speeches.

The moment the last word had been uttered the Espokelots and the Haidas rushed back to their bargaining. The trade was lively for the Tsimshians were eager for the Queen Charlotte Island potatoes and the Haidas, their ammunition now depleted, were anxious for powder and shot.

At this point, Cacas, the Tsimshian chief who ruled over the north end of the Tsimshian Peninsula, came upon the scene. With horror he and his band watched the Espokelots handing over ammunition to the arch en-emies of all Tsimshians. They registered their protest by firing at the Espokelots who dug into their trade goods to fire back. "While this was going on," says Mr. Work, "the poor Haidas made off with themselves (it being perfectly dark at the time) in 2 canoes leaving 8 behind and a quan-tity of potatoes which the Tsimshians soon took possession of — the number killed & wounded as far [as] we could learn, 3 Tsimshians & one Tongass wounded & 3 Q.C.I.rs killed."

While trading quarrels brought on many a bloody clash, the Indian code that made revenge mandatory accounted for even more. It bound the tribes hopelessly in chains of atrocities. Every outrage called for a retaliation which called for a counter-retaliation which called for … until we have a prolif-eration of entries similar to:

September 24, 1841 (two days after the Haidas "made off with them-selves"): "All quiet among the Indians — one of the bodies whom we bur-ied yesterday had the head cut off and Scalped and disfigured in many respects by the Tsimshians — a Tsimshian Chief who visited Queen Charlotte's Islands a few years ago was shot and his body mangled in this inhuman manner by the identical person."

August 24, 1840: "The Cogueles came upon a party of Sabassa Indians (28 in number) who had been 'Sea-Otter' hunting and cut the throats of the whole of them as a retaliation of the great haul they kidnapped of Newitties 2 years ago."

Witchcraft or suspected witchcraft could precipitate a fight any day. June 24, 1856: "An Indian was treacherously shot in the bush, he was a Medicine man & was *supposed to be* the cause of the death of a young woman. His friends and the murderer's friends at each other in the evening, by *understanding*."

And gambling, even in 1842, was a violent sport: "Two Indians gambling quarreled, a Spachaloid and one of Neeskamek's men. Two shots fired which wounded 2 men and a woman. Another woman had her head fractured with a stone and died. At present firing occasional shots in order to show that they are on their guard."

Slaves were an inflammatory element of coast life. Tribes from north, west and south and from the east by way of the rivers, converged on Fort Simpson, bringing their slaves with them. Painful meetings and desperate rescue attempts were inevitable. In one case the Hudson's Bay Company stopped the altercation just short of shooting but also just short of a happy ending.

In the early 1830s the Skidegates had attacked a party of Tongass. They had killed all the men but had taken the little son of one of their victims, as a slave. On a day in May 1837, some Tongass people discovered the boy in the Haida camp at Fort Simpson and set about rescuing him. Guns bristled on both sides. The Skidegates had a strategy for such occasions. They launched their canoes, the boy confined in one, leaving a war party on shore to cover their retreat. As the Tongass prepared to shoot into the canoes and the war party prepared to shoot into the Tongass, the fort rolled out its big guns and promised to send a ball into whichever side fired the first shot. Meantime the Skidegate canoes paddled out of musket range.

Mr. McNeill's theory that women were the root of all west coast evil was upheld from time to time by small woman-instigated wars. Austine's face (before it was mutilated) may not have launched a thousand ships but it certainly sent forth a few canoes. In July of 1837, a party of Tongass Indians arrived with news of their battle with the Port Stewart Chilkats. They told of eight Tongass and fifteen Port Stewart warriors killed. It was not Mr. McNeill but Mr. Work who wrote up the report:

"It appears that the quarrel and all this bloodshed [was instigated] by a woman named Austine, who had been the wife of Quintal, one of our men, sometime. She had a quarrel with a Port Stewart or Cape Fox Indian about two blankets which she affirmed he had cheated her out of, and about 8 or 10 months ago at the fort here she ripped open his cheek with a knife. In order to make up the matter, her friends (for she has powerful connections), had paid him blankets and other property and he appeared satisfied but it was only in appearance, for, on meeting her with her friends — some time ago he attempted to cut open her Cheek as she had done his, her relations interfered to prevent him and a quarrel ensued in which he was shot. His friends took up the cause and this battle and the loss of so many lives have been the result. The affair is not yet settled — Austine and 2 other women are said to have been taken captive by the opposite party[;] the other two were stripped naked and released but she was retained to be cut and mangled and treated without mercy as the cause of so much mischief."

While a war could simmer for months, completely disrupting the lives of two tribes, it was not as horrifying as the single, hit-and-run canoe raid that was the specialty of coast peoples. Once, an elderly woman of our village was moved by my size and age, four or five, to reach back into her memory for the bright pieces of *her* fifth year and to show them to my sister and me. The most vivid were of a Haida raid on a fishing camp — of her mother grabbing her off the beach where she was playing; of the sight, over her mother's shoulder, of black canoes with black paddles sweeping around the point; of her hiding place between two logs, in the woods behind the camp; of the long and silent, cold, hungry, frightened wait for her mother to come back for her; of the return to the still camp with the other women and children; of the finding of their smashed canoes, their plundered boxes; of the three bodies of their men rolling in the light surf where she had played; of the wailing through the night. Her memories were corroborated by many a Fort Simpson journal note and letter:

"A short time ago a marauding party of Haidas from south end of Queen Charlotte Island fell treacherously on a party of Cape Fox Indians, killed 10 men and carried off all the women and children and took their property."

"3 canoes arrived from Victoria and Nanaimo, 17 days … They killed 4 men and brought 4 women prisoners belonging to the Kwakiutls."

"Yesterday a canoe of MacKenzie's people arrived from a war party. They brought 3 women prisoners also 2 heads."

It is plain to see that the depleted and deserted villages cannot be blamed wholly on the white man's diseases. Not quite so clear is the proportion of blame that should be attached to the white man's liquor.

In Fort Simpson's first decade, rum rippled through the Indian camps, if not gently, at least in a somewhat controlled flow. The factor kept a firm hand on the shut-off valve and used it occasionally. Those were the days when the Company traded liquor officially and accepted some responsibility for its consequences. In recording the case of a double murder the journal keeper ended with a contrite note: "Rum I regret to add has been the cause of these 2 peoples' deaths."

The second decade brought the Russian American Company-Hudson's Bay Company pact that ended their sale of liquor to Indians. It did not do away with rum in the villages — there were a few Boston traders and other ships dispensing liquor and there was the odd Hudson's Bay Company "gift" of rum to a chief. But the flow of spirits was reduced to a trickle and alcohol-induced atrocities were uncommon.

Then came the 1850s and the north coast Indians' discovery of Fort Victoria. Their canoes slipped down the Inside Passage, plundering as they went and returned laden with prisoners, spoils, disease and whiskey. When the sale of liquor to Indians was banned in Victoria, the tribesmen simply moved on across the Strait of Juan de Fuca to American territory where whiskey and loot were easy to come by. And before the 1850s ended, Victoria discovered the north coast Indians. It loosed its fleet of rapacious tangle [whiskey] sellers upon them and simultaneously the canoes and the sloops gushed alcohol that turned Fort Simpson into a sea of violence. In those times, every night in the village was like a night of modern television programs; there were beatings and stonings and strangulations and axe attacks and drownings, natural or otherwise, and shootings and stabbings — but the blood was not ketchup.

By the 1866 ending of the journals the flood seemed to have crested and the men-o-war to have reduced the flow, at least sporadically, but the horror of what had happened to the natives is still with us.

HUBERT EVANS (1892–1986)

For most of his ninety-four years Hubert Evans was a professional writer. Born and raised in Ontario, he worked as a newspaper reporter until enlisting in the Canadian army in 1915. At the end of the war, he married and moved with his wife to British Columbia where he worked for several years for the Provincial Hatcheries, first on the Skeena River and then near Vancouver. In 1927 he built a home in Roberts Creek and from that time forward made his living chiefly as a writer, publishing hundreds of stories in American and Canadian magazines and more than sixty serials and plays for CBC radio. His thirteen book titles represent a variety of genres: animal stories, war stories, children's fiction, poetry, memoir, biography and the novel. More cohesive are the themes which recur in these diverse works — a love for animals, an understanding of native peoples and their cultures, but above all a passionate concern for the environment and the preservation of wildlife. The novel *Mist on the River* (1954) is usually regarded as Evans' most significant work, written when he and his wife moved back for a few years to the Skeena, where she taught in one-room schools for native children. It delineates the plight of a Gitksan youth who must choose between the lure of mainstream society in Prince Rupert and the call of his traditional village inland. The novel has been highly commended for its anthropological authenticity, but also for its remarkable cross-cultural sympathies and insights. Equally sensitive to their subjects are Evans' writings about the natural world in *The Silent Call* (1930) from which "The Spark of Death" is taken. In this description of fish habitat and a forest fire, human beings are absent and genre is ambiguous. *The Silent Call* is a collection of animal stories, but this piece is closer to a meditation on nature that anticipates the environmental writings of Roderick Haig-Brown and Mark Hume. Today, a prestigious B.C. book award is named "the Hubert Evans Non-Fiction Prize."

THE SPARK OF DEATH

I

HALF-MOON LAKE lies in its basin of granite, tucked away in a fold of the timbered hills. Hemlock, cedar and vine maple come close to the water and peer dreamily at their reflections there. At the upper end Half-moon Creek makes stately curves through the heavy timber and across a beaver meadow to join the lake. A mile away, at the lower end of the lake, it leaves and throws itself over a hundred-foot cliff and is wafted as mist upward through the dark green branches. There are no other streams either into or out of Half-moon Lake.

In Half-moon Lake there reigns a race of cutthroat trout; superb creatures, lusty of fin and hard of flesh. During the longer evenings they dimple the water at the upper end where the inflowing creek carries their food to them from the warmer water of the beaver meadow where it is bred so lavishly. Blind channels of slow waters almost choked with rich vegetation sprawl like idle fingers across the meadow. Here the fly larvae, the bronze-backed water beetles and the minute crustaceans multiply and downstream, where the coiling water joins the tranquil blue of the lake, the trout are bountifully fed.

Half-moon Creek does more than feed the trout. In the spring the breeding fish ascend it to spawn. No rushing mountain stream this, to carry away the precious eggs or, springing madly into freshet, scour out the nests among the gravel, but a stream whose well aerated water flows evenly and unfailingly over beds of fine clean-washed gravel. Here healthy trout are hatched and here, in the dancing pools below the riffles, the fry and fingerlings play and feed and learn to swim and dart at the food particles the stream brings down to them. During the summer they graduate to the lake and feed lustily until, before winter creeps down from the snow peaks far above and seals the lake in ice, they have grown to be three or four inches long, well-formed and broad of back.

In April the ice goes first from the upper end of the lake. Schooling closer in toward the creek mouth come the trout in answer to the age-old spawning urge. Rounded females, heavy with eggs, lie poised in the current just where the bank at the creek mouth drops steeply off into the deep lake waters. Thin-sided males, their under parts already taking on the darker spawning colours, cruise restlessly. These all are the larger trout. The younger ones follow after a week or more.

Then one evening, when the purple dusk creeps up the sidehills and the stars, with their reflections for partners dance coldly on the polished lake surface, the first schools enter the creek, move purposefully through the lower reaches of the beaver meadow and gain the narrower stretches beyond, where the water flows evenly, smoothly over the clean, well-rounded gravel. Then in little pools or close against an overhanging bank they wait before moving onto the shallow spawning beds.

Exciting times these, when the males dart truculently at one another until the stronger have won the approval of a mate and have discouraged their less persistent rivals. A shallow hole is scooped out in the loose gravel, the eggs are deposited until in a week each pair have entrusted a thousand to the stream. Secured in the gravel that covers them and supplied with oxygen from the water that circulates through it, they will remain until the embryo develops and breaks through the soft shell.

Their annual pilgrimage up the stream completed, the trout drop downstream and feed prodigiously at the creek mouth and grow prime and lusty again. Sudden freshets would scour out the nests and carry the eggs into lifeless backwaters where silt would filter down and smother them; a drought would leave them stranded above the water level and they would die. But in Half-moon Creek the flow of water is uninterrupted, even. The drenching rains are held back by the many square miles of root-woven forest floor and distributed evenly in times of drought.

A month or more later the eggs will hatch. Then for a few weeks the little fish, with their cumbersome yolk sacs attached to their undersides, will lie in the gloom of the gravel that covers them, until this nourishment is consumed. Then wriggling upward toward the light they become free-swimming and sidle across the gentler wisps of current, feeding. When, during the summer, they outgrow their nursery in the narrow pools, they drop down to the deeper reaches of the beaver meadow and into the lake. Zealously, unfailingly, the kindly waters of Half-moon Creek have for centuries reared and guarded each generation of the trout that come to maturity in its placid lake.

II

One August the air hung motionless for many days above Half-moon Lake. Its bright mirror became tarnished. The trout listlessly disregarding food, sank deeper into the cool waters. Only a few, coming to the surface in the evening to course half-heartedly below it, broke water sluggishly as they took the food that floated there. Day after day the sun cleared the eastern ridges, floated across a sky of monotonous brightness and sank sullenly in the west again. An unsettling sense of foreboding filled the creatures of forest and water.

One noon a wind broke the quiet of the hidden valley. It charged up the lake, sending frightened cat's-paws scampering before it and buffeted the trees that walled the shore. It was hot, like the blast from some great furnace door, suddenly opened. Green twig tips and the shaded fronds of ferns seemed to cringe and wither before it.

Soon it found the spark of fire it wanted — a spark that had hidden, waiting and vicious, in the side of a sun-baked rotten log — and hurried it into flame. Within an hour a giant column of biting grey smoke had reared itself higher than the sheltering hills and was spreading like a colossal grey toadstool, against the flattened, copper sky. Baffled and angry, the sun hung poised above it, peering vainly at the increasing havoc below.

The fire from the rotten log spread like an opening fan as it raced to keep pace with the wind. The growling advance guard of the flame paused only long enough to deal slashing blows at the sun-heated timber, then leaped ahead, an insatiable demon, biting and throwing aside each morsel for the wall of slower fire that followed, like a dense pack of jackals, to feast upon the stricken victims. A premature, eerie twilight crept below the low cover of sullen smoke that back-eddied and filtered flakes of grey ash on the pallid water; now and then a twig, glowing and hot, fell to the water with a choking hiss.

That night the army of fire had passed up the valley, marching more leisurely now, confident of victory and unhindered pillage. Where the mature forest had been, charred stubs glowed evenly or stabbed the red night with sudden jets of searching flames. The bottom land, and the sidehills that held it, were like a vast city that had been looted and left. Occasionally the fearsome, muttering night-hush was shattered by the wrenching crash of a giant tree whose butt had been gnawed through by the worms of fire. Half-moon Creek bore heavy loads of charred limbs and bark and left them to circle in the lake at either side of its mouth.

A month passed and no rain fell. The surface of the lake was tainted, unpurged by any ruffling breeze. The trout went deeper. Through the lanes of what had been a city of towering trees sluggish flames prowled, feasting on the fallen giants, eating their way deep into the sponge-like carpet of roots and mould.

And then the rain, like reinforcements that came too late, fell on the rear guard of the fire and annihilated it. But the day was already lost. Relentlessly the rain teemed down. The foliage that had formerly broken its fan was gone and it smote the baked sidehills smartly, wearing deepening watercourses down the scarred faces. The elastic fibrous roots that had kept the mold in place were killed and brittle. They gave way before the sagging weight of drenched soil. Like the hide showing through the fur of a moth-eaten rug, the bare granite slopes appeared where their covering was being washed away. Overturned trees, their roots in air, were left stranded on the rocks, skeletons of wrecked ships where the tide receded.

With only brief pauses the heavy rains continued until the freeze-up in November.

III

Next spring the trout once more ascended Half-moon Creek. The shelving bar at its mouth now was cut through by a deep channel. The reach through the beaver meadow, too, was deeper. The slack water, the blind channels and pockets where food had bred in other years, were above the level of the hurrying water, dry and already crisping before the warming May sun. Farther upstream, where had been wide, smooth-flowing riffles, dappled with shade, were harsh channels torn through a wilderness of blackened snags. The water was fast now, the spawning beds scoured out and the precious gravel mixed with the tangles of uprooted stumps and matted branches.

The fish spawned where they could. Some overcrowded the few remaining patches of smooth gravel and in their frenzy scooped out each other's nests and gave the eggs to the angry water to whirl downstream and kill. Others spawned in the main channel among boulders where the eggs could not be secured and hatched. It was the same spawning period with its old frenzy and restlessness, but all the natural conditions were against, instead of aiding, propagation. When it was over, the trout hurried to the creek mouth to feed and regain vigour and weight.

But this year there was scarcely any food. The luscious reaches in the beaver meadow were baked and lifeless, their water vegetation a dry and tangled mat of mud-caked stalks. The supply of food that had come from it for so long had been stranded and killed. Since the fire the sponge-like carpet of the wide valley above did not hold the rains and melting snow and release them evenly through a thousand tiny feeders. The roots and the filtering soil they kept in place had been washed down by the heavy rain. The creek, instead of being sparklingly clear, was sullied and silt laden.

With every rain it boomed and in dry weather shriveled to a twisted ribbon of water among the outscoured boulders. Savagely, unappeased, the trout cruised off the mouth, viciously darting at what pittances of food — a dislodged caddis or a drowned fly or bee — the stream might bear.

For the first time in centuries the trout of Half-moon Lake did not regain their prime condition. All summer, gaunt and spent-looking, they waited for the feast that never came. And up the creek where the splendid spawning beds had been outraged, Nature was exacting her toll of what fry had come from the almost sterile hatching places. In other years the fry had appeared in thousands, now there were only hundreds; thin-bodied they were, deprived of the mosquito larvae and smaller food the stream had carried in its bounteous years.

Then before they tried to leave the creek, came the crowning tragedy. The bright days of July brought no rain, the creek shriveled. In places it seeped into the gravel, appearing again farther downstream and trickling through the torn channel in the blackened timber. The trout fingerlings tried to follow it and could not. They were trapped, left to mill about in a dozen narrow ponds a few yards long. The kingfishers found them and shrieked their triumph.

Each day the pools, like patches of snow on a southern sidehill, shrank, each day the fish became more crowded in them. Sometimes in the late afternoon the pools almost disappeared, then with the cool of evening partly filled only to shrink when the sun grew hot on the unshaded channel.

One day the pools went altogether dry. The condemned captives struggled to force their way downward into the cool gravel on the trail of the departed water. The sun struck full upon them. The stones became warm, hot. That evening there were hundreds of crisp wisps of silver littering each dry pool, shining like twisted bits of tin-foil against the arid stones.

Over each pool beady-eyed flies buzzed.

That night the moon, a balloon of cold fire, freed herself from the beckoning arms of the gaunt tree skeletons that lined the skyline. It saw that the end of the line of cutthroat trout in Half-moon Lake was near.

That must have been many years ago. For Half-moon Lake is barren now.

M. WYLIE BLANCHET (1891–1961)

Muriel Wylie Blanchet was born and educated in Montreal and came to live in British Columbia in the 1920s when her banker husband was transfered to Sidney on Vancouver Island. There they bought a small cruising boat (25 feet) and planned to travel the coastal waters with their five children, but her husband went missing on a fishing trip, and only the boat was ever found. An independent and quietly practical woman, Blanchet was determined to carry out the family's dream: acting as captain, navigator and engineer, as well as mother, she took her boat and children up and down the inside passage, summer after summer, exploring the islands and the deep fjord-like inlets of the mainland. They ranged as far as Queen Charlotte Strait at the north end of Vancouver Island, encountering storms and rapids, fog and wild animals, meeting eccentric individuals living in isolation, and exploring the ghostly villages of the native people whose populations had either died out or gone to the canneries to work for the summer.

Later in life, Blanchet set down her memories of those adventures in a series of sketches, four of which were printed in *Blackwood's Magazine* in Britain. She also published pieces in yachting magazines in the U.S. and in the prestigious pages of *Atlantic Monthly*. In 1961 Blackwoods published a book-length volume of these sketches which she titled *The Curve of Time*. The foreword begins unpretentiously: "This is neither a story nor a log; it is just an account of many long sunny summer months, during many years, when the children were young enough and old enough to take on camping holidays up the coast of British Columbia. Time did not exist; or if it did it did not matter, and perhaps it was not always sunny." Beneath these simple statements there are complex reflections on time and the nature of happiness. Gray Campbell, Blanchet's friend and Canadian publisher, points to the haunting lyricism beneath her plain style when he writes that she "combined history and the environment as seen through the eyes of an artist" and "painted scenes and characters, mysticism and moods that were fast disappearing."

Blanchet never knew how widely read and deeply loved her book would become. Little attention was paid when it was first published, and she died six months later while working on a sequel about the house in which she had raised her family. But in 1968 the Canadian edition was published and a reviewer for the *Ottawa Journal* predicted it could one day become a Canadian classic. With three different editions of the book to date and at least fourteen printings to supply a continually growing readership, one can say that this prophecy has already been fulfilled in British Columbia. Blanchet's book is not alone in describing the pleasures and hazards of boating: *Upcoast Summers* by Beth Hill (1985) is an edition of the diaries kept by Francis Barrow in the 1930s when he and his wife also travelled as far north as Queen Charlotte Strait in their small boat. Barrow describes many of the same places and people as Blanchet, and includes an encounter with Blanchet herself. Blanchet's book also appears to have influenced the American writer Edith Iglauer, whose *Fishing with John* (1980) is similarly evocative of coastal life.

From THE CURVE OF TIME
THE CURVE OF TIME

ON BOARD OUR BOAT one summer we had a book by Maurice Maeterlinck called *The Fourth Dimension,* the fourth dimension being *Time* — which, according to Dunne, doesn't exist in itself, but is always relative to the person who has the idea of Time. Maeterlinck used a curve to illustrate Dunne's theory. Standing in the Present, on the highest point of the curve, you can look back and see the Past, or forward and see the Future, all in the same instant. Or, if you stand off to one side of this curve, as I am doing, your eye wanders from one to the other without any distinction. In dreams, the mind wanders in and out of the Present, through the Past and the Future, unable to distinguish between what has not yet happened and what has already befallen. Maeterlinck said that if you kept track of your dreams, writing them down as soon as you woke, you would find that a certain number were of things that had already happened; others would be connected with the present; but a certain number would be about things that had not yet happened. This was supposed to prove that Time is just a dimension of Space, and that there is no difference between the two, except that our consciousness roves along this Curve of Time.

In my mind, I always think of that summer as the Maeterlinck summer — the year we wrote down our dreams. The children always called it — the Year of the Bears.

Towards the end of June, or it might have been July, we headed up Jervis Inlet. This inlet cuts through the Coast Range of British Columbia and extends by winding reaches in a northerly direction for about sixty miles. Originally perhaps a fault in the earth's crust, and later scoured out by a glacier, since retreated, it is roughly a mile wide, and completely hemmed in on all sides by stupendous mountains, rising from almost perpendicular shores to heights of from five to eight thousand feet. All the soundings on the chart are marked one hundred fathoms with the no-bottom mark … right up to the cliffs. Stunted pines struggle up some of the ravines, but their hold on life is short. Sooner or later, a winter storm or spring avalanche sweeps them out and away; and next summer there will be a new cascade in their place.

Once you get through Agamemnon Channel into the main inlet, you just have to keep going — there is no shelter, no place to anchor. In summertime the wind blows up the inlet in the morning, down the inlet from five o'clock on. In winter, I am told, the wind blows down the inlet most of the time — so strong and with such heavy williwaws that no boat can make against it. I know that up at the head of the inlet most trappers' cabins are braced with heavy poles towards the north.

For some reason that I have forgotten, probably the hope of trout for supper, we decided to anchor in Vancouver Bay for lunch. Vancouver Bay is about half-way up Jervis, and only makes a very temporary anchorage good for a couple of hours on a perfectly calm day. It is a deep bay between very high mountains, with a valley and three trout streams. You can drop your hook on a narrow mud bank, but under your stern it falls away to nothing.

After lunch I left the youngsters playing on the beach, and taking a light fishing line I worked my way back for perhaps half a mile. The underbrush was heavy and most uncomfortable on bare legs, and I had to make wide detours to avoid the devil's club. Then I had to force my way across to the stream, as my trail had been one of least resistance. It was a perfect trout stream, the water running along swiftly on a stony bottom; but with deep pools beside the overhanging banks, cool shade under fallen tree trunks. The sunshine drifted through the alders and flickered on the surface of the running water. Somewhere deeper in the forest the shy thrushes were calling their single, abrupt liquid note. Later, when the sun went down, the single note would change to the ascending triplets. Except for the thrushes, there was not a sound — all was still.

I didn't have a rod — you can't cast in this kind of growth, there is no room. I didn't use worms, I used an unripe huckleberry. An unripe huckleberry is about the size and colour of a salmon egg — and trout love salmon eggs. Almost at once I landed a fair-sized one on the mossy rocks.

Another … and then another. I ran a stick through their gills and moved to another pool.

But suddenly I was seized with a kind of panic … I simply had to get back to my children. I shouldn't be able to hear them from where I was, if they called. I listened desperately … There was just no sense to this blind urge that I felt. Almost frantic, I fought my way back by the most direct route — through the salmonberry, salal, and patches of devil's club.

"Coming — coming!" I shouted. What was I going to rescue them from? I didn't know, but how desperately urgent it was!

I finally scrambled through to the beach — blood streaming down my legs, face scratched, hands torn — blood everywhere. Five wondering faces looked at me in horror. The two youngest burst into tears at the sight of this remnant of what had once been their Mummy.

"Are you all right?" I gasped — with a sudden seething mixture of anger and relief at finding them alive and unhurt.

After an interval, the three girls took my fish down to the sea to clean, the two little boys helping me wash off the blood as I sat with my feet in the stream. Devil's club spikes are very poisonous and I knew their scratches would give me trouble for days.

"There's a man along at the other end of the beach," volunteered Peter. "He's been watching us."

"All day!" broke in John. "And he's all dressed in black." I glanced up — a tall figure was standing there, against the trees, up behind the drift-logs at the top of the beach. Just standing there, arms hanging down, too far away to be seen plainly. Peculiar place for a clergyman to be, I thought inanely; and went back to the more important business of washing off the blood. Then I put on the shoes I had washed.

"Mummy!" called Elizabeth. I glanced up. The three of them were look-ing towards the other end of the beach.

"The man is coming over," said Fran. "He's …!"

"Mummy!" shrieked Jan. It didn't take us two minutes to drag the din-ghy into the water, pile in and push off. The man was coming — but he was coming on all fours.

The bear ate the fish that the children had dropped. Then, as we pulled up the anchor, not thirty feet away, she looked at us crossly, swung her nose in the air to get our scent, and grumbled back along the beach to meet her two cubs. They had suddenly appeared from behind the logs and were coming along the beach in short runs. Between runs they would sit down — not quite sure what their mother was going to think about it. She didn't think it was a good idea at all. She cuffed them both, and they ran back whimpering to the logs. She followed, and then stood up again — tall, black, arms hanging loosely down, and idly watched us leave the bay.

"Mummy!" demanded the children, when they were quite sure they were safe. "That bad dream you had last night that woke us all up that you said you couldn't remember — was it about bears?"

"No … at least, I don't think so." But even as I spoke, I could remember how very urgent and terrifying something had been in that dream. I hesitated — and then I decided not to tell them about the strange, blind panic I had felt by the stream — I could have smelt the bear downwind. But I knew that the panic and sense of urgency by the stream, and the feeling in my dream, had been one and the same.

Marlborough Heights flanks the northern side of Vancouver Bay, swinging boldly out in a ten-mile curve and making the inlet change its course. It rises straight up out of the sea, and straight up to six thousand feet. And nobody knows how deep it goes. The chart just states in chart language — one hundred fathoms, no bottom, right off the cliffs. The children always hang over the gunwale trying to see — they don't know quite what — but it must be something awful in anything so deep.

Peter and John were still moaning about the trout the bear had eaten — so I said I would stop and we would try to see what mysterious something we could catch. I stopped the engine, and Elizabeth held us off the cliff with the pike-pole, while we knotted all our fishing lines together. We tied on a two-pound jigger, which is a flat, rounded piece of lead, with a rigid hook at the lower end. Then we baited it with bacon, and down … down … down … and everybody watched and pushed for better places to see. After a while I thought I could feel something like bottom — it was so far away that I couldn't be sure. But I jigged the line up and down — up and down. Then something caught and held it and jigged back — somewhat like getting in touch with another planet.

I pulled in, and in, and in … The children watched breathlessly, but still there was more to come. It was now definitely something. I told Jan to bring the dinghy in closer, and I leapt the gap, still pulling. I didn't know what might live at that great depth — I'd bring it alongside the dinghy, have a look at it first and then decide.

Foot after foot … after foot … Then "Ah's!" from the children. A bright scarlet fish was goggling at me from beside the dinghy. It was about two feet long and thick through. It didn't struggle — it just lay there gasping. I took the gaff and lifted it gently into the boat by its gills, for water didn't seem to be its proper medium. Again it didn't struggle. It just lay on the floorboards and gasped and goggled as though it would have liked to tell me something, but couldn't.

"Put the poor thing back! Put it back!" pleaded the children, wringing their hands.

But just then, a great inflated tongue-like thing came out of its mouth and stayed out. Then I remembered what the fishermen up at the Yuculta Rapids had told us about the Red Snappers that were sometimes chased up from great depths. Without the pressure of the depths, this sack or bladder inflates, and they have to die. They can never go back to where they belong — and just flounder about on the surface until the eagles or seagulls put them out of their misery. They are very good to eat — but after seeing this one's goggling eyes and listening to its pleading gasps, I didn't think any of us would want to. I killed it quickly and put it over the side.

The wind hit us as we came opposite Britain River, just as it usually does. It blows out of the deep valley of the Britain River, and then escapes out through Vancouver Bay. After we had slopped ahead out of that, we met the wind that blows out of Deserted Bay and down the full length of Princess Royal Reach. So for the next ten miles or so we battled wind. It is not a nice wind in among the mountains. It picks you up in its teeth and shakes you. It hits you first on one side and then on the other. There is nowhere to go, you just have to take it. But finally, everybody tired and hungry, we rounded Patrick Point into the gentle Queen's Reach — and there, there was no wind at all.

An hour or so later we were at the entrance to little Princess Louisa Inlet. But the tide was still running a turbulent ten knots out of the narrow entrance — so we tied up to the cliff and ate our supper while we waited for slack water.

We were inextricably associated with Captain George Vancouver, R.N., in our summer-long trips up the coast. He explored, surveyed and charted the coast of British Columbia in 1792, and named practically every island, inlet and channel — names that are still used. Every bay we anchor in, every beach we land on — Vancouver or his lieutenants had been there first.

Vancouver of course had no charts — he was there to make them. But from old sources he had certain reports of a great inland sea in those latitudes — and he seemed to be convinced that it existed. Even when he was confronted with the whole stretch of the snow-capped Coast Range, he was still sure he was going to find a channel through the mountains to that mediterranean sea.

In June of that far-off summer of 1792, Vancouver left his ship, the *Discovery,* and the armed tender, *Chatham,* at anchor down in Birch Bay

— just south of what is now the international boundary. Then, with Archibald Menzies, the botanist of the expedition, and perhaps four others in the little yawl, and Mr. Puget in charge of the launch, Vancouver set off to examine the coast to the north.

After exploring part of Burrard Inlet, on which the present city of Vancouver is built, they sailed up Howe Sound, just a little north of Burrard Inlet. Captain Vancouver clearly did not like our high mountains. The low fertile shores they had seen farther down the coast near Birch Bay, he says, "here no longer existed. Their place was now occupied by the base of a tremendous snowy barrier, thin wooded and rising abruptly from the sea to the clouds; from whose frigid summit the dissolving snow in foaming torrents rushed down the sides and chasms of its rugged surface, exhibiting altogether a sublime but gloomy spectacle which animated nature seemed to have deserted. Not a bird nor a living creature was to be seen, and the roaring of the falling cataracts in every direction precluded their being heard had any been in the neighbourhood."

Again — "At noon I considered that we had advanced some miles within the western boundaries of the snowy barrier, as some of its rugged mountains were now behind and to the south of us. This filled my mind with the pleasing hopes of finding our way to its eastern side." Then they proceeded up to the head of the inlet — "Where all our expectations vanished, in finding it to terminate in a round basin, encompassed on every side by the dreary country already described."

They sailed up the coast for about sixty miles, taking observations and soundings. Eventually, they entered Jervis Inlet. Starting off at four a.m. as usual — "The width of the channel still continuing, again flattered us with discovering a breach in the eastern range of snowy mountains, notwithstanding the disappointment we had met with in Howe Sound; and although since our arrival in the Gulf of Georgia, it had proved an impenetrable barrier to that inland navigation of which we had heard so much, and had sought with such sanguine hopes and ardent exertions hitherto in vain to discover."

Later — "By the progress we had this morning made, which comprehended about six leagues, we seemed to have penetrated considerably into this formidable obstacle, and as the more lofty mountains were now behind us and no very distant ones were seen beyond the valleys caused by the depressed parts of the snowy barrier in the northern quarters, we had great reason to believe we had passed this impediment to our wishes, and I was induced to hope we should find this inlet winding beyond the mountains."

After dinner they proceed… "Until about five in the evening, when all our hopes vanished, by finding it terminate, as others had, in swampy low land."

Vancouver's whole outlook on these beautiful inlets was coloured by this desire to find a seaway to the other side of the mountains. Some of the party must have been impressed with the beauty and grandeur. Menzies, the botanist, is more enthusiastic. In his diary he notes, "Immense cascades dashing down chasms against projecting rocks and cliffs with a furious wildness that beggars all description."

Even he doesn't say that the cascades start away up at four or five thousand feet. That mountains six and seven thousand feet high flank either side of the inlet beyond Marlborough Heights, and show great snowfields in the upper valleys.

Coming back from the head of the inlet that evening, Vancouver and his party, who had noticed the entrance to Princess Louisa on the way up and decided it was a creek, found the tide running swiftly out of it. The water was salt and the entrance shallow. They gave up the idea of spending the night there and rowed until eleven o'clock past high cliffs to find shelter behind Patrick Point.

The youngsters were delighted that Vancouver had missed Princess Louisa Inlet — very scornful that he had thought the entrance shallow.

"He didn't even try the right entrance, he was on the ledge," said Peter.

"Well, he couldn't have got in anyway, with the tide running out," said Jan, defending him.

He certainly couldn't have got in. Even we, who knew the way, were tied up to a log, eating our supper while the pent-up waters of Louisa poured themselves out through the narrow entrance in a ten-knot race.

It was also understandable that they should have mistaken it for a creek. From the outside where we waited, you can see nothing of the inlet beyond. Two steep four-thousand-foot mountains, one on each side of the entrance, completely obscure the inlet and the mountains beyond. The entrance is a little tricky to get through at low tide unless you know it, but there is plenty of water. From water level, the points on one side and the coves on the other fold into each other, hiding the narrow passage. It is not until you are rushed through the gap on a rising tide that the full surprise of the existence and beauty of this little hidden inlet suddenly bursts on you. It is always an effort to control the boat as you hold her on the high ridge of the straight run of water down the middle. Then, as you race past the last points, the ridge shatters into a turmoil of a dozen different currents and confusions. Your boat dashes towards the rocky cliff beyond the shallow cove on your right; and the cliff, equally delighted, or so it seems, rushes towards your boat. You wrestle with the wheel of your straining boat, and finally manage to drag the two apart … and you are out of danger in a backwater.

The inlet is about five miles long, a third of a mile wide, and the mountains that flank it on either side are over a mile high. From inside the entrance you can see right down to the far end where it takes the short L-turn to the left. At that distance you can see over the crest to where all the upper snowfields lie exposed, with their black peaks breaking through the snow. The scar of a landslide that runs diagonally for four thousand feet is plainly visible. At certain times of the day the whole inlet seems choked with mountains, and there is no apparent line between where the cliffs enter the sea and where the reflections begin.

Three miles farther down the inlet, the high snowfields become obscured — the mountains are closing in. You turn the corner of the great precipice that slightly overhangs — which they say the Indians used to scale with rocks tied to their backs: the one who reached the top first was the bravest of the brave, and was made the chief …

Then suddenly, dramatically, in a couple of boat-lengths, the whole abrupt end of the inlet comes into sight — heavily wooded, green, but rising steeply. Your eye is caught first by a long white scar, up about two thousand feet, that slashes across … and disappears into the dark-green background. Again, another splash of white, but farther down. Now you can see that it has movement. It is moving down and down, in steep rapids. Disappearing … reappearing … and then in one magnificent leap plunging off the cliff and into the sea a hundred feet below. As your boat draws in closer, the roar and the mist come out to meet you.

We always tied up at Trapper's Rock — well over to the left of the falls, but not too close to the mile-high, perfectly vertical cliff. It is a huge piece about twelve by twelve with a slight incline.

"Did this fall off that cliff too?" somebody asked, as they took the bow-line and jumped off the boat onto Trapper's Rock. I was busy trying to drape a stern anchor over a great sloping rock that lay just under water, ten feet astern, and avoided answering. Dark night was coming on rapidly and the cliffs were closing in. Night was a foolish time to answer unanswerable questions. I was glad we couldn't hear the waterfall too loudly at Trapper's Rock. That waterfall can laugh and talk, sing and lull you to sleep. But it can also moan and sob, fill you with awful apprehensions of you don't know what — all depending on your mood … My crew soon settled down to sleep. On the other side of the falls I could see a light through the trees.

The Man from California, who had started building a large log cabin last year, must be there — in residence. I didn't want to think about him, for he would spoil much of our freedom in Louisa ... Then I started feeling the pressure of the mile-high cliff, worrying about the two huge rocks we were moored between, and all the other monstrous rocks that filled the narrow strip behind us. As you stepped off Trapper's Rock onto the shore, you stepped into a sort of cave formed by an enormous slanting rock that spread out over your head. A little stream of ice-cold spring water ran on one side, and dropped pool by pool among the maidenhair ferns down to the stony shore. A circle of blackened stones marked our cooking fires of other summers. The back and top of this prehistoric cave were covered with moss and ferns and small huckleberry bushes. All the slope behind was filled with enormous rocks. They were not boulders, worn and rounded by the old glacier. They had sharp angles and straight-cut facets; in size, anywhere from ten by ten to twenty by twenty — hard, smooth granite, sometimes piled two or three deep — towering above us.

They were undoubtedly pieces that had fallen off the cliff, the cliff that shut off the world and pressed against me. The first night's question always was — was Trapper's Rock one of the first to break and fall, or was it one of the last, which fell and bounced over the others to where it now lay? In back of the rock, the masses are piled one on top of the other. There are deep crevices between them that you could fall into — no one knows how many feet. It would take rope-work to get on top of some of them. None of us is allowed to go in there alone.

The stars had filled up the long crack of sky above me. Brighter stars than you see anywhere else ... bright ... so bright ...

Somewhere in that uneasy night I dreamt that I was watching a small black animal on a snowfield, some distance away. I don't remember why I was so curious about it, but in my dreams it seemed most important for me to know what it was. Then I decided, and knew most certainly, that it was a black fox playing and sliding on the edge of the snowfield. Then moving closer to it, as you sometimes do in a dream's mysterious way, I saw that it wasn't a fox at all, but a small black pony. I remember that it looked more like a pony that a child had drawn — low-slung and with a blocky head — sliding on a most unlikely snowfield.

In the wonderful bright morning the cliffs were all sitting down again — well back. All the fears and tensions had gone. We had a swim in the lovely warm water. The sun wouldn't come over the mountain edge before ten, but a pot of hot porridge, toast and coffee kept everybody warm. I made the children laugh about my dream of a black fox that turned into an ugly black pony. Everyone decided that it must have been the man in black down in Vancouver Bay that turned into a bear. I couldn't think why it hadn't occurred to me before. It's just as well to have dreams like that in the Past.

Over on the other side of the falls we could see a big float held out from the shore by two long poles — new since last year. Somewhere in behind lay the log cabin and the intruder. His coming last year had changed many things. We used to be able to stay in the inlet a couple of weeks without seeing another boat. Last summer, when the cabin was being built by skilled axe-men, there were always a few boats there — coming and going with supplies. And the men who were building the cabin were there all the time. We had only just met the Man from California, and we had stayed for only two days.

On the other side of the inlet, on the right-hand cliff beyond the falls, which is not as perpendicular and is sparsely wooded with small pines, there is a great long scar. You can see where it started as a rockslide four thousand feet up. It had carried trees, scrub and loose stones in front of it — gradually getting wider as it scraped the rock clean. In rainy weather a torrent races down tumbling noisily from pool to pool. But in summer-time only a thin stream slides over the smooth granite, collecting in an endless series of deep and shallow pools. Heated by the sun on the rock, the water is lukewarm. We used to climb up perhaps half a mile, and then slide down the slippery granite from pool to pool like so many otters. We found it too hard on the seats of our bathing suits, and had got into the habit of parking them at the bottom. Now, with the coming of the log cabin, we had to post a guard or else tie our bathing suits round our necks.

Boat scrubbed and tidied, sleeping bags out in the sun, everybody had their jobs. Then we collected our clothes for washing, piled into the din-ghy and rowed across to the landslide. There was a green canoe turned over on the wharf; no sign of the owner. He probably didn't even know that anyone was in the inlet, for you can't hear a boat's engine on account of the falls.

The three lowest pools of the landslide were called Big Wash, Big Rinse, and Little Rinse. All snow-water, all lukewarm — so washing was easy. And we carry only one set of clothes, pyjamas, and bathing suits — so there is practically nothing to wash anyway. We scrubbed our clothes — we washed our hair — we washed ourselves. That, interspersed with slid-ing, took some time. Then, all clean and shining bright, we gathered up our things. The three girls said that they would swim on ahead. Peter wanted to go too, but he swims with only his nose above water, and it is hard to see if he is there or not. So I said that he could help John and me gather huckleberries first.

When we followed later in the dinghy, Peter with his snorkel up, swimming beside us, there were the three girls sitting on the wharf, talking to the Man from California. He said he hadn't had anyone to talk to for a month — except old Casper down at the entrance, and he always brought back a flea when he went to visit him. He asked us to come over and have supper with him that night and see the new log cabin. The children held their breath ... waiting for me to say — yes.

After lunch, needing to stretch our legs, we started off to scramble up through the mighty chaos that lay behind Trapper's Rock. Peter carried a coil of light rope for rescue work, and John his bow-and-arrow, ready for you can never tell what. We had to be pulled and pushed up some of the biggest barriers. Devil's club made impenetrable blocks around which we had to detour. Then suddenly we found ourselves on a well-defined trail that skirted all the biggest rocks and always seemed to find the best way.

"Who do you suppose this nice person was?" asked John.

"Trapper, I should think," I said, very thankful for it.

Then it ended in a big hole between two great rocks that overhung our way. The youngsters were intrigued with the thought of a real cave and wanted to explore it. But there was a very strong smell coming from it.

"Just like foxes," someone said. "No, like mink," said somebody else.

Certainly it was something, and we decided to skip it. We had to go partly through the entrance to get past ... for some reason I could feel the hair standing up along my spine.

The trail led beyond as well. The huckleberries were ripe and the cave forgotten. Then we could hear the roar of the river ahead, so we left the trail and cut down towards the sea. We soon wished we hadn't, for the going was heavy and we were very vulnerable in bathing suits. Finally we broke through to the shore close to the falls; and there being no other way, we had to swim and wade back to our rock. I waded, with John sitting on my shoulders, up to my neck at times. The sun was off the rock, but the cliffs hold the heat so long that we didn't miss it. Later, each of us dressed up in his one set of clothes, we rowed leisurely across to the float, probably as glad to have someone to talk to as the Man from California.

The cabin was lovely. The whole thing, inside and out, was made of peeled cedar logs — fifteen and twenty inches in diameter. There was one big room, about forty by twenty feet, with a great granite fireplace. A stairway led up to a balcony off which there were two bedrooms and a bathroom. A kitchen and another bedroom and bathroom led off the living-

room. Doors, bookcases, everything was made of the peeled cedar logs —
even the chesterfield in front of the fireplace, and the big trestle table. A
bookcase full of books … A lot of thought and good taste, and superb axe-
manship, had gone into the construction.

After supper, sitting in front of a blazing log fire, the children were telling him of our climb back into the beyond.

"And there was a cave, and it smelt of foxes," Peter burst out.

"Dead foxes," added John.

I asked if there were any foxes around here.

"What on earth made you think of foxes?" the man asked. "There are no
foxes in country like this."

Then he asked questions as to just how far back we had been, and just
where. Then he told us — a she-bear and her cub had been around all
spring. One of the loggers who were building the cabin had followed her
trail, and it crossed the river on a log some distance above the falls. He had
found the den in the cave. Although he had a gun with him, he had not
shot the mother on account of the cub.

Then, of course, the children had to tell about my dream of the fox that
had turned out to be a black pony … shaped much more like a bear than
a pony, I now realized. It all more or less fitted in. But what about the man
down at Vancouver Bay who had turned out to be a bear? Maeterlinck was
beginning to spoil our summer — if the dreams were going to work both
ways we would soon be afraid to get off the boat.

The Man from California, who hardly knew us, was full of the perils of
the surrounding terrain. We were perfectly willing to say we wouldn't go
near the bear's den again — we knew as well as he did that bears with cubs
are dangerous. But we forbore to tell him that we were going to climb up
four thousand feet the next day to get some black huckleberries we knew
of at the edge of the tree line. After all, *he* was the intruder — probably
attracted the bears. Black bears like hanging around the edge of civilization. And this man and his log cabin made the first thin wedge of civilization that had been driven into our favourite inlet.

Judging by the enormous stumps, at one time there had been a stand of
huge cedars in the narrow steep valley. Just behind the new log cabin there
is an old skid road — small logs laid crossways to make a road to skid the
big logs down to the sea, with a donkey engine and cables. The skid road
goes up to about six hundred feet — back the way the old glacier had
retreated. Cedar grows quickly, and in this moist valley, with heat and
rotting ferns, the growth would be rapid.

Six hundred feet high doesn't mean that you get there by walking six hundred feet. It must have been two miles back to the little trapper's cabin at the end of the skid road. The road slanted at quite an incline, and every muscle screamed with the punishment before we got there. We had to stop to get our breath every hundred feet or so — all except John and Peter who ran around in circles. At the cabin we dropped exhausted … then drank and bathed our faces in the ice-cold stream.

The skid road ends there, and we had to follow a trapline marked by axe blazes on the trees. The traplines are only used when the snow is on the ground, so there is no path to follow — just the blazed or white scars on the trees. We rested often, as the going was really hard — soft earth, moss and rolling stones. We had to walk sideways to get any kind of foothold. Then we came to the cliff. The boys thought it was the end of everything. But the blazes led off to the right, to the bottom of a chimney with small junipers for hand holds. John went up directly in front of me. If he were going to slip, I would rather be at the beginning of it, before he gathered momentum. It had its disadvantages though; for he filled me up with earth and stones which trickled down inside my shirt and out my shorts.

At last — on the edge of a flat near the end of the treeline — we reached the huckleberry bushes. Wonderful bushes! Waist high and loaded with berries twice the size of blackcurrants. Growing where they did, in the sun with the cliffs behind to hold the heat, and all the streams to water them — they are sweet and juicy. In no time we had our pails full — you just milked them off the bushes. And then we just sat and ate and ate and ate — and our tongues got bluer and bluer.

It was Peter who started sniffing, swinging his head in a semi-circle to pick up the direction … "I smell foxes — no, I mean bears," he said. I had smelt them some time ago — bears like huckleberries too. But I hadn't climbed four thousand feet to be frightened by a bear. Also, I was getting tired of Maeterlinck conjuring up bears in our life. By now, everybody was sniffing.

"Bang your lids against your tins," I suggested. "That will frighten them away."

So we all banged and banged. Then, as our tins and ourselves were full, I eased everybody on down the trail — just in case. As was perfectly natural, everybody had dreamt of bears the night before. Well — Maeterlinck may have some kind of a plausible Time theory, but the children are not sure how he manages about the bears. If they are going to climb onto both ends of the Curve it will be a little too much.

Going down a mountain is easier on the wind, but much harder on the legs. The back muscles of your calves, which get stretched going up, seem to tie themselves in knots going down — trying to take up the slack.

We tried to sneak past the cabin to our dinghy at the float, but the Man from California was lying down there in the sun.

"Where have you been all day?" he asked. "I've been worried about you."

"We smelt bears," offered John. "And we banged our tins at them, and they were all as afraid as anything."

The man groaned ... his paradise spoiled, I suppose. But what about ours? I hastily showed him the huckleberries and asked him to come over and eat huckleberry pie with us on Trapper's Rock — two hours after the sun went over the top.

Then we rowed home and fell into the sea to soak our aches and pains and mud away — around the rock, out of sight. We couldn't wear our bathing suits, for now our only clothes were dirty again, and we had to keep our bathing suits for supper.

We made a big fire on top of the rock to sit by; and cooked our supper on the little campfire in the prehistoric cave. A big corned-beef hash with tomatoes and onions — our biggest pot full of huckleberry dumplings — and coffee. I had warned the children not to mention bears again, so beyond a few groans when he heard where we had got the berries, we had a pleasant evening.

Clothes had to be washed again — the mountain climb had certainly ravaged them. So we spent the morning away up the landslide while our clothes dried. The man had paddled off in his canoe early, to get mail and provisions that some boat was to leave for him at Casper's — so we had the inlet to ourselves.

I had snubbed everybody at breakfast-time who tried to report a bear-dream — and felt that I had things back on a sane basis again. I had dreamt of climbing all night — my legs were probably aching. It wouldn't do for me to write mine down when I had been snubbing the children for even talking about theirs. By breakfast-time the only thing I could remember about it at all — was hanging on to a bush for dear life, while something — water I think — flowed or slid past ... It had been terrifying, I know.

Later in the day we climbed up beside the falls. The stream above was very turbulent — you would certainly be battered to death on the big boulders if you fell in. And if you escaped that, there were the falls below to finish you off. Quite a long way farther back there was a large tree across the stream which made a bridge to the other side. We crawled across on our hands and knees — no fooling allowed. I brought up the rear, holding John's belt in my teeth ... The others were across and had gone on ahead before John and I got safely over ... I swear that either the tree or the shore shook with the force of that raging water.

The others were out of sight and I called to them to wait. When we caught up, we started to follow them over a steep slope of heavy moss. They were romping across, clutching onto the moss and completely ignoring the torrent sixty feet below at the bottom of the slope. Suddenly I was sure I felt the sheet of moss under my feet slip — as moss will on granite. I shouted to the children not to move, and worked my way up a crack of bare granite, pushing John ahead of me — then anchored myself to a bush. I made the children crawl up, one by one, to where there were some bushes to hang onto. From there they worked up to a tree.

Elizabeth had to come to our help. Holding onto a firm bush, she lowered herself down until John could catch hold of her feet and pull himself up and past her. Then holding onto Elizabeth's feet, I put one foot on the moss and sprang forward, clutched a bush and then somebody's hand ... The youngsters were all safely anchored to a tree and I to a bush — and we sat there watching in horror as the big sheet of moss, to which I had just given the final push, gathered momentum and slid down and over the edge.

"I want to go home," wailed John.

"So do I," echoed Peter, his superior years forgotten.

"Don't be sillies!" I said sharply, recovering my breath.

"How ... ?" they all moaned.

"How what?" I snapped.

"Get home ... ?" they meekly sniffed.

Well, I wasn't quite sure at that stage. Besides, I was shaken. As soon as the moss slid, I had recognized the bush I was hanging on to — it was the bush in my dream.

Straight up seemed to be the only way we could go. Tree by tree all linked together, we finally got onto quite a wide ledge. And there on the ledge was a distinct trail.

"Why, it's that old she-bear's track again!" cried somebody.

"And that must have been her bridge!" said somebody else.

"Well, she certainly knows how to choose a good safe path," I said — wishing I knew which way she and her cub might come strolling.

I certainly didn't want to go over the trembling bridge again so we followed the trail the other way. Going by the logger's tale, it should lead us to the old skid road and then down to the cabin. "Isn't she a nice old bear to make this nice path," said John hopefully — tightly clutching my hand.

"Silly!" said Peter, clutching onto my belt behind.

"Let's sing," I suggested.

So, all singing loudly, we followed the nice bear's trail … A *nice* bear — whom I fervently hoped didn't care for singing.

MIKE

THE FIRST TIME we met Mike must have been the very first time we anchored in Melanie Cove. It was blowing a heavy southeaster outside, so we had turned into Desolation Sound and run right up to the eastern end. There the chart showed some small coves called Prideaux Haven. The inner one, Melanie Cove, turned out to be wonderful shelter in any wind.

We anchored over against a long island with a shelving rock shore. The children tumbled into the dinghy and rowed ashore to collect wood for the evening bonfire, while I started the supper. Away in at the end of the cove we could see what appeared to be fruit trees of some kind, climbing up a side hill. It was in August, and our mouths started watering at the thought of green apple sauce and dumplings. There was no sign of a house of any kind, no smoke. It might even be a deserted orchard. After supper we would go in and reconnoitre.

We were just finishing our supper when a boat came out of the end of the cove with a man standing up rowing — facing the bow and pushing forward on the oars. He was dressed in the usual logger's outfit — heavy grey woollen undershirt above, heavy black trousers tucked into high leather boots. As I looked at him when he came closer, Don Quixote came to mind at once. High pointed forehead and mild blue eyes, a fine long nose that wandered down his face, and a regular Don Quixote moustache that drooped down at the ends. When he pulled alongside we could see the cruel scar that cut in a straight line from the bridge of his nose — down the nose inside the flare of the right nostril, and down to the lip.

"Well, well, well," said the old man — putting his open hand over his face just below the eyes, and drawing it down over his nose and mouth, closing it off the end of his chin — a gesture I got to know so well in the summers to come.

"One, two, three, four, five," he counted, looking at the children.

He wouldn't come aboard, but he asked us to come ashore after supper and pick some apples; there were lots of windfalls. We could move the boat farther into the cove, but not beyond the green copper stain on the cliff. Later, I tossed a couple of magazines in the dinghy and we rowed towards where we had seen him disappear. We identified the copper stain for future use, rounded a small sheltering island, and there, almost out of sight up the bank, stood a little cabin — covered with honeysuckle and surrounded by flowers and apple trees. We walked with him along the paths, underneath the overhanging apple branches. He seemed to know just when each tree had been planted, and I gathered that it had been a slow process over the long years he had lived there.

Except for down at the far end, where the little trellis-covered bridge dripped with grapes, the land all sloped steeply from the sea and up the hillside to the forest. Near the cabin he had terraced it all — stone-walled, and flower-bordered. Old-fashioned flowers — mignonette and sweet-williams, bleeding hearts and bachelor's buttons. These must have reached back into some past of long ago, of which at that time I knew nothing. But beauty, which had certainly been achieved, was not the first purpose of the terraces — the first purpose was apple trees.

He had made one terrace behind the house first — piled stones, carted seaweed and earth until he had enough soil for the first trees. From there, everything had just gradually grown. Down at the far end, where terraces were not necessary, the trees marched up the hillside in rows to where the eight-foot sapling fence surrounded the whole place. "The deer jump any-thing lower," said Mike, when I commented on the amount of time and work it must have taken. Then he added, "Time doesn't mean anything to me. I just work along with nature, and in time it is finished."

Mike sent the children off to gather windfalls — all they could find — while he showed me his cabin. There was a bookshelf full of books across one end of the main room, and an old leather chair. A muddle of stove, dishpan and pots at the other end, and a table. Then down three steps into his winter living room, half below ground level. "Warmer in winter," he explained. He saw us down to the boat, and accepted the two magazines. Then he went back to the cabin to get a book for me, which he said I might like to read if I were going to be in the cove for a few days.

"Stoort sent it to me for Christmas," he said. I felt that I should have known who Stoort was. I couldn't see the title, but I thanked him. The children were laden with apples — and full of them, I was sure.

Back in the boat, I looked at the book by flashlight. It was *Why be a Mud Turtle,* by Stewart Edward White. I looked inside — on the fly-leaf was written, "To my old friend Andrew Shuttler, who most emphatically is not a mud turtle."

During the next couple of days I spent a lot of time talking to old Mike, or Andrew Shuttler — vouched for by Stewart Edward White as being, most emphatically, worth talking to. The children were happy swimming in the warm water, eating apples and picking boxes of windfalls for Mike to take over to the logging camp at Deep Bay.

In between admiring everything he showed me around the place — I gradually heard the story of some of his past, and how he first came to Melanie Cove. He had been born back in Michigan in the States. After very little schooling he had left school to go to work. When he was big enough he had worked in the Michigan woods as a logger — a hard, rough life. I don't know when, or how, he happened to come to British Columbia. But here again, he had worked up the coast as a logger.

"We were a wild, bad crowd," mused Mike — looking back at his old life, a faraway look in his blue eyes. Then he told of the fight he had had with another logger.

"He was out to get me ... I didn't have much chance."

The fellow had left him for dead, lying in a pool of his own blood. Mike wasn't sure how long he had lain there — out cold. But the blood-soaked mattress had been all fly-blown when he came to.

"So it must have been quite some few days."

He had dragged himself over to a pail of water in the corner of the shack and drunk the whole pailful ... then lapsed back into unconsciousness. Lying there by himself — slowly recovering.

"I decided then," said Mike, "that if that was all there was to life, it wasn't worth living; and I was going off somewhere by myself to think it out."

So he had bought or probably pre-empted wild little Melanie Cove — isolated by 7,000-foot mountains to the north and east, and only accessible by boat. Well, he hadn't wanted neighbours, and everything else he needed was there. Some good alder bottom-land and a stream, and a sheltered harbour. And best of all to a logger, the southeast side of the cove rose steeply, to perhaps eight hundred feet, and was covered with virgin timber. So there, off Desolation Sound, Mike had built himself a cabin, handlogged and sold his timber — and thought about life ...

He had been living there for over thirty years when we first blew into the cove. And we must have known him for seven or eight years before he died. He had started planting the apple trees years before — as soon as he had realized that neither the trees nor his strength would last forever. He had built the terraces, carted the earth, fed and hand-reared them. That one beside the cabin door — a man had come ashore from a boat with a pocket full of apples. Mike had liked the flavour, and heeled in his core beside the steps.

"Took a bit of nursing for a few years," said Mike. "Now, look at it. Almost crowding me out."

He took us up the mountain one day to where he had cut some of the timber in the early days, and to show us the huge stumps. He explained how one man alone could saw the trees by rigging up what he called a "spring" to hold the other end of the saw against the cut. And how if done properly, the big tree would drop onto the smaller trees you had felled to serve as skids, and would slide down the slope at a speed that sent it shooting out into the cove. He could remember the length of some of them, and how they had been bought for the big drydock down in Vancouver.

I got to know what books he had in the cabin. Marcus Aurelius, Epictetus, Plato, Emerson, among many others. Somebody had talked to him, over the years, and sent him books to help him in his search. He didn't hold with religion, but he read and thought and argued with everything he read. One summer I had on board a book by an East Indian mystic — a book much read down in the States. I didn't like it — it was much too materialistic to my way of thinking, using spiritual ways for material ends. I gave it to Mike to read, not saying what I thought of it, and wondered what he would make of it. He sat in his easy chair out underneath an apple tree, reading for hour after hour … while I lay on the rocks watching the children swim, and reading one of his books.

He handed it back the next day — evidently a little embarrassed in case I might have liked it. He drew his hand down and over his face, hesitated … Then:

"Just so much dope," he said apologetically. "All words — not how to think or how to live, but how to get things with no effort!"

I don't think anyone could have summed up that book better than the logger from Michigan.

Atlantic Monthly, Harper's — he loved them. I would leave him a pile of them. At the end of the summer, when we called in again, he would discuss all the articles with zest and intelligence.

Mike's own Credo, as he called it, was simple. He had printed it in pencil on a piece of cardboard, and had it hanging on his wall. He had probably copied it word for word from some book — because it expressed for him how he had learnt to think and live. I put it down here exactly as he had it.

"Look well of to-day — for it is the Life of Life. In its brief course lie all the variations and realities of your life — the bliss of growth, the glory of action, the splendour of beauty. For yesterday is but a dream, and To-morrow a vision. But To-day well lived makes every Yesterday a dream of happiness, and every To-morrow a vision of hope. For Time is but a scene in the eternal drama. So, look well of to-day, and let that be your resolution as you awake each morning and salute the New Dawn. Each day is born by the recurring miracle of Dawn, and each night reveals the celestial harmony of the stars. Seek not death in error of your life, and pull not upon yourself destruction by the work of your hands."

That was just exactly how Mike lived — day by day, working with nature. That was really how he had recovered from the fight years ago. And later how he had pitted the strength of one man against the huge trees — seven and eight feet in diameter and two hundred or more feet high. Just the right undercut; just the right angle of the saw; just the right spots to drive in the wedges — using nature as his partner. And if sometimes both he and nature failed, there was always the jack — a logger's jack of enormous size and strength that could edge a huge log the last critical inches to start the skid.

He lent his books to anyone who would read them, but the field was small. For a time there was a logging outfit in Deep Bay, three miles away. They used to buy his vegetables and fruit. Some of them borrowed his books. He talked and tried to explain some of his ideas to the old Frenchman in Laura Cove — old Phil Lavine, who was supposed to have killed a man back in Quebec. After Mike was dead, old Phil commented to me, almost with satisfaction, "All dem words, and 'e 'ad to die like all de rest of us!"

But the next year when we called in to see him, old Phil had built bookshelves on his wall — around and above his bunk, and on the shelves were all Mike's books. Phil was standing there proudly, thumbs hooked in his braces, while some people off a yacht looked at the titles and commented on his collection … Phil the savant — Phil who could neither read nor write.

Among Mike's circle of friends — lumbermen, trappers, fishermen, people from passing boats that anchored in the cove — not many of them would have stayed long enough, or been able to appreciate the fine mind old Mike had developed for himself. And the philosophy he had acquired from all he had read in his search to find something that made life worth living.

I can't remember from whom I heard that Mike had died during the winter. When we anchored there the next year, the cove rang like an empty seashell. A great northern raven, which can carry on a conversation with all the intonations of the human voice, flew out from above the cabin, excitedly croaking, "Mike's dead! Mike's dead!" All the cliffs repeated it, and bandied it about.

The cabin had been stripped of everything — only a rusty stove and a litter of letters and cards on the floor. I picked up a card. On the back was written, "Apple time is here again, and thoughts of ripe apples just naturally make us think of philosophy and you." It was signed, "Betty Stewart Edward White."

Apple time was almost here again now, and the trees were laden. But apples alone were not enough for us. We needed old Mike to pull his hand down over his face in the old gesture, and to hear his — "Well, well, well! Summer's here, and here you are again!"

MURIEL KITIGAWA (1912-1974)

Muriel Kitigawa was born in Vancouver a Nisei, that is to say a second-genera-
tion Canadian of Japanese ancestry. This was a generation in limbo: it was
turning its back on Japanese family traditions and customs, eager to embrace
being Canadian, but Canadians of Asian ancestry did not enjoy full citizenship.
They were not yet franchised and were excluded from some professions —
pharmacy and law for instance — and could not work for government or hold
public office. In her early twenties, Muriel Kitigawa became politically active
as a writer for two publications, *The New Age* (1932), which emerged from
the Young People's Society of the Japanese United Church, and its successor,
New Canadian (1938), both styled the "Voice of the Nisei" and published in
English. These community newspapers allowed Kitigawa to express herself on
topics like arranged marriages and women's liberation, but the programme of
emancipation from older immigrant values came to a sudden halt with the
bombing of Pearl Harbour on December 7, 1941 and, under the War Measures Act, the almost instant uprooting of the Japanese-Canadian community in
British Columbia.

Between January and October of 1942, approximately 22,000 Japanese
Canadians were removed from the B.C. coast which was designated a "protected area." As Roy Miki, active in the Japanese redress movement and editor
of Muriel Kitigawa's papers, has observed: "Lives were utterly disrupted, families and friends torn apart, properties and belongings confiscated, and liberties
suspended." Road project camps were established for men in the interior of
B.C. and in Ontario, while their families were housed in what were livestock
buildings in Hastings Park. Families used to farming were sent to Alberta and
Manitoba to work on sugar beet farms, while for the rest detention camps
were set up in the B.C. interior in tiny communities such as Greenwood and
New Denver, and in ghost towns such as Sandon. Again as Miki observes,
"With no one to speak on their behalf, with no rights of appeal ... the Kitigawas
and other 'persons of Japanese race' became voiceless exiles in their own
country."

The sequence of letters printed here were written by Muriel Kitigawa to her
brother, Wesley Fujiwara, who was a medical student at the University of
Toronto. Muriel was married to Ed Kitigawa, an employee at the Bank of

Montreal. They had two daughters, Shirley and Meiko, with Muriel undergoing a difficult pregnancy that would result in twins just as the disruption of the community began. Muriel's letters (again in Miki's words) "are dramatic, impassioned documents from the time in which the living words, the descriptions and statements, were set down — sometimes frantically — in the heat of the turmoil." She was determined to keep the record straight: "Her community was an innocent group of individuals who became the victims of racist policies and actions." Kitigawa's letters would become a source of inspiration and factual detail for the highly acclaimed novel *Obasan* by Joy Kogawa.

From THIS IS MY OWN
LETTERS TO WES

DECEMBER 13, 1941

Dear Wes:

Just got your second airmail letter, and instructed Eddie to send you a wire. Keep your chin up. We've got to endure this with all the courage we have.

Dad is getting along in his usual way, and Doug is OK. So far we have had no word of any bad news in the family, so don't worry.

Doesn't the fact that you are Canadian-born do you any good in getting a job? Dad's been in this country for over forty years. That's more than a lot of Occidentals can say.

Just get through your exams and we'll parley after.

Love from all of us, and don't get discouraged.

Mur.

(Expect big parcel soon. Just some "eats.")

December 21, 1941

Dear Wes:

I hope first of all that you have as merry a Christmas as you can, and that you will splurge with this money on a real dinner with the trimmings. Of all times for me to be helpless. We have already felt the effects of my not being able to lead the house into the festivities. Everything is upside down, and I just have to go without some of the "musts" of other years. Eiko is going to cook for the family, and since there is no Christmas Ball this year, I think she will have plenty of time to wash dinner dishes too … with Fumi to help. There were so many things I wanted to do for you, but it is just a physical impossibility. I will make up for it as soon as I can. My problem now is to hang on till the 25th, so I won't miss the kids' getting up and finding things. This year is for the kids mainly …

So far as the new war affects us, I really haven't much to say. It is too early to estimate the effects. On the whole we are taking it in our stride. We are so used to wars and alarums, and we have been tempered for the anti-feelings these long years. It has only intensified into overt acts of unthinking hoodlumism like throwing flaming torches into rooming houses and bricks through plate glass … only in the West End so far. What that goes to prove I don't know. We've had blackouts the first few nights but they have been lifted. Bad for the kids, because it frightens them so. Of course we have to be ready just in case and I sure hope there won't be any emergency … not with the kids around. All three Japanese papers have been closed down. We never needed so many anyway. It is good for the *New Canadian* though, as it can now go ahead with full responsibility, though at first it is bound to be hard on the inexperienced staff. All Japanese schools have been closed too, and are the kids glad! Of course I have never intended my kids to go anyway so it doesn't affect us in the least. I am glad in a way that they have been closed down. I hope for good. But it is hard on the teachers who depended on them for a living.

There have been the usual anti-letters-to-the-editor in the papers. Some of them are rank nonsense, and some of the writers think like that anyhow, whatever the provocation. The majority of the people are decent and fair-minded and they say so in letters and editorials. The RCMP is our friend too, for they, more than anyone else know how blameless and helpless we are, and they have already in one instance prevented tragedy when the City Fathers proposed cancelling all business licences, to say that we did not rate such harsh treatment. Now the North Vancouver Board of Trade goes on record to demand that all our autos be confiscated, but I hardly think that could be practical. What then would our doctors and business-men do? Also, it is hard to take everything away from 22,000 people without the rest of B.C. feeling some of the bad effects. The dog salmon industry is already short-handed because the Japanese cannot fish any more. How they will make up the lack in the next season I don't know, though the 'white' fishermen seem to be confident, if they could use the fishing boats now tied up somewhere in New Westminster.

There was one letter in the *Province* protesting this confiscation of the right to earn a living from 1,880 people … said it wasn't democracy. Yes sir, when a people get panicky, democracy and humanity and Christian principles go by the board. Rather inconsistent, but human nature I guess.

Some silly mothers even go so far as to say what right have the black-haired kids to go to school with their own precious? One schoolteacher had the courage to say to one of the "white" pupils who wanted all Japs to be kicked out of school — how they reflect their parents' attitude! — that there were no Japs, and in any case they were far better Canadians than the protester. Strange how these protesters are much more vehement against the Canadian-born Japanese than they are against German-born Germans, who might have a real loyalty to *their* land of birth, as we have for Canada. I guess it is just because we look different. Anyway it all boils down to racial antagonism, which the democracies are fighting. Who said it was Woman … or the Moon that was inconstant? Oh well, it is only the occasional one here and there. I personally have had no change in my relationship with my neighbours, or my Egg-man, who told me not to worry. Most of the hakujin deplore the war but do not change to their known Japanese friends. It is the small businesses that are most affected … like the dressmakers, the corner store, etc., because the clientele are rather shy of patronising in public such places, whatever their private thoughts may be. Powell Street is affected too, in that they have a slightly increased volume of sales to people who usually go to Woodwards etc. But so many have been fired from jobs that belts are tightening everywhere. I don't know yet how all this is going to affect Dad. Most of his patients are fishermen or farmers. So far the farmers haven't been touched.

Last Sunday, the national President of the IODE [Imperial Order of the Daughters of the Empire], who must live far from contact from the Nisei because she didn't seem to know the first thing about us, made a deliberate attempt to create fear and ill-will among her dominion-wide members by telling them that we were all spies and saboteurs, and that in 1931 there were 55,000 of us and that that number has doubled in the last ten years. Not only a biological absurdity, but the records of the RCMP give the lie to such round numbers. The trouble is that lots of women would like to believe their president rather than actual figures. Seems to me illogical that women who are the conservers and builders of the human race should be the ones to go all out for savagery and destruction and ill-will among fellow humans. They are the ones who are expected to keep the peace with their neighbours in their particular block, but when it comes to blackballing some unfortunate people, they are the first to cast the stone. In times like this I always think of that line: "If there be any among you that is without sin, let him cast the first stone." Or words to that effect. And certainly we Nisei are neither harlots nor criminals. We're just people.

But more to the point, how are you getting along there? Is the feeling worse in Toronto where they don't know the Nisei as B.C. does? How does the war affect you personally? Can you get a loan to get through next year and the year after? After all, you are Canadian-born, and the Army needs MDs. How has it affected your living conditions at the Lethbridges? Or your acquaintance with Dent and others? Has it affected the wearing of your uniform? Your standing in class and lab? Have you heard from George Shimo? Please let me know fully. So far Doug hasn't let me know by word or line how he is, but he's never one to write, and he's carefree. I think he is all right. If he doesn't lose his job through this, I'll ask him to send you what he can every month. Dad and Nobi are getting along but I think Nobi's kind of sad that he won't see Mom again, and he does miss a home life. But I can't do a thing to help as Dad rejects every offer. I guess that when gas rationing starts Dad won't be able to use that darned car so often in its really affronting sleekness. He has to report every month to the RCMP, just because when he first came to B.C., which was over forty years ago, and plenty of time to naturalize, he didn't look far enough ahead to know how it would have helped his children. That! for people who live only day to day. Politics never meant a thing to him, and doesn't yet. So long as he can eat and swank in his car he lets important things slide.

We're getting immune to the hitherto unused term "Japs" on the radio and on the headlines of the papers. So long as they designate the enemy, and not us, it doesn't matter much. The Chinese here were indecently jubilant … paraded and cheered in their quarters when the war was announced. They are rather childish that way. Of course, now they hope that both the U.S. and Canada will fork over a lot more help than they have so far. I think they are naive. War nowadays is too complicated and can't be compared simply to a street fight. I am glad however that the Russian army is licking something out of Hitler's troops. The sooner Hitler stops his enslaving of conquered people … you know, ship-loading them into Poland or into Germany proper to work for nothing in the fields and factories far from home and children; his way of stealing food from the conquered peoples; his system of captive labour; shooting hundreds in reprisal for one … then the sooner will the little peoples have a chance at life again.

Ugh! I hate wars, and I've had one already, though I wasn't old enough to know anything then. Now I'm going through a worse one. War, active war, is easier to bear with courage than this surging up of mass hatred against us simply because we are of Japanese origin. I hope fervently that it will not affect the lives of Shirley and Meiko and the unborn son, as the doctor believes. After all, my kids, as only proper being my kids, are so thoroughly Canadian they would never understand being persecuted by people they regard as one of themselves. Already Meiko came crying home once because some kid on the block, whose father is anti, said something. Yet I try to rationalize things for them, so that they won't be inundated by self-consciousness. Children are so innocent, but they are savages too and reflect faithfully their parents' attitudes. That was the one thing my doctor was worried about. Otherwise he, with most of the others, tells us not to worry. We're Canadians and can expect decent treatment from decent people.

Remember when Shirley was little she was more shy of Japanese strangers than she was of the hakujin? She used to stare goggle-eyed at them. Because they, even now, rarely see Japanese people out here, and the ones they see they are so used to that they don't even see the difference in colour. One day they asked me whether they were Japanese or Chinese or English or Scotch or what in the world? It made me laugh. I told them they were Canadians, and that is what they sincerely believe. They are a couple of the most reasonable kids you ever saw, barring Meiko's lapses into "yancha." [Japanese for "naughty" or "mischievous."] We haven't picked a name for the newcomer yet, but if it is a boy he will be Jon, without the "h." I'd like a girl to be named Jennifer, if the opposition won't be too loud. Can't think of a Japanese name at all. I like Phillip, too. Jon is short for Jonathan, you know. While I'm not fussy about the longer one, I do like Jon. What do you think?

Gosh! I never knitted so much in all my life! Guess what: I made three sweaters for Shirley, two for Meiko, one heavy golf cardigan for Eddie, one for Nobi, one for you, those two toques and two pairs mitts, a scarf for Eddie … this last is a secret yet … three jackets (infant), two pants (also infant), two bonnets (ditto), four socks (ditto), one vest (ditto), all in this last couple of months. I'm slightly surprised myself.

Don't let things get you down. You've got to get through. You are far from home, but you know we are backing you up, and we'll never let you down. You are a decent Canadian-born citizen and can depend on it that decent people will always be decent. Let us not think of the dark side, but hope for the best.

We are giving the kids a real Christmas as usual. So have yourself one too. I have written a special column for the Christmas issue of the NC [*New Canadian*]. If it comes out, read it well. I also hope they will print the slightly inebriated verse about the milkman. We can do with some laughs.

Cheerio and thumbs up! A merry Christmas and a happier New Year to you and all of us.

Love,

Mur.

January 10, 1942

Dear Wes:

You'll be properly flabbergasted, I hope, when you get this. It's twins!!!! Born on the 7th.

Boy — 7 lbs. 15 1/2 ounces, 11:00

Girl — 6 lbs. 12 ounces, 11:04

And did it cause a sensation. Wowie! Eddie hasn't quite recovered from the shock. I gave up "Jennifer" for the girl but still cling to "Jon" even if I have to have the rest of it.

Had a bit of trouble after, but they say "no wonder."

Love,

Mur.

January 21, 1942

In bed at home.

Dear Wes:

I gathered from your last letter that the fact that I have twin babes left you in somewhat of "a dither." It has created something of a furor here, and people have quite overlooked the fact that two other Nisei families have had infants at about the same time. Such is the world.

Well, to go into detail. Since October, I had been unable to locomote, so either stayed in bed, or sat propped up in the "wing" chair with my knitting. Seriously, I thought I would bust. The skin and tissues of my abdomen had stretched so much that there was a real danger of them tearing — so thin they were! (As a matter of fact, after I had the babies, I chanced to glance at my tummy when I was horrified to see long thin streaks of coagulated blood. Apparently I was beginning to tear.) Around Christmas I couldn't bear the weight any more, so I begged the doctor to let me have it over with, but he said it was too dangerous both for the babe and for me. On Jan. 6, my patience snapped. I told him I was going to the hospital and that he would just have to do something. On the 7th (Wednesday) he gave me instructions (castor oil etc. etc. — ugh!) and that evening at 7 p.m. I went. It had started showing that very day. For the next five days I was one mass of cramps, backache, stomachache, and general discomfort — and was dosed constantly with Frosst 292, sleeping pills and laxative oils. Then slowly things began to mend, and on the ninth and tenth days after, I was feeling rather good, so the doctor let me come home on the condition that I have a trained nurse stay with me for a week. Jon is a little hog and Ellen is as sweet as an elfin fairy. I think both names suit them remarkably well. Jon is a good two pounds heavier than Ellen, and looks very, very pudgy, while Ellen is light and all eyes and a wide mouth. She is slightly spoiled already. She was so popular at the Hospital she got carried around extra and now knows when she's picked up. We've been figuring out ways and means of parking them into what space we have. We're not getting the attic finished yet — prices have gone up and fixings have disappeared from the market.

About this "moving" business. I'm afraid it will affect Dad and Doug: Dad because he's not naturalized, and Doug because he will be unemployed pretty soon, if not already so. No clear details yet. I still really can't say how it is going to affect this particular family. If Dad goes we'll have to take in Nobi — feed, clothe and educate him on the little we have if Dad makes no money, or if Doug doesn't send any when he is entered into this "Civilian Corps." I really don't know whether to be glad or sorry, and Mom and Kath aren't here to add to the burdens or to relieve me of them. I have tentative plans made just in case.

Since they are moving the unemployed Nisei first, I don't think Ed will be affected. After all, they could hardly expect him to leave a good job for road work when he has a big family to feed. I have my fingers crossed — all ten of them. Of course, since I have been house-bound from October, I haven't felt the full force of the changes since Dec. 7th.

[Alderman Halford] Wilson and his bunch are making political hay out of this. He does so with bland half-truths and falsehoods and hypocrisies enough to turn your stomach. So does the *Sun* paper. They are deliberately inflaming the mob instinct and inciting the irresponsible elements to a bloody riot — the kind they had in 1907, the one in which Wilson's father had a dirty hand. Once the flames catch, Powell Street will be in for a bad, bad time, not mentioning the scattered but large number of families in certain suburban districts. How that Wilson can square his conscience, eat three meals in peace, with his brand of patriotism that stinks to hell — I don't know.

The Province and *News-Herald* have been editorially condemning Wilson and his bunch are appealing to B.C. at large to give the local Japs a chance. Acts of vandalism make the headlines, and there has been one murder. Yoshiyuki Uno was shot to death by a seventeen- or nineteen-year-old bandit.

Gosh Wes, sometimes I wish you were here with us if only for moral support. The twins are sure going to kick someday when they find out that they missed your brand of nursemaiding. This year we are planting a lot of vegetables and fewer flowers. The front lawn will be dug up for potatoes. It seems a pity after all the work you put into it, but as we are told that spending brings on inflation, we try not to, of course. These last few days, money slips through my fingers like water. I've had to double my order for diapers, bottles, gowns, panties, sheets for the crib etc. and we have to buy another crib. It's been a holocaust really. The department stores and the drug stores both hail the twins as a slight "boom."

You can see by the writing that I am in bed. Hope you can make out what I wrote. If ever I need help, Wes, I'll holler for you — if you're within reach and not in the Army. With four kids and Nobi, I will need a couple of stout masculine helpers.

So just keep your shirt on and hope for the best. Someday I'll show you some clippings I've kept to prove that there are a lot of decent people in this mad world.

Study hard, and try not to quit. What of the one-hundred-and-fifty others if the loan doesn't come through? Do they quit too? Please let me know further developments.

My regards to Roger Obata if you see him. I haven't seen him for so many years now.

Chin up and cheerio!

Love,

Mur.

February 19, 1942

Dear Wes:

How's things? That was a good letter you wrote to the N.C. [*New Canadian*].

Well, I guess you've read in the papers that there isn't a province in Canada that will take the "Japs," and B.C. just has to have us whether she will or no. Ian Mackenzie has again come out with "Volunteer or else —" Vancouver City Fathers have petitioned Ottawa to put the OK on a ban of trade licences to Japanese here — eight-hundred-and-fifty or so. Won't the Relief offices be flooded then! How on earth the Wilsonites expect us to eat, I don't know. They don't care anyway — under their hypocritical Christian faces. It beats me how they can mouth "Down with Hitler," and at the same time advocate a program against "Japs" (four-letter syllable in place of "Jews"). Now that attack on this coast is becoming more of a concrete threat, feeling is running pretty high — tho' the individuals in most cases are pretty decent. The rabble-rousers and the mob — haven't we learned about "mobs" in Roman days and in Shakespeare's works? — they are the ones to cause all the trouble. Even the Youth Congress has come out with a plea to move us all out someplace, anywhere except on the coast.

Doug was here the other day so I asked him when his work would stop — and darn him, he wanted to know why! After telling me his job was so insecure. Apparently it's OK. Anyway I'm not sure what to believe these days. Dad takes no thought of his eventual transfer to a camp. (They're moving the over-forty-five year olds after they get the first batch settled.) In fact, if the war comes any closer we'll all be kicked out.

Gosh, but hasn't 1941 been the awfulest year in our life?

Love,

Mur.

March 2, 1942.

Dear Wes:

What a heavenly relief to get your letter. I was just about getting frantic with worry over you. That's why I hope you'll forgive me for writing to Jim Carson. Eddie and I thought that was the only way to find out what really was happening to you. Oh Wes, the things that have been happening out here are beyond words, and though at times I thank goodness you're out of it, at other times I think we really need people like you around to keep us from getting too wrought up for our own good.

Eiko and Fumi were here yesterday, crying, nearly hysterical with hurt and outrage and impotence. All student nurses have been fired from the [Vancouver] General.

They took our beautiful radio … what does it matter that someone bought it off us for a song? … It's the same thing because we had to do that or suffer the ignominy of having it taken forcibly from us by the RCMP. Not a single being of Japanese race in the protected area will escape. Our cameras, even Nobi's toy one, all are confiscated. They can search our homes without warrant.

As if all this trouble wasn't enough, prepare yourself for a shock. We are forced to move out from our homes, Wes, to where we don't know. Eddie was going to join the Civilian Corps but now will not go near it, as it smells of a daemonic, roundabout way of getting rid of us. There is the very suspicious clause "within and *without*" Canada that has all the fellows leery.

The Bank is awfully worried about me and the twins, and the manager has said he will do what he can for us, but as he has to refer to the main office which in turn has to refer to the Head Office, he can't promise a thing, except a hope that surely the Bank won't let us down after all these years of faithful service. Who knows where we will be now, tomorrow, next week. It isn't as if we Nisei were aliens, technical or not. It breaks my heart to think of leaving this house and the little things around it that we have gathered through the years, all those numerous gadgets that have no material value but are irreplaceable. My papers, letters, books and things … the azalea plants, my white iris, the lilac that is just beginning to flower . . . so many things.

Oh Wes, the Nisei are bitter, too bitter for their own good or for Canada. How can cool heads like Tom's prevail when the general feeling is to stand up and fight.

Do you know what curfew means in actual practice? B.C. is falling all over itself in the scramble to be the first to kick us out from jobs and homes. So many night-workers have been fired out of hand. Now they sit at home, which is usually just a bed, or some cramped quarters, since they can't go out at night for even a consoling cup of coffee. Mr. Shimizu is working like mad with the Welfare society to look after the women and children that were left when their men were forced to volunteer to go to the work camps. Now those men are only in unheated bunk-cars, no la-trines, no water, snow fifteen feet deep, no work to keep warm with, little food if any. They had been shunted off with such inhuman speed that they got there before any facilities were prepared for them. Now men are afraid to go because they think they will be going to certain disaster … anyway, too much uncertainty. After all, they have to think of their families. If snow is fifteen feet deep, there is no work, and if there is no work there is no pay, and if there is no pay no one eats. The *Province* reports that work on frames with tent-coverings is progressing to house the two thousand expected. Tent coverings where the snow is so deep! And this is Democ-racy! You should see the faces here, all pinched, grey, uncertain. If the Bank fails Eddie, do you know what the kids and I have to live on? Thirty-nine dollars. For everything … food, clothing, rent, taxes, upkeep, insurance premiums, emergencies. They will allow for only two kids for the Nisei. Six dollars per., monthly. It thas just boiled down to race persecution and signs have been posted on all highways … JAPS KEEP OUT. Mind you, you can't compare this sort of thing to anything that happens in Germany. That country is an avowed Jew-baiter, totalitarian. Canada is supposed to be a Democracy out to fight against just the sort of thing she's boosting at home.

And also, I'll get that thirty-nine dollars only if Eddie joins the Chain Gang — you know, *forced to volunteer* to let the authorities wash their hands of any responsibilities. All Nisei are liable to imprisonment I sup-pose if they refuse to volunteer … that is the likeliest interpretation of Ian MacKenzie's "volunteer or else." Prisoners in wartime get short shrift …

and to hell with the wife and kids. Can you wonder that there is a deep bitterness among the Nisei who believe so gullibly in the democratic blah-blah that's been dished out. I am glad Kazuma [Uyeno] is not here.

There are a lot of decent people who feel for us, but they can't do a thing.

And the horrors that some young girls have already faced … outraged by men in uniform … in the hospital … hysterical. Oh we are fair prey for the wolves in democratic clothing. Can you wonder the men are afraid to leave us behind and won't go unless their women go with them? I won't blame you if you can't believe this. It is incredible. Wes, you have to be here right in the middle of it to really know.

How can the hakujin face us without a sense of shame for their treachery to the principles they fight for? One man was so damned sorry, he came up to me, hat off, squirming like mad, stuttering how sorry he was. My butcher said he knew he could trust me with a side of meat even if I had no money. These kind people too are betrayed by the Wilsonites … God damn his soul! Yet there are other people who, while they wouldn't go so far as to persecute us, are so ignorant, so indifferent, they believe we are being very well treated for what we are. The irony of it all is enough to choke me. And we are tightening our belts for the starvation to come. The diseases … the crippling … the twisting of our souls … death would be the easiest to bear.

The Chinese are forced to wear huge buttons and plates and even plac-ards to tell the hakujin the difference between one yellow peril and an-other. Or else they would be beaten up. It's really ridiculous.

And Wes, we are among the fortunate ones, for above that thirty-nine dollars we may be able to fill it out by renting this house. Now I wish I hadn't given my clothes to Kath. We will need them badly. Uncle has been notified to get ready to move. Dad will be soon too.

There's too much to say and not enough time or words.

Can't send you pictures now unless some hakujin takes the snaps … STRENG VERBOTEN to use even little cameras to snap the twins … STRENG VERBOTEN is the order of the day.

My apologies to Jim Carson.

Love,

Mur.

March 3, 1942

Dear Wes:

This is just to warn you: Don't you *dare* come back to B.C., no matter what happens, what reports you read in the papers, whatever details I tell you in letters. You stay out of this province. B.C. is hell.

Rather than have you come back here, we'll come to Toronto if we can.

I'll keep you posted by letters, but I repeat, there is nothing for you here. Even if you quit school, stay in Toronto — anywhere east of the Rockies.

Yoshi Higashi went to Camp last night with seven hours' notice.

Eddie will be about the last to go anywhere, whether to another branch bank or elsewhere. If I really need you I'll come to Toronto. *Remember!*

For the love of God, don't you come here. Not you, a single male. You'll be more help to me and to others if you stay where you are — free — even if starving.

Love,
Mur.

March 22, 1942
Dear Wes:

Well, things are swiftly getting worse out here. If we stick around too long we and the kids are going to be chucked into Hastings Park. The way it is now it is awful. Miss Hyodo is helping the women there and she says the crowding, the noise, the confusion is chaos. Mothers prostrated in nervous exhaustion, their babies crying helplessly, endlessly. Families torn from their fathers without a farewell — leaving home and belongings behind — all crammed into two buildings like so many pigs. Children taken out of school — no provision made for future education — more and more people pouring into the Park — forbidden outside of the barbed wire gates and fences — the men can't even leave the building — police guard around them — some of them fight their way out to come to town to see what they can do about their families. Babies — one thousand of them on the way to be born — motherless children stranded because their father got taken to camp (the oldest child in eight is thirteen years old).

Miss Hyodo said the women were going to be mental cases. Rev. Kabayama and family got thrown in too. Oh Wes, this is going to be an ugly fight to survive among us. They're making (they say) accommodation for twelve- to thirteen-thousand women and children. In that little park! Bureaucrats find it so simple on paper so they translate it willy-nilly into action, and the muddle resulting is kept "hush-hush" from the public who are already kicking about the "luxury" allowed to Japs.

There is a little Napoleon and his henchmen running things arbitrarily with the OK of the RCMP and now Kunio and Tom are in bad with them. It's a case of "obey or be interned." In short Der Reichstag has been set up with Nappy as der Fuehrer. There's even a Goering and a Goebbels. Uncle Fred was going to Westbank, but now he can't. He has to go to Camp. If the women and children stay here, as is now most likely, they'll be kept like animals in the Pool. In that case Eddie might just have to stay on at the Bank to look after their small accounts. But me and the kids might not get preferred treatment. We might have to go to the Park too. So I've asked Eddie to send us to Toronto if he can get the Bank to guarantee his job and salary. We are then going to rent this house to have that much extra for food for us. I don't know though, if the war goes bad for Canada, would we be safe in the Park — or on our own in Toronto? That's what we try to answer in planning one way or the other. Among our relations, we are the only ones who at present seem to be the luckiest — being Nisei, a good permanent (I hope) job, a home — but then our fate is the most uncertain. Mine is the only place (among our relatives) with small babies needing special care, and I dread the thought of being dumped onto one straw pallet with four kids. No privacy — fight for share of food — and all the complex tragedy of being caged.

We can't make any definite plans. If we can go to Toronto, then you must find me a house, perhaps not too far from the campus so that you can stay with us. If I can feed you, perhaps you can get your degree. I don't know though what we are going to do. Everything is so uncertain.

What do you think? Do you think we might be worse off in Toronto? Of course we couldn't go unless I was sure of a steady income.

I'll close now, and get back to work.

Lovingly,

Mur.

April 11, 1942

Dear Wes:

Just got your letter. You know, Wes, I wonder what I'd have done without you to sort of keep me balanced. Every time I get one of your "preachy" letters I feel as if I'd been hysterical for nothing ...

As for faith — well, it depends on the person. I can't say anything for other people, but for myself it's this. I have faith in this land — not in any political group, not in any MP and their codes (or tricks maybe), not in any system of government — but in the land and the people on the land.

Mickey Maikawa's father came back from Grand Forks where he was stuck. He's bought land for his family and is buying a tomato farm for Mickey and Kiyo. Mr. Maikawa went to see Greenwood, the best (?) of the ghost towns and says the accommodation being fixed for the lowly Jap is worse than Hastings Park. In Greenwood there are only shacks and big frame buildings. No central heat of course. We'll all be in cages, so to

185

speak. Hundreds will be housed in one building. There'll only be double-decker wooden bunks and community stoves. Eddie went to see the Pool bunkhouse for men (the former Women's building) and was nauseated by the smell, the clouds of dust, the pitiful attempts at privacy. The Livestock Building (where the women and kids are) is worse, plus manure smells. Those straw ticks get damp and mouldy. There are no fresh fruits or vegetables. Kiyo Maikawa ate there one day to see what it was like. She had two slices of meat, bread and butter and tea. That's all. For supper it was two slices of bologna and some bread and tea. That's all. Those who have money go out to buy lettuce and tomatoes and fruit. Nothing for babies, yet. We're asking for improvement in that quarter.

You know Wes, my one obsession is privacy. Ever since I could remember I liked being in a place to myself — in fact I needed it. I'll go nuts if I have to stall with a lot of clacking females and crying kids. If I could have a house to myself and the kids — if Ed and we could be transferred to York — if — if — if …

Sab earns about two dollars a day at the Pool helping out, minus board, of course.

I forgot to enclose the snaps last time so here they are. You can see that Jon is fairer than Ellen. They are beginning to "coo" at each other.

By the way, how's the drinking water there? Bet you can't beat Vancouver water? That's what I'm going to miss.

I'll have to rent this house partially furnished. Have to leave the chesterfield suite, dining suite, range, refrig, rugs, linoleum etc. etc. We aren't allowed to sell our furniture. Hits the dealers somehow. I don't understand it, but so they say. The Council is representative of only its backers now. Other organizations have their own delegates to the Commission, ever since Fujikazu raised that fuss. Awfully unwieldy business — this evacuating. Very few entrain for work camps. The rest just "buck." There's a "wanted" list of over a hundred names of Nisei. More added every time the boys won't budge. They're chased all over town. Doug may be one of them yet. Will write again.

Love,
Mur.

Hastings Park Description
April 20, 1942
Dear Wes:

I went to the Pool yesterday to see Eiko who is working there as steno. I saw Sab too who is working in the baggage … old Horseshow Building.

Sab showed me his first paycheque as something he couldn't quite believe
… $11.75. He's been there for an awful long time. Eiko sleeps in a parti-
tioned stall, she being on the staff, so to speak. This stall was the former
home of a pair of stallions and boy oh boy, did they leave their odour
behind. The whole place is impregnated with the smell of ancient manure
and maggots. Every other day it is swept with dichloride of lime or something, but you can't disguise horse smell, cow smell, sheeps and pigs and
rabbits and goats. And is it dusty! The toilets are just a sheet metal trough,
and up till now they did not have partitions or seats. The women kicked so
they put up partitions and a terribly makeshift seat. Twelve-year-old boys
stay with the women too. The auto show building, where there was also
the Indian exhibit, houses the new dining room and kitchens. Seats three
thousand. Looks awfully permanent. Brick stoves, eight of them, shining
new mugs … very, very barrack-y. As for the bunks, they were the most
tragic things I saw there. Steel and wooden frames with a thin lumpy straw
tick, a bolster and three army blankets of army quality … no sheets unless
you bring your own. These are the 'homes' of the women I saw. They
wouldn't let me into the men's building. There are constables at the doors
… no propagation of the species … you know … it was in the papers.
These bunks were hung with sheets and blankets and clothes of every hue
and variety, a regular gipsy tent of colours, age and cleanliness, all hung
with the pathetic attempt at privacy. Here and there I saw a child's doll and
teddy bear … I saw babies lying there beside a mother who was too weary
to get up … she had just thrown herself across the bed … I felt my throat
thicken … an old, old lady was crying, saying she would rather have died
than have come to such a place … she clung to Eiko and cried and cried.
Eiko has taken the woes of the confinees on her thin shoulders and she
took so much punishment she went to her former rooms and couldn't stop
crying. Fumi was so worried about her. Eiko is really sick. The place has
got her down. There are ten showers for fifteen-hundred women. Hot and
cold water. The men looked so terribly at loose ends, wandering around
the grounds, sticking their noses through the fence watching the golfers,
lying on the grass. Going through the place I felt so depressed that I wanted
to cry. I'm damned well not going there. They are going to move the Vancouver women first now and shove them into the Pool before sending
them to the ghost towns.

I'm getting kind of frantic because we haven't heard yet from the Bank.
The manager wrote again on the 17th. If they would only hurry up and
say something one way or the other. If they say no, I shall send you a wire
and then you know what to do. If only Eddie can get a job that pays

enough to make it worthwhile staying out of the work camps, something we can eat on and save a little. He's quick with his hands, but he knows figures best. He's worked twenty-one years with the Bank of Montreal. If I can, I am going to take Eiko with me as nursemaid. I don't think it would be wise to take Obasan [aunt] with us because she is a national's wife, and she is going back to Japan anyway as soon as she can, while Eiko and we have no such intentions.

The other day at the Pool, someone dropped his key before a stall in the Livestock Building, and he fished for it with a long wire and brought to light rotted manure and maggots!!! He called the nurse and then they moved all the bunks from the stalls and pried up the wooden floors. It was the most stomach-turning nauseating thing. They got fumigators and tried to wash it all away and got most of it into the drains, but maggots still breed and turn up here and there. One woman with more guts than the others told the nurse (white) about it and protested. She replied: "Well, there's worms in the garden aren't there?" This particular nurse was a Jap-hater of the most virulent sort. She called them "filthy Japs" to their faces and Eiko gave her "what-for" and Fumi had a terrible scrap with her, both girls saying: "What do you think we are? Are we cattle? Are we pigs, you dirty-so-and-so!" You know how Fumi gets. The night the first bunch of Nisei were supposed to go to Schreiber and they wouldn't, the women and children at the Pool milled around in front of their cage, and one very handsome mountie came with his truncheon and started to hit them, yelling at them, "Get the hell back in there." Eiko's blood boiled over. She strode over to him and shouted at him: "You put that stick down! What do you think you're doing! Do you think these women and children are so many cows that you can beat them back into their place?" Eiko was shaking mad and raked him with fighting words. She has taken it on her to fight for the poor people there, and now she is on the black list and reputed to be a troublemaker. Just like Tommy and Kunio. I wish I too could go in there and fight and slash around. It's people like us who are the most hurt … people like us, who have had faith in Canada, and who have been more politically minded than the others, who have a hearty contempt for the whites.

Fujikazu and his bunch are working with what Kunio calls a "shyster lawyer" who has told his clients one thing and the Commission another, and in front of Tommy and Kunio, got bawled out by Taylor. There has been some sort of pamphlet they put out that has been uncovered by the police and the stink is rising again.

The cop that nabbed Sab was so drunk he had to be propped up by his assistant, and he weaved around and tried to poke Sab. Sab wisely did not retaliate.

By the way, we got a letter from Uncle … or rather Auntie got it. He's the gardener, and has to grow vegetables and flowers on the side. Takashima is cook and gets fifty dollars clear. Uncle only nets about ten dollars. All cards and letters are censored, even to the Nisei camps. Not a word about sit-downs, gambaru-ing [resisting] or anything makes the papers. It's been hushed. Good thing for us. I wondered why I didn't read about it. I haven't been to meetings so long now that I don't know what's going on. Uncle's camp is eight miles from the station up into the hills. Men at the first camps all crowd down to the station every time a train passes with the Nationals and hang onto the windows asking for news from home. Uncle said he wept.

But the men are luckier than the women. They are fed, they work, they have no children to look after. Of course the fathers are awfully worried about their families. But it's the women who are burdened with all the responsibility of keeping what's left of the family together. Frances went to Revelstoke, bag and baggage and baby. When I heard that I felt choked with envy, and felt more trapped than ever. Eiko tells me: "Don't you dare bring the kids into the Pool." And Mr. Maikawa says Greenwood is worse. They are propping up the old shacks near the mine shaft. Sab went through there and says it's awful. The United Church parson there says of the Japs: "Kick them all out." Sab knows his son who had the room next to him at Union College. Vic and George Saito and family went to the beet fields. Sadas are going tonight. They are going to hell on earth, and will be so contracted that they cannot leave the place or move. Whites will not go there.

I pray that Kath and Mom are safe. Mom's got to live through this. Now that Japan proper has been bombed they will come here.

I'll write again soon.

With love,

Mur

May 4, 1942

Dear Wes:

Honest, Wes, if you have to work and if Ed does too — if we can get east you can stay with us and it'll save you board anyway.

As it is now, we don't know which way to turn.

The Bank accountant phoned just now to tell Ed (he's home today be-cause I've got acute pharyngitis, tonsillitis, quinsy and a touch of flu. I'm

dosed with some kind of powder that takes the ache right out of me) …
well, the Bank phoned to say they would use what little influence they had
to get Ed a job in a ghost town. The catch is — we won't be a family unit.
The Commission isn't having any able-bodied male in any ghost town,
and even if Ed gets a job there, he couldn't live with us. He couldn't help
me with the twins, and we'd have to sleep six to eight to a room. Depending on the size of the room, they put in two or four double-deckers. I'd
have to wash everything by hand which even now with all conveniences at
hand I can't do, so I send some to the laundry. I wouldn't be able to keep
the babies' milk fresh — and it is more work than ever to make it every
four hours. Then most likely I'd have to teach grade school.

The pay, irrespective of ability, is two dollars a day, minus Sundays. Out
of which we have to feed and clothe four kids and try to keep them in a
semblance of health. Honest, Wes, I wonder if the "Whites" think we are
a special kind of low animal able to live on next-to-nothing needing no
clothes replacements, disregarding the kids who still outgrow their clothes
as fast as you make them, able to survive without the vitamins that they
need, money for school books, shoe repair, medicine. (Oh they are going
to be sick!!) It isn't as if this place had been bombed and *everybody* was
suffering. *Then* we'd be together and our morale would be high. As it is,
the wives get twenty dollars, the first child five dollars, the next four get
four dollars each. The rest get nothing. Families of internees, widows and
single women get relief. The families have to buy food at the local stores
around the ghost town. Those merchants are bound to raise prices. How
far do you think a mother and eight children can live on forty-one dollars
including clothing and medicine? And most of those children are old enough
to eat a heck of a lot. Not like Emi and Meiko who have the appetites of
birds. That's why I have to feed them cod liver oil and B1 to supplement
what they don't get. They don't eat enough to get even their proteins.

We were talking about farm work. Ed was sighing that he's so out of
shape, it'd take him six months to get used to hard work. If we could get to
Salmon Arm — the work there is seasonal — but being a steady farm hand
is another thing the more we discuss it. Ye gods! What *does* one do in times
like these?

What *kind* of work is there for Ed to do that would ensure his not getting sick through unaccustomed hard labour — for then we'd be without
pay. There are so many complex angles in this business my head aches. Mr.
Matsubayashi just phoned that there is no electricity in McGillivray. What
does one do without electricity? When have we ever been without it? How
do they iron anyway since the old flat irons are as extinct as dodos. How

am I to wash for six? In the hot summer how am I to keep milk and butter and meat fresh?

Another thing that's bothering us is the cost of transportation and freight to Ontario. We can take only our clothes, bedding, pots and pans and dishes. Ed's going to find out. We've sold our dining-room suite and our piano. I'm selling everything else I can't take. Mr. and Mrs. Lock are going to store our valuables for us, our irreplaceables, like books and good dishes (my Japanese ones) and pictures, etc. Also our Hoover.

Ed is so worried he goes around in a daze wondering what to do. We've so little time. The manager was so "yukkuri" [slow] about things up till the 30th of April when we got the "No" answer from HO. It's really too late to do much now except hope. I'm afraid Ed's going grey-haired over this. I can see more white now than ever before. What would you suggest? If we go to a ghost town then it's going to be one hell of a life. Waiting in line to wash, waiting in line to cook, to eat, maybe sleeping with strangers. The Yamadas are going to Alberta. Aunt Toyofuku still has a chance to go to Westbank.

At the Pool, confinees have lost as much as nine pounds in the month they've been there. There's a lot of repressed hysteria, which is so contagious. The red tape is ferocious.

What a hell this mess is. The Bank manager tried to get Ed a place in the more temperate beet fields, but that's out. Once we go to a beet farm we're stuck by contract; the same with a ghost town. If we didn't have to depend on the say-so of every town Council!

Well I've got to go to sleep. We've got to pack yet.

Did you find the diapers? It's either disposable diapers or Kleinerts refill pads (if this last, get two panty covers). Mrs. Pannell or Mrs. Mack ought to know. If we go to McGillivray, we've got to go in a week or so. They won't wait. If you can get the diapers, send them quickly. If they're not available, let me know. I've got to borrow some — somewhere.

Love,

Mur

[The Kitigawas were among a few, with either enough wealth or with relatives and friends in the East, who were allowed to live outside the "protected area" on their own resources and with few restrictions placed on them. Later in May of 1942 the Kitigawas joined Muriel's brother in Toronto where they were sponsored by a minister of the United Church.]

RODERICK HAIG-BROWN (1908–1976)

Roderick Haig-Brown's reputation as a writer and conservationist is based in appreciation: of landscape, of wild animals, of rivers and fishing, and of the place humans make for themselves within nature. As he says in the essay included here, "any given generation of men can have only a lease, not ownership, of the earth; and one essential term of the lease is that the earth be handed on to the next generation with unimpaired potentialities." No Canadian has stated the fundamental truths of conservationism with more simplicity or power. Born in Sussex, England, but never entirely comfortable with the codes of English society, by 1931 Haig-Brown found his natural home on Vancouver Island, eventually settling at Campbell River. He worked as a logger, trapper, guide and local magistrate, but increasingly made his living as a writer. His output was large, and varied. There were animal stories in the tradition of C.G.D. Roberts and Hubert Evans — *Silver: The Life of an Atlantic Salmon* (1931), *Ki-Yu: A Story of Panthers* (1934); novels for adults — *Timber: A Novel of Pacific Coast Loggers* (1946), *On the Highest Hill* (1949); juvenile fiction — *Starbuck Valley Winter* (1943), *Saltwater Summer* (1948), the latter a winner of the Governor-General's Award; books on fishing which were both personal and technical — *A River Never Sleeps* (1946), *A Primer of Fly-Fishing* (1964); and environmental meditations such as *Measure of the Year* (1950), from which "Let Them Eat Sawdust" is taken. Haig-Brown cast his net wide, but as one of his biographers has noted: "Through all his work ... there runs a unifying thread: the message that man must respect the natural world of which he is an integral part." For this message alone, Haig-Brown holds an honoured place in the ranks of the province's early conservationists. Fittingly, the British Columbia Book Prize for regional writing has been named after him.

LET THEM EAT SAWDUST

I HAVE BEEN, all my life, what is known as a conservationist. I am not at all sure that this has done myself or anyone else any good, but I am quite sure that no intelligent man, least of all a countryman, has any alternative. It seems clear beyond possibility of argument that any given generation of men can have only a lease, not ownership, of the earth; and one essential term of the lease is that the earth be handed on to the next generation with unimpaired potentialities. This is the conservationist's concern.

It is in the history of civilizations that conservationists are always defeated, boomers always win, and the civilizations always die. I think there has never been, in any state, a conservationist government, because there has never yet been a people with sufficient humility to take conservation seriously. This is natural enough. No man is intimately concerned with more than his lifetime, comparatively few men concern themselves seriously with more than a fraction of that time; in the last analysis all governments reflect the concerns of the people they govern, and most modern democratic governments are more deeply concerned with some brief, set term of office than with anything else. Conservation means fair and honest dealing with the future, usually at some cost to the immediate present. It is a simple morality, with little to offset the glamour and quick material rewards of the North American deity, "Progress."

Living near a settlement like Elkhorn, one sees both sides of the argument lived out, and inevitably takes part. Elkhorn is entirely dependent on natural resources in their first state. Almost the whole of Vancouver Island is, or was, timber; possibly the finest softwood saw-log timber in the world. Next in importance to timber are the recreational assets, game, game fish and scenery; after these, commercial fishing, coal mining, agriculture and water power. Elkhorn is touched by all of them, but timber is overwhelmingly the most important factor in its existence; the whole forty-year life of the village has been built on service to the logging camps and loggers of the surrounding country. And during those years the importance of a tourist trade based mainly on sport fishing has steadily increased.

It would be logical to suppose that everyone in Elkhorn would be interested in forestry and forest conservation, but almost no one is. Vancouver Island's forests were at first considered "inexhaustible"; then, as it became clear that they were being rapidly exhausted, the forests became an expendable asset, to be used in "opening up the country" so that some unspecified phenomenon, probably "industry," could come in and take over. In spite of some very half-hearted attempts at a sounder forest policy by the government, that is where things rest at present. Elkhorn and other little towns like it watch the big logging camps draw farther and farther away as the more accessible timber is cleared off; they know vaguely that the end of saw-log timber is in sight, that millions of deforested acres are reproducing only slowly if at all; yet they retain a mystic faith in the future, a belief that "progress" in the shape of roads and wharves and airplanes and hydro-electric power will somehow lead them on to a continuously more abundant life. Perhaps they will. But even that could not excuse or justify the fire-destroyed acres, the incredible waste of timber in logging, the long barren years through which magnificent forest land has grown little or nothing.

Elkhorn is in no way unique. This frantic dream of progress and development has cursed nearly every hamlet and village in North America at some time or another, bringing with it premature sidewalks and false-front stores, fantastic real-estate projects, fierce neon signs and an orgy of public services planned with a solidity that might better have gone into the jerry-built houses. Usually it is a recurrent frenzy, starting with each sizable economic boom, dying back between whiles to surge up again on some new promise of oil or minerals or large construction, any high and easy road to sudden wealth. And it is not wholly bad. It has built a continent's material civilization, blatantly, wastefully, with an enormous cruelty in the shattering of men's hopes and dreams, and frequent distortions of true values; but it has built it, and perhaps it was necessary to build so fast and so extravagantly.

But now that the continent is crossed and secured, the method seems stupid, the haste merely destructive. The sanctity of "progress" with its tricky little catch phrase, "We can't stand in the way of progress," seems suddenly false and treacherous. It is a good time to ask, "Why can't we?", to pull progress apart and take a new look at it, to examine everything called "development" in terms of values that already exist, in its relationship to the economy of the whole nation and the whole continent; above all, in its relationship to human happiness.

Progress seems to mean, all too often, the projection of slums into the wilderness. Incredibly, for all its village size, Elkhorn achieved slums for itself on land that had been bush only a year previously. This came about in a sudden flux of temporary jobs on a major construction project; people poured in, found high wages, then paid higher rents for tar-paper shacks set in mud, where each family shared a single room and a dozen families shared a hand pump for water, and an outside toilet. The project was finished, many of the families moved out and the village had time to wonder what had happened to it. Meanwhile the timber has drawn back two or three years farther into the mountains. But more people than ever before are dependent on it.

So the more abundant life has arrived briefly and departed, much of it spent in failure and waste. High wages have little meaning if they will buy only tar-paper shacks or transient homes for growing children. Boom and progress and development add up to high real-estate prices, houses scattered among vacant lots that no one can afford to buy, a few short lengths of sidewalk, some no-parking signs and a multiplicity of stores with little reason to be doing business. And the village settles back to consolidate. Strangely, there is something to consolidate. More people are living in the community, even though there is apparently less reason for them to be doing so. There is a framework of community organization, something beyond the simple mutual help of the older days. There are many improved services, such strange exotic things as street lights and an up-to-date water system and an extremely modern school. Some of these things may prove difficult to maintain and pay for; but they exist and merely by doing so they make a village out of what had been only a settlement. Somehow timber and tourists will support them until another boom comes and a few more of the vacant lots between the houses are filled and a small town begins to grow out of the village. But the solidity, the real existence of the town, as of the village, will be built only slowly, between the booms.

It is difficult to know how much or how little human happiness grows out of such a boom, but the total seems less than before. There are more worried and anxious and uncertain people than there were before. Even small businessmen who have done well are strained by their expansion, working harder, worrying more, remembering the quieter, more logical times with regret. Even the most ambitious of them speak regretfully of simplicities they loved in the earlier Elkhorn, which now seem lost in the surge of the progress they called for. Yet they must seem to call for more progress because the deity is sacrosanct; no North American businessman can deny her lip service, no matter what may be in his heart.

A conservationist fights many battles, varying in scale all the way from the attempted protection of some individual species of wildlife to the supreme issue of proper use of soil, air and water; and every fight is complicated, if not forced, by the false urgency and outdated sanctity of progress. The speed of modern development is such that the conservationist is always under attack, rarely has time himself to attack. He needs only breathing space, a little time for thought to creep in and temper progress with wisdom. Development is rarely a matter of urgency. Timber, soil, fisheries, oil and minerals, even water power, become more, not less, valuable with delay. The problem is to use the self-reproducing resources within their safe yield and to develop the wasting resources without injury to others already producing.

Elkhorn, when a government was damming its river, had to fight and fight hard to save the salmon run on which its tourist trade is built. She had to fight again, still harder, to win clearing of the land that would be flooded by the dam. She expects, and needs, a pulp mill; probably it will come one day and if it does she will have to fight again, harder than ever before, to save her waters from pollution.

Such conflicts as these go on throughout the continent, and none of them is necessary. Hydroelectric developments, pulp mills and other such manifestations of progress are not dreamed up overnight. There is always ample time for mature and careful consideration of every issue involved. But early planning is always left to the single-track minds of the developers, often buried in deepest secrecy for purely commercial reasons, and the conservationist is left with a last-ditch battle. In this way the burden of proof is always forced upon him. He is standing in the way of progress, reactionary, narrow, without real vision.

It seems clear to me that all the destruction it causes should be reckoned in the direct cost of any project, and that no preventable destruction should ever be permitted. Obviously, flooded land is no longer land in any useful sense; but it should be cleared of timber and debris before flooding so that a lake with good bottom and clean shores will take its place. If the cost of this is too great for the project to bear, then the project is uneconomic. Runs of game and commercial fish can be destroyed by poorly planned dams; but sound planning can always find some way to compensate and may even save the whole resource. The onus here is just as clear, if not clearer, since a run of fish properly looked after will maintain itself indefinitely into the future, while a hydroelectric development may be outdated within twenty years, almost certainly will be within fifty years. Pollution of air and water by industrial plants is the simplest issue of all. There are adequate means of preventing all such pollutions. Admittedly they are sometimes costly, but if the industry cannot support the cost it is economically unsound. No nation can afford polluted air or polluted waterways.

These are sweeping statements, and I mean them to be. A civilization built on foul air and polluted water, on destroyed timber lands, overgrazed ranges, exhausted farm lands, on water sucked from one river system to make cheap electricity on another, is too costly and too insecurely based to last. I saw recently a newspaper editorial happily forecasting that before very long the world's timber supplies will be too valuable for any such simple use as building houses or making paper; they will all be needed for human food — processed, no doubt, into pulpy palatability, but still essentially sawdust. Any civilization that can cheerfully contemplate such a morbid future for its multiplied grandchildren needs a new philosophy.

Industrial development has produced such an enormous material prosperity, so widely spread, that its sanctity is easy to understand. But in North America it has done so largely by using capital assets as income. That is why conservation is now far more important than further development. It seems to me that the people of the continent, both Canadians and Americans, have everything to gain, nothing to lose, by stopping to take stock and understand what they have got and how it can soundly be used. Exhausting a continent and overpopulating it to the point at which its inhabitants must start eating trees seems a strange way to a more abundant life.

It is difficult to believe the theorists who say that a nation to be sound must have an increasing population. Thousands of years ago the human race had to breed tolerably fast to survive. After that nations had to grow large populations in fear of wars. And there was always the idea that man must multiply until he had overrun the earth. He seems to have achieved this and surely he can be allowed to pause to recognize that there is no virtue in population for the sake of population; if there were, India, China, even Russia would be more prosperous nations than they are. It is difficult to believe that there is any true morality in producing children, or any essential immorality in not producing them. Certainly there is little to be said for raising men to be slaves to "progress" and cities, to industry and all the machines of a civilization frantically producing substitutes for the natural things it has destroyed.

Conservation is wise use of natural resources, which ultimately are the whole life of any country, even one that imports most of its natural resources. And it is axiomatic that no special interest, whether it is industrial or governmental, can be trusted to use a natural resource wisely. All resources are interdependent; soil, for instance, cannot be separated from water tables, nor water tables from forests; and all life that moves on the land, in the water, or in the air is affected by every use of these resources. Government departments work independently and with blind irresponsibility to achieve specialized departmental ends; British Columbia has an Electric Power Act that restricts the function of a powerful commission to the production of cheap electricity; it has a Water Act that recognizes fourteen uses for water, but does not include its use by fish, though the commercial salmon fishery is one of the three or four main resources of the province. The logging industry has to pay only slight attention to forest regeneration, none at all to economical use of timber stands, preservation of soil or water resources. So it is through the whole picture. The conservationist's hope — perhaps dream is the better word — is to change all this, to establish a co-ordination of effort that will make sure that every factor is properly weighed and every resource fully protected against exploitation or wanton destruction. There are a few slow signs that we are beginning to think on these lines; the existence of a minor government department called the Land Utilization Branch is one of them, and an annual conference of experts on natural resources initiated by this branch is another. But this is a feeble result for the last west, with a whole continent's lessons of waste and destruction to draw on. Perhaps I take too much pleasure in prophesying doom, perhaps I am too much countryman and woodsman to understand the dream of progress through cities and machines, to feel the romance of the bulldozer and the earth mover, the concrete mixer and the four-lane highway. But I think we are on our way through the whole tragic story, that we shall live well on it. Our children and grandchildren and great-grandchildren will have to solve the slow, difficult problem of restoration as best they can. Perhaps atomic power will help them. It seems to be our only legacy.

GEORGE WOODCOCK (1912–1995)

Poet, novelist, essayist, political philosopher, anarchist, literary critic, spiritual seeker and memoirist — George Woodcock was unquestionably one of Canada's most distinguished and prolific men of letters. He wrote between 125-150 books but was always reluctant to count the total. Among the most important are: *The Anarchist Prince: A Study of Peter Kropotkin* (1950); *Anarchism* (1962); *The Crystal Spirit* (about George Orwell, and winner of the Governor-General's Award, 1966); *Faces of India* (1974); *Thomas Merton: Monk and Poet* (1978); *Caves in the Desert* (about Chinese philosophy and spirituality); *The Monk and His Message* (about Woodcock's friendship with the Dalai Lama); *Northern Spring* (1987, about Canadian literature); and specifically about B.C. — *Ravens and Prophets* (1952); *People of the Coast* (1977); and *British Columbia: A History of the Province* (1990). Woodcock's last book of poetry was *Tolstoy at Yasnaya Polyana* (1991). He was also the founder and editor-in-chief of *Canadian Literature* at U.B.C. (1959-1977).

Woodcock was born in Winnipeg, Manitoba, but his parents returned to England soon after his birth, and he only returned to Canada in 1949 as a political exile (and, it is said, inspired by the philosophy and life concepts of the Doukhobors). One of his early essays on this pacifist sect — "Encounter with an Archangel" — is a portrait of a radical breakaway group which established a community at Hilliers on Vancouver Island not far from where the Woodcocks then lived. Woodcock went on to write, with Ivan Avakumovic, *The Doukhobors* (1968) — the standard work on this group, in which a more mature understanding of Doukhobor history and community practice are on display. Woodcock's imaginative life and social commitments were protean, and one catches glimpses of this range in the essay "Playing to the People," about B.C. premiers W.A.C. Bennett and Dave Barrett; the essential political nature of the province is captured in a few deft brushstrokes — but Woodcock's fundamental commitments to human dignity and freedom in art, in politics and in spiritual life were unwavering. In the second volume of his memoirs, *Beyond the Blue Mountains* (1988), Woodcock writes of his desire to have his ashes scattered on Anarchist Summit just east of Osoyoos, gateway to the Boundary and Kootenay regions. In this desire, we see Woodcock's almost complete identification not only with a lifelong philosophy, but also with his adopted imaginative homeland. His death on January 28, 1995 marked the passing of a great Canadian humanitarian.

ENCOUNTER WITH AN ARCHANGEL

I FIRST KNEW THE Doukhobors as shadowy figures of legend in my English childhood, when my father would compensate for a dull life in a small town beside the Thames by weaving nostalgic threnodies on his young manhood in the Canadian West. Evenings on the prairies, with the great pink-bellied hawks settling down; Cobalt in the silver boom; fishing camps on the pristine shores of the northern lakes; and the great winter fires of the cities where burnt-out buildings became palaces of ice. Against such scenes the necessary characters moved in the cinema of my brain with the exaggerated gesticulation of Japanese actors. Lefty Louis and Zip the Blood shot it out with the police from a Winnipeg streetcar; Charlie Chaplin clowned through the one-elevator hamlets with Fred Karno; Chinese in blue gowns and pigtails scurried along Portage Avenue; strange Russians cleared snow in the prairie towns and were given to stripping in public, regardless of sex.

I realized the Doukhobors were something more than eccentric shovellers of snow when I read Tolstoy and Kropotkin and discovered that for these great Russians the Doukhobors were a group of admirable peasant radicals — Nature's anarchists. During the thirties I found in Doukhobor anti-militarism a strain that appealed to my own pacifism, and I accepted Tolstoy's impression of a libertarian sect who took their Christianity neat and had turned their settlements into Utopian communes. Like Tolstoy, I was unaware that this simple view took no account of certain fundamental aspects of Doukhobor philosophy and practice. Unlike Tolstoy, I learnt my error.

When my wife and I returned to Canada in the spring of 1949, I found that on Vancouver Island, where we settled, there was a small group of Doukhobors who had migrated from the interior of British Columbia and had founded a colony at Hilliers, sixty miles north of the village where we were clearing land and carpentering a house in search of that Tolstoyan *ignis fatuus*, the marriage of manual and mental work.

The people of our village talked reluctantly about the Hilliers community, yet even their hostile comments told us something. The leader of the group — a heretical offshoot — was a prophet who called himself Michael the Archangel. He openly preached the destruction of marriage, and this our neighbours vaguely envisaged as a complex and orgiastic pattern of shacking-up which provoked and offended their Presbyterian imaginations at one and the same time.

Since Hilliers was near, we could easily go there to see for ourselves, but we knew already that chronic bad relations with the Canadian authorities had made the Doukhobors distrustful of strangers. However, I wrote to the community, and by return I received a letter from the secretary, whose name was — almost predictably — Joe. He not only welcomed my interest, but invited us to stay at Hilliers as long as we wished. I was a little surprised at the enthusiastic tone of his letter, but the reason became evident once we reached Hilliers.

One day in August we set off northward, hitchhiking, and it was late afternoon when the last driver turned off the seacoast road into the broad valley, hot and still of air, where Hilliers lies in the lee of the hard mountain spine that runs down the length of Vancouver Island. The older, non-Doukhobor Hilliers was a whistle-stop on the island railway, and the entrance to the community stood opposite a siding filled with boxcars. A high cedar fence faced the road. A large board was nailed to it. *Union of spiritual communities of Christ,* it said, in Russian and English. The wide gates stood open; looking between them, the eye encompassed and then recognized with some surprise the unconscious faithfulness with which a Russian village of the Chekhov era had been reproduced. Low cabins of logs and unpainted shacks were scattered along a faintly marked trail that ran between grass verges to end, a furlong on, at two larger two-storeyed houses standing against the brown background of the mountains, with the grey bubble of a communal baking oven between them. Each cabin was surrounded by a picketed garden, where green rows of vegetables and raspberry canes ran over the black earth in neatly weeded symmetry, and ranks of sunflowers lolled their brown and yellow masks towards the light.

An old woman with a white kerchief shading her face was hoeing very slowly in the nearest garden. She was the only person in sight, and I went up to her fence. Could she tell me where to find Joe? Her English was so broken that I could not follow what she was trying to tell me. By this time our arrival had been observed in the cabins, and a little wave of younger women in bright full petticoats, and of blond, crop-headed small boys, came towards us hesitantly. There was nothing of the welcome we had expected. Inge spoke to one of the women. "Joe ain't here," she answered. "He's at the other place." She waved vaguely northward, A pickup truck drove in through the gates, and two young men got out. The women called to them, and they talked together in rapid, anxious Russian. Then one man got back into the truck and drove off, while the other came up to us. He was dark and nervous, dressed in an old blue serge suit, with chaff whitening the wrinkles. "I'm Pete," he said, "Joe's brother. Joe's coming." He paused. "Afterwards … you'll see Michael … Michael Archangel," he added hesitantly, and then fell silent. The small boys gave up interest and went to play in the boxcars.

Joe was so different from Pete that it was hard to believe them brothers — blue-eyed, wiry, jumping out of the truck to run and pump our hands. "Michael Archangel knew you were coming. A long time ago," he shouted. I had written only a week before. "A long time ago?" I asked. Joe looked at me and then laughed. "Yes, before you wrote!" Then he grabbed our rucksacks, helped us into the truck, and drove wildly for a couple of miles along a rough track beside the railway to a large old farm house in a quadrangle of shacks and barns surrounded by propped-up apple trees that were ochre-yellow with lichen. "This is the other place," Joe explained. "Most of the young people stay here. The old 'uns live up there with Michael Archangel."

We went into the kitchen. Two young women, fair and steatopygous as Doukhobor beauties are expected to be, were preparing the evening meal. A small girl showed us to our room and stood, avid with curiosity, while we unpacked our rucksacks and washed our faces. Then Joe took us around the yard, showed us the new bakehouse on which a hawk-faced man like a Circassian bandit was laying bricks, and tried to entice us into the bathhouse. I looked through the doorway and saw naked people moving like the damned in the clouds of steam that puffed up whenever a bucket of water was thrown on the hot stones. In a couple of seconds I withdrew, gasping for breath. The bricklayer laughed. "You never make a Doukhobor," he said. "Add ten years to your life," said Joe, coaxingly.

When everyone stood in a circle around the great oval table for the communal meal, we began to see the kind of people the Doukhobors were. There were twenty of them, singing in the half-Caucasian rhythm that penetrates Doukhobor music, the women high and nasal, the men resonant as bells. Most had Slavonic features, their breadth emphasized among the women by the straight fringes in which their hair was cut across the brow. But a few, like the bricklayer, were so un-Russian as to suggest that the Doukhobors had interbred with caucasian Moslems during their long exile in the mountains before they came to Canada. They sang of Siberian and Canadian prisons, of martyrs and heroes in the faith. "Rest at last, ye eagles of courage, rest at last in the arms of God," they boomed and shrilled.

The singing was solemn, but afterwards the mood changed at once and the meal went on with laughter and loud Russian talk; now and then our neighbours would break off repentently to translate for our benefit. The food was vegetarian, the best of its kind I have ever tasted; bowls of purple borscht, dashed with white streaks of cream, and then casha, made with millet and butter, and vegetables cooked in oil, and pirogi stuffed with cheese and beans and blackberries, and eaten with great scoops of sour cream. Slices of black bread passed around the table, cut from a massive square loaf that stood in the middle, beside the salt of hospitality, and the meal ended with huckleberries and cherries.

Afterwards Joe and Pete took us to drink tea in a room they used as an office. It was furnished with a table and benches of thick hand-adzed cedar, but a big blue enamel teapot served instead of a samovar. This was the first of a series of long conversations in which the ideas of the community were imparted to us, principally by Joe, who spoke English more fluently than anyone else at Hilliers. Except for a few phrases, the details of the dialogues have become blurred in my memory during the thirteen years that have passed since then, but this, in substance, is what we were told on the first evening.

The community began with the experiences of Michael Verigin, a backsliding Doukhobor. Michael had left his home in the mountains, opened a boarding house for Russians in Vancouver, and prospered there. After a few years Michael began to feel the malaise which many Doukhobors experience when they go from their villages into the acquisitive outside world, and he returned to the mountain valley of Krestova. Krestova is the Mecca of the Sons of Freedom, the fire-raising and nude-parading radical wing of the Doukhobor sect. Michael rejoined the Sons of Freedom and was regarded with deference because he bore the holy name of Verigin and was a distant cousin of Peter Lordly, the Living Christ who presided over the Doukhobors' first years in Canada, and died mysteriously in a train explosion during the twenties.

"Then Michael had a vision."

"A dream?"

"No, a vision. He was awake, and he said there was a voice and a presence."

"He saw nothing?"

"That time he didn't. The vision told him he was no longer Mike Verigin. Michael the Archangel had gone into him. He was the same man, but the Archangel as well."

"How did he know it was a real vision?"

"He just knew." Joe looked at me with the imperturbable blue-eyed confidence of a man used to assessing the authenticity of supernatural messages. "The vision said Michael must prepare the world for the Second Coming."

The Second Coming did not mean the return of Christ. According to Doukhobor belief, Christ is returning all the time in various forms. The Second Coming meant the establishment of God's earthly kingdom and the end of time and mortality.

As the chosen pioneers in this great mission, the Doukhobors must purify themselves. The Archangel began by proclaiming that they must renounce not only meat and vegetables, but also tobacco and musical instruments. Joe himself had abandoned playing the violin, which he dearly loved. As he told me this, a radio was playing loudly in the kitchen. "That's OK," Joe reassured me. "A radio ain't a musical instrument."

Above all, the lust for possession must be rooted out. This meant not only a return to the traditional communistic economy from which the Doukhobors had lapsed under evil Canadian influences, but also the destruction of that inner citadel of possession, marriage. No person must have rights over another, either parental or marital. Women must be liberated, sexual relations must be free, families must wither away.

Two or three hundred of the Sons of Freedom, mostly seasoned old veterans of the nude marches and the pre-war internment on Piers Island, accepted the Archangel's teaching. Their neighbours showed disagreement by burning down the houses of those who followed Verigin. At this point the Archangel very conveniently had another vision.

Two of his followers must visit Vancouver Island. There they would find a town where a clock had stopped at half past two, and then they must proceed eastward until they saw a white horse by the gate of a farm. Joe and another man went on the expedition. They found the clock in Port Alberni, and the horse by the gate of a three-hundred-acre farm that was up for sale at a knockdown price. And, for what the fact is worth, I should record that after I had heard Joe's story I happened to visit Port Alberni, and there, on the tower of a fire hall, I saw a dummy clock whose painted hands stood unmoving at half-past two.

The farm was bought with the pooled resources of the faithful, and Michael the Archangel led two hundred of his disciples on the exodus to Vancouver Island. Immediately after leaving the mainland he added to all the other prohibitions a ban on sexual intercourse — to conserve energies for the great task of spiritual regeneration. Complete freedom was only to be won by complete self-control. So much for the stories of Free Love rampant.

I wanted to find out the actual nature of the power that enabled Michael the Archangel to impose such restrictions. Tolstoy once thought that, because they opposed the state, the Doukhobors lived without rulers. Other writers had suggested that the Living Christs, like Peter the Lordly Verigin and his son Peter the Purger, had been rulers as powerful as any earthly governor.

"Michael is just our spiritual leader," Joe explained blandly.

"But he still seems to have a great say in your practical affairs."

"It depends on what you mean by say. He gives no orders. We are free men. We don't obey anybody. But he gives us advice."

"Do you always accept?"

"If we know what's good for us, we do."

"Why?"

"Because we know Michael the Archangel is always right."

"How do you know?"

"We just know."

The next day we met the Archangel. He had sent a message early that morning summoning us to his presence, and Joe drove us to the hamlet where we had arrived originally. The Archangel's house was one of the larger buildings, but we were not allowed to go in. We waited outside. The Archangel would meet us in the garden.

A tall man in his late fifties came stepping heavily between the zinnia borders. A heavy paunch filled his knitted sweater, and his shining bald head loosened into a coarse, flushed face with a potato nose, a sandy moustache, and small eyes that glinted out of puffy sockets. It was a disappointing encounter. The Archangel bowed in the customary Doukhobor manner, but without the warmth most Doukhobors put into their greeting. He shook hands limply. He spoke a few sentences in Russian, welcoming us and wishing us good health, and he affected not to understand English, though we learned later that he was effectively bilingual. He picked two small pink roses from a briar that ran along the fence and gave one to each of us. In five minutes he was gone, retiring with dignified adroitness and leaving our intended questions about archangelic power unanswered. Joe led us away, loudly declaring that the Archangel had been delighted with us, and that he had given many messages which he, Joe, would transmit in due course. Our whole relationship with the Archangel took on this elusive, indirect form, with Joe acting like a voluble priest interpreting and embellishing the laconic banalities of the oracle.

For the rest of the second day we wandered around the community, talking to the people we encountered. I pumped the handle of a primitive hand washing-machine, and learned from the girl I helped a curious instance of Doukhobor double-think. A spaniel bitch trotted across the yard, followed by a single pup. "She had four," the girl volunteered. "Did you give the rest away?" "No, they were drowned." "I thought you didn't believe in killing." "We didn't kill 'em. The Mountie sergeant drowned 'em for us." She chuckled, and quite obviously felt no guilt for merely condoning a killing someone else had carried out.

Under the prophetic discipline there were certain signs of strain. I found empty beer bottles in a corner of one Doukhobor field, and in the shelter of the ten-foot plumes of corn which were the community's pride a young man begged a cigarette and smoked in hasty gulps to finish it before anyone came in sight. Yet there was also an atmosphere of dogged devotion. Much of the land had been irrigated, and it was growing heavier crops of corn and tomatoes and vegetables than any of the neighbouring farms, while the houses were surrounded by rows of hotbeds and cold frames where melons and gherkins ripened. The younger people talked constantly of schemes for new kinds of cultivation and for starting light industries, but the younger people were so few. There were too many children, too many old visionaries.

Sunday was the climax of our visit. Our arrival had coincided with the community's first great festival. In the afternoon the only child so far born there was to be handed over to the care of the community as a symbolic demonstration against conventional ideas of motherhood and the family. Since the Archangel had forbidden fornication we were rather surprised that a being whose very presence seemed to defy his will should be so honoured. From my attempts to discuss the situation I gained an impression that the Doukhobors applied a rather Dostoevskian equation — considering that, if the ban itself was sacred, so must be the sin against it. "Free men ain't bound by reason," one young man rather unanswerably concluded a discussion on this point.

The day began with morning service in the bare meeting house. Flowers and plates of red apples had been brought in, and the sunlight played over the white head-shawls and bright cotton dresses of the women. Bread and salt stood symbolically on the small central table, and also a great ewer of water from which anybody who happened to feel thirsty would stop and drink as the service went on. The women ranged to the right of the table and the men to the left. On entering the hall each person bowed low from the waist, and the bow was returned by the whole assembly; the salutation was not to the man, but to the God within him. The Archangel stood at the head of the men, benign and copiously sweating; despite his celestial nature, he did not attempt to offend Doukhobor precedent by acting like a priest. Today, in fact, as a child was to be the centre of the festival, the children led off the service, choosing and starting in their sharp, clear voices the Doukhobor psalms and hymns for the day. Almost every part of the service was sung, and the wild and wholly incomprehensible chanting of the two hundred people in the small meeting house produced in us an extraordinary sense of exaltation such as I have only experienced once since then, in a church full of Zapotec peasants at a festival south of Oaxaca. At the end of the service we all linked arms at the elbows and kissed each other's cheeks, first right then left, in traditional token of forgiveness.

Later in the day we reassembled in the open air, forming a great V with the bread and salt at the apex. The singing rose like a fountain of sound among the drooping cedar trees, and between lines of women waving flowers and men waving green boughs the mother carried her child to the table. She was one of the young women we had met at the farmhouse on our arrival. As she stood there, her fair face grave and melancholy within the white frame of her head-shawl, she looked like the dolorous Mother of some naive ikon. The singing ended, the old hawk-faced bricklayer prayed before the table, and the mother, showing no emotion, handed the child to another of the women. The Archangel began to speak, in high, emotional tones; Pete, standing beside me, translated. The child would be named Angel Gabriel. The fruit of sin, he contained the seed of celestial nature. It was he who would fulfil the great destiny of the Doukhobors and lead mankind back on the great journey to lost Eden.

The women brought out pitchers of kvass and walked among the people as the orators began to speak. Emblematic banners were unfurled before the assembly. One, representing women dragging the ploughs that broke the prairies during the hard early days of the sect in Canada, was meant to celebrate the coming liberation of the sect from all forms of bondage. Another, covered with images of clocks and other symbols of time, was carefully expounded by the Archangel, who found in it the fatal dates that charted the destiny of the world. Then everyone spoke who wished — elders and young women; a Communist lawyer who had come in from the blue; even I, under moral coercion, as the enquiring Tolstoyan I then was. It was hot and tedious work as the sun beat down into the bowl among the mountains, and Sunday trippers from Qualicum Beach gazed in astonishment through the palisades.

We walked back to the farmhouse with a Canadian woman who had married into the Doukhobors. "You've seen what Mike wants you to see," she said bitterly. "You don't know all there is to know about that girl. Now she'll go up to stay in Mike's house. They won't let her talk to anyone, and they'll pay her out in every way they can for having a child by her own husband. Purification! That's what they talk about. I call it prison!" The mother of the Angel Gabriel was not at the evening meal, and we never saw her again. We asked Joe what had happened to her. She had gone willingly into seclusion, he answered; for her own good, of course.

Indeed, Joe had more important things to talk about in that last conversation. "You have a great part to play in the future of mankind." He fixed me with a sharp, pale eye. "Michael's vision has told him that the end of the world is very near. Now we have to gather in Jerusalem the hundred and forty-four thousand true servants of God mentioned in Revelation. This time Jerusalem will be right here."

"Here? On Vancouver Island?"

"On this very spot."

"But how do you know?"

"We ain't worrying. We just know. And the Archangel had a vision about you. He knew you were coming a long time ago. He knew you were a writer. He knew you were being sent here so you could tell the world what we're doing."

I must have looked at him very dubiously, for he flapped his hands reassuringly. "I ain't asking you to do it. Nor is Archangel. We just know you will. You'll write about us, and people will come to us, and then you will come back and be marked with the sign and live forever among the servants of God."

We left the next day. The Archangel saw us once more in the garden, gave us a white rose each, and said we should meet again before long. "It's a prophecy," Joe whispered.

And indeed it was. One day, months later, I was broadcasting in Vancouver when Ross McLean, who was then a radio producer, said he had heard Joe was locked up in the court house. I went over, but I could not see him. The Mounties were holding him incommunicado. But as I was leaving the station Michael the Archangel was brought in, and for a couple of minutes, in that grim barred room, I was allowed to talk to him. He was pleased to be recognized, and even willing to talk a little English. "I am free soon," he said, as he was led away to the cells. Not long afterwards he and Joe were sentenced on some rather nebulous charges of disturbing public order. And a few months later Michael the Archangel died in jail.

Ten years afterwards we drove through Hilliers, turning off our road on a nostalgic impulse. The palisade was still there, opposite the railway siding, and for a moment everything looked unchanged. But inside, where Jerusalem should have been rising, there was only the ghost of what we had seen on the day the Angel Gabriel was named. Most of the buildings had gone, but falling fences and squares of thistles still marked out the theocracy where the Archangel had ruled.

PLAYING TO THE PEOPLE

IN DEMOCRATIC politics successful leaders are the good actors who project the personal fantasies of their constituents. Only when we know the kind of image people in a specific country or region develop of themselves can we begin to understand the style that succeeds in their local politics. In Canada it is most of all a matter of regions. Politically, one hundred and ten years after Confederation, we are even yet hardly a nation. There is really no such thing as an all-Canadian Canadian, which is why national popularity is so precarious among us, and why Ottawa politicians always find that whatever image they project sooner or later antagonizes that key section of the community on which they had relied for enduring power. There are, in fact, only Canadians who are first of all Québecois or Newfoundlanders or Manitobans or British Columbians. Each region in Canada has its own environment, its own history, even its own ethnic mix. Each expresses itself — despite the vast efforts of the CBC and CRTC to make us all feel uniform — in a special way that shows itself in literature and the arts, in lifestyles, and especially in political approaches.

The image of a region — the way its people see their setting and their neighbours and themselves — is not something to be learned quickly, and that applies most of all to my own region of British Columbia. Once I used to describe myself as "Canadian by birth and British Columbian by adoption." It took a long time for the graft to work. Now, twenty-seven years after crossing the Continental Divide, I reverse the order. "I am British Columbian by choice, Canadian by birth."

And, as a British Columbian by choice, watching people from over the Rockies trying to grapple with the local political scene, I realize how easy it is for the great mountain ranges to form a mental as well as a geographical divide.

It isn't only that British Columbians live in narrow valleys and on islands and river deltas that are scanty footholds in a "sea of mountains." It isn't only that even today British Columbia remains far more dependent on exploiting largely non-renewable natural resources — minerals, timber, fish, fossil fuels, hydro power — than on agriculture (like the Prairie provinces) or industry (like Ontario). It isn't only that British Columbia started out before Confederation on its own separate history of settlement by sea from Britain and Asia, and by land from California, and so established its peculiar mix of peoples and traditions. It isn't that British Columbia — at least the thickly inhabited areas around Vancouver and Victoria — enjoys a bland, rainy climate that combines with mountains and sheltered waterways to foster a uniquely hedonistic existence, the renowned lotus life of the shores of the Gulf of Georgia. All these things, of course, go toward giving British Columbian life its special character, but they gain human meaning only through the peculiar self-image that emerges from them.

When we look at that self-image, we realize that the British Columbian, no matter how heartily gregarious he may seem, sees himself dramatically as a loner in a world of loners. This highly individualized personal image makes him susceptible to the kind of politics that ends in a cult of people rather than of classes, and sees the people as a participating consensus of individuals rather than as a ladder of social gradations or a mosaic of ethnic groups. British Columbia man is a populist.

Thus the far western province, jammed between mountains and sea, presents the paradox of being perhaps Canada's most individualistically oriented region while enjoying a highly localized socialist tradition that goes back for more than eighty years, that has given the province a consistently socialist official opposition in the Legislative Assembly since the late 1930s, and has allowed it to experience [a] period of NDP government, from 1972 to 1975.

But there is a great deal more than that to British Columbia's political oddity. For almost a quarter of a century, west of the Divide, the federally powerful Liberals and Conservatives have been derided provincially and reduced to minute forlorn hopes of parties, while the CCF-NDP has shared the great majority of British Columbian votes and legislative seats with the Social Credit Party, which in 1952 blew up literally out of nothing to form the Government of British Columbia. By the 1975 provincial election, Social Credit (the winning party) and the NDP shared over ninety percent between them. Provincial Liberals on the West Coast have become somewhat scarcer than anarchists.

British Columbian politics, in other words, is now polarized between two parties unknown until the 1930s, neither of which had ever held power federally — or seems likely to do so. Moreover, both Social Credit and socialism in British Columbia are quite different from their counterparts in other provinces, and much more alike than they appear at first sight. Both of them have realized the need to mirror the British Columbian's personal myth of himself as at once a loner and a good man of the people.

I've now been a politician-watcher in British Columbia for twenty-seven years. As an arch-loner — an avowed anarchist — I've found myself drifting into the company of the mildly eccentric political failures that decorate the fringes of every British Columbian party, including the old ones, since to be a provincial Liberal or Tory west of the Rockies has by now become the wildest form of quixoticism. I reach my personal level among those gently cynical but hard-working failures whom the tough tacticians of every party expend as standard-bearers in forlorn-hope constituencies. Still, a province is by definition provincial, and therefore intimate, and inevitably one rubs shoulders with the local mighty, which for [a] quarter of a century meant that melodramatic trio of Victoria premiers, with names like the members of an old-fashioned attorney's firm, Bennett, Barrett and Bennett.

With that cunning, durable master of regional politics, W. A. C. Bennett (who ruled British Columbia for twenty years), it was literally a matter of rubbing shoulders, once passing in a corridor of the legislative buildings in Victoria and once jostling on the B.C. Ferries at Tsawwassen, as we made our respective ways to the car deck. Each time I was struck by a peculiarly fabricated look to the man, with his massive jaw and set nervous grin, as if he were being doubled by Madame Tussaud's effigy of himself. I thought of those masked intelligences who were the insect rulers of the moon as H. G. Wells envisaged it. Since then I have had the same kind of reaction watching other leading Social Crediters, like … Bill Bennett, and that handsome but chilling kingmaker Grace McCarthy (the onetime teenaged flower seller who created a chain of British Columbia florist's shops before she entered politics to become — eventually — provincial secretary, and who by sheer frenetic energy pulled Social Credit from defeat in 1972 to victory three years later.)

In contrast, my first encounter with Dave Barrett was indubitably human, even humane. I remember the occasion clearly because it emphasized strongly for me the two special characteristics that have distinguished … political leaders in British Columbia — the image of the battling outsider, and the complementary image of the man who speaks not for any one class but, with conviction and emphasis, for that vaguest but most seductive of political abstractions, *the people*.

By the time I met Dave Barrett, in 1970, he had been ten years on a rocky political trail. In 1959, as a social worker at the Haney Correctional Institution in British Columbia, he was sacked for seeking nomination as a CCF candidate. With loner's luck, he won the election and displaced the Social Credit labour minister. In 1969 he tried for the NDP provincial leadership and was beaten by Tom Berger. But Berger lost in that year's provincial election, and — loner's luck again — Dave Barrett was voted into leadership of the Opposition by the NDP caucus in the Legislative Assembly. The 1970 NDP convention had little alternative to confirming Barrett's leadership of the party, which it did by acclamation, though the local Canadian Labour Congress bosses were not enthusiastic.

The convention was held at the Bayshore Inn, then Vancouver's plushest hostelry. At the time, I was writing a CBC documentary on what had happened to unionism since the days of the Tolpuddle Martyrs, and I turned up to take a look at the delegates enjoying themselves like unregenerate capitalists. Barrett had arrived, but he was kept out of the inner conclaves. I went to get a tape from him on an idea he had recently been propounding. Why not let out-of-province — even foreign — firms set up plants in British Columbia, with ownership fifty-one percent socialized, the province holding thirty percent and the workers twenty-one percent of the shares? I liked the idea. It seemed a way to break down the ritualized antagonism between labour and industry that even unionists agree has scarred the British Columbia economy in recent years. The union bosses, who realize that power and perquisites wither in industrial peace, hated the idea.

After the taping I stayed awhile, and we got into a drift of conversation that I have always remembered as illuminating in relation to Barrett's later actions. He remarked that it was pointless to idealize the workers ("There are as many bloody a____s among the workers as anywhere else"), and that it was also pointless for men like him or me — or the union bureaucrats for that matter — to pretend we knew how men or women felt about their work. "Our whole way of life's different from a blue-collar worker's. We've gone away from all that. We don't have much idea how he really feels at the workbench. But nobody's just a worker. He's a member of society in all kinds of ways, and if you think of helping people in general toward a more equitable society, you're automatically helping the workers, which you don't do if you try to separate them from everybody else." His remarks, which impressed me and clung in my memory, showed the other side of the typical British Columbia leader: the triumphant loner is also the tribune of the people rather than the representative of vested class interests.

I remembered those words vividly after Barrett came to power in 1972, and particularly in 1975, when he legislated three unions back to work (the supermarket workers, the B.C. Railway workers and a section of the Teamsters) because he believed their continued absence from work was militating against the interests of British Columbia people in general. The union bosses who had snubbed him in 1970 were forced to obey, rather than face responsibility for defying British Columbia's first socialist government. Left-wingers within the NDP were critical, arguing that it was a working-class party and should defend the interests of the workers as a class. Populist Barrett disagreed.

There are extraordinary resemblances between the Barrett pattern and his predecessor W. A. C. Bennett's career. Bennett, a retail hardware millionaire from the farmland interior of British Columbia, entered politics when he was elected a Tory MLA in 1941. Defeated in a bid for the Conservative leadership in 1949, he resigned from the party and in 1952 fought and won the provincial election as leader of the newly founded British Columbia Social Credit League. Bennett's appeal was to the province's outsiders: to people in the towns and villages of the interior and the north who felt their interests neglected by city-based politicians; to the congregations of rural clapboard churches who believed morality and prosperity alike were going to hell in a handbasket; to small farmers and shopkeepers on the edge of failure; to ill-paid workers ignored by union aristocrats. The appeal was answered, and even by some who had once been devoted followers of the CCF. For, as historian Martin Robin admitted in *Pillars of Profit,* the Social Crediters "like the CCF, were outsiders."

Between them, Social Credit and the CCF had in one election destroyed the old-line parties and opened the province to populist politics. In a purely physical sense, as well, this change opened up the province. Bennett began a vast program of road and railway building that made the neglected parts of the province accessible, and unlocked the northland to a far more thorough exploitation of its natural resources than ever before.

Bennett ruled the province continuously for twenty years. His later Cabinets included lawyers, doctors, even an odd university professor, as well as back-country merchants, enhancing the image of a movement that embraced people of all kinds and classes.

There were loud protests from the lumber barons in 1952 when he imposed higher royalties on them, just as there would be lamentations when Dave Barrett imposed higher royalties on the mining industry in 1973. Bennett enjoyed the cut and thrust of political debate, and became a kind of parliamentary smiler-with-the-knife who slaughtered his opponents with an easy grin. He was adept at reviving the persecuted-outsider image by presenting his regime — "this poor little government" as he would call it while literally weeping in the legislature or on election platforms — as the victim of forces hostile to the British Columbian people as well: the lumber combines, the unions, the national railroads, the great hydro complex of B.C. Electric, and always the federal government, dominated by parties that honest British Columbians had dismissed as corrupt and antediluvian.

Bennett did not flinch even from the "socialist" expedient of nationalization. In 1958 he established a provincial fleet of large, handsome ferryboats plying between Vancouver Island and the mainland. And after the CCF urged a public takeover of B.C. Electric in 1961, Bennett — who had his own populist grudges against BCE for neglecting the unprofitable outlying areas of the province — surprised the Opposition by introducing takeover legislation. He thus forced the embarrassed CCF to support him in one of the very few unanimous votes in British Columbia history — fifty to nothing. It was not surprising that in 1963 Bennett should claim that "Social Credit is the party of the working people." Note that he said working *people*; not working *class*. This could include professionals and millionaire shopkeepers as well as men in overalls, and so, later on, Bennett was able to claim that Social Credit was virtually all things to all men: "The Social Credit government is more conservative than the Conservatives in financial matters, more liberal than the Liberals in terms of providing the nation's highest old age and social assistance benefits, and even more in favour of public ownership than the CCF because of our ferry system and hydro program."

No democratically elected regime lasts forever. Bennett's Social Credit rule died from many causes. The voters got bored with the same aging Cabinet faces; Bennett became less adept at finding new issues and making new promises; corruption showed up and the premier hated to admit the frailties of old supporters; British Columbian society was becoming more urbanized, producing new upwardly mobile classes of which the Social Credit politicos did not take enough notice; the young were restive, the old getting resentful.

Yet the election of 1972, which Wacky Bennett lost, showed that his tried formula was still the best — the rejected loner who rides in to establish himself as tribune of the people and who unites enough interests to create an elective majority in a deeply divided province. Until 1970 there had been no CCF or NDP leader flexible enough for the role. Dave Barrett succeeded where his predecessors had failed by watching Bennett and adapting the old magician's methods to his own program. In a different way from Bennett, he was gifted with an engaging ugliness — multiple chins and a beer belly that appealed to cartoonists and suggested a man not so caught up in socialist dogma as to be indifferent to proletarian pleasures. Yet he had an educated mind, sharpened by Jesuit teachers, and shared Bennett's power to wield either knife or bludgeon with a joking grin. He hectored opponents without mercy but never quite destroyed them, leaving in listeners' minds a feeling that he was not a bad chap after all. He needed that image, since he spread his net wide. He gathered in discontented teachers and academics, upwardly mobile new suburbanites, itinerant workers in the north and thousands of the underprivileged who found themselves swept into the ragbag of welfare as an automated society made them redundant. As Martin Robin remarked, Barrett was "no doctrinaire or ideologue." In 1970, when he became leader of the NDP, he admitted: "In all practical reality we'll be living with a mixed economy for a long, long time."

In other words, Barrett made himself a populist politician like Bennett, appealing to a constituency of varied interests, rather to the left of Social Credit's but overlapping to compete for the drifting voters. Bennett was tired and familiar enough for them to elude him; Barrett was new and vital enough for them to swim into his net. So in 1972 the electoral results were dramatically reversed; Social Credit slumped from thirty-six to ten seats, and the NDP gained an overwhelming majority with thirty-eight seats.

What happened afterwards exemplified the sad old tag that the more things change, the more they remain the same. As every sensitive observer has known for years, British Columbia's economic ills, especially its waves of high unemployment, are due to the predominance of primary industries. The revolutionary solution would be to set up factories to process British Columbia raw materials on the spot and create a stable employment base of secondary industry. Instead, Barrett imitated Bennett with another grand scheme to thrust roads and rails into the north and gouge the land for the last of its raw materials. Before being elected, Barrett had criticized Bennett for divisive and separatist inclinations, and was especially scathing about the links between British Columbia Social Credit and Réal Caouette's Créditistes. But once elected, Barrett defied the national policies of his own party, the NDP, to explore a working alliance with the Parti Québécois.

In some palliative ways Barrett did bring about improvements. He slowed down the sale of farmlands to developers; he improved the legal system; his welfare programs were more compassionate than those of his predecessors. But in distinctively socialist areas, like the take-over of industry, Barrett was notably slow; his threats to socialize the British Columbia Telephone Company never materialized, and acquisition of a couple of pulp mills due for abandonment by their owners compared poorly with Social Credit's take-over of B.C. Electric.

Barrett fought his campaign in 1975 largely on the old Bennett theme of the persecuted loner, this time "fat little Dave," whom his opponents wanted to get rid of, but his defeat was as dramatic as his victory in 1972. When the dust had settled, Social Credit, led by Wacky's son Bill Bennett, was up again to thirty-six seats, the NDP was down to seventeen, the Liberals and Tories almost eliminated, and Barrett defeated in his own Coquitlam constituency, where young, upwardly mobile voters turned the scale. Later on, Barrett did get back into the legislature, but only because a by-election was arranged in Vancouver East, one of the few traditionally solid socialist constituencies in Canada.

Why did Barrett fail after three years? Partly because, while the socialists are strong in British Columbia, they have never come near a majority of the voters, and the marginal electors who gave Barrett his victory in 1972 were easily scared back to Social Credit in 1975 by a drumfire of media warnings of what might happen if socialism gained a lockhold on the province. But Barrett himself was as much to blame in failing to respond to the feelings of his varied constituency. He co-operated with Minister of Education Eileen Dailly to aggravate university and schoolteachers, school boards and parents by erratic budgeting based on untested educational theories rather than real need. He angered everyone except the recipients by doubling MLAs' salaries and raising his own to fifty-two thousand dollars, four thousand more than Pierre Trudeau was then receiving. He let his social worker past blind him to the fact that Human Resources Minister Norm Levi's openhanded welfare system was being exploited by thousands of frauds, as well as benefitting thousands of needy people unaided before. Unlike Wacky Bennett in his prime, Barrett neither counted his enemies nor kept his friends, and he fell …

In the last resort, democratic politics depends on the economy. Wacky Bennett was able to rule by gifts for twenty years because throughhout his reign the British Columbia economy expanded. Dave Barrett tried to be a giver in a stagnant economy and failed … The populist politician — unlike the old-style party hack in a world of sharply defined loyalties — depends on a shifting balance of support in a population educated enough to remember promises (even promises of austerity) and to demand their fulfilment. That is the new politics, as men in Ottawa are learning to their cost.

GILEAN DOUGLAS (1900–93)

Gilean Douglas was a newspaper reporter, a copyeditor and, throughout her life, a freelance writer. Born into an affluent family in Toronto, she moved to British Columbia in the late 1930s, leaving behind the "needless complication" of marriages and the conventions of female domestic life. From 1939 to 1947 she lived in a small wilderness cabin in the Cascade mountains, which was only accessible by wading a river or crossing over it in a metal cage on a pulley; and she survived in almost complete isolation there on the produce of her garden and her harvest of the wild. In *Silence is My Homeland* she describes with ecstasy the moment when she was fishing the river and first saw "gazing into [her] face with its deep-set windows" the abandoned miner's cabin that she would claim as her home.

> It was the great moment of my life when I waded the Teal River
> with my packboard on my back and stood at last on my own ground.
> I can never describe the feeling that surged up inside me then ... I
> felt kinship in everything around me, and the long city years of noise
> and faces were just fading photographs.

Douglas wrote two books that describe her hermit's existence and that celebrate her almost mystical communion with the natural world. *River for My Sidewalk* (1953) was published under the male pseudonym of Grant Madison because readers at that time might have questioned the authenticity of a woman surviving alone in the circumstances she describes. More philosophical versions of these experiences appear in *Silence is My Homeland* (1976) from which "The Pilgrimage" is taken. (Note that the break two thirds of the way through this piece is the author's, not the editors'.)

Gilean Douglas eventually made her home on Cortes Island, B.C., where she worked as a weather observer for Environment Canada and continued her writing. Reminiscent of Emily Carr in attitude, Douglas' style of living anticipates by twenty years the popular back-to-the-land movement that emerged in the 1960s, and her books anticipate the work of such writers as Chris Czajkowski who in *Cabin at Singing River* (1991) describes her construction of a log cabin on Lonesome Lake near Bella Coola. Douglas' other publications include *A Protected Place* (1979) and four volumes of poetry.

from SILENCE IS MY HOMELAND
THE PILGRIMAGE

And smale fowles maken melodye,
That slepen al the night with open yë
(So priketh hem nature in hir corages);
Thanne longen folk to goon on pilgrimages.
> — Chaucer

I DO NOT NEED the red squirrels sliding down my roof, the robins uttering plump chirps on the lawn or a hermit thrush whistling by my woodshed to wake me on a June morning. When the heights of Evergreen [Mountain] are still dark outside my window and the earth is silent in sleep, I am out in the vegetable patch hoeing, weeding and transplanting. This is one of the loveliest times of day. The air is cool and fragrant and that holy feeling of communion with the soil fills me completely. Such an exultancy wells up in me as I walk among my growing things! It is second — and by only a small margin — to that terrible joy I feel in the creation of a piece of writing. Here, in my gardens, I have not given birth myself but have only assisted in the delivery room. Yet the two experiences are so closely bound that it seems that one could not have come into existence without the other.

I put more stakes in for the tomatoes and see that the pea vines are bearing up under their load. There will be lettuce, radishes, onions and small raw carrots for lunch, with swiss chard and potatoes for dinner. Turnip and beet tops provide variety, while soon the pea pods will be bursting with fullness and the bush beans will be long and tender as well as green. Achillea, scarlet phlox and polemonium make the borders of my useful plots patriotic and ornamental. The flower pot stumps sing clearly in red, white, blue and yellow, and the beds are filled with the blossoms of spring and early summer together with the buds of July. The pocket-handkerchief lawn is green and soft, with red and yellow salmonberries hanging deliciously over it. My heart is so happy that surely it also must burst into flower!

Very early on these mornings the light comes "forth with pilgrim steps, in amice grey," and even the highest trees on the mountain are still in shadow. Then rosy little clouds come drifting over Evergreen, and the sun begins to creep down the tall trunks, lower and lower until it strikes the topmost branches of Home Wood and slides goldenly to the mossy ground. The cabin and its garden are still in shade, but the river is sparkling with sun. Bushes are dew spangled and the fresh, earthy smell is like the very scent of heaven. Why do we build cathedrals of brick and stone when there are hills, woods and rivers where we can worship so much more simply and beautifully? How far we have come from that divine simplicity taught by Christ! He went away from cities into the solitude of the mountains and he preached beside the sea. To us a tree is so much timber, a river so much power and a hill — well, in a hill there may be gold.

When I was a child, I lay on the summer grass looking up at the big, white clouds and imagining that they were the towers and turrets of heaven. How simple everything was in those days! Now, for me, it is simple once again, after long years of needless complication. I know this: there has been thanksgiving in my heart every hour of every day since I came to this place. Here I have found faith, courage, truth and such beauty that even if there is no heaven after all, in the clouds or above them, yet I shall have walked its paths and sat beside its streams.

Now the sun is stretching long fingers across the knoll to touch my writing chair and table there — both built from old chopping blocks and painted green — and I know that I must bathe, breakfast and do house and woodshed chores, which are no chores really, but merely part of the great pleasure of living in this place — or of just living. Mr. and Mrs. Robin are listening for worms nearby and the dawn chorus is in full voice when I turn to go back to the cabin. Scales, arpeggios and trills cascade down from the trees as warbler, thrush, wren, Say's phoebe and blackheaded grosbeak pour out silver melody to flow upon golden sunlight. The robins join them and then, shrill with envy, jay, woodpecker and kingfisher go shrieking across the clearing. In the pauses the crystal notes of the water ouzel rise up from the river accompanied by the wren's own liquid, rushing song. Bees stir sleepily in blossoms and hummingbirds hover above the window boxes. It will be difficult to leave all this, even for a little pilgrimage to my neighbour's.

My neighbour is Bill, an old prospector with "a certain jollity of mind pickled in the scorn of fortune," who has roamed these mountains or others like them for over seventy years. Some of his tales are taller than he — and he is well over six feet still, only a little bowed by years and many packboard loads — but all of them are told with such dry humour and with such twinkling of blue eyes in a brown parchment face, that they are irresistible. Bill, praise be, will always "want that glib and oily art, to speak and purpose not." He knows that his stories are stretched to snapping point — and he knows that I know it. This is half the fun of the whole thing, but his herbal lore is sound. I can testify to that after using the young shoots of yellow arum as a spring tonic, the grated root stalks of false solomon's seal (wild onion does just as well) as a poultice and Oregon grape roots for a stomach upset.

Pansy, arabis, iberis, alyssum, armeria, aubrietia, helianthemum, lobelia, gentian,

God made a little gentian;
It tried to be a rose
And failed, and all the summer laughed,

ice plant, tunica and verbena are jewelling the rock gardens, and my wildflower plot is blooming joyfully as I go down to the Teal with my lunch and a few gifts for Bill in my knapsack. The water is still high — too high for wading — so I swing out on the cage with a breeze of my own making in my face and the roar of the river below me. I doubt if any visitor will ever forget that cage, especially the ones who arrive by train in the middle of the night and have to walk miles along the railroad track and then across and down a mountain by bush trails. At the end of that arduous journey they find a homemade ladder rising fifteen feet up into the air with a frail platform on top where the cage swings on a thick wire rope attached to a big hemlock.

The ladder wobbles a bit and the platform distinctly moves, while the river roars below with what might pass anywhere for savagery. There is only one small lantern to push back the darkness, and it seems that we are going to launch ourselves into a black void on three unsubstantial boards. My guest climbs on, I unfasten the hook and follow and then we are rushing through the night as though we were riding the wind. In a moment the sound of the river is behind us and we are pulling over small willows up to the home landing with our lantern swinging from the prow. That trip is something to be remembered, especially when the rivers are in flood and there seems to be no sound in all the world but that of thundering water.

But by daylight it is a bright, familiar thing and I find it very pleasant this June morning to idle slowly across, stopping every now and then to look up and down the Teal. It is the same scene, yet never the same. Now coral honeysuckle flashes its bright trumpets from between the huge leaves of broadleaf maple on the opposite shore, a sharp-shinned hawk drifts lazily overhead and from somewhere hidden comes the spiralling song of the olive-backed thrush. That sound reminds me of Maestro. Maestro is a

Sierra hermit thrush who sings outside my bedroom window each dawn and dusk from May until September. Yes, even in September he essays a few pathetic notes, a stammering travesty of his full, rich song of summer. There are a great many hermit thrushes nesting near my cabin, but Maestro is the most glorious singer of them all. One of his relatives sounds like a rummage sale, he is always in such a hurry to finish; another is off key; still another gives the effect of having a wee bottle under his wing.

But with Maestro each note is rounded, each song complete. He is an artist. He is also, I believe, somewhat of an albino for his thrush markings are barely visible, and his chest is a much paler grey than that of the usual Sierra hermit. When his throat puffs out with singing, it is almost white. But his eye is a roving dark one, and he is very plump and trim in his brown morning coat, which seems to have become a bit green as to back and slightly rusty as to tail — from wear, no doubt. We have long conversations together, although I believe he is almost ready to give me up as a singing pupil. I am no credit to him, certainly, and when he hides "his head under his wing,/Poor thing," he probably has horrible dreams of my roving the woods, emitting those ear-revolting discords that I think are his beautiful song. But I *have* mastered his call note and now he gives it night and morning — and occasionally through the day — until I answer. I have also acquired the "weet" with which he talks to himself and his cronies, but his "snore" — in broad daylight with his eyes wide open! — is beyond me.

One of Maestro's rackety relatives opens up as I walk away from the ladder northward toward Fireweed with alder, aspen, willow and cottonwood all around me and berry bushes brushing against my thighs. Fern and foamflowers mingle, rather aloofly, with the unsociable devil's club, while the delicate twinflower and miner's lettuce clamber over logs or picture themselves against the smooth green of moss. Now there are maples and young conifers and then an open, park-like space with hemlock, fir and cedar standing straight and tall within green space and quietness. The sunlight, slanting through the tree trunks on to mossy ground so beautifully clear of underbrush, has the colour of tokay and the air, it's full and fragrant sweetness. Water once came through here in spring and fall, so logs were laid down many years ago, which are welcome even now because of the swampiness of those seasons.

At the far side of this enclosure wrens are bustling about and a brown creeper is insect hunting. A red-eyed vireo — that not very solemn "preacher bird" — flings leisured melody across yellow avens and blue brookline. A great wild rosebush, nearly six feet tall, is the lovely signpost at the intersection of Main Street and Swamp Road. I have been following the former

— so called because it is one of the main trails up over Fireweed mountain to the railroad, crossing Village Road on the way — but it is by the latter that I shall probably come home. Swamp Road and Timber Trail duplicate Mountain and Home Wood trails on the other side of the Teal, running, as they do, west to the village and east toward a tiny railroad community six miles beyond Bill's cabin. His house stands almost at the intersection of Swamp Road and Cougar Trail, which skirts the eastern end of Cougar mountain and runs through the high passes of the Cocoosh country, past Chert Lake and a hill town, to Gold Road.

Trappers, prospectors, travellers and settlers toiled along Cougar Trail and Gold Road in years gone by, and even now these are wide, open ways for the most part, easy to find and follow. Before the railroad came and a recent highway, which runs thirty miles south of Gold Road, they were the east-west, north-south arteries of this mountain land. But, used only by a few hunters and prospectors now, it will not be long before they are overgrown by brush and obstructed by windfalls, with sections of them lost forever in one deep canyon or another.

After its meeting with Swamp Road, Main Street begins its climb, running through heavy timber for a mile or so to where it meets the broad Village Road. This wooded section is at its best in spring and early summer. I remember coming home late one night in early June with the soft light of my lantern falling on false Solomon's seal, twisted stalk, foamflower, a few alum root, starflower, alpine beauty, dwarf cornel, yellow violet, bleeding-heart, crimson salmonberry blossom, white thimbleberry and blackberry flower, the blushing wild currant, white trillium turning to crimson, Oregon grape, red columbine, pink twinflower, blue larkspur and the white bells of black nightshade — all in glorious bloom together. It was an unbelievable sensation to walk through such drifts and pools and hanging gardens of scent and colour, flashing my light here and there to watch them come strangely and impressively out of the soft darkness. That was one night I said, with Faustus:

Stand still, you ever moving spheres of heaven,
That time may cease ...

And also, like him, for my soul's salvation.

Early June prefers the woodlands, but late June comes into its own on the open Village Road and the untimbered upper slopes of Fireweed. It was at this wide trail that the firefighters were able to stop the great flames that swept over the mountain a few years ago, leaving little but skeletons and ash behind. So now the slopes, as I walk east toward Bill's, have nothing living on them that is more than bush tall. But what bushes and what flowers between them! Fireweed shouts with colour on this mid-summer day and my heart shouts too, with joy that I am here to see it. Indian paintbrush, pink fleabane, yellow fennel (which once crowned victorious gladiators), Queen Anne's lace, white daisy, sagebrush, cow parsnip with its lacy leaves, and wild clover — there seems to be no end to the hues and patterns woven through this glorious cloak thrown protectingly across devastated Fireweed. But it is not all shouting here; there are whispers also. Along the dry stream beds, which are such torrents in spring and fall, the delicate bluebell companions the elfin yellow monkey-flower which closes at a touch; maidenhair fern creeps from rock crevices to background blue beardtongue and the white stars of field chickweed; the wild yellow lily nods to the tiny blue florets of speedwell, which the villagers call forget-me-not.

I want to run and sing as I go! I want to fling my arms wide to all this radiance and raise a paean to this golden hour! The sun shines down in noon warmth; the bridal perfume of syringa drifts intoxicatingly by; river, mountain and forest are spread out before me like a promise of heaven "framed in the prodigality of nature." I am drunk — I am quite delirious! It is too much for me or for any man.

The shade of a blue elderberry bush is just the right luncheon spot, as I munch raw vegetables and sourdough bread with cymes of white flowers waving over me and pert western buttercups peering up from below. "Lettuce," says Charles Dudley Warner in his sketch, *My Summer in a Garden,* "is like conversation: it must be fresh and crisp, so sparkling that you scarcely notice the bitter in it," but it is only the elderly who may become bitter. The tang of wild onion and the tonic breath of sage mingle, very suitably, with the flavour of my young, sweet leaves, while the fragrance of wild strawberry proclaims what my dessert will be. The taste of this small red berry is so much sweeter than that of the cultivated fruit, that sugar would be "coals to Newcastle." But it hides so skillfully under its low green leaves that picking becomes a treasure hunt and one devoutly wishes for "a cast-iron back, with a hinge in it."

There is one thing that distinguishes Village Road from most of the other trails I follow: it is the silence; "silence more musical than any song." On Timber, Mountain, Swamp and Home Wood trails and in my little cabin, the sound of running water is steady and insistent until, after a little while, it so weaves itself into the consciousness that you are not aware of its presence unless you wish to be. Yet it is always there. In summer and winter it is a sedate and quiet singing, but in autumn and spring it is a roistering mountain chorus. Yes, whatever I do has the sound of water running through it — until I climb Main Street and hear it grow fainter and fainter below, standing at last on Village Road in a core of silence. I feel suddenly deaf then, as though I were climbing to the peaks or losing altitude in an airplane, and it is several minutes before my ears can adjust themselves enough to distinguish those softer sounds usually hidden under the voices of my rivers. Then the drone of a bee becomes audible, the whirr of a dragonfly, the roll of a pebble, the faraway note of a tree toad and the swift slither of a striped garter snake through last year's leaves.

But the rivers can still be seen. They are grey threads running through green cloth one thousand feet below. Bone mountain, graveyard of another forest fire that is usually hidden behind Cougar, comes into view. A flock of yellow warblers (they share the name of a "wild canary" with the common goldfinch) flies down near a clump of false box, and some Brewer blackbirds go over in the direction of Bill's cherry trees.

These trees are a glorious sight in May — as are also, to a lesser degree, the wild cherry trees that grow near my cabin and on various trails — while down near the village the Oregon crabapple makes spring a delight. The dwarf bilberry grows near the village too and that is where the purple violets, those "deep, blue eyes of springtime," can be found in April with the glorious Pacific dogwood rising white above them. (Actually the flowers of this tree are green-yellow and small; it is the large white flower-bud scales that are so sensational and usually mistaken for the flower itself.) And right now, on this June day, the beautiful evergreen rhododendrons will be growing in the mountains high above the village; rosy banks of them in the dark passes where snow and wind go hurtling through in winter and where, even now, the ground is moist and cold. It is one of nature's many miracles that a conservatory bloom like this should flourish in such surroundings.

Where Cougar Trail crosses Village Road and lunges down the mountain toward Bill's, stonecrop, shrubby cinquefoil and wild mustard make a lovely farewell to the flowers of dry and sunny places before I return to those of the cool woods. I twist swiftly down Cougar Trail, through shade and dappled light where salal grows and the melody of the song sparrow comes sweet and clear. Through a gap in the trees I can see Bill's bachelor cottage ("A cow is better than a woman; a woman uses too much wood") with its red roof, but there is no sign of the owner, so I sit down on a fir stump beside the shining leaves of silver-back and unship my binoculars for a bird hunt. Roughwinged swallows skim high above the cabin and the black caps of a flock of pileolated warblers bob up and down in the little orchard. I have discovered eight different families of the warbler clan in this district, but two of them — orange-crowned and Audubon's — are usually in the higher mountains during the summer. The black-throated grey, MacGillivray, Calaveras and Townsend chirp around my cabin until September, but for the others — pileolated and yellow — I have to come up here. The killdeer plover is not a rare sight down near the village, while on the higher slopes of Fireweed the ravens sometimes get together. Cooper's and the sharp-shinned hawk make life rather miserable for Bill's chickens, and flocks of purple finches occasionally do the same for his fruit trees. The less said the better of that astute robin family who built their nest on a cherry tree limb so that they might have breakfast in bed!

One of the ones that Midas touched,
Who failed to touch us all,
Was that confiding prodigal,
The blissful oriole.

That "fire bird" and "golden robin," Bullock's oriole, has proved here, by keeping down the insect pests in the orchard, that he can be useful as well as decorative. An old grandaddy of a pileolated woodpecker — called "cock o' the woods" — can be seen any day around this clearing, and the Say's phoebe turns up every now and then, while pipits and pine siskins make this a favourite way station in the fall.

"Songs are sung and tales are told, darkness dreams upon the sky" when I set out for home. A full moon is rising over Sable mountain as I leave Bill's clearing and strike into the forest. My path follows a stream bed of ferns and mossy boulders precipitously down to the Teal and then swings directly west just along the bank, where the hungry river is nibbling at the trail. Beyond, the salmonberry brush is higher than my head and I have to find my way through it by the feel of the path under my feet. At the edge of the clearing where there are two old logging cabins, stinging nettles rake across my arm and I stand still, thinking for a moment that I can see the graceful dancers of the ballet Swan Lake move across the moon-flooded clearing toward the glimmering water. The princess of that tale was not the only person who wove nettles into cloth; Europeans and Asiatics have made fine linen from them for centuries. The Indians here wove them into cord and the cord into fishing nets, besides using both roots and leaves as food. I can see tiny tents of the red admiral caterpillar on these leaves and if it were daylight, I am sure that I would find the green caterpillars of the tiger swallowtail on the nearby bitter cherry, embryo Compton tortoiseshell butterflies on the willows and most certainly the misleadingly named saltmarsh caterpillar of the dainty — and equally misnamed — saltmarsh tiger moth.

This night is too lovely to say goodnight in so, with the moonlight full on my face, I slip quietly past some deserted cabins and sit down on a log at the river's edge. As always, the hypnotism of its flowing is like a soft, compelling hand across my eyes and never more so than now when each ripple is enchanted to onyx or to silver, and darkness is a changeling of the moon.

A little way downstream I can see the shadow of the big cedar that was felled for a footbridge and now stretches from bank to bank. A young lad who was placer mining here a few years ago admitted to me that when he crossed it once at high water, he was so scared he "cooned" it along the tree trunk. I can imagine how the river snarled below him, reaching up with clammy, urgent fingers to loosen his grip of the narrow bridge. For the course of the Teal is direct and steep, so at all seasons of the year its voice can be heard — softly in midwinter and midsummer, loudly in fall and spring when the heavy rains and the freshets of melting snow turn it into a brown monster, raging from bank to bank and driving the driftwood before it. Bridges go out then and the growl of rolling boulders can be heard night and day.

The Teal has come seventeen miles to these cabins — from Teal Lake at an altitude of four thousand feet — and has twenty more to go before it merges with the big Mallard River and travels with it to the sea. There is not even a village on its way until it reaches the Mallard — only a few small, grey cabins huddled at intervals along the banks. Tributaries like the Wren flow into it here and there, coming down from the mountains of the Cocoosh and Endahwin Ranges. Accumulation of glacial debris has changed its course somewhat, but for the most part it follows the same channel as in pre-Pliocene times except that during the ages of its life it has cut down deeper and deeper between Fireweed and Cougar so that its bed now is a much narrower one than in, as the Indians say, "old time."

Where the Teal begins the snows lie deep in winter, and the handfuls of people who live at Teal Lake find the white ocean rising to their rooftops and have tunnels instead of paths connecting their houses. Fishermen from outside have almost emptied the lake of fish, but in the river and its tributaries — especially those like the Wren that are fairly inaccessible — rainbow and Dolly Varden trout dart and gleam and it is not difficult to get a good string at almost any time. In Dubh Glas, just outside my cabin, the big steelhead may be found — and caught on salmon eggs. "There is a river in Macedon, and there is also moreover a river at Monmouth … and there is salmons in both." On late afternoon of spring and summer I can see them jumping as dragon or damselflies flit over, but when I go after them with rod and line, they suddenly discover that the bouldered bottom of the pool is much more desirable than the exposed surface. That is when I know with Izaak Walton, that "angling will prove to be so pleasant that it will prove to be, like virtue, a reward in itself." Yet sometimes there are more material rewards also.

The night-scent of earth and the river-scent of water mingle in my nostrils as I walk slowly along my favourite part of Swamp Road: a clear, wide pathway carpeted with moss and leaves and roofed with evergreen and maple branches. Quietness lies here like deep velvet, with only the sound of cool water stirring it. No other large animal seems to be abroad tonight, but now and then a wood rat agitates the bracken. Moonlight filters through the trees, arabesques the forest floor and, where the trail contacts the river, makes pinpricks of argent light on ripple and tiny waterfall.

The way seems unbelievably short and almost before I know it, I am at the Main Street intersection once again. I never come out on the shores of the Teal just at this place without feeling a surge of joy at the sight of my little cabin snugged down between the mountains and the forest. It is so simple and real and lovely. Here is everything I want and more than I ever hoped to have. The green roof, the bark walls, the flowers, the vegetables, the filled woodshed — every tree, bush and stone, every foot of earth is dear to me. Inside, the words of friends fill my bookshelves, and my companion, fire, will come when I call him. There is no harsh speech, no lies, no bitterness anywhere; nothing but generosity, beauty and peace. I never knew before the real meaning of the word "home."

Now the cabin is just a dark outline silhouetted by the moon, but it is there and it is mine. Swiftly I climb the platform to the cage and launch myself out over the river. In a few moments I am mounting the stone steps by the rock garden and walking along the path toward my front door. Whenever I come back, even after only a few hours' absence, I want to touch each flower and each tree I pass, to tell them something of my joy because I am here with them again. But I think they know it. There is no lamplight to welcome me now, but there is the moon to give a lovelier glow. There are no human voices to call to me, but there is the river's music and the night wind in the trees and all the faint stirrings of woodsy things. Human voices quarrel and say ugly words; human light is not always kind. When I have come back to people, I have expected much and been disappointed or, not knowing what to expect, I have dreaded the return. But here all is rooted in beauty and in peace and there is surety everywhere. This is home.

[Source of quotations: *And smale fowles maken melodye* — Chaucer, *The Canterbury Tales; ... forth with pilgrim steps, in amice grey* — Milton, *Paradise Regained; ... a certain jollity of mind* — David Grayson, *Adventures in Solitude; ... want that glib and oily art* — Shakespeare, *King Richard III; God made a little gentian* — Emily Dickinson, "Fringed gentian"; ... *his head under his wing* — Anonymous, "The North Wind Doth Blow"; *Stand still, you ever moving spheres of heaven* — Marlowe, *The Tragedy of Dr. Faustus; ... framed in the prodigality of nature* — Shakespeare, *King Lear; ... a cast-iron back, with a hinge in it* — Charles Dudley Warner, *My Summer in a Garden; ... silence more musical than any song* — Christina Rosetti, "Rest"; ... *deep, blue eyes of springtime* — Heine, "*Die Blauen Frühlingsaugen*"; *One of the ones that Midas touched* — Emily Dickinson, "The Oriole"; *Songs are sung and tales are told* — Gilean Douglas, "Night Song"; *There is a river in Macedon* — Shakespeare, *King Henry V; ... angling will prove to be so pleasant* — Izaak Walton, *The Compleat Angler*].

ARTHUR ERICKSON (1924–)

The first Canadian architect to be widely known internationally, Arthur Erickson was born and educated in Vancouver but achieved world renown for buildings he designed for his native city. In 1953, after army service in Asia and a period of travel in Europe, he opened a private practice in Vancouver in partnership with Geoffrey Massey. It was their 1963 design for Simon Fraser University on the summit of Burnaby mountain that brought Erickson international attention, and a series of major commissions followed. In Vancouver they include the MacMillan Bloedel office tower (1969), the Museum of Anthropology at UBC (1973), and the Law Courts and Robson Square complex (1971-77). Elsewhere, Erickson's significant public projects include Roy Thompson Hall in Toronto (1982), the Canadian Embassy in Washington, D.C. (1988), as well as numerous commissions in middle eastern countries and Japan.

The popularity of Erickson's architecture derives to a great extent from his ability to create, out of simple materials, places of great drama that arise naturally from their specific setting. It also derives from a connection to what is usable from ancient cultures. At Simon Fraser University, advanced studies and aspiration are embodied in the mountain-top setting, but also in the rise of steps and the pyramid motif inside the academic quadrangle; at the same time the central mall under glass creates a very contemporary place for community on the campus. Erickson has been strongly influenced by west coast First Nations architecture, especially evident in the geometric lines of the courthouse building and the Museum of Anthropology. The latter is built in longhouse fashion on Point Grey and looks out on a vista of beach, water and sky. Erickson believes strongly that climate determines culture and arranged the three rooms in the great hall of the museum to reflect the increasingly symbolic forms of carving as one moves from the southern to the northern tribes and towards the decreasing amount of warmth and light. Erickson's theory is that the fully-rounded natural figures of animals and humans released from wood by the Salish carvers give way to the more symbolic masks of the Kwakwak'wakw (Kwakiutl), and then to the unpainted poles of the Haida and Tsimshian where the form of the tree still dominates and the carving is abstract, almost mystical. Many commentators argue that Erickson's best work is on the West Coast and deals with elemental issues of landscape and climate, especially the lack of strong light.

Erickson's ideas continue to be as dramatic as his buildings. In a May 1999 interview in *Two Chairs*, he reflects on cities and communities of the future. "In 2020 there will be no more countries," he suggests. "Countries are becoming an artifact ... They were necessary for cultural and defense reasons, that sort of thing, but in the age we're going into it isn't necessary. So we will have city-states. I've always believed that history is going backwards. When we come to 2000 we'll go back to 1000."

[The 1964 interview that follows was found in a volume of typescripts at UBC titled "Speeches by Arthur Erickson." Attempts to locate the interviewer, identified simply as "me," have not been successful. The interview is in very rough format and labelled "extra" (probably a photocopy of a carbon copy); some words and lines at the bottom of the pages are indecipherable. Nonetheless, this particular interview was chosen for this volume because it brings together so many of the ideas that repeat themselves in the speeches and interviews Erickson has given over the years and that the architect himself still holds as central to his thought.]

NOTES FROM AN INTERVIEW WITH ARTHUR ERICKSON, ARCHITECT, JANUARY 16, 1964

AE: I have a favourite theory. In B.C., as pioneers, we didn't make a significant contribution until a few years ago. As a matter of fact we are the first in Canada to demonstrate contemporary housing. This was about fifteen years ago — just after the war. The rest of Canada was a way behind and there was an article in *Canadian Art* by Bob Hubbard which was written — after he had visited the West Coast — just about 1952-53 or 53-54. It was called "Climate for the Arts." Suddenly B.C. did have this fresh spirit — both in painting, architecture, poetry — all these things — and it was very much on top of the heap at that time — as far as Canada was concerned. There was a time lag in which the rest of Canada, in a sense, caught up, then really took over, because I think one thing that characterizes what we do — whether it is architecture, painting, or anything else — is a hangover of being pioneers, and that is innovation. We had no traditions, nothing tying us down, no ancient architecture, no tradition of building materials that stopped us from making a fresh and interesting experiment at that time. I think this spirit still exists here to a certain extent.

As with the pioneer, you do tackle your new environment with fresh eyes, you are able to innovate, but I think also that when you are asked to make your first spurt, you become a tired old homesteader. I think this happened in B.C. The place settled too quickly. A type of house was built like the post and beam which has been repeated and repeated. This was actually a good solution for the small house. But it was never — and this is the interesting thing — it was never really developed into a fine building type. And I would say that is somewhat characteristic of B.C. — that you don't have the maturity, at least a maturity isn't reached. Post and beam was experimented with but it was never refined. Never perfected.

Everyone who came here had to deal with unusual conditions. There were siting problems. You tried to put up a traditional house, but then you found you had to do something else with underpinnings and therefore the whole contractor's field involved more innovation. And, I think, one of a higher standard than perhaps anywhere else in Canada. I was amazed going up into Capilano Highlands, no matter how awful you think the houses are or out at Bay View, the standard is quite extraordinary. When compared to contractors' houses elsewhere. Elsewhere in Canada. Elsewhere in the States on the West Coast.

There is a kind of vernacular here that comes from the challenge of using local materials and settings.

We confuse innovation and experiment with the design. We don't take it as far as we can — but go on to something else.

I think at that time there was a lot of courage in British Columbia in all the arts — architecture included — which does not exist now. Right at the moment, one of my greatest contentions is the lack of courage in B.C. Looking at the history of the city, I am surprised how few people of vision or people of courage have made their mark here. We seemed to be cursed with timidity. And it makes me mad. For instance, the man who built Lions Gate Bridge, A. J. T. Taylor, was not a Canadian. The people who put the C.P.R. into this area were from elsewhere. The people who created Stanley Park ... had nothing to do with the resident population.

Me [Interviewer]: What you are saying is that outside of some superficial things, we are still living on the foresight of other people?

AE: Yes ... What can develop is a spirit that pervades everything. I think it existed when B.C. was first beginning. I think now it exists in Quebec, maybe brutally, and in Ontario. And I think it is coming back here. Now ... the degrading of the profession of architecture has had a lot to do with the lack of spirit here lately. It is a disrespect of professionalism. It has been said lately that an architect is no better than a contractor — there is no difference between an engineer and an architect. They will try to get the cheapest thing possible without respecting, basically, that you have a knowledge at their disposal; that you are a professional. We should have the same respect as a doctor has.

I think we are cursed with the do-it-yourself magazines, which is the curse of Western America. I think the home should express the way a person lives, but I think that the creativity which goes into making furniture and things like that, is the wrong way. You should walk into a home and say: this home has character. It represents an attitude toward life that these people have made in it. But not that this is a piece of furniture that the owner made himself — and he is not really a carpenter. This, unfortunately to me, is common to the West Coast. It is all through California right up to here. Not on the East Coast. And I think that this again might be partially due to the wave of settlement across the continent. The people who came to the West Coast were not professionals. They stayed in Quebec, in Montreal, in Toronto, if you will. You didn't find architects immigrating out here in the very beginning. The people who were here had to solve their problems. The do-it-yourself person is the pioneer. He had to do it himself. Therefore I think we have the values of the pioneer because the arts were late in coming across the continent — painting and music are still a little suspect. The painter isn't considered as important as the plumber. In Mexico, the painter is an extremely important person and often a Mexican would forego plumbing to have a painting.

Me: Jessup says we are still in our adolescence.

AE: Don't forget that sometimes when there are signs of youth there is also disintegration of old age. I am afraid — and this is common to North America and more specifically in the West — that the important things are given the most unimportant places. The fact that the houses are heated and that the plumbing works and the roof doesn't leak is the most important thing in our lives. But to some people there are other things much more important than these things.

Me: But can you marry aesthetics with the necessaries — like a roof which will keep out three inches of rain such as we had last night?

AE: It is a confusion of fundamentals. The Sicilian would consider certainly that the roof being watertight was essential — but just as important is the place of his native image. It is not something he brings in afterwards to decorate the house. Unfortunately, what happens is that most of the arts including architecture are thought of as decoration. It is not thought of as absolutely fundamental.

Me: In some ways, architecture is thought of as luxury?

AE: Yes, and this is a completely ass-backwards situation.

Me: Now ... does all this apply to office buildings and plants?

AE: Certainly, because ... Mind you architects suffer here from lack of training and experience and challenge that creates good architecture. There is a more competitive situation in the East. Certainly they have a much greater sense of becoming better architects. There just isn't the challenge here in this respect. But whatever it is, factory or office building, you are providing an environment of some kind. I feel this is the most important thing in our lives. We are so influenced by our environment, so conditioned by it, and we are always creating it.

Look at San Francisco which is a much older city than ours. The strongest thing is a pattern of thought, a pattern of acting, a way of thinking, what you have is very difficult to spell out. For instance, I am very conscious when I go east of how different my thinking is from theirs.

Me: What is the reaction of the people listening?

AE: Very responsive, but I find also that they, with their experience, consider things more carefully — that I would perhaps be impatient of a problem, but I am sure that I see the problem freshly and that my ideas are valid. Therefore the response to them is good. I also find that there too is a lack of courage, but it comes from not being able to see a problem freshly — almost being burdened.

Me: You mean they are seeing things in a more limestone-fronted manner?

AE: In modern terms.

Me: Are you angry?

AE: Consistently.

Me: Is there a pride in the city?

AE: No … I don't think people take pride in this city. I think this is one of the reasons people don't give money to the city or to the university beyond a token few, who do more than their share.

Me: Do you think that people live here purely because of the easier climate, being more or less opportunists — not putting anything back into the city?

AE: Yes. I think this still persists.

Me: Is this then a reason for a sense of moral laxity in politics, a sense of letting things slide by just because we haven't much interest and are only using the place to live nicely?

AE: Yes. And I think this is the reason why we can't have a well-run Grey Cup parade without hoodlums and that sort of thing — because if you have a shoddy place it is treated shabbily and if you have a good-looking place it is treated well. This has been proven time and time again.

Me: There was a news story on that. There were one-hundred thousand people who attended the Rose Bowl Parade, New Year's Day, in Pasadena. They milled all over the downtown for two nights. The police reported not one case of hoodlumism.

AE: People expect something that is beautiful. For instance, you don't have a defacement of Stanley Park.

Me: What are some of the problems of building in B.C.?

AE: Unskilled labour. You just can't get skilled labour to do anything. I don't think there is a climatic problem whatsoever. But I think there is in aesthetic terms. The main problem is light. Natural light. With the overcast skies. It has not been answered in architectural terms. It needs a rich profile and this has not been answered. And also, we need to get light into our buildings, both light and shadow. It is a drab, depressing light. The main problem is to use the rain, and take advantage of it as is done in

Japan. Japanese architecture makes the rain beautiful. But no one else's solution is adequate for this. An architect always imagines his building in sunlight and casting shadows, but here there aren't strong shadows, no highlights. In a sunny climate you are dealing with a white ground and a dark sky. It is the reverse here. You have a dark ground and a white sky. This means you see things in silhouette, without highlight, and psychologically it can be unpleasant. One is in a dark area and the light is above as at sunset — a melancholy feeling. This is the situation we live in most of the time. Somehow we have to overcome this. Somehow we have to replace it not with lamps and artificial sunlight. The problem is to try to live with it. The Filberg House was the one where I did try to experiment with the problem of light.

The most important thing is the creation of harmony. The role of the architect is to bring the human into harmony with the environment. You have to work with the idea of harmony right from the beginning. If you have a depressing outlook, sky, etc. how do you make this pleasant. This is a very real thing we have to do. How to let one enjoy this landscape. I think B.C. is one of the blackest places on earth. Black trees. Black mountains. The minute you go to California, they are not black. The redwoods are bright green. Other countries are a different green entirely. Black-grey and black-green — how to make one see the softness and subtlety of the colour. I remember when I flew back from Japan — Japan makes you very conscious of colour, because it never uses colour — they use it only for festivals and things like that — and somehow you become conscious of all the subtle gradations in colours. In a garden, there will be no flowers and you see all the differences of green and how they have been used. Very often in their gardens they cut them off because it is jarring. The flowers they treat as a kind of festival event. For instance, they will have in a garden, which is all green, one pool of iris which come out only once a year. Or perhaps an area of cherry trees which are out once a year. Everything is kept in harmony. And I noticed when I returned here and I was flying over the country, it was a beautiful day of sunlight — and then for a week afterwards when I was driving up-Island, how brilliant the greens are in Japan and what a rich and splendid variety they have of greens in their foliage and how very different our greens are. But how beautiful they were in a different way, in a soft way. They are all greyed here. Everything is greyed. Now, if we could build so that people began to see these lights and colours and the softness of them, and understand their own response to them, they would realize the marvels of the environment we live in. This question of environment ... people hate to walk out of doors and be spat on by rain. It is a kind of affront. I think there is an antagonism to the environment. I know a psychiatrist who felt in B.C. that there was a real, deep-seated hate of nature and therefore we treat it violently in the way we clear and the way we build. We go out of our way not to create this harmony.

The Indian village is a wonderful example of adaptation to an environment. Their livelihood came from the sea and the forest. They had plenty to eat and therefore didn't have to organize into any greater cultural unit than the village. The village was placed on the dividing line between the forest and the sea. Nothing was done to the forest. They built along the beach. The village was strung in perfect juxtaposition between these two environments which gave them their livelihood. This is harmonious positioning in the strongest sense. The beach gave a shape to the village. On it they built their magnificent houses ... I must say the Haida House at UBC is the one great piece of architecture in B.C. A copy built by Bill Reid. It has everything that great architecture has — that is, it takes common material at hand and fuses it with spirit and uses it with skill and inspires you. How simple the idea of the house is ... the size of the great timbers and how beautifully they are put together. Then, for the special things, because they were involved with the animals and fish, the other animate creatures become deified. They decorated the poles with these — and the pole was nothing but a cedar tree raised on the beach. It stood just as a cedar tree against the backdrop of cedars, but painted in the colours that they saw on the backs of the sea ducks or the whales — the dark browns, the brilliant whites. The cedar tree decorated this way was a harmonizing of the forest and the sea. Everything that was in the forest, everything that was in the sea, became part of the village. This was a primitive village and a simple society — but our job of much greater complexity is eventually to do this. We have to come to terms with our environment. In the meantime we are destroying it. We have no respect for it. And this is the tragic thing. The fact that we are creating parking lots in Stanley Park when really what we should be doing is taking the cars out altogether and using some kind of public transport or horse and buggy and not allowing people to drive through — letting it become more primitive. I think the climate has a tremendous influence on our minds. You can almost pinpoint the different characteristics of the peoples of the world by the kind of climate they live in and I find I respond very quickly to a climate change. My whole attitude changes. I remember when I was in Syria in the desert, finding that this whole country was so completely different and I changed. I became conscious of attitudes within me I never knew before. I became suddenly more sensitive to my senses there — odours, colours, stimulated my senses. Here there is the smell of wetness and it is hard to differentiate between odours. And this is the same in Japan. The main odour in Japan is sour — almost like sewage, but not quite the same. In the desert you begin to see forms very clearly and your mind becomes sharper to form. The sunlight plays on shapes and you become more conscious of form. There is a more heightened sense of life. It is more stimulating and it is celebrated. Here the greyness penetrates right through our lives. The people are rather lethargic, spiritless. But where there is a lack of spirit, there is a great sense of poetry. In painting, architecture and literature the poetic sense is stronger. The forms and structures are not as important as the moods and the poetic inference of the forms.

Me: What do you think of the women in Vancouver?

AE: They are rather fashionless. I don't think they take advantage of their beauty. I think in general they are handsome, but they look dowdy and ill-kempt as though they just got out of bed. The men appear to lack adventure in their minds. I think people here are indifferent to morality. It is a very amoral place and it is a kind of climate that sponsors amorality and [in reaction to this, on the other side,] you have a lot of prudishness. People here are easygoing. Very casual. Very lax in maintaining social responsibilities. Their friendships are not deep but they are very friendly. The Swedish people are the same. In the winter they hibernate. I think the same thing happens here.

Me: That is a summation of your students?

AE: I find the same thing.

AE: (speaking of civic pride) I think there is an artificial pride here. People are proud of their mountains, proud of the site and certainly this is the most beautiful site of any city besides Rio. You can't really be proud of something that nature has done, you have to be proud of what you have done and we have not done justice yet. I intend to stay because the potential is fantastic and because there are so few places left in the world with this emergent aspect.

Me: What do you see in Simon Fraser [University]?

AE: We haven't had time to develop the initial ideas. We were thrown almost from a cartoon into working drawings without going into a lot of soul-searching as to how this should evolve. Therefore I think we lost a lot. We haven't had time for the refinement, the development. It is a monumental scheme. It is going to be the one monumental thing that people in Vancouver will see. They have never seen anything like it and probably never will again. It will have great spaces which I felt were important — in scale to the landscape and the site. It will unfortunately be rough, brutal, and I feel that it is better to be rough and brutal in the materials and in the way it is built, rather than to pretend refinements, when there hasn't been time to apply these. It will be as I think architecture should be in this city — down to earth, rank, open, no nonsense, applying itself with as much harmony as possible to its setting and to the climate and within itself — and also something that takes the human out of his ordinary, human fireside existence. Ennobles him, lifts him.

ERIC NICOL (1919–)

Three times the recipient of the Stephen Leacock Medal for Humour, Eric Nicol has been one of Canada's most popular humorists. He was born and raised in Kingston, Ontario, but he attended the University of British Columbia and, after three years service in the Royal Canadian Air Force, he made his home in Vancouver. He worked there as a radio and television scriptwriter and as a syndicated columnist for the *Vancouver Daily Province*. Most of Nicol's more than thirty books consist of pieces collected from his newspaper columns. His sketches usually treat everyday domestic concerns — pets, houseplants, cars, shopping, house parties — but also include irreverent reflections on political and national topics such as those reprinted here from *Still a Nicol* (1972). There has always been a strong regional component to his work, especially in his plays which usually find their subject matter and their audience in the lower mainland area of British Columbia. His most successful play, for example, *Like Father Like Fun* (1967), which also had a Broadway run, satirizes some of the province's leading lumber barons; *Ma!* (1981), on the other hand, is a play about the famous newspaperwoman from Lillooet, known as Ma Murray. *The Clam Made a Face* (1972) was written for a young audience and evokes British Columbia native lore. Nicol's writing is always light and humorous, meant to be read with a grain of salt. The immense popularity of his work is an index to the tastes and interests of his time and today sometimes reveals unacceptable attitudes to race, gender and sexuality. While Nicol is often referred to as a satirist, he is probably more accurately described as a punster and a gag writer because his work contains no sustained comic vision.

FIRST PROVINCE ON THE LEFT

ALTHOUGH VANCOUVER, British Columbia, is more than sixty years old and its population is nudging the half-million mark, many strangers, including some Eastern Canadians, still don't know exactly where it is. Responsible for this geographical vagueness are several false impressions:

for instance, the common belief that British Columbia is a steaming colony in the heart of the South American jungle. Something about the name, British Columbia, apparently suggests a tattered Union Jack fluttering over a few square miles of monkeys and malaria.

As a result of this loose notion about our latitude, those of us who visit other lands and there mention that we are natives of British Columbia often draw surprised comment on our mastery of the English tongue, and on our ability to handle a knife and fork without injury to ourselves or to others, although we never entirely dispel our hosts' suspicion that we may be concealing a blowgun, or carrying a shrunken human head in our coat pocket.

Another popular misconception about Vancouver's location is that it is on Vancouver Island. In Toronto, Montreal and throughout the United States there are small but well-organized groups who insist that the logical place for Vancouver is on Vancouver Island and who are liable to turn ugly if you try to prove otherwise. Actually, of course, they are confusing Vancouver with Victoria, the capital of the province, thereby annoying the citizens of Victoria, who resent being associated with the continent of North America.

Victoria, it may be noted incidentally, has gained considerable celebrity as "a little bit of Old England." When a British colonel anywhere in the world is wounded or feels death at hand, unerring instinct leads him eventually to the windswept waste of whitening flannel that is Victoria, and there, after snorting defiance through the local press, he passes on.

Thirdly, there are a few persons who fail to distinguish Vancouver, B.C., from Vancouver, Washington, which sits just below the border and refuses to go away. And lastly, some people haven't the faintest idea where Vancouver may be, other than perhaps a forest-bound clearing periodically traversed by Indians and Nelson Eddy singing excerpts from "Rose Marie."

The truth is, of course, that Vancouver lies on the mainland, at the foot of the snow-tipped coastal range, between Burrard Inlet and the mighty Fraser River. You can't miss it, the first province on the left.

In 1946 Vancouver celebrated her Diamond Jubilee, enjoying a bumper crop of American tourists, a hardy staple which comes up every year. Many Vancouver residents insisted that the house they were renting was obviously more than sixty years old, failing to realize that, although the city wasn't incorporated until 1886, there was a shack town here for some time before that, known variously as Hastings, Gastown and Granville. Vancouver was so tough in those days she *had* to keep changing her name.

Vancouver became so excited about being incorporated that she got overheated and burned down. But the hardy pioneers merely spat on their hands, a questionable habit, and built her up again. This discouraged her so thoroughly that she has never tried to burn down since.

The original settlers around Vancouver were, of course, the coastal Indians, who were great canoe-makers and who thought nothing of paddling hundreds of miles to visit another tribe. The Indians were interrupted in these cheerful pursuits by the arrival of the Spanish explorers, who sailed in and planted the flag of Spain, only to have the English come right along behind and dig it up. For, just as the Spanish were leaving, Captain George Vancouver rowed in triumphantly. (There is no historical corroboration of the story that, as he passed the Spaniards' ships, Captain Vancouver yelled over: "How many miles do you get to the galleon?")

Anyhow, Captain Vancouver, as the sharp students in the front row have already guessed, was the man after whom Vancouver was named. Yet, at the time, Vancouver thought he was barquing up the wrong inlet until he saw the Indians' welcoming committee standing on the shore. Approaching the Indians in his yawl, Vancouver hailed them:

"I am Captain Vancouver. I come in my yawl."

"How yawl," drawled the Indians, who belonged to the southern tribes. "Have you any cheap beads or worthless bits of glass you'd care to trade for these priceless furs?"

"Now that you mention it," chuckled Vancouver, "I have."

Thus the morning was filled with gay chatter and one-sided trading. Captain Vancouver, well-satisfied with the site of the city that was to be named after him, sailed away in his gallant little *H.M.S. Discovery,* the prow of which was already dinted from repeated attempts to find the North-West Passage.

Some years later the Hudson's Bay Company opened a trading post near Vancouver, and soon the traders were busy breaking glass up into worthless bits and destringing cheap beads. Most of the early trading was done at Victoria, which was a lot quieter than Vancouver, where people like Alex McKenzie and Simon Fraser kept bursting out of the bush every few years expecting to be congratulated and put up for the night.

The next big moment in Vancouver's life was the Gold Rush. We may as well face it — a good many of Vancouver's early lovers were interested in her for her money. This was the period of building and lawlessness, when men worked the mines and women worked the miners. Bands of ruffians roamed the streets, until one day Queen Victoria made the whole place into a crown colony, giving Vancouver a respectability from which the city has never recovered.

Shortly afterward the gleaming rails of the Canadian Pacific Railway came down the Fraser Valley, to stop short at Port Moody, about fifteen miles east of Vancouver. The C.P.R. had it on good authority that Port Moody was where the ocean began, and saw no point in taking its locomotives any farther (they would get soaking wet for one thing). While Port Moody was still thumbing its nose at Vancouver (they never had got along very well), a champion, Van Horne, arose to persuade the company to extend the line to Vancouver, the City with a Future. Impressed with the personality of this virile town, which had just burned itself down (Port Moody had never burned *itself* down — a pretty stuffy place), the C.P.R. extended its line. It was a gay and stirring sight as the first transcontinental train puffed into the station, covered with people and freight rates.

The rest of the story is one of phenomenal growth, of Vancouver's rise to the position of third largest city in Canada. The largest and second largest are two places called Montreal and Toronto, situated inland. There is a legend that when the good people of Toronto die they go to Vancouver. "Retiring to the West Coast," they call it, to this spawn of mountain and sea, home of the world's heaviest dew — our Vancouver.

EARTHQUAKES I HAVE KNOWN

IN VANCOUVER, at 10:14 a.m. on the sunny Sunday morning of June 23, 1946, I was lying in bed musing on the possibility of remaining there indefinitely, when suddenly the air was filled with a sighing sound, a peculiar whoosh of wind, accompanied by a low rumbling that was felt rather than heard. Father, I thought, is having another bilious attack.

Jumping out of bed I was surprised to find the floor quivering under my feet, then see a nearby picture of two leering Scotties swing out from the wall as if to bite me. I quickly realized that there was more than father's dyspepsia behind this: it was an earthquake. Naturally, I was shaken. I kept my head, however; after I and the other members of the family had knocked one another down several times in unco-ordinated flight, I called a halt and got us all running in the same direction — into a clothes closet, unfortunately. Since the 'quake had lasted only twenty seconds, much of this activity was unnecessary, as we realized later, and we all came out of the closet pretty sheepishly.

We joined the crowds of neighbours, mostly in night attire, who had flocked into their back yards to reveal the interesting fact that nobody in our block was at church or had any intention of going to church. The moment I ran out in the back garden I could see there was great excitement. At first I thought this was because of the earthquake, then I realized that in such emergencies one pays the penalty for sleeping without one's pajama pants, and I ran back into the house.

I returned in time to see the old gentleman who lives next door, and who is quite deaf, potter out in his slippers wanting to know what had happened.

"It was an earthquake," we shouted, happy to inform someone of the event.

"Felt like an earthquake," shouted the old man.

"It was an earthquake," we blared back.

"Could have sworn it was an earthquake," he hollered, and shuffled into the house leaving us livid with frustration.

Also out were those people, admittedly few, who had "slept right through it." These persons were of the type that never fails to be damnably superior about sleeping right through earthquakes, thunderstorms and train wrecks. We ignored them.

I myself was content to appear blasé and nonchalant about the whole upheaval, an effect weakened somewhat by the fact that my teeth were still chattering. Actually, though, this was not my first encounter with an earthquake. It just seems that no matter how many 'quakes you experience you never really come to feel at home in one.

My first trembler occurred in Ottawa in September, 1944. A minion of the RCAF at the time, I was living out, having outbid a band of termites for a room in a human honeycomb on Lisgar street. Located in the loft of the house, this room, a wall-papered sarcophagus, was cheaper than the others because whoever slept in it served as a living air-conditioning unit, his breathing sucking the bad air up from the lower floors. There was also rather limited light from the window, which wasn't so much a window as a hole in the roof that had been glassed over.

My landlady, Mrs. Kaloone, was a charming woman who went out of her way to see how her guests were getting along, usually through the keyhole. In order to charge the legal limit for the room, Mrs. Kaloone rented it to me as a double, necessitating my signing the register as "Sgt. and Mrs." This fictional wife became more and more of a mystery to the snoopier of the other residents, who consulted the register when Mrs. Kaloone wasn't looking (there was a brief period on Sundays, just before dawn, when Mrs. Kaloone wasn't looking).

Since I was the only person ever seen entering or leaving the room, the story developed — I learned later — that I kept this wife locked in, possibly chained to the bed. There came to be dark doubts that the poor girl was my wife. At first, therefore, I couldn't understand why the other boarders hissed at me whenever we met on the stairs. I had heard that easterners were cool to strangers, but never expected such a sibilant display of antipathy. After a few weeks the tension became so acute that Mrs. Kaloone cornered me in the hall and harshly informed me that I had better take my girl friend and get out of the room.

"But, Mrs. Kaloone," I protested, "you suggested that I sign as 'Sgt. and Mrs.' so that you could charge extra for the double room …"

"I'm running a respectable place here," rasped Mrs. Kaloone, loud enough for the other roomers to be able to hear her without straining. "Now get out by 6 p.m. or I'll call the police."

I left immediately, carrying a duffel bag, which a small, silent send-off party of roomers stared at as though it might contain a dismembered female corpse.

But all this was incidental to the earthquake, which occurred shortly before I left. It was one of those hot, sticky late-summer nights when you are kept awake by the drip, drip, drip of your own perspiration. Every time I rolled over, the mattress rolled with me.

I was just dozing off when I was abruptly awakened by the bed shaking violently. For one wild instant I thought Mrs. Kaloone was attacking me (my rent was paid to the end of the month, so she had little to lose), and it was with some relief that I realized it was merely an earthquake. The air was filled with the sighing, rumbling sound of our more recent 'quake, and Mrs. Kaloone's house seemed to be making a determined effort to imitate Fred Astaire. Situated as I was in the crow's-nest, I quickly decided that my best move would be to get closer to the foundation in case the fine old firetrap fell flat on its façade. The floor was still shuddering as I bounced out of bed, and I was delayed a moment while I attempted to slip my arms through my slippers and got my feet tangled in my bathrobe.

I could hear a woman screaming downstairs, conclusive evidence that the weaving of the walls wasn't just the result of a fried egg sandwich eaten before retiring. I then heard somebody running down the stairs yelling incoherently, and we all had a good laugh when it turned out to be me. The other roomers, having fled their burrows, were congregated in the hall. This was an enlightening display in itself, for never before had occasion demanded the whole lot to be ferreted out en masse, and the size of the milling crowd created as much astonishment as the 'quake itself, which had now subsided.

Some people emerged from doorways blinking molishly, as though they hadn't seen light for many months. Naturally the affair developed into a field day for Mrs. Kaloone, who was running around like a cat on a kipper counter, putting the finger on these rarely-seen tenants for their back rent. I then noticed several people glaring at me, and realized I was being despised for saving myself first, abandoning my "wife" under the roof. I was about to slink back upstairs when somebody noticed that, for the first time in the memory of living persons, the bathroom was unoccupied. A savage rush promptly broke out, in which several roomers were trampled. These were the only local casualties I heard of resulting from the Ottawa earthquake of 1944, and those of us from the west were agreed that the earth couldn't have chosen a better place to have a movement.

CHIEF DAN GEORGE (1899–1981)

A hereditary Coast Salish chief, Dan George (or Teswano) of the Burrard Inlet Squamish Band worked as a longshoreman, logger and itinerant musician until age sixty. He was discovered as an actor in 1959 when the CBC was looking for someone for the role of Ol' Antoine in "Cariboo Country," a TV series written by Paul St. Pierre. This was followed by a succession of Canadian television roles in which he played the wise and gentle Indian elder, and a moving role in the original production of George Ryga's play, *The Ecstasy of Rita Joe* (1967). In the 1970s he made a series of Hollywood films including "Smith," an adaptation of St. Pierre's *Breaking Smith's Quarter Horse*, and "Little Big Man," which garnered him an Academy Award nomination. He accepted a number of acting parts, but he would only play "good" Native characters. His mission was to elevate the popular image of Native people.

Much of George's work involved speech-making at theatres, clubs and public celebrations. His recitation of "Lament for Confederation," which speaks of First Nations defeat and resurgence, was one of Vancouver's most publicized Centennial events in 1967. *My Heart Soars*, a slim collection of poetic oratory, was published in 1974 and became a British Columbia bestseller. It was followed in 1982 by posthumous volume of similar material entitled *My Spirit Soars*. These writings were attributed to "Chief Dan George," but his friend Hilda Mortimer, who has written a book with and about him entitled *Call Me Chief* (1980), has said that these books were ghostwritten and largely the work of a local Catholic priest. Similarly, we are told of his speech-making: "He had a mentor and a guide who dictated most of what he uttered."

It is clear that the person and the writings that we know as "Chief Dan George" are complicated constructions of First Nations and European values – which may help explain their popular appeal to a white audience. Today, we most often see them as stereotyping First Nations people into benign but powerless beings. Like the humour of Eric Nicol, the "writings" and persona of Dan George represent a phase of cultural history in British Columbia that now seems incorrect or out-of-step. Still, they are worth examining for what they tell us of our past. In themselves, the writings of Dan George have a particular appeal because they come from an oral culture. They are perhaps most clearly understood and appreciated as performances.

MY VERY GOOD DEAR FRIENDS

Was it only yesterday that men sailed around the moon ... And can they now stand up on its barren surface? You and I marvel that man should travel so far and so fast ... Yet, if they have travelled far then I have travelled farther ... and if they have travelled fast, then I faster... for I was born a thousand years ago ... born in a culture of bows and arrows. But within the span of half a lifetime I was flung across the ages to the culture of the atom bomb ... And from bows and arrows to atom bombs is a distance far beyond a flight to the moon.

I was born in an age that love the things of nature and gave them beautiful names like Tes-wall-u-wit instead of dried-up names like Stanley Park.

I was born when people loved all nature and spoke to it as though it had a soul ... I can remember going up Indian River with my father when I was very young ... can remember him watching the sun light fires on Mount Pay-nay-nay as it rose above its peak. I can remember him singing his thanks to it as he often did ... singing the Indian word "thanks" ... so very, very softly.

And then the people came ... more and more people came ... like a crashing wave they came ... hurling the years aside!! ... and suddenly I found myself a young man in the midst of the twentieth century.

I found myself and my people adrift in this new age ... but not a part of it.

Engulfed by its rushing tide, but only as a captive eddy ... going round and round ... On little reserves, on plots of land we floated in a kind of grey unreality ... ashamed of our culture, which you ridiculed ... unsure of who we were or where we were going ... uncertain of our grip on the present ... weak in our hope for the future ... And this is pretty well where we stand today.

I had a glimpse of something better than this. For a few brief years I knew my people when we lived the old life ... I knew them when there was still a dignity in our lives and feeling of worth in our outlook. I knew them when there was unspoken confidence in the home and a certain knowledge of the path we walked upon. But we were living on the dying energy of a dying culture ... a culture that was slowly losing its forward thrust.

I think it was the suddenness of it all that hurt us so. We did not have time to adjust to the startling upheaval around us. We seemed to have lost what we had without a replacement for it. We did not have time to take our twentieth-century progress and eat it little by little and digest it. It was forced feeding from the start, and our stomachs turned sick and we vomited.

Do you know what it is like to be without moorings? Do you know what it is like to live in surroundings that are ugly and everywhere you look you see ugly things ... strange things ... strange and ugly things? It depresses man, for man must be surrounded by the beautiful if his soul is to grow.

What did we see in the new surroundings you brought us? Laughing faces, pitying faces, sneering faces, conniving faces. Faces that ridiculed, faces that stole from us. It is no wonder we turned to the only people who did not steal and who did not sneer, who came with love. They were the missionaries and they came with love and I for one will ever return that love.

Do you know what it is like to feel that you are of no value to society and those around you? To know that people came to help you but not to work with you, for you knew that they knew you had nothing to offer ...?

Do you know what it is like to have your race belittled and to come to learn that you are only a burden to the country? Maybe we did not have the skills to make a meaningful contribution, but no one would wait for us to catch up. We were shoved aside because they thought we were dumb and could never learn.

What is it like to be without pride in your race, pride in your family, pride and confidence in yourself? What is it like? You don't know for you never tasted its bitterness.

I shall tell you what it is like. It is like not caring about tomorrow, for what does tomorrow matter? It is like having a reserve that looks like a junkyard because the beauty in the soul is dead and why should the soul express an external beauty that does not match it? It is like getting drunk for a few brief moments, as an escape from ugly reality, and feeling a sense of importance. It is most of all like awaking next morning to the guilt of betrayal. For the alcohol did not fill the emptiness but only dug it deeper.

And now you hold out your hand and you beckon to me to come across the street ... come and integrate, you say ... But how can I come? I am naked and ashamed. How can I come in dignity? I have no presents ... I have no gifts. What is there in my culture that you value? ... My poor treasure you can only scorn.

Am I then to come as a beggar and receive all from your omnipotent hand? Somehow I must wait ... I must delay. I must find myself. I must find my treasure. I must wait until you want something of me ... until you need something that is me. Then I can raise my head and say to my wife and family ... listen ... they are calling ... they need me ... I must go ...

Then I can walk across the street and I will hold my head high, for I will meet you as an equal. I will not scorn you for your demeaning gifts and you will not receive me in pity. Pity I can do without, my manhood I cannot.

I can come only as Chief Capilano came to Captain Vancouver ... as one sure of his authority ... certain of his worth ... master of his house and leader of his people. I shall not come as a cringing object of your pity. I shall come in dignity or I shall not come at all.

You talk big words of integration in the schools. Does it really exist? Can we talk of integration until there is social integration? Unless there is integration of hearts and minds, you have only a physical presence ... and the walls are as high as the mountain range.

Come with me to the playgrounds of an integrated high school ... See how level and flat and ugly the blacktop is ... but look ... now it is recess time ... the students pour through the doors ... soon, over here is a group of white students ... and see ... over there, near the fence ... a group of native students ... and look again ... the black is no longer level ... mountain ranges rising ... valleys falling ... and a great chasm seems to be opening up between the two groups ... yours and mine ... and no one seems capable of crossing over. But wait ... soon the bell will ring and the students will leave the play yard. Integration has moved indoors. There isn't much room in a classroom to dig chasms, so there are only little ones there ... only little ones ... for we won't allow big ones ... at least, not right under our noses ... so we will cover it all over with blacktop ... cold ... black ... flat ... and full of ugliness in its sameness.

I know you must be saying ... Tell us what do you want? What do we want? We want first of all to be respected and to feel we are people of worth. We want an equal opportunity to succeed in life ... but we cannot succeed on your terms ... we cannot raise ourselves on your norms. We need specialized help in education ... specialized help in the formative years ... special courses in English. We need guidance counselling ... we need equal job opportunities for graduates, otherwise our students will lose courage and ask what is the use of it all.

Let no one forget it ... we are a people with special rights guaranteed to us by promises and treaties. We do not beg for these rights, nor do we thank you ... we do not thank you for them because we paid for them ... and God help us, the price we paid was exorbitant. We paid for them with our culture, our dignity and self-respect. We paid and paid and paid until we became a beaten race, poverty-stricken and conquered.

But you have been kind to listen to me and I know that in your heart you wish you could help. I wonder if there is much you can do, and yet I believe there is a lot you can do ... When you meet my children in your classroom, respect each one for what he is... a child of our Father in heaven, and your brother. Maybe it all boils down to just that.

And now it is the end. May I say thanks to you for the warmth of your understanding.

NORMAN NEWTON (1929-)

Norman Newton's book *Fire in the Raven's Nest* (1973) has been described as "neither a formal history nor a contemporary chronicle"; rather, Newton offers a multifaceted personal view of Haida culture on the Queen Charlotte Islands. He brings together a wide variety of materials ranging from raw documentary materials such as interviews and statements on tape, to traditional oral narratives, and ancient myths and legends. The two excerpts included here draw on the Haida's story of how smallpox came to destroy their culture and the traditional villages of their islands, and on interviews with Bill Reid, the great Haida artist. Written with a perceptive and sympathetic understanding of the lives of indigenous peoples, *Fire in the Raven's Nest* came out at a time when it was still possible for a non-native writer to work without potential charges of cultural appropriation. In fact, Newton's commitment to indigenous cultures runs very deep: *Fire* was preceded by *The Big Stuffed Hand of Friendship* (1969) — a novelist's portrait of a B.C. coastal town and the often strained relations which exist between natives and whites. In the same year, Newton brought out the historical work, *Thomas Gage in Spanish America*. Before this, Newton published two historical novels: *The House of Gods* (1961), which examines the golden age of Toltec culture in Mexico from the fifteenth century, and *One True Man* (1963) based on Aztec and Mayan legends of conquerers who preceded the Spanish arrival by centuries. Newton is a man of diverse talents and wide interests. In addition to novels and historical non-fiction, he has written two books of poetry, opera libretti, verse plays for radio and theatre, and musical scores for concert, radio, and television. Newton was born in Vancouver in 1929 and lived there for much of his life while he worked for the CBC, first as a freelance director and writer of plays, and later as a music, drama and documentary producer. He now keeps a residence on Gabriola Island.

From FIRE IN THE RAVEN'S NEST
CHAPTER 1

Open the clouds with your hands —
Look down.
Ah, all your body and your face!

VANCOUVER, British Columbia, once thought of itself as "The City of Imperial Destiny" and "The Constantinople of the West." These slogans date from that time between the latter part of Queen Victoria's reign and the abdication of Edward VIII when the British Empire was developing a mystique rather like that of the Roman. Vancouver was to be a great port through which would flow much of the Far Eastern trade of the Empire. The imperial dream survives in street names, carvings over the doorways of public buildings, fountains and statues in public squares, and even in the design of old houses. Hence Vancouver, incorporated in 1886, carries beneath its modernity something of the melancholy of a lost hope and a certain indefinable air of the false antique.

Yet Vancouver is really much older than the British Empire. A mythological chronicle of one of the Fraser River tribes begins "In earlier times this Fraser River resembled an enormous dish that stored up food for all mankind." At the very beginning, it says, there were no deciduous trees, only evergreens; there were only clams and mussels in the sea, since the more highly developed fish had not yet appeared; and there were no mammals at all. Then God created groups of people in various places, and one of these he settled at Musqueam on the outskirts of Vancouver, by the banks of the Fraser River.

Most of the prominent natural features of the Vancouver area have legends attached to them. In this respect it is part of a mythical landscape whose supernatural features are as well delineated as those of the landscapes surrounding the cities of ancient Britain, Greece or Mesoamerica.

To most of its white inhabitants, their roots shallow or untraceably widespread, such an idea would appear an antiquarian fantasy. Not to the Indians, though. The oldest of them still remember the legendary springs beneath the concrete, the monster-concealing lakes which have become ponds in public parks, the sacred peaks on which ski resorts have been built, the spirit-haunted creeks which have disappeared or become part of sewage systems. Young Indians are disturbed by such memories, though they cannot remember the names.

To the Haida, geographically unable to lay claim to these myths which belong to the Squamish and related peoples, Vancouver is still the capital of the world. All roads lead to it. To some it is a whirlpool into which they will be dragged, to be spewed up later as mere Indians, indistinguishable from Tsimshian, Kwakiutl, Nootka or even visiting Iroquois. To others it is a kind of bath from which they hope to emerge shining, scrubbed almost white and carrying briefcases.

Few make it. Some sink quickly to the moral disaster area around Cordova and Columbia Streets. Some return, defeated, to Masset or Skidegate on the Queen Charlotte Islands. Some go on welfare. Some drift helplessly from one ill-paying job to another. Some — a few — find permanent and moderately well-paid employment. Some — a very few — become low-status professional men. Some become artists and carvers, and perhaps these are the only ones who really make it.

The Indian artist may achieve a passing local fame. The newspapers will praise and even over-praise him; the big department stores will ask him to demonstrate his craft before the public, who will crowd about him, between the millinery and the photo supplies, to ask him silly questions about his work ("How long does it take you to make a carving?"); and fashionable women in Shaughnessy and the British Properties will wear his silver bracelets and argillite medallions.

The best are very good indeed, and some are able to support themselves: Patrick McGuire, a young Haida artist who died of an overdose of heroin in December, 1970, made, on occasion, up to one hundred dollars a day. The dean of Haida artists is William Reid, the grandson of Charlie Gladstone, a well-known carver of an earlier time. When Reid began carving some twenty years ago the tradition was almost dead and was being kept alive by white interest rather than by an inner compulsion in Haida society itself. Even the older carvers were copyists working, without any real understanding of the stylistic language involved, from photographs of old carvings in anthropological books. It was Bill Reid and the white United States carver and dancer, Bill Holm, who first analyzed this language in a manner useful to artists, something earlier writers on the subject had failed to do.

Reid is a laconic man, usually amiable and entertaining, but sometimes terrrifyingly direct in his rejection of importunate bores and fools. He has the rich chesty voice of a radio announcer, which he once was, and an impressive head of grey hair. He believes the spirits of his noble ancestors, among them the best carver of all, his great-uncle Charles Edenshaw, are with him when he works, though he may sometimes rationalize their inwardly-heard voices are those of his super-ego. Yet he is far removed — it could hardly be otherwise — from the world of the ancient Haida, who knew no art style very different from their own. His art, though very close to the tradition in the language it employs, has that intellectuality and nervous refinement which distinguishes a self-conscious and idiosyncratic style.

Reid has built a "Haida village" in a small treed park on the campus of the University of British Columbia in Vancouver. It consists of two memorial posts, and two wooden houses in the Haida style, each with its frontal pole. One of the memorial posts is a richly carved gravebox, set on high between two massive trunks, and bearing the stylized representation of a dogfish. The other is a beautiful mortuary pole carved with an eagle and figures from the Bear Mother story — a grizzly bear with his human wife and their two children. The complex is only a few miles from the suburb of Marpole, beneath which are buried the remains of an ancient village which produced a miniature stone art with curiously Mesoamerican resemblances. When seen late at night, perhaps in the moonlight, with no traffic on the road which passes by, it takes on the quality of a private vision of nearly epic proportions. The great poles tower into the dark sky; the road is a black river and the only sound is made by the gravel underfoot.

"I attempt to stay within the convention established in Haida art," Reid once told me, "at the same time making all my designs original; that is, there are not any direct copies, and I certainly have developed through the years a distinctive style, which I think is my own. Now, whether this would fit into the traditional pattern of Haida design as it reached its height during the last century, I really couldn't say. I think that's for the future to decide."

"You talk about getting through to the roots of Haida art," I said. "I know it's very difficult to put visual ideas into words —"

"I think it could best be described as variations on a single theme. Through the centuries — and I believe Haida art could extend back as far as maybe four or five thousand years — they have simplified the whole basic concept down to one essential form which you've probably seen, the flattened oval, the eye form. And practically all aspects of this art are variants of this one form, either in two or three dimensions. This oval can take innumerable shapes, long and narrow or practically round. It's a kind of non-geometric geometry, if you will, based on this one very subtle, extremely tense kind of construction. It's not something you can draw with a great sweeping curve; it's something you have to draw painfully, bit by bit."

"Do you think the traditional style has any power of growth in it? Is it a flexible art language, something that can continue adapting and changing?"

"I wouldn't say this is absolutely out of the question, because individuals can perform quite marvellous things in the world of the arts. I think it's unlikely, though. I think it grew out of a set of social circumstances that demanded this form of expression. These social circumstances no longer exist, and all that people such as I can do now is carry on in an eclectic sort of a way, looking for precedents. If we want to do something, then we check and look for a precedent on which to base this, and then figure it's all right to go ahead. If you don't do that, then you get a degenerate form, which is unfortunately all too common today, where the work that is being produced bears very little resemblance to the great art of the past, and actually is not really art at all, but a sort of crude folk-craft."

I later went to Reid's studio to talk to Robert Davidson Jr., a twenty-five-year-old Haida who was occupying it while Reid was away in Montreal. I drove through the downtown area, turned a corner and went down a lane between two office buildings. I came to a low wood building, very old and apparently near collapse — a relic of Vancouver's old West End.

At one time the West End was an enclave of such wooden houses, most of them fairly large, with some stone mansions among them. They were not beautiful: they cheapened, miniaturized and ruthlessly forced together elements from the entire architectural history of Eurasia. Looking over the roof-tops one could see Greek pediments, Gothic spires, Norman turrets, pagoda eaves, Moorish fretwork facades, onion-domes, mansards and plain gables, all in wood and all at war with each other. Stained-glass windows, set on either side of the brass-knockered front doors, cast a coloured gloom over the dark hat stands and umbrella racks inside: banal wooden scrollwork festooned the verandahs. Apartment buildings, two-storey cubes covered with stucco and possessing pseudo-baronial names (Balmoral, Argyll, Norfolk, Kent) sheltered hordes of shabby-genteel spinsters. Muddy lanes passed between back gardens planted with vegetables and flowers and the streets were dotted with steaming mounds of dung from the horses which pulled the milk and ice wagons. It was all absolutely tasteless and mediocre, yet I look back on it with a certain nostalgia. Each house was a little folly, a dream castle, representing the last Western stand of the small man's private vision and his malformed love of traditional beauty. The sons and grandsons of the men who built them now live in gigantic apartment houses with courtyard fountains, Muzak in the elevators and names resembling those of kitchen appliances and rock groups — Viking, Belmac, Pacific Surf.

Robert Davidson, in stocking feet, took me up the dark stairs to the studio. He is a handsome well-built young man who has spent much of his life outdoors; his face is coppery, but has a more European than Indian cast; his smile is wide and engaging and has a kind of innocence. He speaks slowly and cautiously, in the relaxed manner of the countryman, but without an accent.

As we went through the anteroom door at the head of the stairs, I heard a high-pitched yapping: two German Shepherd pups, apparently hungry, were trying to climb out of a fenced-in enclosure. On the wall were blow-ups of some marvellous photographs of Edward Curtis, pictures which were taken at the beginning of this century but which might have been taken thousands of years ago, they seem so remote: a naked Nootkan spearing a fish; another, also spearing a fish but dressed in a bark-cloth robe, who looks like some bearded prehistoric Norseman; and the canoes of a Kwakiutl wedding party under sail. A number of books on literature and art were on a shelf by the kitchen door.

We went from the anteroom into the kitchen, which was decorated with fashionably humorous posters, picked up two pottery mugs from the cluttered sideboard and poured ourselves coffee. The sugar spoon was a delicately moulded imitation, in miniature, of a Haida horn spoon.

In his workroom I was struck again by nostalgia. I was reminded of my youth in the West End, which had by then become a miniature Bohemia. Along with other painters, poets and novelists, I lived in a pleasant clutter: we were saving up for fares to Mexico, London, Paris or the Balearics. We had all valued craftsmanship and I was moved by Davidson's obvious devotion to craft — he seemed the survivor of an earlier generation. His dusty workbench was spread with silver-worker's tools. He used them with remarkable deftness while we talked, cutting tiny oval forms into the bracelet he was carving. A Haydn trumpet concerto played softly on the record player; beside it were records of Bach, Mozart, Bob Dylan, Joan Baez and some rock groups. A bookcase contained more art books and a few paperbacks of poetry and general literature. His bench was set before a window which overlooked the harbour and the roofs of a few two-storey office buildings.

He frowned at the pattern he was cutting. Under his hard steady pressure the silver peeled off from the graver in a thin ribbon. He was now used to Vancouver, he told me; he had a number of white friends and received much flattering attention. When he had arrived from Masset, a nineteen-year-old, he had been very much a country boy.

"When I first came down here, I used to say hello to everybody and people would look at me and say, 'is he crazy or something?' And now I've become the same way. If somebody says hello to me on the street, I have the same reaction, 'Is he crazy or something?' I've just completely changed."

The city is a solvent of conventional values, those values which are supported not by inner conviction but by habit and social pressure.

"I used to believe in God — for one reason, I was brainwashed into believing in Him. I was told to go to church, so I went to church. They said, 'it will bring you good luck,' so I went every Sunday, sometimes twice a day. For about a year after I came down here I used to go to church every Sunday and believed in it very strongly. But I started thinking about it — why am I going to church? What is it doing for me? I sort of enjoyed sleeping in on Sundays. This Sunday I decided not to go to church and nothing happened, so I decided not to go again."

The traditional Indian value system, now defunct, provides no substitute for Christianity. Even among the oldest, very few believe in it. Some may defend it warmly as being superior to Christianity, but usually their belief is a kind of vague pantheism which owes as much to white sources as Indian ones. A few who look upon themselves or are regarded by others as tradition-keepers may retain some knowledge of the old religious system, but they treat it like a bundle of intellectual artifacts: they open it every so often, admire the objects within and wrap them up again. For most of the people, all that remains is a number of incoherent superstitions and folk beliefs.

Davidson is typical of the young Haida in that the old religion means nothing to him. Later, when I was sipping my third cup of coffee and looking at his silverwork, he said:

"You've got to remember they were living in a different age. So I just have no feeling about it now, what with having cars and jet planes and things like that. It's hard. Like when I was going to the art school I got very frustrated because people were interpreting paintings that were done in the sixteenth century. I got tired of them doing this, because I felt they had no right to interpret them. They were living in a different age, and they thought differently, and I don't think we can interpret it. I find the same thing happening with Indian art — people trying to interpret it in our age. And they find it strange. I'd find it strange myself."

"If you had your choice, and obviously there's not much choice under the present circumstances, but if the people of Masset were making a good living, and they weren't poor, and they had a degree of cultural independence, would you prefer to live in Masset or to live in Vancouver?"

"I'd prefer to live on the Queen Charlottes any day. One of the reasons I'm down here — well, there's nothing up on the Queen Charlottes any more. The museums have it all; they have all the old stuff, all the things that were made up there. Also I need contacts with people for my art. It's the only means of supporting myself."

As I waited for the elevator, my anger and unease returned. Every time I talk with Indians I become aware of a painful split in the corporate personality of British Columbia, and, I suppose, Canada as a whole. We pretend to a desire to welcome Indians into the "mainstream." Yet how can we do this when we fail to understand either our own society, which we are destroying (what is attractive about the "mainstream" of a disintegrating society?), or the place of the Indian in it, which is that of an inferior being?

I first became interested in Indian matters as a poet, and then I was most interested in what might be called "the matter of British Columbia." I had written two novels about early British Columbia and Mexico, and I had discovered in the process a rich store of myth. Thus I had started with myth and poetry and had ended in social consciousness — a not-unusual route, especially in our time, when prevalent social relations have become anti-mythical and anti-poetic.

The British Columbia of my previous conception — a vast undeveloped province, an administrative unit in a federal system governed politically by Ottawa and Victoria and economically by the United States — began to change. I began to see the province as it had been: a collection, on the one hand, of ancient coastal and river-oriented village states, some of them of great age, varying from small to tiny, and, on the other, of larger less well-defined inland territories exploited by nomadic or semi-sedentary tribes. The British Columbia of my time was another country which had settled down atop the old one, squashing its contours, but not obliterating them entirely. Some of its cities, towns and villages lay over old sites, some did not; some of its roads followed old trails, some did not; some of its industries exploited resources known to the ancient inhabitants, others exploited resources unknown to them.

Were our sins, in a sense, finding us out? Were we paying, in a growing sense of purposelessness which produced an agony something like that of dismemberment, for our violation of the land? When did I first become aware that something was wrong at the root of things, something I had no name for? Was it during a boyhood walk in the woods, when I became aware of an alien life in the cedars and hemlocks, something which seemed to say *You do not belong here?* Did it happen one day in my adolescence when I was walking along the sea-beach at Texada island, and passed a logged-out patch, a dreary expanse of dead splinters, lopped branches, rotting stumps and stagnant pools of water? I remember it as a dry summer day; the sun shone like a floodlight, and the sky was its enamelled blue reflector. I felt thousands of square miles of desolation closing in on me, a wilderness full of rusty barbed wire, splintered tree trunks, broken beer bottles, abandoned bulldozers and old Eaton's catalogues and pulp magazines lying, half drowned, in black pools bordered by garish and malodorous skunk cabbages.

[In the following passage taken from Chapter 8, Newton reflects on European images of the native, and the collapse of traditional Haida culture on the Queen Charlotte Islands due to smallpox. The story which he recounts has the qualities of a dark myth. The James Douglas referred to was Governor of Vancouver Island and later Lieutenant Governor of the Queen Charlotte Islands in the mid-nineteenth century. His wife was part native, and he himself is thought to have possessed African ancestors.]

Let us look at some of the "disgusting" aspects of Haida life, as they are described in books of the last century. They smeared themselves with grease for protection against the winter cold; though they bathed, they did so inefficiently by late nineteenth-century standards (it was not until the eighteenth century that whites began to think of Indians as "dirty"); the men sometimes went in loincloths or naked; they kept the heads of their enemies instead of their medals and flags; crude commoners and slaves sometimes cracked and ate their own lice. Their summer camps were littered with fish bones and bits of discarded fish, though this was not true of the longhouses in the permanent villages. They used a hair lotion made of bear grease perfumed with herbs, or of parsnip roots and dogfish oil, and washed their hair (and skin) with urine: a harmless practice after all, since normal urine is sterile (the Haida had no soap, and the chemical properties of urine make it a practical detergent).

Then there was the question of godliness, so close to cleanliness in the mind of the time. The devout were told that the Haida were godless pagans. However, they believed in a God at least as definite as that of the deists. For that matter, most Victorians, in spite of the neo-orthodoxy of the established churches and the revivalism of the sects, were not so much Christians as deists who inconsistently adhered to a sort of Christian mythology. If some Haida rituals were dark and terrifying in nature, they were not, at least until the introduction of ritual slave-sacrifices and pseudo-cannibalism, which were both late developments, much more sinister than some of the rites of Freemasonary, to which cult, strangely enough, belonged many of those who attacked Indian religions in the name of Christianity.

To say this is not to idealize Haida civilization nor to deny that it was, at its worst, grim, narrow, crude in its material satisfactions and deadeningly conformist as only isolated and archaic village civilizations can be. Yet to equate it with "savagery" is grotesque. The word "savage" was a propaganda term, an attempt to restructure reality to suit a political end. The "savage" does not own land, and may safely be treated as a kind of permanently displaced person, with nothing to lose but his lice.

In the late 1850s, Victoria, by then a great trade emporium, was visited by north coast Indians in the thousands, and among them were the Haida, who made a trip of six hundred miles down a very difficult coast, navigating by that oral piloting tradition which has unfortunately been lost to us. They had no charts, though of course it is probable that they had a way of indicating rough distances and directions in some pictographic form. They do not seem to have used celestial navigation to any considerable extent; members of the crew, familiar with the contours of the coastline and the local behaviour of winds and currents, would act as pilots.

The Indian sailing canoe was a common sight along the coast in those days. Old photographs of Indian canoes under sail, dating from a later period, are most attractive and full of romance. One can see by the white wake behind the canoes that they went very fast with the wind aft or quartering. Solomon Wilson, who thought the sail pattern was aboriginal, explained it to me. Such a canoe could run with a quartering, aft or beam wind, but could not tack effectively, Wilson said. Perhaps the sail would permit tacking of a sort, though not very close to the wind, but the canoe's lack of a keel or centreboard would result in too much leeway. The smaller Viking ships were not much larger than these canoes, and the inhabitants of Victoria felt understandably uncomfortable when the Haida fleet entered the harbour.

On April 23, 1859, the *British Colonist* reported the arrival of nearly a thousand Haida carrying "several very fine specimens of gold-bearing quartz and some fine gold. We are not informed," the paper says, "as to what part of the island they obtained their gold from." No doubt the Haida had found a new vein, whose location they were keeping to themselves. On one of these trips, some chiefs, including Edenshaw, protested to [Governor James] Douglas about the seizure by fiat of the Queen Charlotte Islands, but to little effect. Meanwhile the Indian encampments outside Victoria were reflecting, in a concentrated and hideous form, the demoralization of the Indian and the degeneration of his society. Victoria merchants were selling as whiskey a concoction of raw alcohol, "bluestone vitriol" (obtained by dissolving copper oxide in sulphuric acid) and nitric acid, which may be used, though in highly dilute form, as a diuretic. Another concoction was a solution of red pepper in diluted alcohol. The manufacturers of this poison were respected citizens, who ran what they called "importing" wholesale liquor establishments. D.W. Higgins, a newspaperman and politician of the time, wrote in *The Passing of a Race:*

> Did the police know that this infamous business was being carried on under their eyes and noses, the reader will ask. The answer is that they were well aware of the methods by which the Indians were being cleared off the face of the earth. They knew that the hot stuff for which a dollar a bottle was paid by the Indians did not cost the maker ten cents. The maker and seller could well afford to cut the profits in two and still realize handsomely. For the makers and dealers to refuse to divide meant exposure and ruin for men who went to church regularly or occupied a good position in society. Did they divide? It cannot be said with any certainty that they did; but it was a notorious fact that certain firms were never disturbed. They were immune from the visits of constables …

In 1860, the Haida almost attacked Victoria. They were frustrated, directionless and crazy with drink at the time. The young men wanted to attack the whites, but one Haida (Higgins thinks he may have been in the pay of the Hudson's Bay Company) urged them to attack the Tlingits instead. A man was stabbed and soon a feud developed between Haida and Tlingit factions. Gunboats were called in from nearby Esquimalt and stood by to bombard the encampment. As the feud between Haida and Tlingit grew, a thousand more Haida arrived. Once again they prepared to attack Victoria. The superior force of the whites, supplemented by the skillful diplomacy of Douglas and Edenshaw, who was playing his now-established role of peacemaker, prevented what might have been an Indian war. A threatened Haida attack on the coal-mining town of Nanaimo was averted by the dispatch of a gunboat. The Haida left.

In May of 1861 the Haida attacked and stripped of its valuables the schooner *Laurel*, whose captain had sold them a keg of whiskey which he had diluted by half with sea water. The gunboat *Forward* set out in pursuit, and a battle ensued between the Haida, who were firing from shore fortifications, and the ship. When one of their chiefs was killed and another severely wounded, the Haida surrendered. The prisoners were later released without charge.

In 1862, the disaster occurred which finally broke the spirit of the Haida and other coastal Indians — the smallpox epidemic. Douglas, in all good faith, had warned the Indians encamped around Victoria that a man had arrived from San Francisco with smallpox and an epidemic was more than possible. He ordered them to leave. But the Haida chiefs looked upon this as a ruse to make them go home. In addition, they could not afford to obey an order from Douglas, who had up to now treated them as if they still retained some independence, because such obedience would have been an acknowledgement of British claims to sovereignty. Douglas then ordered out the police, Royal Marines and the Navy. Gunboats fired warning shots into the encampment. The Indians were rounded up at gunpoint and forced into their canoes, which were roped in long lines behind Navy craft. They were then towed out of the harbour and up the coast.

Edenshaw could not accept this. He cut his tow rope, the other men of his clan followed his example, and they headed back to Victoria. It was a gesture in support of their right of free access to the town. They stayed there long enough to establish their defiance of Victoria's pretensions to authority over them, and left again. But as they sailed and paddled north, hoping to catch up with those who had gone before, they found only corpses. They saw canoes rolling aimlessly in the waters of quiet coves, where their crewmen had headed to die. As they approached the Queen Charlottes, men in their own canoes were dying. The epidemic spread along the coast. Among the Queen Charlotte Haida the population shrank from the estimated seven to ten thousand of the late 1700's to a mere thousand.

Solomon Wilson told me a story which he claimed to have heard from the carver, Henry Young, who was born ten years after the incident he describes. His own uncle, John Brown, had vouched for the story, he said, which described the origin of the great smallpox epidemic.

A boat had arrived from China, according to Wilson, flying the flag which indicated there was smallpox aboard. At this time the Haida were paying their annual visit to Victoria. They had left their blankets and furs, for safekeeping, with a certain merchant whom the Haida have come to call "The Man with the Pitchy Hair." There was no written agreement indicating the goods were theirs.

One of the significant items of trade at that time was molasses, which was used liberally as a condiment. The merchant lusted after the great pile of blankets and furs left in his keeping. So he obtained access to the corpse of one of the smallpox victims put ashore for burial, and cut off a finger. He immersed this in a keg of molasses, which he gave to the Haida as a present. Shortly after, the Haida began to fall ill of smallpox. Desperate with fear, they fled Victoria as quickly as they could, leaving their goods with the merchant.

As they went up the coast they continued to die. People of other tribes, seeing the empty canoes guarded only by corpses, came to take the goods left in them. They too died, but not until they had spread the plague to Vancouver Island and the mainland. Very few Haida returned. It was not until they were nearly home that they discovered, in the nearly empty keg of molasses, the finger of a dead man. The Victoria merchant caught small-pox himself, and died before he was able to realize a profit on the blankets he had kept.

This is the story as Wilson told it to me. It has a distinctly Grand Guignol quality, and bears a certain resemblance to the folklore that springs up around events so catastrophic or wonderful that they demand bizarre ex-planations, like the Angel of Mons or Mrs. O'Leary's cow. The epidemic is still vividly remembered. "My people's bones are scattered up and down the coast," Chief Weah is in the habit of saying.

As ancient families died out, titles and prerogatives were available to anybody who could afford the expensive ceremonial feasts needed to claim them. Commoners competed shamelessly for position; wives and daugh-ters were prostituted in order to accumulate goods for the feasts; the con-tenders engaged in gigantic give-aways and offered whiskey at their feasts in order to attract the witnesses necessary to ratify their claims. Hundreds of totem poles, many of them quite mediocre, were carved for these parve-nus.

Douglas, now Sir James Douglas, retired in 1864.

HUGH BRODY (1943–)

The back cover of Hugh Brody's critically acclaimed study of Athapaskan native culture — *Maps and Dreams* (1981;1988) — identifies the author as "a writer and a filmmaker," and lists his titles: *Indians on Skid Row* (1971), *Inishkillane: Change and Decline in the West of Ireland* (1973), *The People's Land* (1975), *Living Arctic* (1987) and, with Michael Ignatieff, the screenplay for *1919*. He is also the author of a book of short stories based on fact, *Means of Escape* (1991). Brody has established himself as a scholar, teacher, documentary and feature director, non-fiction writer and artist. In the wide range of his accomplishments, *Maps and Dreams* (two chapters of which are excerpted here) may stand out as a masterpiece. Paul Theroux, writing of Brody's achievement, calls *Maps and Dreams* "a wonderful book, full of travel and people. Most of all it is superb anthropology, challenging many of the accepted notions about the lives of hunters."

Maps and Dreams recounts Brody's initial undertakings as a researcher and anthropologist, and his gradual entering into the deeper lives of the Dunne-za or "real people." Known to Europeans as the Beaver Indians, the Dunne-za have been hunters from time immemorial on B.C.'s remote northeastern plateau, leading a traditional life which has been little known, understood or valued by outsiders. Yet, as Brody comes to recognize, "Perhaps nowhere else in the New World can Indians more properly affirm that theirs is a cultural presence and an economic entitlement of a depth and significance beyond our comprehension." Mapping this rich cultural presence, Brody introduces us to one unforgettable character — Joseph Patsah, the elder to whom *Maps and Dreams* is dedicated — a man who embodies the collective humanity and wisdom of his people. It is Joseph Patsah who leads Brody to a first understanding of the dream maps which guide his people; Joseph who takes the author to Quarry in winter — the lovely Sechin River region where the Dunne-za people carry out their winter hunting; and Joseph who gives a final lesson in both pride and acceptance when he tells the author: "Better to be on the trapline, at Quarry. And even if you die up there, that's fine." Joseph Patsah in fact died shortly after Brody completed the writing of *Maps and Dreams*. One understands that for Brody, as well as for readers of his book, the lives of these hunters are maps which lead beyond stereotypes — reminders of "how much prejudice and misconception [we all have] to shed." Brody has said that the theme that unites all his work is a determination to render the invisble visible; to give voices to those whose voices are suppressed or ignored. Hugh Brody does much of his work in the United Kingdom, where he was born, but keeps a residence in Vancouver which he visits frequently. Excerpts from two chapters of *Maps and Dreams* — "Maps of Dreams" and "To Quarry in Winter" — are presented here.

from MAPS AND DREAMS
MAPS OF DREAMS

THE RIVERS OF NORTHEAST British Columbia are at their most splendid in the early fall. The northern tributaries of the Peace achieve an extraordinary beauty; they, and their small feeder creeks and streams, are cold yet warm — perfect reflections of autumn. The banks are multicoloured and finely textured; clear water runs in smooth, shallow channels. The low water of late summer reveals gravel and sand beaches, textures and colours that are at other times of the year concealed. Such low water levels mean that all these streams are easily crossed, and so become the throughways along the valleys that have always been at the heart of the Indians' use of the land. In October those who know these creeks can find corners, holes, back eddies where rainbow trout and Dolly Varden abound.

The hunter of moose, deer, caribou (and in historic times, buffalo) does not pursue these large animals without regard to more abundant and predictable, if less satisfying, sources of food. The man who tracks and snares game, and whose success depends on his constant movement, cannot afford to fail for much more than two days running. On the third day of hunger he will find it hard to walk far or fast enough: hunger reduces the efficiency of the hunt. Hunger is inimical to effective hunting on foot; yet continuance of the hunt was, not long ago, the only means to avoid hunger. This potential source of insecurity for a hunter is resolved by his ability to combine two kinds of hunting: he pursues large ungulates in areas and with movements that bring him close to locations where he knows rabbits, grouse, or fish are to be found. These are security, but not staples. Hunting for large animals is the most efficient, the most rational activity for anyone who lives in the boreal forest. But such a hunter would be foolhardy indeed to hunt for the larger animals without a careful and strategic eye on the availability of the smaller ones.

In October, only a month after Joseph Patsah and his family first spoke to us about their lives, they suggested that I go hunting with them — and, of course, fishing. By now the rainbow trout would surely be plentiful and fat. Joseph said that he also hoped we could go far enough to see the cross. One evening, then, he proposed that we should all set out the next day for Bluestone Creek.

Between a proposal to go hunting and actual departure there is a large and perplexing divide. In the white man's world, whether urban or rural, after such a proposal there would be plans and planning; conversation about timing and practical details would also help to build enthusiasm. In Joseph's household, in all the Indian households of northeast British Columbia, and perhaps among hunters generally, planning is so muted as to seem nonexistent. Maybe it is better understood by a very different name, which is still to suppose that planning of some kind does in fact take place.

Protests against the hunting way of life have often paid hostile attention to its seemingly haphazard, irrational, and improvident nature. Before the mind's eye of agricultural or industrial man loom the twin spectres of hunger and homelessness, whose fearsome imminence is escaped only in the bright sunlight of planning. Planners consider many possibilities, weigh methods, review timing and at least seek to deduce what is best. To this end they advocate reason and temperance, and, most important, they are thrifty and save. These ideas and dispositions, elevated to an ideal in the economics of nineteenth-century and secular puritanism, live on in the reaction of industrial society to hunters — and in the average Canadian's reaction to Indians. And a reaction of this kind means that a person, even if inclined to be sympathetic to hunters and hunting, has immense difficulty in understanding what planning means for hunters of the North.

Joseph and his family float possibilities. "Maybe we should go to Copper Creek. Bet you lots of moose up there." Or, "Could be caribou right now near Black Flats." Or, "I bet you no deer this time down on the Reserve …" Somehow a general area is selected from a gossamer of possibilities, and from an accumulation of remarks comes something rather like a consensus. No, that is not really it: rather, a sort of prediction, a combined sense of where we *might* go "tomorrow." Yet the hunt will not have been planned, nor any preparations started, and apparently no one is committed to going. Moreover, the floating conversation will have alighted on several irreconcilable possibilities, or have given rise to quasi-predictions. It is as if the predictions are about other people — or are not quite serious. Although the mood is still one of wait and see, at the end of the day, at the close of much slow and gentle talk about this and that, a strong feeling has arisen about the morning: we shall go to Bluestone, maybe as far as the cross. We shall look for trout as well as moose. A number of individuals agree that they will go. But come morning, nothing is ready. No one has made any practical, formal plans. As often as not — indeed, more often than not — something quite new has drifted into conversations, other predictions have been tentatively reached, a new consensus appears to be forming. As it often seems, everyone has changed his mind.

The way to understand this kind of decision making as also to live by and even share it, is to recognize that some of the most important variables are subtle, elusive, and extremely hard or impossible to assess with finality. The Athapaskan hunter will move in a direction and at a time that are determined by a sense of weather (to indicate a variable that is easily grasped if all too easily oversimplified by one word) and by a sense of rightness. He will also have ideas about animal movement, his own and others' patterns of land use … But already the nature of the hunter's decision making is being misrepresented by this kind of listing. To disconnect the variables, compartmentalize the thinking, is to fail to acknowledge its sophistication and completeness. He considers variables as a composite, parallel, and with the help of a blending of the metaphysical and obviously pragmatic. To make a good, wise, sensible hunting choice is to accept the interconnection of all possible factors, and avoids the mistake of seeking rationally to focus on any one consideration that is held as primary. What is more, the decision is taken in the doing: there is no step or pause between theory and practice. As a consequence, the decision — like the action from which it is inseparable — is always alterable (and therefore may not properly even be termed a decision). The hunter moves in a chosen direction; but highly sensitive to so many shifting considerations, he is always ready to change his directions.

Planning, as other cultures understand the notion, is at odds with this kind of sensitivity and would confound such flexibility. The hunter, alive to constant movements of nature, spirits, and human moods, maintains a way of doing things that repudiates a firm plan and any precise or specified understanding with others of what he is going to do. His course of action is not, must not be, a matter of predetermination. If a plan constitutes a decision about the procedure or action, and the decision is congruent with the action then there is no space left for a "plan," only for a bundle of open-ended and nonrational possibilities. Activity enters so far into this kind of planning as to undermine any so-called plans.

… Hunters at rest, at ease, in wait, are able to discover and enjoy a special form of relaxation. There is a minimum of movement — a hand reaches out for a mug, an adjustment is made to the fire — and whatever is said hardly interrupts the silence, as if words and thoughts can be harmonized without any of the tensions of dialogue. Yet the hunters are a long way from sleep; not even the atmosphere is soporific. They wait, watch, consider. Above all they are still and receptive, prepared for whatever insight or realization may come to them, and ready for whatever stimulus to action might arise. This state of attentive waiting is perhaps as close as people can come to the falcon's suspended flight, when the bird, seemingly motionless, is ready to plummet in decisive action. To the outsider, who has followed along and tried to join in, it looks for all the world as if the hunters have forgotten why they are there. In this restful way hunters can spend many hours, sometimes days, eating, waiting, thinking.

The quality of this resting by the fire can be seen and felt when it is very suddenly changed, just as the nature of the falcon's hover becomes clear when it dives. Among hunters the emergence from repose may be slow or abrupt. But in either case a particular state of mind, a special way of being, has come to an end. One or two individuals move faster and more purposively, someone begins to prepare meat to cook, someone fetches a gun to work on, and conversation resumes its ordinary mode …

In retrospect it seems clear that they felt the right time had come for something. Everyone seemed to give the few moments it took for this change to occur some special importance. Plainly the men had something to say and, in their own time, in their own way, they were going to say it. Signs and movements suggested that the flow of events that had begun in Joseph's home and Atsin's cabin, and continued with the fishing at Bluestone Creek, was about to be augmented. Something of significance to the men here was going to happen. I suddenly realized that everyone was watching me. Sam joined the group, but said nothing. Perhaps he, as a younger man, was now leaving events to his elders, to Atsin, Jimmy, and Robert. There was a brief silence made awkward by expectancy, though an awkward pause is a very rare thing among people who accept that there is no need to escape from silence, no need to use words as a way to avoid one another, no need to obscure the real.

Atsin broke this silence. He spoke at first of the research: "I bet some guys make big maps. Lots of work, these maps. Joseph, he sure is happy to see maps."

Silence again. Then Robert continued: "Yeah, lots of maps. All over this country we hunt. Fish too. Trapping places. Nobody knows that. White men don't know that."

Then Jimmy spoke: "Indian guys, old-timers, they make maps too."

With these words, the men introduced their theme. The tone was friendly, but the words were spoken with intensity and firmness. The men seemed apprehensive, as if anxious to be very clearly understood — though nothing said so far required such concern. Once again, it is impossible to render verbatim all that they eventually said. I had no tape recorder and memory is imperfect. But even a verbatim account would fail to do justice to their meaning. Here, then, in summaries and glimpses, is what the men had in mind to say.

Some old-timers, men who became famous for their powers and skills, had been great dreamers. Hunters and dreamers. They did not hunt as most people now do. They did not seek uncertainly for the trails of animals whose movements we can only guess at. No, they located their prey in dreams, found their trails, and made dreamkills. Then, the next day, or a few days later, whenever it seemed auspicious to do so, they could go out, find the trail, re-encounter the animal, and collect the kill.

Maybe, said Atsin, you think this is all nonsense, just so much bullshit. Maybe you don't think this power is possible. Few people understand. The old-timers who were strong dreamers knew many things that are not easy to understand. People — white people, young people — yes, they laugh at such skills. But they do not know. The Indians around this country know a lot about power. In fact, everyone has had some experience of it. The fact that dream-hunting works has been proved many times.

A few years ago a hunter dreamed a cow moose kill. A fine, fat cow. He was so pleased with the animal, so delighted to make this dream-kill, that he marked the animal's hooves. Now he would be sure to recognize it when he went on the coming hunt. The next day, when he went out into the bush, he quickly found the dream-trail. He followed it, and came to a large cow moose. Sure enough, the hooves bore his marks. Everyone saw them. All the men around the fire had been told about the marks, and everyone on the Reserve had come to look at those hooves when the animal was butchered and brought into the people's homes.

And not only that fat cow moose — many such instances are known to the people, whose marks on the animal or other indications show that there was no mistaking, no doubts about the efficacy of such dreams. Do you think this is all lies? No, this is power they had, something they knew how to use. This was their way of doing things, the right way. They understood, those old-timers, just where all the animals came from. The trails converge, and if you were a very strong dreamer you could discover this, and see the source of trails, the origin of game. Dreaming revealed them. Good hunting depended upon such knowledge.

Today it is hard to find men who can dream this way. There are too many problems. Too much drinking. Too little respect. People are not good enough now. Maybe there will again be strong dreamers when these problems are overcome. Then more maps will be made. New maps.

Oh yes, Indians made maps. You would not take any notice of them. You might say such maps are crazy. But maybe the Indians say that is what your maps are: the same thing. Different maps from different people — different *ways*. Old-timers made maps of trails, ornamented them with lots of fancy. The good people.

None of this is easy to understand. But good men, the really good men, could dream of more than animals. Sometimes they saw heaven and its trails. Those trails are hard to see, and few men have had such dreams. Even if they could see dream-trails to heaven, it is hard to explain them. You draw maps of the land, show everyone where to go. You explain the hills, the rivers, the trails from here to Hudson Hope, the roads. Maybe you make maps of where the hunters go and where the fish can be caught. That is not easy. But easier, for sure, than drawing out the trails to heaven. You may laugh at these maps of the trails to heaven, but they were done by the good men who had the heaven dream, who wanted to tell the truth. They worked hard on their truth.

Atsin had done most of the talking this far. The others interjected a few words and comments, agreeing or elaborating a little. Jimmy told about the cow moose with marked hooves. All of them offered some comparisons between their own and others' maps. And the men's eyes never ceased to remain fixed on me: were they being understood? Disregarded? Thought ridiculous? They had chosen this moment for these explanations, yet no one was entirely secure in it. Several times, Atsin paused and waited, perhaps to give himself a chance to sense or absorb the reaction to his words. These were intense but not tense hiatuses. Everyone was reassuring himself that his seriousness was being recognized. That was all they needed to continue.

The longest of these pauses might have lasted as much as five minutes. During it the fire was rebuilt. It seemed possible, for a few moments, that they had finished, and that their attention was now returning to trout, camp, and the hunt. But the atmosphere hardly altered, and Jimmy quite abruptly took over where Atsin had left off.

The few good men who had the heaven dream were like the Fathers, Catholic priests, men who devoted themselves to helping others with that essential knowledge to which ordinary men and women have limited access. (Roman Catholic priests have drifted in and out of the lives of all the region's Indians, leaving behind fragments of their knowledge and somewhat rarefied and idealized versions of what they had to preach.) Most important of all, a strong dreamer can tell others how to get to heaven. We all have need of the trail, or a complex of trails, but, unlike other important trails, the way to heaven will have been seen in dreams that only a few, special individuals have had. Maps of heaven are thus important. And they must be good, complete maps. Heaven is reached only by careful avoidance of the wrong trails. These must also be shown so that the traveller can recognize and avoid them.

How can we know the general direction we should follow? How can anyone who has not dreamed the whole route begin to locate himself on such a map? When Joseph, or any of the other men, began to draw a hunting map, he had first to find his way. He did this by recognizing features, by fixing points of reference, and then, once he was oriented to the familiar and to the scale or manner in which the familiar was reproduced, he could begin to add his own layers of detailed information. But how can anyone begin to find a way on a map of trails to heaven, across a terrain that ordinary hunters do not experience in everyday activities or even in their dream-hunts?

The route to heaven is not wholly unfamiliar, however. As it happens, heaven is to one side of, and at the same level as, the point where the trails to animals all meet. Many men know where this point is, or at least some of its approach trails, from their own hunting dreams. Hunters can in this way find a basic reference, and once they realize that heaven is in a particular relation to this far more familiar centre, the map as a whole can be read. If this is not enough, a person can take a map with him; some old-timers who made or who were given maps of the trails to heaven choose to have a map buried with them. They can thus remind themselves which ways to travel if the actual experience of the trail proves to be too confusing. Others are given a corner of a map that will help reveal the trail to them. And even those who do not have any powerful dreams are shown the best maps of the route to heaven. The discoveries of the very few most powerful dreamers — and some of the dreamers have been women — are periodically made available to everyone.

The person who wishes to dream must take great care, even if he dreams only of the hunt. He must lie in the correct orientation, with his head towards the rising sun. There should be no ordinary trails, no human pathways, between his pillow and the bush. These would be confusing to the self that travels in dreams towards important and unfamiliar trails which can lead to a kill. Not much of this can be mapped — only the trail to heaven has been drawn up. There has been no equivalent need to make maps to share other important information.

Sometime, said Jimmy Wolf, you will see one of these maps. There are some of them around. Then the competence and strength of the old-timers who drew them will be unquestioned. Different trails can be explained, and heaven can be located on them. Yes, they were pretty smart, the men who drew them. Smarter than any white man in these parts and smarter than Indians of today. Perhaps, said Atsin, in the future there will be men good enough to make new maps of heaven — but not just now. There will be changes, he added, and the people will come once again to understand the things that Atsin's father had tried to teach him. In any case, he said, the older men are now trying to explain the powers and dreams of old-timers to the young, indeed to all those who have not been raised with these spiritual riches. For those who do not understand, hunting and life itself are restricted and difficult. So the people must be told everything, and taught all that they need, in order to withstand the incursions presently being made into their way of life, their land, and into their very dreams.

TO QUARRY IN WINTER

AFTER THEIR RETURN from Bluestone, Joseph and the family stayed at the Reserve. The men hunted all day long on or close to Reserve land, returning every night to their houses. By Christmas time, in the wake of Alan's sickness and the many accidents, and after the celebration of the midwinter festivities, Joseph began to grow restless. "Better to be at Quarry," he remarked, "far away from these flats."

… "That's how to make life better," he liked to say. "Move to a good cabin where there are no neighbours. Lots of real work, and the best of food." It was no surprise, then, when he made it known that he would soon leave again for his cabin on the Quarry River, deep inside his registered line. Anyone was welcome to come along. If no one wished to be up there with him, all well and good. He would stay there alone. "No use down here, on the Reserve. Too much trouble."

Is Joseph too old for another winter's trapping? Too weak? Might his heart give out? His family asked these questions, sometimes directly, sometimes in the form of cryptic or discouraging remarks. Joseph himself stated the issue in characteristic fashion. With his hand over his heart, he shook his head and said, "Maybe no good. Not long now. Not long now." But his answer to his own and others' remarks was plain enough: "Better to be on the trapline, at Quarry. And even if you die up there, that's fine." That way, said Joseph, he would die in the place where his first wife and others with whom he had spent the best years of his life had already died.

These questions were asked many times in the week before Joseph actually set out. When the hunters returned after dark from their day trips, they liked to sit in Joseph's house, discussing by candlelight the day's hunt and hunting in general, and basking in the intense heat thrown off by the wood stove. Speculation followed speculation about animal movements and the prospects for trapping at Quarry. But there was the usual long hiatus between Joseph's declared resolve to set out and any outward sign of his getting ready. Then, one morning, as I sat visiting in another house, someone remarked that Joseph had been preparing to leave since daybreak. Maybe he would leave that same afternoon …

During the first morning at Quarry, Joseph announced that he would like a fat cow moose to be killed. This would provide a supply of the best meat. In midwinter most bull moose are still lean and their meat is inferior. Two rabbits were found in the snares Sam set the night before, and a multitude of rabbit tracks showed that we were not likely to be short of rabbit meat. But the hunters wanted a moose — or, maybe, a caribou, though so far no one had seen any caribou tracks. During that day we found four sets of moose tracks close to the cabin. For a while we followed a pair travelling together.

In winter snow, tracks are comparatively easy to read. The texture and shape of a fresh hoof mark or of droppings clearly show just when animals have been in an area. The angle at which urine has hit the snow tells a hunter whether the moose he is close to is a cow or bull. The distances between hoof marks show an animal's speed and indicate, also, changes in speed. When Atsin set out to hunt the two moose close to the cabin, he gesticulated as he read the signs. With his right arm, he waved, pointed, and explained. The quick movement of his fingers showed the direction in which the animal was going. Opening and closing his hand, his arm stretched out level to the shoulder, he showed the direction the wind was blowing (here, in winter woods, hardly more than the drift of a breeze). The sweep of an open palm echoed the undulations of the terrain. Finally, with decisive pointing he established — given the lie of the land, the way the animal was moving, and the wind's direction — the particular course that he was going to take. Those behind him could follow if they wished.

With much excited signalling — he had deduced from tracks and droppings that a large cow was only minutes away — Atsin attempted to circle around to catch up with the moose from the side, and to surprise it from down wind. Three times he turned off from the animal's track. Twice he circled too late: the moose was deeper into the woods than Atsin had expected. The third time the manoeuvre was almost exactly right, but Atsin came so close to the moose that it was alarmed before he had a clear enough view to take a shot. That night we ate rabbit stew again.

On the second day we drove to Clay Flats, a small, open, and grassy area a little to the west of the cabin. Atsin and Sam hoped to find marten or lynx tracks and so decide where they might best set traps. Of course, everyone was on the lookout for moose. Only a mile or two from the cabin we spotted a magnificent bull. The hunters watched it for a few moments, as it browsed within easy range; then we continued on our way — Joseph had said he wanted a cow. After inspecting Clay Flats, we drove for some miles to the southeast, in the direction of the Alaska Highway, to take a look at Juniper Flats, another place important to the people, and where Atsin's family had always trapped. This took us away from the mountains towards the most settled land in the Quarry area. We were heading towards ranch and ranchers. These are established but small-scale ranchers, some of whom supplement their incomes by trapping. The Indians who once lived at Quarry know them well and think of some of them as neighbours. There are pleasant memories of helping and being helped by one another.

When we approached the ranches, a matter of no more than four or five miles from Clay Flats, the hunters put their guns away — even insisted that they be more or less hidden. Too many farms this way, they said. It would be better not to do any hunting here, even though these small farms are on or at the edge of lands on which the Indians hunt and trap just as much as they do anywhere else in the neighborhood of Quarry. There was an immediate and pervasive sense of conflict. It may be all right to trap beaver in the spring on Crown lands near the farms, but it is as well not to hunt too close to them in fall or winter. More specifically, it is best not to be seen hunting there.

Some way down the valley, Atsin proposed that we visit one of the ranchers. There was a household of old-timers only a little way ahead, he said, and we would be sure of a warm welcome there. He had known them for twenty years, and he always liked to call in on them, to recall old days, see and hear what had been happening in the area. Atsin particularly hoped to talk about his suspicion that strangers had been poaching his old trapline. Everyone agreed, and we turned off the snow-packed road into a driveway that led to a cluster of shacks and farm buildings. To one side of these, on the wide bank of a frozen creek, stood a small but well-finished log house. Atsin led the way; but before he got to the door, it was opened by a short middle-aged woman, who, recognizing the Reserve people, pressed us to come inside for coffee. There, in a warm and comfortable ranch kitchen, the Indian visitors, nervous but full of curiosity, sat in a ring of chairs at one end of the room. In an armchair facing them sat a heavy-set man. He was a neighbouring rancher, also visiting, well known to the hunters. The man of the house sat at the kitchen table. He joined his wife in urging everyone to accept the offer of coffee and to help themselves to slices of a large cake that was passed around.

The ranchers teased the Indians. "Trapping out of a pickup these days, eh? Don't suppose you guys bother to do much walking no more!" Such remarks were addressed to men who hunt and trap on foot or horseback, who only occasionally have the use of a pickup, and whose home community has never had more than a total of two functioning vehicles. But the Indians did not explain or contradict. They did not even tease back. They simply laughed along with the jokes. Sam was complimented on the particularly nice pair of moccasins he was wearing, but then one of the ranchers commented that Sam must be the only person left with such footwear. "I guess nobody makes them things. Forgotten how, eh?" This remark was not made in jest, but as an observation of undeniable fact. Once again, no one resisted the implications or reacted to the assured tone of the question. They kept laughing along with their hosts and, with this show of amusement, may even have reinforced a stereotype of modern Indian life. Yet every Indian in the room belonged to a household where moccasins are made. All the hunters in the cabin at Quarry River wore moccasins nearly every day of the year.

Even in the kitchen of a family that the people had known for twenty years, the Indians' identity was somehow effaced. They accepted the condescension, the barely concealed air of superiority. At one point the visiting rancher commented on the fact that the girl with us, Joseph Patsah's daughter Shirley, was pretty. He spoke of her in the third person, as if she were not there: "Yeah, I heard about her the other day. She's a good-looking gal, too." His remark was addressed to everyone and to no one, a thought out loud. The girl blushed, and later she said that she had been angry. But no one replied to the rancher, just as they had not bothered to challenge remarks about pickups and moccasins. The Indians observed, accepted coffee and cake, waited on the ranchers' conversation, and presently left them with their ways, opinions, and attitudes unruffled. Much as the Indians' land is taken and cleared, so also were the people themselves over-ridden by the settlers, whose assumed dominance the Indians seemed to have granted.

Within minutes of our leaving, conversation in the pickup turned to the Whites we had just visited: to the details of their homes, their life styles, and what they had said. Some of their remarks were considered to be lies, others were laughable. Some of their jokes and teases were picked up and exchanged within the Quarry group. The visit had been an entertainment, a spectacle — not an occasion for participation. The ranchers' homes were living theatre. Their stereotyping of Indians appeared to reach no deeper than that. And on the way back, at the edge of the farmland, Atsin spotted a cow moose among the trees. After a brief hunt he killed it.

The afternoon was unusually cold, even by the standard of sub-Arctic winters. As usual, we built a large fire as the hunters began the butchering. The intensity of the cold gave some reason for haste, and the men felt an additional urgency because of our proximity to the ranches. Atsin kept repeating what we all knew: Indians have the right to hunt for game, even on land that belongs to a farmer. "We have to get meat. Out trapping you have to kill your meat. This is all Indian land. We can go any place to get our food." He spoke in apparent defiance, but he could not entirely conceal his apprehension and nervousness.

The moose was butchered hurriedly but properly. As always, virtually every part of the animal was taken: the digestive system was cleaned out, the intestines separated from other entrails, the liver and heart carefully set aside. Despite the cold, and whatever uneasy feelings were inspired by the thought that others might say we were trespassing, the hunters observed the rules and conventions that govern the butchering of a moose. On this occasion they observed also the conventions that surround the treatment of an unborn calf. First, they prepared a thick bed of partially digested browse which they poured from the animal's stomach. Then, painstakingly, they began to remove the foetus. Each part of the surrounding reproductive system was disconnected from the womb and set aside. Then the womb itself was placed on the bed of the cow's stomach contents and sliced open. As the amniotic fluids flowed from it, Atsin very carefully guarded against their running onto the snow. His son David, who had been building up the bed of stomach contents, almost allowed a trickle of amniotic fluid to escape. Atsin leapt forward and, with his butchering knife, remoulded the mushy, half-digested grasses into a better barrier. "You've got to be careful," he shouted. "If the water goes on snow, then right away the weather will go hard and cold. And pretty soon we'll all be frozen to death!" Finally, Atsin pulled the tiny calf from the womb.

A well-developed foetus is used as food. This time there was some discussion about whether or not it should be taken, but the hunters in the end decided that it was too small. So the foetus was carefully laid on the mat of stomach contents, protected with more digested grasses and some membranes, then covered over with spruce boughs and a few dead branches. Only when all the remains were entirely hidden away was the butchering finished. Such respectful treatment of the foetus was as automatic as any other part of the butchering. Even if it did cause some delay, there was no question of its not being carried out …We spent much of the next days eating and resting … Sam walked each day looking for caribou, or whatever he might come across. But the weather was bitter cold. The temperature ws never above −25° F and often as low as −40° F … The coldness of weather became the focus of pessimism and a justification for a prolonged but untroubled inactivity which had their real source in the failure of that winter's trapping.

Conversation began to turn towards the Reserve. Is everyone O.K. down there? Do you suppose they have enough meat? Maybe the kids are hungry. Maybe no one is doing much hunting. No doubt it is even colder on the flats. Maybe some of the good hunters have gone out to work as slashers on the new seismic cuts. And there could be problems, too. There is still some meat in the cache up here at Quarry. Perhaps someone should take it to the Reserve, help people out. Joseph rarely joined in these conversations. He busied himself with the firewood, made bannock (a slow-fried bread), cooked grouse and rabbits, checked and prepared his traps. Trapping might not be much good right now, he seemed to be saying, but that gives us time to get ready for the spring beaver hunt. The talk of returning to the Reserve went on around him, it was never directed at him. Yet its purpose was probably more to secure his agreement to a return than an expression of any great anxiety about the folks at home. If Joseph resolved to stay at the Quarry cabin, someone had to stay with him. Whatever he might insist to the contrary, however often he declared a willingness to live alone at Quarry, however much he assented to the risks his independence might necessitate, the others would never agree to it: someone would have to stay there with him. As the cold, inactive days wore on, and all hope of busy and profitable trapping was given up, no one much wanted to be the one.

Eventually Sam volunteered to stay with Joseph, at least for a while. Greatly relieved, everyone else set off the next morning.

At the Reserve there was a party, though not a protracted one. We learned that people there had experienced difficulties, but nothing serious. There were some minor shortages of meat. About a week later Joseph and Sam returned. They had hitched a ride from a local rancher. Joseph was not well, and Sam had become alarmed by the possibility that Joseph might fall seriously ill so far from help. Joseph himself insisted he had returned only because Sam was so worried. He would, he declared, spend the next weeks at the Reserve getting ready for the beaver hunt. Soon it would be time to go back to Quarry. By then, he remarked, as if to justify another stay "down on these flats," the horses would be in good enough shape to be taken up there. There would be adequate grazing around the cabin and up the valley slopes. Better, in any case, to have the horses at a real hunting place. Yes, that was how it was going to be as soon as it was time to hunt beaver. He and all his family would move up with the horses, and they would stay there, of course, through the whole spring and summer. It is always best, said Joseph, to be on the trapline during fine weather.

DREAMS OF FREEDOM
Scandinavian Oral Histories

ED. GORDON FISH, FROM THE B.C. PROVINCIAL ARCHIVES

Sound Heritage was a quarterly begun in 1972 that published the oral histories and reminiscences of British Columbians on a wide variety of subjects. Number 36 (1982) in this forty-volume series was devoted to recording the recollections of men and women born near the beginning of the 20th century who grew up in the remote Scandinavian colonies of the coast. These included the Bella Coola Valley, which was first settled in 1894 by a group of Norwegian immigrants from the United States; Cape Scott, established in 1896 by Danish settlers, many of whom were also from the U.S.; and Sointula, set up in 1901 by Finns who were idealistically motivated to establish a co-operative community on Malcolm Island. Gordon Fish, the editor of these particular histories, viewed them as part of a larger pattern of settlement wherein ethnic and religious colonies sprang up throughout the province in the nineteenth and early twentieth centuries. He points to Metlakatla near the mouth of the Skeena River as being something like a prototype; there the Anglican lay missionary, William Duncan, established a sanctuary in 1862 for his Tsimshian parishioners where there would be little outside influence (especially from disease or alcohol) and the converts could live and worship as they chose. Fish points to the Doukhobors in the Kootenays as creating another such community.

The three Scandinavian communities were all partly motivated by a similar search for spiritual and political freedom, by a shared belief in ideals of co-operation and community. They all, however, faced formidable problems: the Norwegians at Bella Coola, who were cut off from the rest of the world for much of the year, lost their religious leader in their third year and met for the last time as a colony in 1909; the Danes in the wild and isolated area of Cape Scott were not only cut off from the world, but from each other by a lack of harbours, roads and bridges and, according to Lester Peterson's elegiac *The Cape Scott Story* (1974), they had all left the Cape by 1914; the Finns had severe financial and leadership problems, such that the co-operative system was abandoned by 1905. In their oral histories, the descendants of these settlers recall vividly a way of life that was based on a strong sense of community but which also required an enormous amount of ingenuity and self-reliance.

Gordon Fish points out that while the settlers inevitably failed in their search for a paradise or utopia, many of them stayed on and established permanent communities even as their original idealism faded into the wilderness around them.

INTO A WILD COUNTRY: NORWEGIANS AT BELLA COOLA

The beginning of a severe depression in the United States in 1893 caused many farmers in the Midwestern states to lose their properties when they were unable to make payments on debts and mortgages. In Minnesota and the Dakotas, where many Scandinavians had settled in the latter part of the nineteenth century, a group of Norwegians became interested in making a fresh start elsewhere. Leading one search for a better area was Rev. Christian Saugstad, a Lutheran pastor in Minnesota. He was actively looking into the possibility of establishing a colony where his congregation would be able to live a happy and virtuous life away from the evils of the world. It seems likely that he saw, or heard about, an article on Bella Coola written by Bernhart Fillip Jacobsen, a Norwegian, who had been to the valley early in 1884. Jacobsen described the area in favourable terms and even suggested that it would be a suitable place for a colony.

MILO FOUGNER: Most of the people that went to Bella Coola were from Minnesota, North Dakota, South Dakota, [Iowa, Wisconsin] and some of the predominantly Scandinavian areas in the Red River Valley. And 1894 was the middle of one of the worst depressions, I guess, that the United States had ever experienced. It was getting harder and harder to sell their wheat. They had several poor crops, they had hail and this, that and the other thing, and they didn't have the wheat that we have nowadays. There was rust, and they were plagued by a number of things, and their economic position was pretty bad.

Reverend Saugstad, who was, amongst other things, I think, an idealist, probably had been thinking for some time about establishing a colony of almost morally perfect people, in an ideal situation away from temptation.

He was to be the leader. So he and two others, Mr. [A.] Stortroen was one, came out to the West, and they examined several possibilities. One, the American government offered them the Yakima Valley and said that they would put in irrigation if Saugstad's group would settle. Then they came to Victoria, and they [the B.C. government] offered them land in the Fraser Valley. And then he and B. F. Jacobsen went up to Bella Coola.

Jacobsen at that time was collecting curios for a museum in Germany and could speak the Bella Coola language; in fact, he could speak two or three Indian dialects fluently and had been on the coast some time. They looked the situation over, and more and more Reverend Saugstad realized that here was the Shangri-la that he was looking for. He could herd his people in there, and they could be supervised, and he could make the valley into a garden.

TED LEVELTON: Now, my personal opinion is they either wore dark glasses or couldn't see at all, because, frankly, I would never have come here when I think of what the country was like when we arrived here. What he could see in the place I'll never know. But anyway, he came back and painted a very glowing picture of the conditions here. There was lots of fish, there was lots of game, there was wild fruit and there was good land and lots of timber. Well, I quite agree with him there — there was lots of these things that he mentioned, mind you — but for a man to move in here with just his bare hands, into a wild country, no transportation whatever except a boat every two months in those days, and that was uncertain … If the weather was bad, they didn't come in here.

He [Reverend Saugstad] came back here and then got busy, and that summer they signed up about eighty-five people. Among them was my dad, Erasmus Levelton. He was a man who had been raised in the timbered country. He'd done quite a number of years fishing the Lofoten Islands, out where the fishing is really tough. You fish in the winter there; you go out there with the cold gales howling and ice and things. Anyway, he got fed up with that kind of life and decided to migrate. We migrated to the United States in the summer of 1892 and went to Minnesota, where a number of relatives had moved in previous years.

ANNIE LEVELTON: Dad didn't like Minnesota. He wasn't used to the flat prairie country and he wanted to go where there was the sea; he was used to that.

TED LEVELTON: They left Minnesota and went up to Winnipeg, where they got on the CPR and the CPR took them into Vancouver. They had to go from Vancouver to Victoria, because that was where the provincial government was, your land department and all that.

MILO FOUGNER: They boarded the old side-wheeler *Princess Louise* and headed for Bella Coola. On the way there it had been decided that first of all they would draw lots for land, a quarter section of land each. Then the four chaps who had drawn the same quarters in the same section banded together, and the idea was that they would build a temporary shelter on the section and the four of them would work together improving their individual properties. This worked out very nicely.

There was no dock there, of course. The Indians came out to meet them in canoes at the mouth of the river, and the colonists were all very surprised that standing right up in one of the Indian canoes was a very, very blonde-haired girl. It turned out she was Bertha Thorson, a daughter of an old sea captain [Thore Thorson] who had retired in Bella Coola. He had come there just prior to the colony and he later joined the colony. It sort of perked them up a bit to see some of their kind there.

Although the colonists were scattered along the valley, the centre of the community was about twelve miles (nineteen kilometres) from the sea. Originally called Christiania, the community later became known as Hagensborg, the location of Hagen Christensen's store.

The first winter was a hard one. The colonists cut a road from Bella Coola, at the mouth of the Bella Coola River, to Hagensborg.

On 6 May, more colonists arrived. Some were families of the men in the first group, and others were Norwegians from different areas of the American Midwest.

TED LEVELTON: We came up here on a boat called the *Danube*. I can remember the old whistle just about scared us to death. We were standing around, you know, watching the shoreline gradually coming closer, and then, all of a sudden, this whistle let out a terrific blast and we kids just about jumped out of our shoes! As soon as the steamer blew its whistle, these Indians all came boiling down in their great big old spoon canoes and surrounded the ship. They had heard about these people coming in and they figured, "Well now, here's a dollar or two for us, you see; we'll be able to take these people ashore."

They would take a whole canoe-load from the boat down there up to the village for a dollar. It'd take three men when the tide was out, because there was a rather rapid current in that river, and they'd have the boat loaded with trunks. There used to be a village on the bank; great big old houses. They would be forty feet wide and probably a hundred feet long — terrific big houses.

When we landed here, Dad already had a house built, and we walked right up six miles that same afternoon. I can remember going up. I was not quite six and I can remember my legs were getting pretty tired by the time I got up there.

ANNIE LEVELTON: Father had a cabin — luckily. He was the only one who really had a good cabin, so we had a home to go to, but it was alarming after having been on the prairies to see those huge trees, you know. And my mother, oh, she just couldn't get reconciled to the fact that she left a beautiful home in the old country, in Norway, with servants and all that sort of thing to look after all us little ones, and to arrive up here and … Oh dear, she didn't know what to do.

BERTHA NYGAARD: I came in the spring of 1895 with my parents. My dad was headed for California; then Reverend Saugstad met him on the street in Minnesota and persuaded him to join the colonists. And that's what he did. He said, "We want men like you, great big husky men."

My first memories of Bella Coola are of the Indians poling us up the river. I was frightened, and they were chanting. They only had blankets around them. The old Hansen place was where we landed, and poor mother — there were five of us — said she was standing out there, she didn't know where to go or what to do, and my dad was then pitching a tent under some trees for the night. And Mrs. Hansen said, "Come with me, this house can hold a few more," and when we got there it was just full of people!

TED LEVELTON: When you're a kid of six, it was a grand place to run around, climb trees and chase squirrels and all this kind of stuff.

You could raise good crops when you got the land cleared, but boy, it was all back-breaking work. The ground was grubbed with a grub hoe. There were no horses or ploughs, and the patches were too small, anyway, for a horse even to turn around on. You'd grub out a little spot for a garden and another little patch for potatoes, and that was it for the first few years. It was the women and the children that did most of this, because the men had to get out and hustle. Most of them who came here, I would say, were down to practically their last dollar when they arrived here. I know certainly my dad was.

ANNIE ENGEBRETSON: They all had to work and they were all together in bunches then, you see. My father started to cut logs for his own house. He just split the cedar logs. I shingled the roof. We were busy all the time. I helped to pull on the crosscut saw, dig up the devil's club and things. I got strong!

TED LEVELTON: Luckily, he was a good woodsman, a good man with a broadaxe.

He could build just about as nice a log house as you'd want to set eyes on. And he was also a fairly good carpenter, so he got a certain amount of work building homes for others here. That's the way he made a few dollars.

BERTHA NYGAARD: My father was a tailor in Minnesota. In Bella Coola he was supposed to be a farmer, but he didn't know anything about farming. He had hands like a woman because he'd done nothing but light work, but he made a success of whatever he undertook. We ended up having one of the biggest ranches there.

MILO FOUGNER: I suppose transportation was their biggest problem. My dad says in one place in his diary: "I got up at five this morning and walked to the waterfront and back," which would be twenty-four miles round trip over a rough trail that they had hacked out. He doesn't mention the fact that on his way back he packed all of the things that he needed possibly for the next two or three weeks. They packed cookstoves on their backs; they packed everything that you need in your home, and that's the only way they could pack it — there were no horses — other than the river itself for canoes. Certainly, you could get it up to the river bank, but in a lot of cases you still had to pack it a long ways.

It's the [Bella Coola] valley that runs east and west, and the part that they settled would be from salt water to twenty-four to twenty-five miles up the valley. And [the Bella Coola River is] quite a large river, lush growth; down in the valley floor itself, huge timber — fir, cedar, hemlock — interspersed with miles of devil's club and underbrush. Then along the river, a thick growth of willow and alder and birch and that sort of thing. There just wasn't anything easy about it. It wasn't these sylvan paths that you hear about going through the forest of *Evangeline* by any means at all. It was tough going.

MILO FOUGNER: The Indian people, they were a very important factor in the life of the colony. I think, perhaps, that both sides discovered integration and segregation wasn't so important as mutual trust — mutual admiration, if you like — for one another's good points and mutual understanding. When I was a boy, you respected the Indian people to the point where you would never intrude on one of their affairs unless you were asked, unless you were invited, and you considered it an honour if you were. By the same token, our affairs were the same. Now, integration says that these barriers should all be cut down, but I'm not prepared to agree that the situation is any better now than it was when I was a boy. In fact, I feel that there was more respect, possibly, between us in those days than there is now.

TED LEVELTON: For a monetary consideration, naturally, they were always willing to take your freight up [river]. They hauled freight all the way to Hagensborg in canoes. These fellows that lived a way up there, say half a dozen of them, would sort of club together and come down and buy maybe a ton and a half of provisions — the heavy stuff like flour, sugar and this kind of stuff. And they'd get the Indians, and they'd take it up for five dollars. Two men would take that canoe all the way to Hagensborg and unload the stuff there and then come home again which saved those fellows a tremendous lot of hard back-breaking work. They'd pole it. Two or three men can take one of those spoon canoes up places that you would swear that nothing but a very powerful motor could drive a vessel up through.

MILO FOUGNER: We grew up with the Indian kids, of course, and could speak with them, and I suppose we heard more of the imagery of the different dances and what it meant and that sort of thing, and knew the different costumes.

When my dad was Indian agent, he had a field matron at Kitimat send in her annual requisition for drugs, and amongst it was a barrel of Epsom salts, which is one hundred pounds of Epsom salts. So my dad wrote to her and he said he'd received her requisition and passed it on, but he said, "What are you going to do with one hundred pounds of Epsom salts, move the village?"

ANNIE LEVELTON: The Indians were surprisingly very good to us. They could have resented us pretty badly but they were awfully good to us. And we were good to them. The settlers, I will say this, were fine men, and never once did we ever hear of any scandal with them, bachelors and all. They never went near the village. They were polite to the Indians and the Indians were polite to them, and they understood each other. You'd go down to the wharf and hear one fellow say, "How many fish did you catch?" and he'd be speaking Norsky. "I got so many fish," and the other fellow would say something in Chinook, and that was fine.

Although the scenery and climate of the valley may have reminded settlers of parts of Norway, one element of the natural life of the area was new to nearly all of them — the grizzly bear.

ANNIE LEVELTON: I saw a bear and never even knew it was a bear when I was a little girl. I didn't know that it was a bear until I saw a picture of one in later years. I thought it was a big dog I'd seen.

Mr. Bakken arrived one morning down at the cabin and he was laughing, he was nearly in hysterics. And Mother said, "What in the world is so funny?" "Well," he said, "I did a funnier thing today than I ever did in my life," he said. He was coming from his home — he lived about four miles up the line, I guess — and he had to cross what we call the Snootli bridge and as he came along on this side down the hill, a big grizzly meandered right out on the road right ahead of him.

The grizzly was so close to him that he didn't really know what it was at first, I guess, and the grizzly just stopped and looked at him. And he just couldn't think of a thing to say, so he tipped his hat and said, "Good morning!"

TED LEVELTON: A very close friend of ours, Karls Christopherson, he was a bachelor, but he used to stay at our place a lot and he was a very comical sort of guy. He was a great man with kids. He would tell us some of the most hair-raising yarns. I'm sure that none of them were true, but boy, he had us spellbound. We'd just sit there with our ears strained right out to make sure we didn't miss anything when he started telling some of these yarns.

He, with several other guys, had been up to what is known as the Salloomt Valley, which runs off the main valley here about twelve miles up. And they'd been prospecting in there and found a very likely looking prospect. And they had this analyzed, and it analyzed very well, and they decided to develop this thing.

Anyway, this one Christopherson, with several other guys, had been up there doing some work. They built a cabin and made a pretty good road in there. And he was coming out again with a big pack of blankets and personal clothing, and he had a frying pan in one hand and a kettle in the other. And he was walking along the trail — this was in early summer — and all of a sudden, a big old grizzly pops right out of the bush, right out in front of him, got up on her hind legs and started roaring and coming towards him. Well, here he was with his big pack on his back and he couldn't get rid of that in a hurry and he figured it was no use running, so he thought the only way is to go right at her and see if he could bluff her out. So he started beating this frying pan and his kettle together and kept walking towards her. And he finally bluffed her! She started backing off, and she backed off and backed off, and she finally got up and beat it. And he said he could feel the cold sweat running down the back of his neck all the time he was doing this. But, he said, when he finally realized what he was doing, the kettle was absolutely flat and the frying pan was all dented up, but he said, "I think it saved my life. I fully expected that old girl would have gone for me, because she had a couple of cubs there."

I can remember we had some terrific winters. The first couple of winters we were here, we had terrific snowfalls. The people up the valley had a hard time because they had to break a road for twelve miles in the snow.

I can remember a good many times those fellows would come down from Hagensborg, twelve miles up, and they'd come down here to Clayton's and get, oh, sixty pounds worth of provisions. They'd put that on their backs and they'd start back up again and they'd get it back up to our place at nine or ten o'clock at night, absolutely pooped out. They were just barely able to drag their feet behind them. They stayed at our place overnight.

ANNIE LEVELTON: My mother was one of the most generous women in the world. She always had the coffeepot on, and it made no difference if they were black, red or white, she fed them all.

TED LEVELTON: I can remember, oh, six or eight or ten of these fellows coming in a bunch. They had no blankets with them, and it meant that we had to put some bedding on the floor, and they'd flake out in a row on the floor.

We slept upstairs. This house was only about seven feet high on the wall, but they'd put some joists in and then they'd laid some boards along the top, about eight feet wide. It was just a very small room up in there, but that's where all us kids slept. Whenever any youngsters came in we'd flake out like sardines in a can, you see, along these boards. I can remember looking down over the edge — they had a board set up on edge at the side of this floor so you wouldn't fall off it — looking down and seeing this row of fellows' faces in the early morning light. You'd see them all lying there with their noses in the air, some snoring away to high heavens, and other fellows with a great big bunch of whiskers on. We used to get a big bang

out of watching the different facial expressions you'd see down below —
some fellow, you know, snoring away in good style!

Although some of the original colonists had left the valley soon after their ar-
rival, newcomers continued to arrive, and by the end of 1896, the colony had
158 members. The men earned some money working on the construction of a
wagon road from the waterfront up the valley. Land for farming was gradually
cleared and cabins built. A church congregation assembled, and a choir was
formed. A post office, a store and a library were established. Gardens provided
a variety of vegetables, the streams were a source of salmon, and there were deer
and geese.

In 1896 the colonists did very well fishing at Rivers Inlet. In Torliev Viken's
words, "the men returned with money in their pockets and courage in their
hearts to return to clearing land."

MILO FOUGNER: The Reverend Saugstad was the first of the colonists
to die. He had great plans, he had organized so many things: a salmon
cannery, sawmills and he also planned a river steamer to bring supplies up
and down the river.

He foresaw the farming, of course, and dairying as being the big thing,
putting in the creameries and exporting the products of the creameries
and also farm products of various kinds. Regular meetings were held and
then annual colony meetings, and they had committees of all types for
administering the colony. It would have been interesting, and I suppose
that has been said many times, as to just what would have happened if they
had continued under his strong leadership.

AWAY FROM THE OUTSIDE WORLD: FINNS AT SOINTULA

The colonies at Bella Coola and Cape Scott were established largely in response
to specific economic conditions in North America. To a certain extent the same
is true for the Finnish colony on Malcolm Island, conceived by a group of
Finnish miners already in British Columbia. However, unlike the other colo-
nies, this one would be utopian.

A considerable number of Finns had worked on the construction of the

Canadian Pacific Railway, and when that work was completed, some of them found work in the coal mines in the Nanaimo area of Vancouver Island. Work in the mines was dangerous, and there were frequent accidents. Wages were low, and any attempt by the miners to improve their situation was firmly resisted by the mine owner, James Dunsmuir. When the North Wellington mines were exhausted, Dunsmuir opened new mines at Extension and then at Ladysmith. The miners had to move their homes each time if they wanted to keep their jobs. With very little work to be found elsewhere in the area, they had no choice but to move. Living conditions in the mining towns were, in many ways, as bad as working conditions in the mines.

WAYNE HOMER (paraphrasing the history of Sointula written in Finnish by Matti Halminen in 1936): Dunsmuir was a slave driver who gave his employees a harsh time and is said to have introduced bootleggers and company beer outlets to ply the disgruntled workers with booze to keep them quiet. It was under these disgusting working conditions that the first Finnish Brotherhood of Temperance Societies was born in Nanaimo. This new revolt against drunkenness and associated vices spread rapidly across Canada and into the United States. It was from this unbearable harassment and miserable working conditions in the coal mines that the idea of establishing a collective workers commune under socialist principles was born.

KAISA RIKSMAN: They had heard of something similar in France. A man named Fourier had had a colony, like a Shangri-la or something. So these people asked the B.C. government for land to which they could move as a group. And then they wrote to Australia to Mr. Kurikka and asked him to come to be the leader of this group. He wrote back and said that he was very ill and he was in hospital and he didn't have a penny to his name; but if they would send him money, he would certainly come. Which he did.

Matti Kurikka was well known in Finland as an author and a playwright. As editor-in-chief of the Helsinki newspaper Työmies (The Worker), *he wrote articles on a wide range of subjects, among them socialism, class struggle, the value and dignity of physical labour, the status of women in the community and the need for universal suffrage. Kurikka had left Finland in protest against the political situation there, but his attempt to establish a Finnish community in Australia was a failure. He arrived in Nanaimo in August 1900.*

KAISA RIKSMAN: When these people asked the government for land, the Land Officer threw a lot of maps at them and said, "Take your choice." And they picked Malcolm Island, because it was by the sea and seemed like the only place where they could have farms, because their idea was to make their living through farming.

Malcolm Island is located at the northern end of Johnstone Strait, between northern Vancouver Island and the mainland of British Columbia. About fifteen miles (twenty-three kilometres) long and roughly two and a half miles (four kilometres) wide, it was heavily forested with cedar, spruce, fir and hemlock.

The first members of the colony to go to Malcolm Island left Nanaimo on December 6, 1901. They travelled in a sailboat owned and captained by Johan Mikkelson. Theodore Tanner was elected leader of the group. The others were Kalle Hendrickson, Otto Ross and Malakias Kytomaa. Mostly they sailed, but sometimes there was no wind and they rowed. After passing through Seymour Narrows a shotgun went off accidently in the boat and Mikkelson's hand was hurt. The others administered what first aid they could and got him finally to Alert Bay. He was sent to Nanaimo on the first steamer. He lost only his thumb although at first the doctors thought his arm would have to be amputated. The others reached Malcolm Island on December 15, and anchored at Rough Bay.
— AILI ANDERSON, *History of Sointula*

KAISA RIKSMAN: It just happened to be during a big storm. In fact, it was such a big storm that there hasn't been any like it since. It blew all the trees down on Haddington Island nearby, and these men had to take shelter in some big tank that some outfit had left. So they didn't think too much of it at the time, but anyway, it didn't scare them enough not to come back. They went back and reported that they found the island favourable, and two more men came who were the builders, the carpenters, and they built the log cabin that's in Rough Bay. They built it, and of course a sauna was the next one.

There were seven altogether, and one, Mr. Wilander, brought his wife along, so she was the first woman. They were the only people here when I arrived; I was twenty-two then. I came from Finland along with this other lady. Our husbands were here in Sointula already. They had heard about Sointula from Mr. Kurikka when he went on his lecture tours. He and Mr. Salmi came here, and then I and Mrs. Salmi and our four children came to Sointula together.

We arrived on June 3, 1902. We arrived here late at night. It was pitch black, of course, and all the bay was covered with these big kelps — these great big snakes in the water with these great big heads on them. The boat tied up to some sort of a slip, and we had to walk along these logs to the shore where this little shack was.

In this log cabin there were five double bunks for all these families. Hay was piled on these bunks for a mattress, and my husband and I and the two children got one of these bunks for our own.

The first meeting to decide on how to proceed and just what they were to do was held in June of 1902. And they held a three-day celebration at that time, where they had meetings and had plays and sang.

They were going to share everything. Everyone would be working for the common good. No one owned anything separately and individually. They planned to farm and log, and all the proceeds would be divided equally.

I think the main idea was to have a free society. Especially, they emphasized that women should have equal rights with men. At that time women had no property rights, they had no rights whatsoever in wages, so this was one thing that was applied here. The women had a dollar a day wages, as the men did, and they had a right to speak at meetings and they had a right to vote. And they had to work. Everyone had to work.

Another thing they wanted was a society where there would be no government church. There would be no liquor vending, and no women should have to sell themselves, whatever that would mean. They could have religion, but no one would be forcing any particular religion, and they could believe as they wished.

The company was to look after all the children — all the expenses, clothing, food and schooling. No one would be charged extra for children. The idea was that later on the children would be the workers and they would look after the elders. All the women went to work in the kitchen or laundry or wherever they were needed, and they had a nursery where their children were sent. They could be left there overnight, but most of the women took their children home in the evening.

That summer the colonists officially named the settlement Sointula — "the place of harmony." There were now over a hundred people in the colony, and the future seemed promising, despite the lack of money to buy essential equipment and supplies.

KAISA RIKSMAN: Each family was supposed to pay two hundred dollars, but that's where the trouble really began. A lot of people arrived and they didn't have the two hundred dollars, so the colony didn't have the money it expected to have. But they didn't turn anyone away, so everything they bought was mortgaged.

The main industry was going to be farming, but they found that it just wouldn't do. This area wasn't meant for farming, and it meant so much work clearing land that they would all starve before they got started. So they turned to logging and fishing.

They weren't really farmers. The people that came here were expert tradesmen in their own line — tailors and blacksmiths and whatever was necessary — and they were educated. They were not ignorant people by any means. Mr. Makela, he was a very well-educated man. He had gone through university in Finland and he was translating English books into Finnish. And they had a doctor [Dr. Oswald Beckman] here, too.

When they saw that they couldn't farm, they had to turn to logging to make a living. And then to make homes for people to live in, they had to build a sawmill. That was the first thing that was built, and then a blacksmith's shop.

RICHARD MICHELSON: I was born in Wellington, B.C., in 1894. My father's name was Takkomaki and my mother's name was Pauna. I was registered under the name Takkomaki, but my father changed his name a little bit afterwards. He came to Sointula in 1902, more or less to get out of slavery in the mines. He used to work in the mines in Wellington and Extension.

For the first couple of nights we stayed in a log house until the tents were raised for the different families. We lived in the tents until the sawmill got around to making lumber for building houses for different families.

ARVO TYNJALA: They opened up dairy places. Of course, there wasn't any open ground here, but they had to feed their cows. They had to go elsewhere for the feed and they went as far as the head of Knight Inlet and the head of Kingcome Inlet to get their grass on the river flats.

Nobody had any private property, or anything like that. It was all one community under a sort of co-operative. It was just like one household, you know — everyone was together. They dined together, worked together and tried to make things go the best they knew how.

RICHARD MICHELSON: I think about once a week they had a general meeting. As youngsters, we used to go to the meetings but we didn't know much about what was going on. I remember one time I went there and I fell asleep against the table. I woke up in the middle of the night and the meeting was all over, and the only one around was a watchman. He didn't wake me up, but when I woke up, well, I just got up and walked home.

A housing shortage caused a great deal of concern. There simply were not enough houses being built to accommodate all the colonists. Living in a tent had been acceptable during the summer, but with the onset of winter, the crowding and discomfort gave rise to complaints and prompted some people to leave. An attempt was made to alleviate the problem, but the result only made things worse.

ARVO TYNJALA: In 1902 a kind of apartment house was being built. The first two storeys were divided into apartments, and on the third storey there was the meeting hall. On the twenty-ninth day of January, 1903, that thing burned down. It was built out of rough, wet lumber — straight green stuff that was newly from the woods. You know how it dries; there were big cracks in the walls and there must have been an awful draft in there.

KAISA RIKSMAN: They didn't have any definite knowledge as to how it started, but they surmised that it had started from where the heating system pipes had been extended with a wooden flue. They didn't have enough money to buy more pipes, so they decided that would do.

When the fire started, most of the people were at a meeting upstairs, so that's one of the reasons that so many people were burnt to death.

I had two children at that time, and the youngest was fretful that evening, so I wasn't able to go to the meeting. I went to bed early, but I was still awake when I heard someone crying that there was a fire. I jumped out of bed and looked around to see what I would take, and then realized that I could only take the children. So I took one under each arm and I went out.

I decided to go out the front entrance, which was one floor lower. And when I got there, there was so much draft the smoke was going through the doorway, along the top of the door and rising up to the top of the ceiling, so that it was all clear, and I was able to get out with no discomfort at all.

Many other people were jumping out of windows because they were afraid to go through the front entrance, because of the kerosene barrel that was stored right by the door, and they expected it to explode.

Eleven people died in the fire — eight children and three adults.

Word was got to Vancouver, and people sent clothing and food from there. Of course, travel was so slow it took quite a while to get word down there, and again for the boat to come up with supplies.

ARVO TYNJALA: That was a big disaster — just about the finish. It would have been worse yet, but we got quite a bit of help from the outside, from Vancouver. People collected and sent clothing and all kinds of help.

Work was quickly begun on the construction of houses for all families with children, but in the aftermath of the fire there was increasing dissension in the colony as people discussed the possible causes of the fire. There were even stories of the fire being started deliberately to hide evidence of the embezzlement of colony funds. Nothing ever came of such stories, but the disaster left bitter division in the colony.

Worse yet, the economic situation was not improving. Logging was not profitable because timber prices were low and operating costs were high. Low prices for salmon meant low incomes for fishermen. Because of the long distances between Malcolm Island and possible markets, the output of the brick factory was used mainly on the island, and while the foundry and the blacksmith shop were of great value to the colony, they did not bring in much income. Only the sawmill showed a profit, and late in 1903 construction of a new mill began. Nevertheless, the population totalled 238 at the end of the year, up from 193 twelve months earlier, and there was renewed hope in the future.

This hope was dashed by another setback.

Kurrika was in Vancouver at the time when North Vancouver notices about bridge building contracts over Capilano and Seymour rivers were in the papers. On the advice of a certain Finnish businessman from Seattle, Kurikka placed a $3,000 offer for the contract in the name of the Kalevan Kansa Colonization Co. Ltd., and $150 down to hold it. This sum would be lost if the colony didn't take the contract.

Many long discussions were held at meetings in Sointula over this, and new estimates made. The general feeling was that it would be wiser to withdraw the offer and lose the $150 than to go ahead. But Kurikka talked them into it. He envisioned better and larger contracts with Vancouver later, once they got in on the building of the city. He insisted that the colony's financial situation was such that it forced them into taking on the contract. All the timber and lumber needed could be taken from Malcolm Island. That would help so much it would surely turn out a profitable undertaking. The contract was signed.

As the work progressed and Kurikka realized the big mistake made in the estimate of the cost, he urged the men to go on strike but no one would listen to him any more.

— AILI ANDERSON

This episode was followed by yet another controversy, this time about Kurrika's views on love and marriage, which he had expressed in articles in *Aika*. When the bridge builders returned to Sointula late in 1904, a special meeting was held to discuss the matter. Many people were concerned about the idea of "free love" seemingly implied in Kurikka's articles. Although there was no suggestion "free love," was practised in the colony, there were fears that outsiders would form a misleading impression from the articles. This, plus the bridge fiasco, seriously divided the colony on the issue of Kurikka's leadership, and Kurikka's old partner, Makela, was now part of the opposition.

The meeting resulted in Kurikka's resignation from the colony. Accompanied by nearly half of the colonists, he moved to Webster's Corners in the Fraser Valley, where they tried to form another utopia. Later he went back to Finland, but returned to the United States once more and eventually died in New York in 1915. The remaining colonists tried to continue at Sointula, but were unable to overcome the problems caused by a lack of manpower and the burden of debt.

PAUL ST. PIERRE (1923-)

Paul St. Pierre has a well-deserved reputation as one of Canada's leading humourists, teller of tall tales and spinner of yarns. He is a man of many parts: newspaper columnist, author, Member of Parliament, junior diplomat and police commissioner. To all his careers he has brought humane intelligence and a wry wit. His first and enduring love is for the country and people of the Chilcotin, both of which are featured prominently in several books: *Boss of the Namko Drive* (1965); *Breaking Smith's Quarter Horse* (1966); *Chilcotin Holiday* (1970); and *Smith and Other Events* (1983). All these books originated in St. Pierre's 1950s CBC television series "Cariboo Country"(which also saw the beginning of Chief Dan George's acting career). Other books by St. Pierre include *Sister Balonika* (1969), a coffee table book, *British Columbia Our Land* (1981) and *In the Navel of the Moon* (1993). The selections included here, "Looking For Horses" and "On Old Horses, Winter and Death," both come from *Chilcotin Holiday*. The hand of the true humourist has left its imprint on each: a sense of the ridiculous and absurd is tinged with pathos over human frailty and desire. As one of his characters says at the conclusion of "Old Horses": "When we die, somebody who never knew us will make a nice speech about us. You may be the lowest type man the country has ever produced, but somebody will say something nice about you. And they'll give you a bunch of flowers that you can't smell. Quite a thing to look forward to, ain't it?" St. Pierre was born in 1923 in Chicago, grew up in Nova Scotia during the Depression and moved to Vancouver in 1945. He now lives in Ft. Langley — once the capital of B.C. for a few weeks in 1858 — "for exactly the reason that nothing much has happened there since then." St. Pierre received the Western Writers of America Spur Award in 1985.

LOOKING FOR HORSES

BECAUSE SO MUCH OF MY TRAVEL was in the ranch country, horses were a subject that constantly recurred. Some readers even got the impression that I liked horses. Personally, I can conceive of a life which is full, rich and rewarding and which has nothing to do with horses. On the occasions when I have been obliged to use them, it was in the spirit that second-class riding is better than first-class walking.

But generations of cattlemen seem to feel otherwise about these animals, and although the economic theory is that ranchers keep horses only because they need them to handle cattle, I have met a few whom I suspect keep cattle only as an excuse for running horses.

In any event, throughout much of the Chilcotin, horses replace weather as a means of opening conversation.

BIG CREEK — A few days ago, when it was twelve below up at the Tee-pee Heart Ranch, Duane Witte suggested that we go looking for horses. Well, I was delighted, of course. As a matter of fact, I didn't really mind very much. Here was a chance to take part in one of the esoteric rites of the Cariboo: looking for horses.

In the Cariboo, it does not matter where a stranger comes to rest, or why. He may be in a moose camp or a duck blind. He may be prospecting or taking pictures of kigli holes. If he but wait a little while, a rider will come by and this rider will say that he is looking for horses.

Sometimes, I have told these riders that yes, I did see some horses that day, and have described the horses. Sometimes, I have been able to describe the brand. Sometimes, I have not seen any horses. One answer appears to please a rider as much as another. He is very grateful for the information, and says "Thank you," and then says that he must be off again looking for horses, and he leaves.

So last Thursday, for the first time, I was introduced to this mystery as a rider, one of the people who asks the questions.

Shortly after noon, when it was warm, we left the ranch. Duane and his wife Marion rode young paints and I was on an elderly bay, sometimes used to pack moose. The snow lay deep and crusted, and the moose, who were rustling for food in the horse pasture, paused in brushing the snow away with their long forelegs and watched us go by. They appeared to wonder what we were doing. But moose have a naturally puzzled expression, anyway, and possibly they were not really interested at all.

By 1: 30 p.m., we had seen two Stellar's jays, three chickadees, one whisky-jack and a Franklin's grouse cock, who came out from beneath the horse's feet with a blast of powdered snow, more like a cannon than a rocket. At 2:00 p.m. we sighted half a dozen horses on one of the long buckbrush meadows of Duane's ranch. They were pawing in the snow for feed, as the moose had been doing — and, like the moose, they paused to look at us as we went past. They were Duane's horses. Unfortunately, they were not the ones he was looking for.

We saw coyote track, lynx track, rabbit track, moose track and squirrel track. Even our stirrups left tracks as our horses walked through the deeper snows.

There were some of Duane's horses on the meadow that we reached at 3:00 p.m. But these also were not the ones that he was looking for.

Duane rode right to look over a spruce swamp, and Marion and I went to the Big Meadow. We found horses in both places. But these too were not the right ones.

We rode by an old corral built by wild-horse hunters. (*Hunting* horses is much different from *looking* for horses. But that is another story.) We rode through the little grove of trees where the rustlers had camped a few years ago. They stole thirty from Duane and are believed to have driven them north to the roadless ranges above his ranch.

When it was late in the afternoon, an east wind began to cut at our cheekbones with little pieces of broken razor blade, and we came home to the ranch house. We had seen, oh, quite a lot of horses, I would say, although not one of those that we had set out to look for. And that is what it is all about.

The only thing I forgot to find out was why we were looking for them. The thought did not occur to me until a day later, when I was hours away on the road out to Hanceville.

Come to think of it, in all the years of meeting riders in the Cariboo, I have never met one who found his horses, nor one who said why he wanted to find them. What an opportunity was mine! I could have penetrated to the very heart of the mystery! There I was, riding with the man. He was there. An expert. All I had to do was ask the question. But I never asked him.

That is the way a man fritters away the great opportunities of life.

ON OLD HORSES, WINTER, AND DEATH

ALEXIS CREEK — Some of us were sitting around talking the other night when the subject of horses arose. Old horses, and what to do about them.

This is winter, when the old gentleman with the scythe passes among the horse herds, making his selections. These selections are usually made among the young and the old horses, for slightly different reasons.

Colts and yearlings do not endure winter as well as mature horses. Some ranchers estimate that only fifty percent of young horses survive to the age of five. They are inexperienced, more prone to falling into spring holes and to other hazards. Also, their inability to endure severe cold has a simple arithmetical explanation. Young animals have a larger ratio of skin area to bulk. Thus, their body heat dissipates quicker. Sometimes they cannot eat enough to fuel their little bodies against the steady drain of cold.

At about twenty-five, another process operates — one less easily explained, except in the two simple words — "old age." These old horses may have done their accustomed work in summer and may have fattened satisfactorily in the golden days of autumn. But they will fade during the long winter.

Even if fed grain, these old pensioners who once rustled for themselves will become gaunt as the winter progresses. The snow will be on their backs. Some will be cast in the snow — unable to rise from a fold of the ground where they have carelessly lain to sleep — and if they do struggle to their feet again they may rise with one side frozen. Ranchers can usually apprehend, before autumn ends, when a horse is facing his last winter. They then sell the old animal to be slaughtered for fox feed or they shoot him.

We were talking of such gloomy matters here last night with Lester Dorsey of Anahim Lake. He was passing through town with more than his usual speed, the back of his pickup laden with sacks of grain. On Lester's range there has been heavy snow, then rain and then a freeze. These are the classic conditions of a mass starve-out and he was in great haste to take feed into those icebound meadows.

Last fall, he had forty pack horses and saddle horses in his hunting territory behind the Rainbow Mountains. When the last of his hunters left, Lester looked over the herd and selected those whose work had ended. With one of his guides, he led them one by one down the meadow and shot them. They were Red, Brownie, Little Joe, Dago Pete, Old Alec and Shanaham.

"I would never sell an old horse for fox feed," he said. "I saw some of those old horses in the yards at Kamloops one time. They were being shipped down to the States to be butchered. I decided right then that it didn't matter how hard things ever got for me, I would never need twenty bucks enough to sell an old horse for fox feed.

"Shooting them used to bother me. Years ago, I used to hire fellows to shoot them for me. But I went out in the meadow one night and found an old horse that had been shot in the afternoon and he was still alive. So that ended that. I always shot my own after that.

"Still, it used to bother me a lot, up until just a few years ago. Then I began to feel differently about it. You just take the heaviest gun in camp — my Ought-Six is pretty good — bring it up fast, just between the eyes, and pull. Usually, there's only one kick when they go down.

"I don't believe they ever know what's happening. They're old anyhow, and it all happens too fast for them to know what is coming. Just *Bang* and they're down, and there are no more hard winters."

So we agreed that we all have to go some time, which is probably the tritest statement of the human condition that can be made.

"In our case," said Lester, "When we die, somebody who never knew us will make a nice speech about us. You may be the lowest type man the country has ever produced, but somebody will say something nice about you. And they'll give you a bunch of flowers that you can't smell. Quite a thing to look forward to, ain't it?"

DENISE CHONG (1953-)

Denise Chong has written that the "crucial difference" for a memoirist "is not between fact and fiction, but rather fact and truth. The question for the writer is to rise above the facts, and ascend to some greater truths. I think when you transcend the facts, somewhere in there is the beginning of art." In her stunning memoir *The Concubine's Children*, first published as an essay in *Saturday Night* in 1988, then expanded into a book in 1994, Chong begins in fact and ascends to some greater truths concerning family. She opens a door on family secrets across two continents: on a grandfather who at the turn of the century leaves behind a wife in south China and comes to "Gold Mountain" — the gritty Chinatowns of B.C.'s West Coast — in search of his fortune; on his concubine, Chong's maternal grandmother, whose earnings in teahouses and gambling parlours in Vancouver support both the grandfather and the family he has left behind in China; and on a small child whose curiosity about missing family members begins with some old photographs. Chong tells her own story within the family — of returning to China in 1987, of two years in that homeland, and of the return with her mother to the family village in search of the truths which will define her. Chong is the product of two cultures — the Chinese traditions which are her past and a broader Canadian society within which she has lived and worked. Raised in Prince George, B.C., Chong went on to work as a western affairs advisor and economist in the federal government and became an economic advisor to Pierre Elliott Trudeau. *The Concubine's Children* has been awarded the Vancouver City Book Prize, the Edna Staebler Creative Non-fiction Prize, and was nominated for a Governor-General's Award. In 1997, Chong edited *The Penguin Anthology of Stories By Women*, and in the preface describes her award-winning memoir in the following words: "Acutely aware that writing a book would violate the privacy my grandmother thought she took to the grave with her, and trespass on my mother's past in the everyday life of the old Chinatowns, I felt vindication would come if I captured the truth of their lives." Chong is currently a freelance writer and economist who lives in Ottawa with her husband and two children. Her most recent book is *The Girl in the Picture: The Kim Phuc Story* (1999).

THE CONCUBINE'S CHILDREN

MY UNCLE YUEN was born with his feet turned backwards at the ankles, and in traditional China no one had the means to fix them. Following him up a set of stairs wasn't easy; we had the sensation he was going down instead of up. At the top, he led mother and me behind the screens of a storeroom in the house their father, my grandfather, had built fifty years ago in Chang Gar Bin, a village in Guangdong province in the south of China. The wood of the screens was decaying, though the marks where carved panels had been lifted out were still faintly evident. Yuen rummaged around, looking for whatever it was Ping, mother's sister, had said she wanted to return to her. What could Ping have to give back? As a child growing up in Canada, my mother had sent only letters, copied at the insistence of Grandfather as an exercise in Chinese brush-writing, to her elder sisters, Ping and Nan, and her younger half-brother, Yuen, in China.

Ping beckoned us out to the balcony, where the light was better, to look at the faded brown bundle Yuen handed to Mother. Shaken out, it fell into the shape of a child's coat. In halting yet sure motion, Mother went straight for its collar, searched for and found its velvet trim. She threaded her arms through the sleeves, tugged the coat over her shoulders, leaving knees and wrists exposed that betrayed when it had last fitted her. When she pulled the sides of the collar together to wrap velvet around her neck and chin, it was as if the coat itself reunited her two families, one in Canada, one in China.

Mother had last worn the coat when she was thirteen. She had paraded the sidewalks of Vancouver in it, arm in arm with her girlfriends. Never had she guessed it had lived out its life in China, that Grandfather had sent the coat in one of his regular care packages to his other family there. Ping herself had sashayed along the village paths in it, enjoying the taunts of the other children: "Foreign lady, foreign lady." The coat had then passed to Nan, the sister who died in her youth, and later to Yuen. He kept it in safekeeping for almost forty years, away from looting Japanese soldiers and Communist vigilantes — stored along with Ping's and his hopes that Mother, their sister, was still alive in Canada.

I had known all my life there might be relatives in China. As a child, I was curious about the black-and-white photograph of two children in the bottom drawer of the cedar chest upstairs in our home in Prince George, British Columbia. If I stared long enough, the two girls blinked. They had to: how could they not, waiting so long for Mother, the sister they would never meet? They even looked ready to be presented, as if they had run in from school, hurriedly rolled their socks to the ankles and smoothed their dresses. I didn't have to use my imagination so much on the other family photographs in the drawer. I had known Grandfather and his concubine, my grandmother, in real life. In fact, I preferred Grandmother's silent beauty in the photographs; in real life, she had scared me. The one portrait of Grandfather showed him with his jaw set, hinting at the temperament that supposedly made Grandmother leave him. Nowhere in the drawer was there a photograph of them together.

Years later, I noticed that Grandfather's portrait had disappeared. I saw that ones of the two sisters and of Grandmother had found their way into an album, each image scissored from its background and pasted down. But it was passing faces in crowds in China that would finally reawaken my childhood curiosity about these relatives. In 1987 I was near the end of a two-year stint working in Beijing, and I wrote to the Chinese authorities asking for help tracing Mother's ancestry. Mother, now a widow, had accepted my urgings to visit and, for my sake, brave her complicated feelings about China. I thought chances were remote that we would find any immediate relatives alive. China's political turmoil would surely have claimed them, lost them among her billion people. I thought the purpose of taking Mother to Grandfather's birthplace would be to fill in some blanks on the family tree, take some snapshots for the Canadian family album.

But the reverberations from the collision of the two worlds shook dust from mirrors. Before this visit, Mother had felt only the shame of her deprived childhood in Canada, the errant ways of her mother, the fact that both of her parents had gone to their graves unloved by her. From Ping and Yuen, she was to find out that Grandmother's money and Grandfather's love had actually been siphoned away from her to the family in China. But the discovery didn't make her bitter; instead, it lifted the burden of her shame. Over the years through war and revolution in China, and the growing acceptance in Canada that Orientals could be Canadians too — events had evened the score between Grandfather's two families. Mother's parents, whose ways she had for years tried to forgive, had endowed her with the gift of a life in Canada. That realization finally turned Mother's shame to gratitude and made her own life at last all of one piece.

My Grandfather, leaving his family behind in rural China, set forth in

1922 to find work in North America. Chinese men before him had gone to the land they called the Gold Mountain, seeking their fortunes in the 1848 Sacramento gold rush; later, they'd been lured to work on the great transcontinental railways. But in Grandfather's time it was not money so much that drove men abroad as it was the constant turmoil and instability that paralysed the economy in his southern province of Guangdong. Canton, not far from Grandfather's village, was the stronghold of Sun Yat-sen, the founding father of modern China. Sun was arming his Kuomintang nationalists and fomenting revolution among rival warlords. Men like Grandfather didn't have the means to buy off warlords and keep roving bandits away. In his early thirties, he had to support one nearly grown daughter from his first wife (who had died), and a second wife — now titled Wife Number One — who had yet to produce children. His one hope of prosperity lay in going abroad.

After an eighteen-day ocean voyage, Grandfather stepped onto the pier in Vancouver, Canada, a fedora gracing his head, his gaunt, nearly six-foot frame attired in a three-piece grey suit. Never was he to be seen in any less casual dress. With his black hair combed to expose a high forehead, and his large, melancholic eyes staring from wire-framed glasses, he didn't look at all like the shifty-eyed, pigtailed Chinamen in the Fu Manchu movies of the day. Grandfather made it on one of the last boatloads of working-class Chinese allowed into the country before Ottawa passed the Chinese Immigration Act of 1923, also known as the "exclusion act." From then until the act was repealed in 1947, Chinese were barred from entering Canada unless they were students or merchants, or had proof of Canadian citizenship.

Chinese fathers who left their families to work in Canada lived in lonely exile. They weren't allowed to bring their families over, yet the white community condemned them as morally depraved, dirty and disease-ridden, believing them to be undesirable citizens who worked only to remit money to China. Grandfather himself took a room in Vancouver's Chinatown and found work running a few tables of mahjong in a gambling parlour, but he resisted the bachelor's condition.

In 1924, a friend of a friend arranged for him to buy, sight unseen, Leong May-ying, a girl from another village in China. She was my grandmother, then seventeen years old. When her aunt, to whom she was probably a child-servant, told her she had been sold as a concubine to a Chinese man in Canada, she kicked and screamed in protest: "I might just as well be a concubine in China!" In her own country, Grandmother, with her penetrating, radiant, ebony eyes and delicate features set in pale skin, could probably have escaped becoming a beast of burden — the usual fate of Chinese women. In wealthy households, concubines led a pampered life. But in China girls did as they were told; it was that or suicide. So Grandmother readied herself to leave, even cutting and curling her hair to look older to conform to the illegally purchased birth certificate Grandfather had sent her. To Canadian immigration officials, she passed as twenty-four-year-old Chung Gim-ching, born in Ladner, British Columbia.

Work was almost all that Grandfather had in mind for her. At first he seemed kindly enough, taking her directly from the boat to have dim-sum at the Peking Restaurant on Pender Street. But then the owner joined them, and Grandfather introduced him as her new boss. It took Grandmother two years to work off the $500 Grandfather had borrowed from the restaurant owner to pay her passage. Lest she dream of running away, Grandfather kept a hunting knife under his side of the mattress. Out of threats, two daughters, Ping and Nan, were born.

If Grandfather was a hateful husband, he was a dutiful father. In 1929, he made plans to take his family to China. As was the custom among Chinese sojourning abroad, he wanted to give his children, then five and two, a Chinese education. For two years in China, havoc reigned as Grandfather tried to keep his two wives under one roof. As a concubine, Grandmother was supposed to be the subservient one, but she took advantage of Wife Number One's gentleness to argue with her, push her around and humiliate her, often reducing her to tears. The one dignity on which Wife Number One stood was that she slept in the privacy of the back room of the two-room house and, usually, in the company of Grandfather. Grandmother was assigned the front room, with the children.

But of the two wives, Grandmother became pregnant first. In her eighth month, she consulted a blind soothsayer — considered closer to the truth than a sighted one who predicted that she was carrying a son. Grandmother wanted him born in Canada where she thought he would have a better chance in life. Grandfather agreed. Ping and Nan were left behind to continue their educations in the care of Wife Number One. In the spring of 1930, fully expecting to return for their two daughters, Grandmother and Grandfather left for Canada. Three days after the boat docked in Vancouver, Grandmother gave birth to my mother in a room above 79 Market Alley in Chinatown.

Grandmother immediately tried to run away to Vancouver Island, to Nanaimo, then a bustling coal town where there were teahouses that always needed waitresses. Grandfather bundled up the baby and followed. He needed Grandmother: only she could put rice on the table for his families in Canada and in China. He couldn't get work with the Depression on and the trade unions agitating against Chinese men taking jobs from whites. But Grandmother was much sought after as a waitress. Restaurant owners knew that male patrons found seductive the way she wired curls and chignons to her hair, stained her lips red and pinned silk flowers at her neck.

When Mother was five, Grandfather again began to make plans to return to China for the sake of a daughter's schooling. But he also wanted to build a house in Chang Gar Bin, as home villagers expected of an overseas Chinese. Grandmother at last saw her chance to get him out of her hair. She offered the money for him to go, but only if she and Mother remained in Canada. To pay for his passage, for the construction of the new house and furnishings, and for the extravagant gifts he must take, Grandmother borrowed heavily. Going empty-handed would be to lose face, or so Grandfather argued. One day in 1935, he set sail for China on an American freighter, *The Presidential.*

"One day of happiness in China is better than a hundred days of happiness in Canada," was the saying Grandfather invoked when he saw Wife Number One again. She was certainly happy not to have the concubine underfoot and was unaware that Grandfather's apparent wealth was not of his own making. Now there was just herself, Ping and Nan — as was her duty, she loved them as her own — to enjoy Grandfather's affection and indulgences: the crates of grapes, salted crackers, and condensed and evaporated milk he brought from abroad. Within months, Wife Number One became pregnant.

Compared to when Grandfather had first left China in 1922, the country was less chaotic. Chiang Kai-shek, who became leader of the Kuomintang upon Sun's death in 1925, ruled a somewhat more unified country. What was left of the Red Army, led by Mao Tse-tung, was in retreat, on the Long March to Yenan, thousands of kilometres to the northwest. In the south, feudal landlords and rich peasants still held sway. Upon his return, Grandfather used some of Grandmother's money to purchase twenty-eight mu (five acres) of land on the edge of the village; he marked off a courtyard and hired workmen to lay the foundations of Chang Gar Bin's first-ever two-storey house. In the countryside of Guangdong, such houses — balustrades and balconies hinting at Western architecture — identified like pins on a map the families whose fathers had gone abroad.

But the cache of Grandmother's money that Grandfather had taken to China was gone before all his fanciful plans for his new house could be fulfilled. Letters were sent to Canada for only one purpose: to ask for more money to complete the house. And Grandmother was willing to work, borrow, do anything, to pay the price of keeping Grandfather in China. Then long before the house was finished, Wife Number One bore Grandfather his first son. The baby, Yuen, was born with crippled feet, but that didn't dent Grandfather's paternal pride. He put on a thirty-table banquet that spilled into his new courtyard.

From their perch on the wrought-iron gate opening into the courtyard, Ping and Nan watched as workmen affixed porcelain tiles to the rooftop. Oversize double portals swung open to reveal the house's expansive reception room, with its fourteen-foot-high ceilings. The balcony that swept around the upper floor's five rooms commanded a view of the entire village and the fields beyond. The overseas furniture crated in the courtyard was at last carried in. Craftsmen began carving wooden panels and inlaying stained glass in screens. Artists were hired to paint landscape scenes on porcelain and portraits of Grandfather and Wife Number One.

But hardly had Grandfather enjoyed the villagers' admiration of his accomplishment than he was booking a return passage to Canada. His son was another mouth to feed. He may also have feared that staying away too long would jeopardize his re-entry; who was to know how the unwavering anti-Oriental mood in North America might harm him?

He issued last-minute instructions to his daughters. Keep clean, he said. Keep your clothes folded away. Study hard: "If you don't, you will be nothing but peasants chasing bugs in the field." Two years later, in those fields, Ping, clutching Nan by the wrist and with Yuen strapped to her back, would be fleeing from Japanese bombs. But for now the fields were for frolicking. After school, the girls in their overseas dresses would offer rides to their playmates in their overseas pram.

During the two years Grandfather was away, Grandmother had taken to dressing their third daughter like the son she had been deprived. At six, Mother, in short pants, a shirt, and suspenders, was still going to the barber in Nanaimo. When it came time to go to school, she enrolled herself. When the teacher wouldn't accept her as "Hing" — it wasn't an English name — she, and her best friend, Elsie, came up with the name "Winnie."

When Grandfather returned from China, he decided that his youngest daughter must learn to read and write Chinese if only to correspond with the family in China. But his teaching and Mother's letter-writing lasted only a year. Grandmother and Grandfather argued constantly — about nothing and everything from Grandfather's putting jam and ketchup on his rice to his buying bonds to help Chiang Kai-shek. Grandmother finally refused to live with him. After he moved out, Grandfather came around only if there was a letter from China that he wanted them to see — and the reality of Ping and Nan soon began to fade.

Grandmother mentioned her older children only in gambling-table chatter — when she won big, she boasted, she would bring them to Canada. Grandfather himself soon became little more than a cardboard figure to Mother. He could find work only out of town, usually bundling shingles. Months, eventually years, passed without contact. Once Mother caught sight of him buying groceries on the other side of the street. Grandmother forced her to turn her head: "Don't address him; he's not your father."

Grandmother, on her own with a young daughter, led a transient life, packing their one metal trunk to follow jobs to Nanaimo, Victoria or Vancouver. The two of them saw little of each other; by the time Mother had come home from public school and then the Chinese school after that, Grandmother had already gone to work at the restaurant or the gambling parlour. When she had no homework, Mother went off to catch the seven o'clock performance of Chinese opera at the local theatre. Well past midnight, she would wander over to the gambling parlour, where she would sit silently by Grandmother's side watching her play fan-tan or mahjong. At about two in the morning, the two of them headed back to the rooming house for a late meal. Never did Grandmother cook anything ordinary: sometimes it was lady-slipper-bulb soup; sometimes a quick slaughter of a pigeon or chicken.

For Mother, Grandmother was at times an embarrassment, at times a burden, but always a stigma that had to be lived down. But in the playground Mother was the challenger to beat at marbles, jacks and double-Dutch. In the classroom, the first desk, the one reserved for the top student, was usually hers. If she had to study for English and Chinese tests in one night, she would sometimes tie the end of a string to her hair and the other end to a light fixture overhead. If she nodded in sleep the string was just long enough to give her a sharp tug. Mother didn't like wasting time. As she watched repeat performances of Chinese opera, she knitted in the dark of the theatre. One year she turned out 112 cotton-knit washcloths, winning the public-school competition for the most washcloths knitted for Canadian soldiers fighting the Second World War.

Grandmother knew nothing of Mother's achievements; she cared less. All she wanted from Mother was obedience, and obedience she got, enforced daily, whether necessary or not, by a stick of discipline on her daughter's legs. The bruises were nothing compared to the shame Mother felt on the day she and her fourth-grade classmates were walking home and noticed a raid in progress at the gambling parlour. "Isn't that Hing's mother being put in the paddy wagon?" the children asked. "That's not her," said Mother.

More and more often, Mother was sent to buy herbs to make the teas Grandmother used to soothe away the effects of too much drink. Then there were trips to B.C. Collateral, the pawnbrokers on Hastings Street. Mother dreaded having to translate as Grandmother bargained a price for her jade and gold jewellery.

In 1940, Grandmother tried to claim back the rites of love and court-ship denied her by Grandfather. She gambled her love on Chow Guen, a loud, shrewd gambling parlour banker twenty years her senior. She met him when she was working at the B.C. Royal Café; he came in every day for a fresh butterhorn. While Guen cared for Grandmother less than she cared for him, he did have the money to help her get what she had always wanted: a son. It was Guen's $300 that Grandmother paid to Granny Yip, a Caucasian midwife who knew expectant Chinese mothers in dire straits. Granny Yip procured a newborn baby and registered Grandmother and Grandfather as its parents. Grandmother named him Gok-leng, but Mother called him Leonard.

Neither Grandmother's husband nor her lover appear in the family por-traits she then commissioned — only mother, son and daughter. But Grand-mother soon began to board her children out as she chased after Guen in an on-again, off-again relationship that lasted fifteen years. Until Leonard was four, he lived mostly with the midwife, Granny Yip. Mother, like checked baggage, waited for Grandmother to claim her in rooms shared with elderly couples or Grandmother's women friends.

When Mother was twelve, Grandfather made one of his infrequent visits in order to tell Grandmother that their second-born daughter, Nan, had fallen ill and died. Mother's sharpest memory of the news was that Grand-mother didn't shed a tear.

Mother's last foster home was back on Market Alley in Chinatown, steps from where she had been born. Her last guardian, the rather thick-headed Mrs. Low, worried more about juggling her boyfriends than about her teenaged daughter or Mother. Like their other friends, the two girls whiled away hours at cafés looking for the initials of future loves at the bottom of their tea cups. Mother found what was written at the bottom of the menu — "White Help Only" — ultimately more upsetting. At seventeen, and in the tenth grade, she began to worry about her own and Leonard's financial security; Grandmother's drinking bouts were worsening. Mother quit school and with the help of a recommendation from her former principal, Mr. Webster, became one of the first Chinese students to enter a three-year nursing program at Essondale Psychiatric Hospital near Vancouver (now Riverview Hospital).

It was 1948, and a good time for Mother to finally get away from Chinatown. Talk in every restaurant booth in the place was of the Communist advance in China. Many of the old-timers were Guangdong compatriots who had helped raise money for the Kuomintang; they were filled with fear for their wives and children back home. Few of them had the money or the connections to get their families out, even though the Canadian government had finally lifted the ban on Chinese immigrants. Grandfather certainly didn't.

After 1949, many old-timers feared the new Communist regime was intercepting their remittances. Grandfather himself feared he was a victim of extortion; recent letters from Yuen and Ping bore little news and asked only for more money. One from Ping said that unless $700 was sent, she would have a nervous breakdown. Mother agreed with Grandfather that recent letters written on Ping's behalf — she wasn't schooled enough to write herself — were unmistakably in a different hand from earlier ones. Grandfather agonized over it, but kept writing and sending money.

The ripcord that would help set Mother free from such obligations was John Chong, a man of quiet resoluteness, who won her heart. She met him when she was eighteen. He was handsome, athletic and from a family of eleven children. After two years of driving up to Essondale on the chance that Mother could avoid curfew by sneaking out a lower-floor window of her dormitory, he gave her an ultimatum — nursing or marriage. Grandmother objected to Mother's choice of a husband: a laundry-truck driver, she said, was a nobody. Mother went to Grandfather. Six months short of graduation, she walked down the aisle on the arm of her father.

In keeping with tradition, the new bride moved into her mother-in-law's house. There were three living in the attic once my parents had their first child, a girl. With six other adults and a baby living downstairs, there was rarely enough water pressure to the attic to wash rice, never mind diapers. When Mother became pregnant again, she and Father found a two bedroom apartment near Chinatown. But they couldn't afford the $40-a-month rent on their own, so Mother invited Grandfather to share the space and the rent. This was home when Mother had me, her second-born, in 1953.

A few months later Grandfather decided that Mother should move again; that she should own a house in Canada; and that he should install her in one. He insisted on giving my parents $900 towards a down payment. Mother wondered how he had come into the money; it turned out that she had been his unwitting accomplice. Months before, she had gone with him to the immigration office on the Vancouver dock to swear that she had a sister in China named Ping. Later, a "Ping" did arrive in Canada, but it wasn't Mother's sister. It was Grandmother who eventually found out that Grandfather had sold Ping's Canadian birth certificate for $3,000, just as he had made money years earlier selling Nan's. She demanded a share of the money, but Grandfather wouldn't give her a penny, reminding her that Guen had never paid *him* for taking his wife.

In return for Grandfather's $900, he moved into the second bedroom of the modest house my parents bought on Gladstone Street, off Kingsway's commercial strip. A letter from Ping arrived at this address, in handwriting again arousing suspicions, telling Grandfather that if more money wasn't sent, his family would have to sell the glass in the windows. Grandfather asked Mother to help out. Father put his foot down: "Let them take the glass out; it will let fresh air in."

Grandfather stayed a little more than a year with us. Though he liked the idea of living in a house, Chinatown was a half-hour away by bus. For company during the day there was only old Mr. Penny tending his flowerbed on one side, or the reclusive Mr. and Mrs. Stewart on the other side, and none of them spoke Chinese. Grandfather went back to living in Chinatown.

At the time, Grandmother and Guen were running the Nanking Restaurant in London, Ontario. But Guen was getting exasperated with Grandmother; the more she drank, the more monosodium glutamate she put in her cooking. He ran out on her, and the bank moved in — foreclosing on the place. Leonard, too, had run away because of her drinking, and was placed in a foster home by the Children's Aid Society. Grandmother left him behind and came back to Vancouver to move into the bedroom Grandfather had vacated. Soon it was our garbage bins that were being filled with her empty bottles. After a year of this, Father asked Grandmother to leave. He ended up almost carrying her out of the house, depositing her at Grandfather's door in a hotel above Chinatown's Ho Ho Restaurant.

Two days later, in a rare united act, Grandfather and Grandmother showed up at our door. They served Mother with a lawyer's letter announcing their intention to sue for Grandfather's $900. Mother countersued, demanding back rent. Both suits were dropped.

Home and family in Chinese are represented by one and the same character — a pig under a roof, a symbol of contentment. Never was there domestic harmony in the Canadian family; rarely had all members lived under the same roof. But in China, Grandfather's family and home were one and the same, though the house, built on his instructions and Grandmother's money, was almost the ruin of them.

War between China and Japan broke out in 1937, and by 1938, Japanese bombs were falling on Guangdong province. When Chang Gar Bin village became a battleground, Japanese soldiers chased Wife Number One and her three charges, Ping, Nan and Yuen, from the house. "Don't be afraid, don't be afraid," Wife Number One chanted, as she and the children stepped on dead bodies and shrank from anti-aircraft fire. When they came back to their village, the bombs had stopped falling but the Japanese occupiers had turned their house into local headquarters: they could keep watch from the second-floor balcony. When the soldiers moved on, they ransacked the house, taking any valuables they could carry.

But Grandfather's Chinese family believed that his lot in Canada was worse. Wife Number One read in Grandfather's letters that the concubine drank and gambled her time away; about how they had separated because he couldn't stand her quarrelling any longer. The fact was he had no trouble being fatherly from afar. He regularly sent care packages. He wrote, encouraging his crippled son to find a way to ride a bicycle. At his insistence, young Yuen learned to write Chinese so he could take over from the schoolmaster the task of writing letters for Wife Number One. On birthdays, Grandfather sent an American coin or two, sometimes even a dollar bill. His children treasured most the gift of three Big Ben alarm clocks, the kind with a loud tick-tock, large faces and two-legged stands, made in Peterborough, Ontario. His remittances, in a foreign currency, bought the family stability, especially during the rampant inflation of the war years.

Still, the family couldn't live on his affection or his money alone. Like all unmarried daughters, Ping and Nan went to work in the fields. One day in the fall of 1942, the fourteen-year-old Nan headed out as usual. Ping and Yuen remember the commotion as she was carried home, haemorrhaging. "Someone scared her in the field," was all Wife Number One would say. After a month in bed, Nan died. That same year Ping was married off. Grandfather wrote wondering if she, at eighteen, wasn't too young, but he said he would approve if Ping was a willing bride. He granted her in-laws three mu of land from his holdings; and for the wedding feast he arranged from afar for one whole roasted pig.

That was to be the last banquet for more than three decades. The first of several serious famines hit Guangdong in 1944. In 1946, the country was plunged into civil war between the Kuomintang and the Communists. By 1948, nothing could stop the Communist advance, neither Chiang Kai-shek's disorganized troops, nor American aid, much of which found its way into the personal coffers of Kuomintang leaders. In October, 1949, Mao proclaimed the People's Republic of China. Chiang's last southern stronghold fell, and he and his troops fled to Taiwan.

Grandfather's house again brought the family trouble. Communist leaders labelled Grandfather's family as "black elements" and set about redistributing his wealth. Grandfather's land was organized into a village co-operative. The "unsightly" opulence of his house was remedied. The wrought-iron gate, the dressers, the wool blankets from Canada, the carved panels in the wooden screens, the stained glass, the tiles on the roof: all were removed or destroyed. The huge portrait of Grandfather that watched over the reception area was cut down, and his house was divided, making apartments for two more families. Villagers were called on to "speak bitterness" against Wife Number One, Yuen and Ping, who were forced to stand for hours on one spot, hands tied, heads bowed in penance for the shame of Grandfather's wealth.

Yuen wrote to Grandfather to tell him it wouldn't be possible for him to return: "You would be too heartsick to see what has happened to what you worked hard for, with your sweat and your ten fingers." Letters arrived from Canada only sporadically, remittances even more so. The last letter came in 1957. In it was a Vancouver Chinatown newspaper notice announcing Grandfather's death at seventy. A note was attached, with Grandmother's name at the bottom, extending condolences to Wife Number One.

Though I was only four years old when Grandfather died, I have vivid recollections of him. I can still see him coming through the back door of our house on Gladstone Street, his arms laden with groceries, him setting the bags down and scooping me up. The first present I remember receiving from anyone was the red and white tricycle he showed up with one day. I remember, too, sitting with my sister in pails of water in the back yard, cooling off on warm summer days, while Grandfather, dressed in a suit, worked nearby in the garden. To Mother's consternation, he would run hot water over the garden tools to clean them off.

I can also remember standing by his graveside, and that there was no weeping. Grandmother wasn't there: she was in hospital with tuberculosis, which she suspected she caught from coughs filtering over the half-partitions in her rooming house. But the first chance she had, six months later, she went through the rituals of worshipping the dead. I remember she prepared several steaming dishes and there was wine and tea in thermoses. I was astounded when she left it all in the shadow of Grandfather's tombstone.

My earliest memory of Grandmother is that she intimidated me into silence. At two, I held out my palm to her, burned on the wood stove, as she applied a stinging salve of fermented oranges. At five, I tilted my head back as she plucked my eyebrows, and then forward as she plaited my hair, always too tight. I couldn't cry out. Grandmother was herself fearless and wouldn't stand for it.

The year after Grandfather's death, Mother decided she wanted to make a final break with Vancouver. Even if Father had changed his mind about it, Mother didn't want Grandmother to live with us again because of the risk of exposing her by now four young children to tuberculosis. The federal government was advertising for radio operators; Father applied and got a job at the Prince George airport. On Christmas Eve in 1958, Mother bundled us into our 1949 Meteor for the 800-kilometre drive north along an icy highway to this northern logging town. We pulled into the driveway of a substandard surplus wartime house on the airport grounds — our home until another house became available — to find frozen water pipes by night and, by morning, neighbours frowning at the prospect of Orientals on the block.

The airport community of twenty-one families, with its own clubhouse and one-room school, was a crucible of assimilation. Mother's advice to us was to feign hard-of-hearing to the taunts of "Chinky, Chinky, China-man"; she soon made it clear to other mothers that she wasn't going to put up with their kids throwing stone-embedded snowballs or waiting in ambush to knock us off our bikes. She was determined that we should be as robust as our playmates: the milk in our glasses was enriched with extra cream. She worried about Leonard too; once he was old enough to be released by the Children's Aid, he came to live with us for a year. At Mother's suggestion, he applied to Essondale Psychiatric Hospital, was accepted, and graduated as a psychiatric nurse.

Grandmother, now in her mid-fifties, would visit us in the summers. From what I remember of her lightning-quick quips and laughter, she was happy to stay with us, especially since, of five of us children by now, three were grandsons. Visiting her in Vancouver was a different story. The Chinatown of my early childhood — a sensuous place of steamy smells, squawking chickens and the clacking murmur of mahjong tiles — was already gone. In the early 1960s, cut off from new blood and commerce and sanitized by local bylaws designed to clean up the "squalor," the Chinatowns of Canada, like the old-timers who lived in them, were dying.

Father would stop in front of whichever rooming house Grandmother was living in and Mother would wait in the car as he and one of us children would climb up the stairs. He would knock on the door and then we would wait in the hallway to see if it would open to us. If it didn't, we knew, but didn't say, that Grandmother would have to dry out first. Her main pastime was still mahjong. But now, when she wanted to gamble, she had to get a ride across town to the suburbs out of the sight of the city police. Grandmother didn't much like riding in cars, trusting only Father and a mahjong buddy, Mr.Pang, to drive her. Just after midnight one night, the elderly Mr. Pang was driving Grandmother home to the Garden Hotel in Chinatown. Two blocks from the hotel, the car was hit broadside by a pickup truck driven by a teenager, out for a spin with his pals.

The story on page fifteen of *The Vancouver Sun* said that a traffic accident had caused the city's third fatality of 1967, killing a sixty-four-year-old woman named Chung Gim-ching. Crushed between two people in Mr. Pang's back seat, Grandmother died of a punctured lung: discounting the false birth certificate, she was only fifty-eight. Mother made one last trip to B.C. Collateral to claim Grandmother's jewellery. Among the pieces, she found a diamond ring that had come from Grandmother's lover. The sale of that ring paid for the funeral.

At the inquest, the coroner found that no one had been at fault. Of more importance to Mother, the pathologist had found no trace of alcohol in Grandmother's blood. When the coffin was lowered into the ground, Mother thought her own past had been laid to rest.

Twenty years later, in her own mind at least, Mother had turned that past to dust and ashes. If she felt anything about Grandmother, it was a slight remorse that no one had left food on her grave — but then, Mother had never worshipped at Grandfather's grave either. Since his death, there had been no word of any relatives in China, nor did Mother know if anyone there knew that she still existed. For a time, all overseas Chinese lost contact with their families in China, because of the xenophobia that reached its height during Mao's Cultural Revolution. When Mao died in 1976, the Gang of Four was officially blamed for the persecution, torture and execution of China's intellectuals and for the wanton destruction of cultural property. Only then was the stage set for leader Deng Xiaoping to usher in the era of an "open door" to the West.

Mother finally walked through that door in the spring of 1987, at my insistence. Still, if she hadn't already been in Hong Kong when she got word that other siblings were still alive, she might have called the whole trip off. The news alone sent her on a roller coaster from shock to jubilation to disbelief and fear.

The Chinese government's instructions were terse: "Go to the Chinese side of the frontier at Macao in two days. Officials will meet you, with your two sisters and brother. Look for a white van." Two sisters? Mother was no longer certain that Nan had died. Could Grandfather have fabricated the story to justify having sold her birth certificate? Perhaps the family had sold Nan? What if, worse, the Chinese authorities had dragged up fictitious relatives? Was the woman using Ping's name in Canada really the fraud? Who was to know who was authentic?

We decided to go no farther than the border, but the decision was in vain: the officials in the white van were an hour late and had no one in tow. After a three-hour ride into China, the van dropped us in the compound of the overseas Chinese office in Chang Gar Bin village. We waited while news of our arrival was sent. Then a thin man, with wavy hair and a face with Grandfather's quiet strength and squareness, shuffled into the room. His feet made a sweeping sound, one at a time, as he limped towards us, like a broken doll whose limbs had been twisted round and stuck — Yuen, Mother's half-brother. I had deliberately withheld from officials our knowledge of his deformity; how could this be contrived? Mother embraced him, feeling the sorrow of his crippled feet but also the joy that they swept away worries that he was not of the same blood. He answered the question of Nan. Yes, she had died, many years before; the officials had just got it wrong.

We went out into the courtyard, and there Mother hugged her sister Ping for the first time. The proud fine lines of Ping's face were like Grandmother's. The quickness of her movements and her girlish laugh were Grandmother reincarnated. Both sisters fumbled for the photographs each had brought for this moment. Mother showed the one photograph she had of her two sisters as children and one of Grandmother posing with her and Leonard. Ping unwrapped the cellophane protecting a photograph of a beautiful young Oriental woman, cradling a baby — Grandmother and Ping. She turned the photograph over. It was imprinted as a postcard, and in the lower left corner was "Vancouver, Canada."

The two sisters walked like schoolgirls, arm in arm, through the village, their younger brother riding his bicycle ahead. They wove their way among black pigs that scavenged for food in the market, past the stalls where one of Ping's sons sold pork and where Yuen's sons sold fresh fish from baskets. They passed the hardware store where Yuen kept the books. Ping stopped often, hailing villagers, to show off "Younger Sister," and some of them remembered a last sight of Grandmother, leaving pregnant for the boat in 1930.

At the other end of the village, through a gate, was an imposing chalk-blue two-storey house. We entered its main room through a small swinging door hinged into massive sienna-painted twin portals. Here, Yuen lived with his wife and three children. This was the house that Grandfather — and Grandmother's money — built.

"Heaven and earth have eyes," said Yuen, as he and his two sisters finally sat in Grandfather's front room, laughing and crying at the triumph of being reunited. For the three days of our visit, Ping poured out the lost stories of family life in China, illustrated by Yuen pointing to the back room where he was born and Nan died, to the places where once stood overseas dressers, where once hung decorative mirrors. To the field beyond where Japanese bombs fell and where now stood a cluster of modern flat-roofed two-storey houses, television aerials on their rooftops. The Communists were allowing limited home ownership again. If Yuen could raise the money to build new houses for the two other families living in Grandfather's house, he could have it to himself. "I am scrimping and saving for the pride of my father," he said.

In the face of Ping and Yuen's devotion to the memory of Grandfather, Mother held back many of her stories — and that she believed he had exploited Grandmother and sacrificed the family in Canada for the sake of the family in China. Let them hold dear their idea of him as a model father. Let them believe the concubine brought him only unhappiness and that Wife Number One, the woman who raised them, was the superior wife.

Ping wanted one memento of her past: she asked Mother to find proof that she had been born as the postcard photo said, in Vancouver, Canada. When times were bad, she had had to endure the villagers' taunts that she had been left behind in China because she "must deserve to suffer." Time and again, she had thought her plight was unfair: "I don't deserve this; I was not born here." Mother didn't have the heart to tell her that another Ping had lived all through those trying years, safe in Canada.

Grandfather had come to Canada to throw off the cloak of poverty, though he and Grandmother never managed it in their lifetimes. The family in China, who had harvested some of the spoils of the Gold Mountain, now had only a few relics of the goods Grandfather had sent from Canada: a metal crib, badly rusted; an RCA Victor phonograph that once played 78 rpm records; Yuen's Big Ben alarm clock; and a $10 American bill. The truth was that Grandfather's penchant for showiness had brought his family in Chang Gar Bin persecution. For Mother, who lived her childhood in the shadow of sacrifices made for the family back home, her parents' act of immigration had been a liberation.

When our Chinese relatives saw us off at the bus station in their village, the weeping was as much for the parting of flesh and blood as it was for the realization that Mother had ended up the luckier of the children. Mother, having left behind her long ago the rooming houses of Market Alley, would return home to Prince George and a life of her own choosing. Ping and Yuen could expect to die in Chang Gar Bin, the birth and burial place of several generations of the family, the village to which the Communist government had assigned them. Ping could nurture only faint hopes that Yuen's or her own children's children — the youngest of which she strapped to her back every day while its mother went to work — would not be peasants. That they might get off the land. Mother's children were college-educated and living their own lives.

The phrases of gratitude that Mother would now express to her parents, if they could be heard in the grave, might be borrowed from a letter Yuen pressed into her hand just before she left. It asked for help in getting one of his children into Canada: "I hope my children can take root in Canada. Then the roots of the tree will grow downward. We will be fortunate; the children will be fortunate; our children's children will be fortunate. The family will be glorious and future generations will have a good foundation."

Mother left the brown coat with the velvet collar behind in Chang Gar Bin. It seemed it still belonged in China, where the threads of Grandfather's hopes were still woven in his children's dreams.

ROSEMARY NEERING (1945–)

Rosemary Neering's account of small town B.C. life — *Down the Road* — won the Hubert Evans Non-Fiction Prize in 1992. "Slocan Dreams" from this volume portrays not so much a town but a state of mind influenced by the blue mountains and narrow valleys of the Kootenay region of British Columbia. Long a refuge for dreamers, wanderers, idealists and charlatans, this region holds a special place in the collective psyche of the province. In her journalistic essay, Neering captures the pride and independence of those loners and seekers of dreams, who are often enough on the run from history and personal circumstance. We are introduced to writers, publishers, communal activists, conscientious objectors and the counter-culture — and to this ferment are added the Quakers and Doukhobors, idealists who have sought sanctuary, and the Japanese, brought here against their wills and repopulating the dying towns of the valley. The Slocan is a valley of ghosts, and of dreams found and lost. In addition to this book, which explores the margins of the province, Neering has teamed with photographer Bob Herger to produce *The Coast of British Columbia* (1989), finalist for the Duthie Booksellers' Choice Award, and with Steve Short to create *In the Path of the Explorers* (1992), which follows along the routes of early European explorers in British Columbia. Neering has also written an historical documentary — *The Continental Dash* (1989) — about the attempt in the 1860s to construct a telegraph line from Seattle to Siberia, and a children's book — *Pioneers* (1990) — which explores the lives of Louis Hebert, Joe Boyle and Catharine Parr Traill.

SLOCAN DREAMS

IN THE VILLAGE OF ROBSON beside the Columbia River, a seeker of truth tries to put into words the sense he has of the Kootenays. On the map, this region is a succession of mountain chains from the Rockies to the Okanagan, wedged apart by the north-south lengths of deep and narrow lakes and circumscribed by the valleys of the Kootenay and Columbia rivers. But the map does not convey the singular beauty of the Kootenays or the healing spirit some people ascribe to them.

"What is it about this place that attracts people who are bleeding?" Jim Terral asks. "I don't know." He searches for words that might describe the special meaning of this region; perhaps it is, he says, a *chakra,* a place of sacred healing, on the Rocky Mountains, the spine of the North American continent. "It's like a continental hospital, somehow. There are all sorts of groups that have come here because of their suffering. The Doukhobors are here, there are people here who came up during the McCarthy era from the U.S., there is a significant community of Quakers. The Japanese people are out here."

And though he has moved back and forth between the coast and the West Kootenay, Jim is here. A deserter from the American army during the Vietnam crisis, he fled to Canada and came to the West Kootenay in the early 1970s with a group of people who wanted to start a co-operative farm. That venture succeeded, and then fell apart. Jim now teaches writing at Selkirk College in Castlegar.

Jim grew up in the American midwest, and went to college and on to graduate school in Seattle. All through his university years, the peace movement in the United States and the protests against the Vietnam war were growing. During the Cuban missile crisis, Jim went with other workers for peace to a movement meeting in Chicago. "I remember being drunk out of my mind on the way back, and throwing up three or four times along the road. It was just sheer anxiety, like really believing that you weren't going to wake up the next morning, that it just all wasn't going to be there."

Berkeley, free speech, the draft, the war: they were all on young American minds during the sixties. In grad school, "I was very much aware that as soon as I got out of school, my student deferment would be up and I would be draftable." He finished his master's degree and went to a teaching job in the midwest. "Almost as soon as I started teaching, I got my notice that I would be drafted. I was not the only person who was in that jam. All my male students were in that situation, except for a handful who had already been through the service. It was really very difficult teaching in that kind of situation. Nobody was motivated. It was terrible. During that year, and in grad school too, I would wake up and it was like being obsessed with a woman or something, the first thing I would be aware of was the word Vietnam in my mind.

"It happened every day, day after day after day. Sometimes I would get ten minutes where I didn't think about it."

Part of the reaction was, of course, fear. "Nobody wants to fight a war, nobody wants to die. And yet, there are probably things I would risk my life for." Jim sighs. The American cause in Vietnam was not one of those things. The more he looked at American motives overseas and the conduct of the American government at home, the less he believed. "Still, all the way through that year, I believed that if I read the newspaper religiously enough, or studied the right book, or heard the right interview on TV, that it would change. So I went in.

"Years after I came here, that was the thing that really troubled me and made me wonder about myself." Why did he enter the army when he opposed the war? By the end of basic training, Jim knew he had made the wrong decision. Twenty years later, in a country he has adopted, every detail of basic training is as fresh in his mind as it was twenty years ago. The training exercises where some soldiers played the part of Viet Cong, where he learned that the massacre of villagers at My Lai was not an aberration but standard procedure. "That was the way it was done, and if you did it any other way, you were stupid, you'd have probably got yourself shot by your buddies." The mind-bending treatment handed out to people who declared themselves conscientious objectors. The recruiting of illiterate men, mostly blacks, teaching them to read and write and sending them to Vietnam to be killed — in a country that refused to teach them to read and write in peacetime. The men who pretended to be crazy to get their discharge, and ended up not pretending. The experience on the firing range with a soldier who spoke only Spanish. "The guy ... gets up and starts waving his hands. There was a tarantula that was coming from the target to the guys, and he didn't know what to do. So the sergeant went over and he took the M16 and he took it off the single shot mode and put it on the automatic mode and blew the living shit out of that tarantula." Jim imitates the rat-a-tat of an automatic weapon, then laughs, the way you laugh when you cannot come to terms with an alien way of thinking. "And if that didn't get him, you call in an air strike. It was symbolic of the whole thing."

The bureaucracy considered Jim's case at its own slow speed, then rejected his request for CO status. Jim deserted from the army. He and his wife went to Seattle. Aided by the Quaker committee, they crossed the border to Vancouver. Once he got his Canadian work permit, he taught on the coast, came to the Kootenays, went back to the coast, came back to Castlegar. Now he's thinking again that he might move.

"The native people somehow had a sense of this as a place that you go to, but you don't stay. When you're finished with it (the continental hospital), and it's finished with you, you should go on. I feel as though I'm at a point

with the Kootenays where I am ready to be released from the hospital."
Behind that decision is a continuing desire to make a difference to a world
that could countenance a Vietnam. He prepared a booklet that set out the
case against uranium mining in the Kootenays, a project defeated by public outcry. Now he wants to try to influence changes in an educational
system that he believes should, but now cannot, create fundamental change
in the way people think about other people.

"I'm looking around for what I need to do next. It will probably involve
more risk, less income, more meaning. It's kind of odd to be thinking
about that as I'm approaching fifty. I'm not going to do some young person's thing. I don't know what it's going to be. I don't know."

From Robson, I head towards the Slocan, one of those narrow river-lake
valleys that characterize the Kootenays. In the last twenty-five years, the
Slocan has drawn hippies, American draft dodgers, back-to-the-landers,
artists, writers: people who seek a lifestyle distant from what they view as
the urban insanities.

If you look at the Slocan road on a map, you'll see half a dozen little
white dots that indicate towns. On the road itself, only the occasional gas
station or wayside café indicates that people live somewhere around here.
The communities themselves are on the west side of the river, near gravel
roads that wind between the poplars and firs along the river, in log cabins,
farms, homesteads, new houses, at the ends of long driveways and behind
the screening trees. Off one of these gravel roads, the youngest students at
the Vallican Whole alternate school are ready for a snack and swim break.
We straggle through the forest, jumping roots and discussing which berries are edible and how the trail has changed since the spring, to the swimming hole next to the river. Some of the children, unself-conscious, strip
off and leap gleefully naked into the water. Others, more modest, retain
their underwear. Two or three, life's planners, have brought bathing suits
with them. I talk, alternately, to a six-year-old about the best techniques of
frog-stroking, and to Trudy, teacher and parent, about the school and the
building it occupies.

"It took a few years for the building to get off the ground — they called
it the 'Hole' to start with, because it was just a hole in the ground. When
they put up the big beams, even the kids were out helping. It was a real
community effort. Every day, different people would show up."

Completed, the Hole became the Whole, a community hall where wed-
dings, anniversaries and birthdays are celebrated. But it also became the
centre for the social activism that characterizes the valley. An annual wom-
en's festival that attracts women from across Canada, environmental im-

pact meetings and political campaign meetings all take place at the Whole.

During the day, the alternate school rents the building. Teacher-administrator Brenda Curry expresses the reasons for the school. "We want to keep the child a child longer (than is possible in the regular school system). We want to nurture them more in their younger years. We want to have a more exciting, stimulating type of education, with more hands-on projects, more field trips where they learn counting and reading at the same time as they see what the community has to offer, what the world has to offer."

Though the school began as an alternative for students up to age sixteen, now two dozen children between the ages of four and ten attend. "They learn all the basics," says Brenda, "reading, writing, math, geography, language arts, painting, music. We hope to get a French teacher, and maybe a Japanese teacher."

We walk back to the school through the woods, and I drive away. And drive back. Unwittingly, I have kidnapped the Whole Cat. I let him out and depart again. No other cars leave dust plumes on the gravel road that leads me north along the Slocan River, its autumn waters fast and shallow over the rocky riverbed.

Close enough to the river that you can almost hear its murmur, an editor and graphic designer are at work at light tables. In Toronto, regional publishing refers to anything outside Toronto. In British Columbia, regional publishers have addresses like Ganges, Madeira Park and Winlaw. Julian Ross runs Polestar Press near Winlaw, one of those well-spread-out Slocan communities. He was a part of eight different businesses in Vancouver over a decade or so, all of which "didn't quite work out." He was the first creative writing graduate of the now defunct David Thompson University Centre in Nelson, bought land at Winlaw because he really liked the mix of creative, artistic people who had gravitated to the Slocan Valley, moved back to Vancouver and Victoria, and finally settled with his family here.

He knew that the odds against financial success were high. "A lot of people come here because it's very beautiful, but they run out of money very quickly. They want to get more training, more money, but they can't afford to leave because they have been out of the work force for so long. There are a lot of artistic people in the valley who do treeplanting and that sort of thing — until their bodies get too old." Left undescribed is the month-to-month struggle to survive, the growing frustration and the recourse to welfare payments that is often the outcome of the struggle.

Julian and Ruth did not intend to lose the struggle. "We went back to Victoria to get more skills, because we felt we didn't have enough skills to prosper, to survive in the valley," says Julian. Then they moved to Creston, east of here, where Julian took a newspaper job as sports reporter, typesetter and layout man. A month later, the newspaper, in business for seventy-five years, folded. The Rosses moved to their property in Winlaw. "We had the land and we had an old barn and a really small cabin. We started doing some typesetting for other people, and then we did some books and some textbooks." Polestar was born. For several years, the press was housed in a small workshop — "at night, you'd be laying everything out and all the bugs would land on the light table" — before moving to their present light, airy, to them palatial, quarters.

For the first few years, Julian tried to distribute his own publications, spending half the time on the road with a trunkload of books and publicity flyers, half the time trying to get reorders out through the post office since there was no parcel service in any nearby town. Finally, Polestar threw in its lot with a Vancouver distributor who acts for several publishers. "On our own, we really weren't big enough for bookstores to bother dealing with us. Now, we have the same sales reps as the other publishers, and our books are treated the same way as theirs. It has always been delightful to me that once our books are in the stores, our book and some multimillion-dollar publisher's book have the same chance of sales."

And he has not lacked for creative talent. "We've been fortunate. We've used a local stained-glass artist to design some of our covers, and an architect, so our covers look fresh and different. We try to use as many people from this area as we can."

Nonetheless, Julian and Ruth must balance their desire to live here against the difficulties of working here. "Anyone in a rural area has to work a lot harder, because there are so many things we don't have the services for. You have to go outside for them, or you somehow have to create them here."

For them, hard work is balanced by the rewards of living in a rural area. "One of the beauties of being here is, I can go to the post office and they know us. If we are short fifteen dollars, they'll lend it to us to get our mail out. Or they'll undo their bags if we're late, and get our things off that day. They are tremendously helpful. And driving to the post office, you get to drive along the Slocan River. Even in the midst of a really crazy day, you get to enjoy the beauty of the place. That's one of the great advantages of being here. Even though it's very busy, you're in a very peaceful setting, and you draw comfort from that."

He finds the rural life they live more complete in many ways than the urban life they left behind. "You have respect for individuals according to who they are, not for what they do. You interact with people on a different level than you would in the city, where you only see people in one role.

Here, you get to see people volunteering in the fire department, or involved in a political campaign, or fighting the logging of a watershed or the possibilities of pollution. Work is just something you do in relation to the many other things a person does.

"I feel very strongly that this is a wonderful place to live, but we are absolutely not retreating. We are connected to a greater world, a world outside."

Rita Moir looks up in mock shock from a book she is laying out. Retreat is not a word in her vocabulary. Feminist, journalist, dramatist, from a very conservative area of southern Alberta, she and her partner came to the West Kootenay for a conference, and tagged along with a friend on a visit to the valley and the first women's festival at the Vallican Whole. "I fell in love with the place. The hall needed caretakers; we applied and moved here five days later.

"Sometimes, there's a sign in your life that says, 'turning point,' and you either do it or you regret that you didn't. A lot of women have moved here because they visit the area and find out there is a place for them here. Women have been outspoken in this community. It's an atmosphere where women have fought and made gains. You think you can have some effect. You're not the Lone Ranger. This is the place where a lot of us have chosen to make our stands."

The first year in the Slocan, Rita and her partner lived in a tent until mid-November. "We were very poor. We moved here with six hundred dollars. But we weren't in any worse shape than a whole bunch of other people. People were very generous to us. They took the time to teach us how to do stuff, to give us a hand."

Many years a journalist, Rita decided to move on to creative writing, fighting against her own impulses to continue writing newspaper stories she thought worthwhile. "I'd gone off to Alberta and worked in the legislature for four months as a press hack. I made enough money to come back and write plays." Her first was presented on CBC radio. Then, with two other women, she wrote a play for the Nelson-based group, Theatre Energy, on the topic of the persecution of women in medieval Europe.

"We wrote that play in just three weeks. The emotional effect was quite incredible." That effect was heightened by the events of the day. During the first rewrite, the federal government cut off funding to women's centres; scant days later, fourteen female engineering students were murdered in Montreal. "Because of our outrage, we moved forward fast. It was like a paradigm shift. We couldn't believe these things had happened."

Theatre Energy presented the play in a leaky tent on the shore of Kootenay

Lake. "It was really like all the goddesses were stirred up. There were huge winds and rainstorms. And the show was about survival and magic and persecution and fighting back and the elements. The play ended with a burning on the lake, and everyone came out in the rain and watched it. It was quite something."

But her own sense of energy and purpose does not blind Rita to the shortcomings of life in the Kootenays. "It depends on who you talk to. I don't happen to work in the forest industry. If you had been here after the university closed and the mills shut down and B.C. Tel workers were shut out … There was a ton of unemployment. It was just a hell of a tough place to live. A lot of people had to leave. They had no choice. But a lot of people stayed, and scraped by on nothing. They built the foundations for the things you see flourishing now. There's a real strength in having gone through those hard times together.

"I don't want to romanticize it, but this place is of a size you can get a grip on. I feel like a lot of people feel about this area, that if I am ever going to do something in my life that really matters, this is the place it's going to happen. It's not going to happen when we move someplace else. We make our stand here."

I drive up the valley, towards Slocan Lake, which curls between the Valhalla and Slocan mountains. Traffic is halted at a road construction project that will widen the dreaded Cape Horn section of the highway that clings, narrow, to the edge of a cliff. Four hundred feet above the road, scalers' safety helmets glint red and silver against the blast-scarred rock and boulders bounce down the cliff to shatter on the road below. The sun blazes full above the western mountains, and the smell of hot oil invades the car, to remain for days.

Jim holds the traffic back with his stop sign. A flagman now, he used to be a scaler, working the province from North Vancouver to Terrace. Not any more. "You're supposed to have some brains by the time you're fifty, and you don't have any brains if you do that." He gestures upwards at the scalers, tiny dots on the sheer and crumbling rock. Every morning, the scalers follow an access road to the top of the cliff, clamber out to the cliff face, attach ropes and slither down the cliff to lever away with their picks rock that has been loosened by blasting. "Do they have rock-climbing experience, training?" I ask. He looks surprised. "Nope. They're just scalers." Ten hours a day they dangle from their ropes, finding footholds where they can. Coffee breaks, lunch breaks and rest breaks come when the bulldozers push the fallen rock over the edge of the highway into the lake and the flagman waves the waiting traffic through. "When I worked the Fraser canyon, the Squamish Highway, it was better than this," says Jim. "It took half an hour for the traffic to go by. Here you got, what, three cars?"

But he insists the work is not dangerous. "Only way you can fall is if a rope breaks — some kind of a fluke." He saw a fluke happen once: a stump caught up somehow when a rope end whipped around it. The rope broke. Did the man live? Jim looks at me pityingly. "He fell a hundred and fifty feet."

Jim was pushing fifty and working out of Vancouver when he decided one day he'd never make his fiftieth birthday if he stayed in the city. "Hassle, always hassle." He was born near here; he and his wife bought a house in New Denver, north of Silverton. He worked "out" on road gangs for the first two years, and took courses in fixing furnaces, refrigerators, what-have-you, skills he thought he could sell in the Slocan. He doesn't need much to live on. And he doesn't miss at all the urban delights. "We were in Terrace, my wife and me, I was working there, and we had some time to kill. We went to the mall, and the first thing I did, I bought a hamster and a cage. The wife said, 'What did you do that for?' I didn't know. First thing I did when I got here, I gave it away."

I have phoned ahead to reserve a cabin at Silverton, just beyond Cape Horn. At the resort, a message is on a slate outside the door: "Rosemary. Cabin 2 is open for you." Hugh has gone fishing. Had I a boat, a rod, a worm, I would do likewise. Bereft, I swim, eat, ponder.

Hugh Wilson returns. His lakeside resort is the end of an odyssey for Hugh. English, he was sent to the United States when he was four years old, as a child war evacuee. Forty years later, he returned to North America, the guest of a North American corporation sponsoring a reunion of war evacuees with their foster parents. All was sweetness and light, Hugh recalls, until Hugh couldn't stand it any more. "What about," he asked, "the situations that didn't work out? What about the abusive foster parents, the ones who worked their newly acquired children half to death, the children who were unhappy?" That didn't make Hugh popular. He left, and began a trek across the continent, looking for something that would change his life.

"I was coming up to fifty. I was happy but I was miserable. I decided if I was ever going to do anything different with my life, this was the time." He ended up one August day in Banff, in the Canadian Rockies. "It was beautiful, but there were so many people." He fled the crowds, and followed his whims down into the Kootenays. At New Denver, he went for a walk in the park. "I thought the town must have been evacuated. There was no one in sight, just one canoe out on the lake." When he discovered that the Slocan was always as beautiful and often as empty of people as this, he knew he had to move here. He immigrated to Canada and began to build this log cabin resort at Silverton.

Yet a man's dream can be a woman's nightmare. After two years, his wife left him. "I was devastated," says Hugh, flatly. He stuffed the few hundred dollars he could scrape up into his pockets and left for Mexico. There, speaking almost no Spanish, with not a plan in his head, he wandered the byways, living cheap and risking danger. He loved it. He learned, he said, that he could survive hardship and find excitement. He returned to the Slocan revitalized. Now he pours his energy into battling any encroachment he thinks could destroy the beauty of his valley.

Eagerly, he thrusts a sheaf of papers into my hands. He has joined a coalition of environmentalists, tourism operators and long-time residents of the Slocan to fight a proposed expansion of the pulp mill downstream in Castlegar. They fight on two fronts: against additional pollution they believe will result from the new mill, and against the converting of the Slocan into an industrial corridor, with chip trucks rolling ceaselessly down the narrow valley road towards the mill. Statistics roll from Hugh's lips: an average of one chip truck every seven and a half minutes, no proper guarantees of pollution control, access for the company to forests that cover half of southeastern British Columbia. The loggers, millworkers and truckers who favour the plan talk about the jobs it will create, the security it will bring. Hugh and the others who fight the expansion are convinced it will devastate the valley. "They aren't widening that road for us," says Hugh, referring to the road work at Cape Horn. "They're widening it for the pulp company." And he asks why the taxpayer should subsidize the mill by paying for road repair and maintenance instead of insisting that the company ship by lake barge or rail and shoulder the real cost.

At dusk, the small village of Silverton, wedged between the lake and a steep cliff that rises towards the mountains, is quiet. Two pyjama-clad children chase a curly-haired black dog across a side street where dish antennas sprout in tiny backyards; the sound of "60 Minutes" spills through an open window. Along the back street, up against the mountain, *For Sale* signs sprout in front of neat houses. A treeplanter's shovel leans against the porch of an old miner's cottage and a row of clean diapers drips from the clothesline. On the main street, a dozen sceptical teenagers listen to a man barely older than they are talk about log books and certification and the bright future in store for those who take the training program he promotes.

Feeding fish create spreading ripples on the lake, in the shadow of the dark mountains to the west. Across the road, a man pauses in the spill of light from the hotel doorway to light a cigarette. He joins his girlfriend on the side of the road, at the edge of town; they stand forlornly by a small suitcase and hopefully stick out their thumbs. When I go to bed an hour later, the hitchhikers are still standing by the road, waiting for a car to appear on the empty highway.

RITA MOIR (1952–)

Rita Moir's essay, "Leave Taking," explores a reality hidden from most human beings: the preparation of bodies for burial, or cremation. The essay deals with an emotionally charged issue in a sympathetic and honest way which has touched readers throughout North America. "Leave Taking" originally appeared in *Event*, the literary quarterly published at Douglas College, and was a co-winner of that journal's creative non-fiction prize for autumn 1989. It has been reprinted in *Best Canadian Essays* (1990) and in one of Norton's anthologies in 1996. Moir says of her essay that "it catapulted me from the observational skills of journalism into creative non-fiction — to a place where journalism doesn't usually get to go." She was formerly a freelance journalist who contributed to regional and national media, both print and broadcast, and has written drama for the CBC. Moir has kept a home for many years in Winlaw, B.C. in the Kootenays, and has been a member of the burial society in her community. (B.C. is the only province where lay people may legally prepare the dead for burial, a practice still sometimes carried out by groups such as the Doukhobors and Quakers). Moir has developed her skills as a writer of creative non-fiction in books such as *Survival Gear* — short-listed for the Edna Staebler Award for Creative Non-Fiction in 1995 — and *Buffalo Jump: A Woman's Travels* (1999). She has co-written with Shirley Bruised Head an essay titled "Light on the Land" set on the Peigan Reserve in southern Alberta which will be published in an upcoming anthology of creative non-fiction by Coteau Press. Moir has long been involved in women's and social issues, and is currently President of the Federation of B.C. Writers.

LEAVE TAKING

WE PULLED DOWN the stainless steel locker door and slid you out. The morgue was warm — a refrigeration breakdown, the nurse said, and it would get warmer as we worked.

I didn't know if I'd know you. I only knew you were Bert Carlson and you died in a motorcycle accident last Saturday in Silverton. Your friends asked our burial society to help prepare you for cremation. The society built the cemetery a few years ago, and some members learned how to do the simple things that help a dead person take leave.

I'd never done it before. I hoped I wouldn't be sick. I hoped I wouldn't be useless.

The hospital wrapping of plastic and linen had loosened around you. I saw your penis before I saw your face. It made you human, needing our help but not helpless.

The four of us, three women you didn't know, and your male friend, lifted you onto the metal table. We searched through a black plastic garbage bag lying with you. The belt buckle your girlfriend asked for lay at the bottom of the bag, broken. It was with another piece of metal, a piece of the car you collided with.

The section of bumper was silver and untarnished. Inside your helmet, the black foam was still wet. Your jeans and sheepskin jacket had blood on them, too. Nothing was awful. Nothing was horrifying.

My friends told me that the autopsy cut and stitching is disturbing. Especially in babies. It's a long cut from your navel to your breastbone, then a Y-shape to your shoulder blades. The coroner bastes you back up with a string heavier than that used on a turkey. They cut open your head, too, and the string hangs from your hair, waiting for the final trim.

You didn't look that damaged. Not like the pictures in the first aid book. Your deadness didn't alarm me. I'd been with death. It was animal death, but there's a connection. Even dead chickens have dignity. Not the kind of chickens bought frozen in the Safeway, but the ones I've had to kill myself. The bears our neighbour shot for fun, then gave us to butcher — they have power, too. My dog howled all night when I tried to boil a head to make bear-head cheese. I learned not to do things like that. There are some things that aren't done. Decent burials are important. Respect is important. Time is important.

When Amanda died in her crib, Penny held her for eight hours. A change came over them both. They found peace together while they were leaving each other.

You needed to find your peace, too. It wasn't just for us, and for your family, that we did this. You weren't three days dead. You weren't gone yet.

The Doukhobors who live in these valleys give the body three days to lie at rest before burial. It goes back to the three days Christ had before rising. I know you're not a Doukhobor, Bert, and no one ever accused me of being religious, but here in this room it makes sense.

We struggled to put on your white cotton socks, tried to make your legs move one more time. Were you one of the long-legged treeplanters who left us short-limbed ones behind? Did you stride so fast a breeze cooled you in the hot spring sun? You called out with joy when fireweed sweetened the air or nettle stung your fingertips, leaving you shocked and laughing.

We couldn't get on your boots, even though we used pruning shears to cut them up the back. Your feet weren't bending. We slipped your jeans on, rolling you sideways, holding you in our arms, the four of us a team.

The hard part was your head. This most vulnerable place, this container with all your thoughts. The head injury and the autopsy cut at the top — we didn't know how to touch it. This was a test, but it wasn't grisly so far. We didn't want to be afraid of you.

The nurse showed us how to move your head. Your man friend washed your face. They brought us swabs, and I cleaned around your eyes and in your nostrils and in your ears. Your friend cleaned your teeth. There was blood in these places. You died from inside.

We wheeled you to the sink. I remembered last week at Margee's hair salon, lying back as the warm water coursed over me, soothing, gentle. We couldn't wash your hair, but we cleaned away the blood with damp cloths.

We snipped the string and I combed your hair. I'll have a hard time looking at my lover for a while. The resemblance is only passing, the same receding hairline, the same mustache.

Sometimes your eyes opened as we washed around them. I closed them. I could see.

We didn't try to lift or bend you to put on your shirt. We used the coroner's scissors from the white towel covered with the tools of his work, and snipped up the back of your yellow T-shirt. The one that says Fleetwood, the name of your treeplanting company. I thought of Fleetwood Mac, rock 'n' roll. The shirt stayed connected around your chest and we slipped it over your arms and tucked it round you.

Your flannel shirt was harder. We figured the only way was to cut it up the back, right through the yoke and collar, slip on the two halves, and button up the front.

Your friend put on the baseball cap you always wore on the slopes.

Months ago Sally made the wood coffin that we kept in stock. Your friends believed you would fit, but they were off by a few inches. You were six feet four.

Until then it had all been gentle. Now we had to use force. The four of us looked at one another, drew our breath, and kept going.

We left you tucked in your coffin with your quilt and pillow, a sheet tucked around your bent legs.

We washed up, then stood aside while your girlfriend came in with the nurse to see you. We exchanged brief hugs. We didn't know her well, and she hadn't cried yet.

She left the room and we screwed down the pine lid, twelve screws, lifted the coffin and wheeled you out to the basement loading dock of the hospital where the treeplanters' station wagon waited for you.

Your six men friends waiting below concentrated on the metal handles of the coffin and didn't look up into our eyes. We passed you on. You were ready to take your leave.

Your face came into my mind even when I left for a long time to go away to work. You'd taken your leave, but now I needed to take mine, from you.

I phoned your girlfriend. I worried she would find my words too personal, impertinent.

She did what I knew she'd do. She took out a snapshot. I braced myself.

There was still the chance that I would recognize you as someone I'd known. But I didn't know you, was just glad to see how thick and dark your hair had been, you leaning against the counter in your plaid shirt, tall man with big mustache and cheeks whipped red and warm by the wind.

Your girlfriend completed the picture, helped me take my leave.

Last night I talked with a friend of mine. While I'd been away working, she had helped prepare a man for burial. She'd never done it before either. She found it moving, although she had not known the man in life. The same nurse said to her, I like the way you people do this. This is so much better than the other way.

Her brother said to her, I hear you've been laying out stiffs in your spare time.

MARK HUME (1950–)

In the opening essay to his first book, *The Run of the River* (1992), Mark Hume tells of killing a porcupine with a bow and homemade arrow when he was a boy. It didn't die when he shot it the first time, so he put his boot on its nose and pulled the arrow out of its head and shot it a second time. Reflecting on that long ago event, he writes "sometimes you go too far and it's terrible when you realize you can't turn back ... I felt sad about it for years." With this cautionary tale he opens his study of eleven British Columbia rivers whose ecosystems are threatened by the logging and agricultural practices and by the industrial pollution of a civilization that he views as going too far.

Born in Victoria, Hume grew up in a family of five boys where he was the only one to develop a passion for fishing. As a teenager he came upon the writings of Roderick Haig-Brown and decided that he wanted both to fly fish and be a writer like the environmentalist and lay magistrate of Campbell River. Hume has made his living as a newspaper reporter (*Vancouver Sun, National Post*), but has written three books in which he argues passionately for a conservation ethic that will preserve the rivers and streams of the province from destruction. In a hard-nosed reporting style, he writes about the dramatic decline in fish stocks at the end of the century and about the specific ways in which rivers are polluted and spawning grounds destroyed. But there is increasingly a fierce lyricism to that style which conveys the passion he brings to his subject and that renders his prose almost poetry. *River of the Angry Moon: Seasons on the Bella Coola* (1998) begins: "The river is fed by the sky. It runs over a bed of shattered mountains, through the dreams of a great forest and into the mouths of ancient fishes. It starts in clouds as grey and heavy as the sea and ends in a windswept estuary haunted by ghosts. It is a place where white swans dance on dark mud flats and salmon lay fragile eggs in nests of stone." Written with Harvey Thommasen, that book laments the biological decline of one of the province's great rivers, but also celebrates what remains and what could be restored. Fittingly, it was awarded the Roderick Haig-Brown Regional Prize for the book that best contributes to the understanding and appreciation of B.C. "Swimming at Night" from *The Run of the River* describes the plight of the steelhead in the Deadman River near Kamloops.

SWIMMING AT NIGHT
The Deadman

THE LAST EXIT before the oblivion of Kamloops Lake is the Deadman River, where steelhead hang an abrupt left and disappear. Months earlier they were gliding over the Emperor Sea Mounts off the northeastern coast of Russia. But turning out of the powerful, clear Thompson River, with the blue waters of Kamloops Lake in sight above them, the big fish head up a small, dirty stream to begin the last stage of their journey. They started here four or five years ago and have been searching for the scent of the Deadman since they entered the mouth of the Fraser in the fall. It must smell to them of topsoil, volcanic rock, rotting trees, shaded cottonwoods and jackpine, of deer bones, alfalfa, diesel and the stink of cattle.

The Deadman is a troubled river that rushes through subsistence ranchland where "for sale" signs mark the retreats of men from their dreams. Perhaps it is the unforgiving, hardbaked earth that has defeated them, leaving their barns and houses to slump like exhausted drunks and their fences to stagger and pitch to the ground. Or maybe it is the five hoodoos that stand on a steep mountainside over the river, so hidden in the timber you can only see them when the light is just right. For some the bad luck runs deep. Crops wither in the summer heat; spring floods erode the narrow strip of bottom land. One rancher stopped to open a gate and was run over by his own truck, whose emergency brake had failed. Now the widow is selling out, but the river isn't waiting for a dignified departure; it has cut sharply into her farmyard, undermining the barn and outsheds, tugging at their foundations, trying to suck them into the current, to blow them out down the valley, to spread the planks from the barn through a thousand log jams and carry the remaining pieces into the big river and on to the great sea.

The Deadman got its name after Pierre Charette, clerk of the North West Trading Company at Kamloops, was killed here in 1817 in what has been reported, rather unsatisfactorily, as a quarrel over the choice of a campsite. Imagine, if you will, the number of places a man could have found to camp in this empty land in 1817. Did people really kill each other over such things? Perhaps they did in the 1800s, when every brook, every murmuring, shining stream seemed to promise gold. The Deadman promised, sparking a rush in the 1860s, but it didn't deliver much until 1930 when a "big play" was found in the upper valley at Vidette Lake. That led to one mine, but the Deadman was no new Klondike. The big play played out, leaving rocky soil that was too poor for farming and natural meadows where the waving grass enticed ranchers with whispers of prosperity.

The Deadman River drains a quadrant of the Fraser Plateau, rising in a series of lakes, running due west then turning abruptly south and winding its way to the Thompson. Along the way it plunges over a fall of 170 feet (which cuts steelhead off from the upper river) and enters a great chasm that is 700 feet deep and from one to two miles wide. Where the chasm opens along the river, the flat land offers the greatest agricultural potential. Ranchers settled where the natural meadows once stood and soon were hard at work clearing more land. In 1919 the British Columbia department of lands surveyed the area and concluded that, although the soil and climate wouldn't permit profitable farming, cattle ranchers could make a go of it. "The chief assets are the abundance of summer feed and good water. Stock do well. All we saw were in good condition and most of the cattle were rolling fat," reported the land agents. They noted plentiful mule deer, grouse and rabbits, but made no mention of any fisheries value in what was originally called *Rivière des Defunts*, or River of the Dead.

Deadman Chasm is a dry land that has broken the hopes of gold seekers and begrudgingly grants a living to those who struggle to ranch it. Despite the hardships, there is magic between the steep hills, and you sense it soon after turning off Highway 97 just west of the sawmill town of Savona.

Ian McGregor's B.C. Ministry of the Environment pickup truck rattles off the end of pavement onto the dirt of the Deadman River road. It is mid-May and the alfalfa fields along the bottom land are lush, fading to lighter shades of green where the bunchgrass and pine forest from the highlands merge at the base of precipitous slopes. He looks on the agrarian landscape without any fondness. His eyes are following the river bank as it twists back and forth across the narrow valley like a deer running in panic.

"We spent $35,000 on that corner right there," he says, slowing the truck as we near an inward curve of the river, here about two lanes wide and fast with spring melt. The corner is piled deep with rip-rap, a jumble of boulders fronting a berm of mixed stone and gravel. The current churns at the bank, deflecting in whorls and back eddies. Inside the protective berm are the fields of a small ranch.

"This guy says he loses five or ten acres a year to the river. He fights against it. He's in there all the time with his Cat, but you can see how it's eaten away at his land farther down. The berm is working, but you wonder how much more would have to be spent to protect his whole place. At what point, you have to ask, are you spending more to save the land than the ranch is worth?"

Farther upstream, passing onto an Indian reserve, McGregor points out where native workers have cabled hundreds of pine trees to the bank, the trunks lashed down, the tree tops waving in the current.

"This is a new technique and it seems to be working really well. The tree branches soften the current, protecting the bank from erosion, and it gives young fish good hiding places. There is lots of shade and cover there. But it's hard work. Last spring about fifty percent of the trees washed away in a flood and they all had to be replaced."

Higher up, softened by Skookum, Snowhoosh and Mowish lakes, and still shaded by vegetation, the Deadman is a gentler river. In places it comes through the forest like a Haydn concerto, with the notes drifting in the deeper pools, spilling through the riffles and dancing down long, smooth runs. Where ranchers have stripped away the streambank cover, however, there is no symphonic proportion to it; the river runs fast, slashing at its banks, trying to cut away the corners so it can go straight to the Thompson.

"This is our biggest problem," says McGregor, stopping his truck to look out on a ranch that boasts alfalfa fields that sweep right down into the river. The early ranchers tried to take out every bloody tree. Every cottonwood they could find they cut down. They devegetated the river. And they have done everything they can to straighten it out, to take out the bends. Ranchers like a river that runs straight. But when you take the curves out, you speed it up and it only causes you more problems. The river is highly volatile now."

The cattle that wander through the grazing pastures are continuing the devegetation. They eat everything in sight. They lumber along the streambanks, chewing at every willow bush, every young cottonwood that takes root, turning the streambank vegetation into cud and green saliva. They trample pathways to the stream, creating muddy wallows. The result: unstable banks that wash away when the water runs high in the spring. You can see it now from up on the roadway; the water is the colour of dark loam. Flood and erosion haunt the ranchers but it is hard to be sympathetic for, to a large degree, they are simply being revisited by the sins of the past.

"It is better now than it once was," says McGregor, trying to find reason for hope. "But it's nothing like it should be. It's nothing like it was historically. You can go to the upper valley and see the Deadman in its natural state with lots of vegetation on the banks. It's a pretty sight."

McGregor first came to Deadman Chasm in 1977, the year after he was named biologist in charge of saving the Thompson River steelhead run. When he started, virtually nothing was known about the big fish that came up the Thompson except that an extraordinary sports fishery had developed at Spences Bridge. Nobody knew how many fish there were, but everyone said there were an awful lot less than there used to be. The sports fishery by then was about twenty years old, and by today's standards it was still excellent. But it wasn't what it had been. So McGregor started to put the puzzle together: How many fish were there? How many should there be? What did they need to survive and flourish?

Just about the first thing he did was to radio-tag a batch of steelhead. He wanted to know where they went after they left Spences Bridge. A few weeks later he found himself heading north up the Thompson in his pickup, past Ashcroft, then west, staying with the mainstem past Walhachin and on towards Kamloops Lake. Above the lake the main river branches into the North and South Thompson, and there is a lot of good water up there for steelhead. He thought that was where the steelhead were taking him. Historically there are references to steelhead as far up the North Thompson as Barrier Creek, seventy kilometres northeast, but biologists now believe those were big rainbow trout from Kamloops Lake, misidentified as steelhead. In fourteen years of radio tracking, not a single steelhead has ever been known to pass through Kamloops Lake. Deadman is the last stop for Thompson steelhead.

McGregor was surprised when he found his truck turning north off Highway 97, heading up the narrow Deadman, honing in on the sharp "pip, pip, pip" of radio signals. The quartz crystals in the transmitters gave each fish its own unique frequency. Running across the dial on the radio receiver, McGregor realized the whole school of transmitting fish was turning up the Deadman. When the road came down next to the river he stopped his truck and walked the bank. Wearing polaroid glasses to cut through the surface glare, it wasn't long before he found his first steelhead, a greenbacked fish hovering over a gravel mound, ghostlike at the tail of a pool. In heavily silted water it is hard to make out fish. You have to know where to look and you have to look hard. You key on shapes, colour tones and movement. What McGregor could see was really no more than a grey shadow vanishing and briefly reappearing as the current shifted veils of silt near an oval of gravel that had been cleaned by the repeated brushing of a fish's tail. Even so, he was elated. He had just uncovered one of the great secrets of the Thompson River steelhead. He had found their birthplace. It was a secret they had kept for ten thousand years before the arrival of

Europeans, and for two hundred years after prospectors and settlers moved in.

"It's amazing," said McGregor, "to think that for all those years these huge fish were coming here to spawn and none of the ranchers here knew anything about them. They slipped in when the river was cloudy with run-off and were gone before anybody knew they were here."

It is little wonder nobody knew about the steelhead. They spawn during a brief period from mid-April to the end of May when the river is silted and running so heavily that nobody thinks of fishing it. They come in when the people of the chasm are distracted with flood problems, calving and seed crops. And just to make sure the secret is kept, the steelhead hold to cover during the day. They move upstream through the open riffles where their backs might show only after darkness falls. They swim at night in the River of the Dead.

Biologist Alan Caverly pulls green waders up to his chest, lifts back two large plywood trapdoors and vaults down into the swirling current of the Deadman. He is waist deep in a small pen that is barred on three sides. The river churns through the bars and boils around his waist. The fourth wall of the cell, downstream, is notched with a V-shaped opening less than a foot wide. Stretching across the stream is a fence that blocks any up-stream movement of fish. When steelhead encounter the Deadman fish trap, set beneath a dramatic, rainbow-hued, volcanic cliff, they nudge back and forth along it until the V-gate leads them into the holding pen. The largest number of steelhead to pass through the fence in a single year was twelve hundred. That was in 1984, when runs peaked. They have been on a downward trend ever since. Total this year, with only a few days left in the season: 144. The Deadman steelhead are falling towards extinction.

It is early afternoon. Caverly has held some steelhead for me from the night before. Some years there have been as many as a hundred steelhead a night pushing their way into the trap. Last night was typical for this year: three. They are stored in long black plastic tubes that undulate in the current. The fish are calm; it is as if they know they are going to be released unharmed. Unzipping a tube slowly, Caverly points the open end towards a dip net. In a sudden explosion a steelhead appears from the blackness, surging out of the current and into the net. The fish is silver and green, with a heavily spotted back and a bold pink stripe riding down its side from cheek to tail. The stripe looks like the tail of an Amazon parrot — brilliant and wild. The fish is as long as a man's leg. The average weight of Deadman steelhead is twelve to fourteen pounds. This one is about twelve pounds.

Caverly wears a woolen glove on his left hand, so he can get a better grip on the fish. He reaches down into the water, his arm disappearing up to the elbow. His face is so close to the river he can feel the cold air above the surface. 'This is a very wet job," he says. "You get used to being soaked day after day." He is searching for the part of the fish that narrows before it flares into a broad, translucent tail. That place is called the wrist. On a twelve-pound fish, the wrist is just about the thickness of a human wrist. It is firm muscle. The fish is as cold as ice and as smooth as a peeled mango. Without a glove, Caverly's hand would slip on the steelhead's protective coating. Most people call the mucous covering "slime," thinking of the clammy, viscous substance that covers a dead fish at the market. But on a healthy wild Steelhead, "slime" is beautiful and functional. The slick, glistening lubricant lets a fish slide through the grit and friction of the current and protects it from bacterial infection.

Caverly gropes in the water like a blind man for a moment, his right hand sliding up the steelhead's belly to rest behind its steel grey head, the plates of the gills gasping with excitement just in front of his fingers. His left hand fixes on the wrist. Then he stops moving and smiles. "Okay," he says and lifts the steelhead. It emerges from the dark water as if by magic; it is an astonishing sight. A brilliantly lit, vibrant steelhead, its mouth slightly agape, its eyes showing alarm, its body rigid. He is holding in his hands a million years of genetic selection — a fish the size of a small child. The colours seem to be neon against the dullness of the river. I look around at Deadman Chasm, at the dry land, the sad ranches and the cliff called Split Rock. I think: this surely is one of nature's great wonders.

Biologists have come to realize that every salmon stream has its own unique genetic coding. Steelhead from the Deadman are biologically identical to steelhead from other systems in B.C., but at the same time they are different. Each stream has a stock that has evolved over thousands of years to perfectly fit its environment. With individual stocks of wild salmon vanishing rapidly throughout the Pacific Northwest, largely because of habitat alterations, fisheries biologists have realized with a sense of urgency that every small brook that produces fish is vital. If the Deadman stock is eliminated it can never be replaced and it will dramatically weaken the larger Thompson run, of which it historically made up about thirty percent. (The remainder of the run comes largely from the Coldwater and Bonaparte rivers, which are in marginally better shape than the Deadman.) Steelhead populations in the Thompson system have fluctuated up and down over the decades, but began a disturbing downward trend in 1985. By 1991 the overall Thompson population had fallen to under a thousand. The system historically had runs of about twenty thousand fish. The Deadman, which should be supporting three thousand steelhead, instead has less than a hundred and fifty. If the unique Deadman strain falls below fifty fish, it may have hit a point of no return, after which extinction is highly probable.

"We have reached the point where we need every fish back. We just can't afford to lose a single one," McGregor has told me. "We are starting to talk about an endangered species here."

Scan Dunn, a sixteen-year-old student on the resource management program at NorKam Secondary School, takes the net handle from Caverly and gingerly lifts the fish from the trap. He wades upstream from the fence, then bends down, catches the steelhead by the wrist and pulls it from the dipnet. He holds it, nose into the current. After a few minutes the fish struggles, its strength coming back. Dunn opens his hand and the steelhead vanishes. Chad Arden, seventeen, another student working at the counting fence, takes a second fish from Caverly. A stocky kid who looks like he could create mayhem in a loose ruck, Arden cradles the big steelhead as gently as if it were a baby. Sports anglers treat wild fish in the same way, and studies have shown more than ninety-nine percent survive release. Arden smiles when he feels the fish kicking for freedom. "There you go," he says, pushing it tenderly into the river. I have to wonder if his kids will ever have the chance to experience that.

Walking up above the fence, Caverly peers into the murky current. "There was a pair spawning just up here the other day," he says, smiling happily. We see a broad, dark tail the size of a dinner plate swirl near the surface, then disappear. "There!" he says. The fish surfaces again. "Oh no, it's not a spawner. It's a kelt. A male that's already spawned, and he's in rough shape." We can see white patches on his head and flanks where bacterial pathogens have invaded the body, attacking in openings where the slime has been worn away. He does not glisten like the fish just released. The shocking pink stripe he once wore has faded to a rust stain.

"We've had as many as ten percent of the steelhead here come back as repeat spawners, but all of them have been females so far," says Caverly, watching the fish struggle in the current. "The males have a rough time. They stay in the stream longer. They wait for the last female to show up, and they fight a lot. They come in first, leave last — and for most of them it is just too much. I don't think that one will make it."

The fish fence will be gone in a few weeks, and when most of the steelhead stop spawning and start to drop back out of the river there will be no bars to block them. They will ride the current down to the Thompson and from there back to the sea. They will not stop to feed or rest. "They'll go as fast as the current will take them," says Caverly.

By mid-July, in two short months, the fry will begin emerging from the gravel. As many as fifty percent of the eggs may not survive. The rate of production would be higher if the stream were in better shape. Floods will scour out some of the redds, grinding up the fragile, orange eggs. Sediment will be a major cause of mortality in the early stages of life. Soil washed from broken banks will physically block the emergence of fry from the gravel, and it will kill more by reducing the amount of dissolved oxygen in the intergravel water. By preventing interchange with surface water, blankets of sediment will literally suffocate eggs in their beds. The fry that do survive will probably emerge into a relatively clean and productive stream. By July, water levels will be down and the sediment load should have cleared, as long as there isn't further disturbance by road building, logging or by ranchers driving equipment into the river to reclaim land.

But the fry will still face problems. The long sunny days that help clear the stream also start to wither crops on the flat bottom lands. As ranchers irrigate their fields, using diversion ditches and pumps that drive water into long aluminum sprinkler pipes, they will draw down the Deadman dramatically. The stream, already stripped of its shade trees, will start to heat up rapidly. Some small fish will get caught in landlocked pools where they will suffocate or be eaten by predators. Others will get killed by the heat. In recent years, irrigation ditches have fallen out of favour as a method of getting water onto fields. That has been a blessing, because the ditches unintentionally diverted hundreds of thousands of fish out of the main stream, then left them stranded in the mud when the ditches were drained onto the fields. There are still many ditches in use, although it is a crude and environmentally devastating process. Fisheries biologists plead with land owners to think of the fish, but have little authority to stop the practice. Under water lease rights, ranchers can draw down the whole river if they want to.

"The water here has all been licensed. The watershed has been licensed away. In the summer, in a drought year, they are capable of withdrawing all the water," says Ian McGregor. "In most years they might withdraw fifty percent. When that happens you get high water temperatures and that causes severe stress in fish."

Water has always been a problem in this arid landscape. Marring the steep slopes above the river is the track of an old flume that once ran down to orchards on the sagebrush benches above the Thompson. Gentlemen farm-

ers from England tried to start an Eden there, but the flume never func-
tioned properly, with most of the water evaporating before it reached the
fruit trees, and the dream of Walhachin turned to dust. The men went
away to World War I and the flume fell apart.

Without liberal water rights some of the small ranches in the Deadman
Chasm might also fail. But by running the tap unchecked, ranchers are
threatening an incredibly valuable and rare resource. For fourteen years,
since the secret of the river was uncovered, the governments of B.C. and
Canada have ignored the problem while steelhead numbers have dwindled. Before it is too late, politicians must weigh the relative values and
then answer this question: what's more important, the production of a few
more steers or the preservation of a unique run of wild steelhead?

The ranchers themselves don't face any moral dilemma. The river eats
away at their land so they take a Cat into the stream and reroute the channel. Their alfalfa fields start to dry out, so they pump the Deadman up
onto the flat fields. Let the steelhead take care of themselves.

"The ranchers don't feel the same way about steelhead that I do. They
don't value them," says McGregor. He pulls his truck over and looks out
across the chasm towards the river. Right there, he says, pointing his finger
out the window; a day earlier, he stopped a rancher who had driven his Cat
into the stream to push gravel from the river bed up against an eroding
bank. Huge clouds of silt poured downstream from around the grinding
treads and were churned up by the massive steel blade. The Cat was in the
river during the middle of the Deadman spawning run, in the middle of
some of the most important steelhead spawning habitat in the world. A
warning was issued, pictures taken, charges contemplated. Upstream, that
same week, another rancher had built a dam right across the river to divert
water into his ditches. The dam was removed, charges contemplated. Under the Fisheries Act it is illegal to deposit deleterious substances into fish
habitat; it is also notoriously difficult to get courts to take such matters
seriously. After all, what's a few dead fish? If convicted, the Cat driver
might be fined one hundred dollars.

I follow McGregor on foot across a field and along a fence that has been
strung by fisheries workers to keep cattle away from the streambank. Vegetation is starting to spring up along the water's edge. One day cottonwoods
may grow here again, but for now they are found only in log jams, where
the discarded trunks have washed together in deep piles. The bankside
grass is long, at least, and willows are taking root. We pass a series of natural springs that bubble up in the fields and run through thickets to the
Deadman. The water entering from the springs is cool and crystal clear.

McGregor hopes the provincial government will buy the ranch on which these springs sit. For two-hundred thousand dollars, the government could get three thousand acres surrounding the most valuable stretch of spawning gravel on the entire river. The springs could be modified to provide perfect, stable spawning beds, a sanctuary — The Deadman Chasm Steelhead Sanctuary. McGregor, daydreaming for a moment, says he could see people coming here, just to watch the great fish. "You know," he says, "we could build a couple of artificial platforms so the fish would spawn right there in front of them. It could really be something."

He is moving quickly, surveying each pool with a glance. We pass the bleached skeleton of a steer. It seems prophetic. "This is a beautiful place to spawn," says McGregor, loping along a section where big cottonwoods overhang the stream on the far bank. "There should be fish all through here." There are not. "There's a redd," he says after a moment. Scooped out behind a granite boulder we can see an oval of clean gravel about half the size of a desk top. The collected silt has been swept away by the repeated arcing of a female's body. The male will have stood by, waiting for hours while she cleared the redd, attacking rival males, chasing away any trout that dared venture close. The redd is placed in knee-deep water where a swift run of current should keep it clean. As long as the silt load isn't too heavy, the eggs may hatch. We go farther up the stream, then turn, retrace our steps to the springs and start down on new water. We see one more redd, a rainbow trout hovering over it, either looking for loose eggs or planning to spawn in gravel cleared by the larger steelhead.

"This is a very fertile system. It has so much going for it," says McGregor, dismayed by the lack of spawning sign. "The Deadman produces the biggest fry in Canada, maybe in North America." The fry emerge in mid-July, small enough to rest on a fingernail. By September they'll be just over three inches — the length of an index finger and twice the size of fry from some other systems. Studies have found that larger fry have a seventy percent greater chance of surviving to adulthood than those that are even a few inches smaller.

The Deadman not only has the ability to produce bigger fry, but it also has the potential to produce more of them per redd than any other river. "The fish here are the most fecund in North America," says McGregor. Deadman steelhead have small eggs compared to steelhead elsewhere, but more of them. A doe in the Deadman will carry twelve thousand eggs on average, while a fish of similar size in a coastal river will have only three thousand. The fish on the Deadman evolved to take advantage of the natural state of the river. Coastal fish must carry fewer, larger eggs so that alevins can emerge attached to expansive yolk sacs. Coastal fish hatch in clear, sterile streams and need to carry more supplies with them for the first weeks of life. The steelhead of Deadman Chasm emerge into a river that is rich in aquatic life. As a stock, they should thrive. That they are not thriving is a condemnation of society's failure to recognize the importance of this special system, and to act to protect it. The biologists know what needs to be done, and so, clearly, do the steelhead.

McGregor stops at a house to say hello to the rancher whose property he hopes will become a sanctuary. "What are those fish called? Steelhead?" asks Pauline Docksteader, casting a skeptical eye at the river. She'd be happy to sell to the government, she says, long as the price is fair. McGregor says he'll get an appraiser in. "Oh, that don't matter to me," she says. "I know what it's worth." The ranch has been in the family since 1956. She mentions, just in passing, that when she was driving on the highway the other day she found herself behind a truck carrying bottled water. Would anyone, she wondered, be interested in bottling the water coming out of her springs? McGregor just shrugs. He knows one thing for sure. The steelhead could use that water a lot more.

Driving out of the chasm later, coming down over the sagebrush flats along the Thompson, McGregor recalls what it was like a decade ago, before the falldown began. One day, fly fishing on the big river, he caught and released fourteen steelhead. It left his arms aching. Now experienced anglers fish five days, on average, to catch one fish. I told him about the big doe I caught at a run known as Martel, near Spences Bridge. "She was holding above the Nicola then," he says. "That means she was coming here, to the Deadman. She's probably in there right now." Of course I knew she was, and I knew where she spawned too — in the gravel runs near the fish fence, under the rainbow-coloured cliffs. That is, if the Cat didn't kill her.

TERRY GLAVIN (1955–)

Terry Glavin has developed a strong reputation for his carefully researched and socially committed books and essays on B.C.'s environment; almost all have a special focus on, and commitment to, indigenous peoples, water and fisheries. After working for ten years as Native Affairs reporter for the *Vancouver Sun*, and receiving a number of national magazine awards, Glavin wrote *A Death Feast in Dimlahamid* (1990), a book which explores Gitskan and Wet'suwet'en cultures in northwest B.C., and was a finalist for the Hubert Evans Non-fiction Prize. That book was followed by a co-written volume, *Nemiah: The Unconquered Country* (1992); *A Ghost in the Water* [about the Fraser River sturgeon] (1994); and *Dead Reckoning: Confronting the Crisis in Pacific Fisheries* (1996). In the same year Glavin published *This Ragged Place: Travels Across A Landscape*, which was a finalist for the Governor-General's Award for non-fiction. "Oolichans," a study of the mysterious and little known life cycles of the pacific candlefish, is taken from this book. But the essay is about more than oolichans. For Glavin, the oolichan comes to symbolize larger cycles of nature, and is a test case for ecosystems tampered with by human ignorance. The harvest and consumption of oolichans enters into a political dimension as Glavin explores the alternating dialogue and incomprehension which exists between indigenous people and non-natives. In a broad sense, Glavin's essay is a meditation on the special human cultures which exist on the margins of rivers and coastlines. Most recently, Glavin has co-written with Charles Lillard a book on Chinook language — *A Great Voice Within Us* (1998) — published in the New Star Press Transmontanus Series, for which he is general editor. Glavin lives in Queensborough, near New Westminster, within sight and smell of the Fraser River.

OOLICHANS

IN THE WHEELHOUSE of the *Escorial II,* making the short jog up the slough from his houseboat to the main stem at New Westminster, Mark Petrunia let on that as far as he was concerned, the sea lions knew what was going on, and the seals probably knew too. Rounding the upriver tip of Annacis Island, where the Fraser River divides to become the Main Arm and the North Arm, Petrunia also let on that to his way of thinking, it might be that the seals and the sea lions had become wretched in their wisdom, lurking in the river the way they were, lying in wait for him to tear his nets.

"They know what I'm doing," he said, just as a seal surfaced about three boat lengths off the port side of his gillnet boat. "They know what's going on."

What was going on that afternoon was that Mark Petrunia was headed for the same spot in the river he had been visiting in his gillnet boat every day since the oolichans arrived a month earlier, accompanied as they always are by clouds of seagulls. Petrunia's daily routine, shared by two other gillnetters – Harold Wolf downriver and Jimmy Adams up at Katzie – involved a fifteen-minute set, on the backup tides, to maintain an exact record of catch for analysts with the Department of Fisheries and Oceans. He was also gathering samples to be sent on to the Pacific Biological Station in Nanaimo, where people in lab coats would analyze oolichan DNA, fish scales, age, sex, milt and eggs so humans might know a little, at least, about whatever it was that the seals and the sea lions knew.

After what had happened that year, there was nobody at the Department of Fisheries and Oceans or the Pacific Biological Station who would lay claim to knowing what had caused the strange and disturbing events that were taking place up and down North America's West Coast involving populations of Osmeridae, the extended family of smelts that includes the oolichan. All anybody knew was that oolichan populations were suddenly disappearing from rivers where they normally spawned predictably and in the hundreds of millions. They were appearing in rivers where they had never been known to spawn. Massive herds of Pacific white-sided dolphins were showing up in inlets where they had never been seen before, and they were feasting on oolichans. Autumn-spawning capelin appeared to have vanished from the waters south of Alaska, and just when their extirpation was about to be pronounced a certainty, an unknown population was found up the fiords of B.C.'s Central Coast, up Wakeman, Knight and Kingcome inlets – spawning in the springtime. Longfin smelt, also saltwater fall spawners, were showing up in the spring, far up the Fraser River, ready to spawn. And in the midst of all the confusion, the Fraser gillnetters who set their nets for oolichan were finding themselves surrounded by herds of harbour seals, California sea lions and those giant, ten-foot brutes known sometimes as northern sea lions and sometimes as Steller sea lions, the old bulls weighing as much as a ton. The herds would move in and rip the fish from the mesh and tear the nets to shreds.

When these bizarre events began to unfold, fisheries scientists were at a loss to make any sense of it because so little was known about the Osmeridae. That's because none of the half-dozen or so species that occur on the B.C. coast were in any way important to the commercial fishing industry, and it's the industry's priorities that determine research effort. There was a time when oolichans were an important commercial fish, but the processors who set up fish-oil plants on the Nass River in 1877 soon found that the Nisga'a ate so much themselves that there weren't enough fish left to render down to oil for export. Around the turn of the century, the fishing companies moved in on the Nass again, and a thriving industry producing fresh, salted and smoked fish kept oolichan in fifth place among the coast's fisheries until 1912, when competition from other smelt fisheries around the world pushed oolichans out of the world market. In the late twentieth century, the only commercial oolichan fishery on the coast had been a small gillnet fleet of a dozen or so boats on the Fraser. Apart from these few gillnet boats, oolichans remained important only to Native communities, and mainly for that peculiar, lardlike product known as oolichan grease, that most precious of aboriginal trade commodities, rendered from tubs of boiled oolichans that have been first left to rot for as long as three weeks.

It can take up to twelve tons of rotting oolichans to produce a mere two hundred gallons of grease, and the practice of grease-making is conducted according to rigid rules, some of which are serious enough that you're expected to potlatch away the shame if you violate one of them, and each set of rules is as unique and distinct as the languages of the peoples who carry on the greasemaking tradition – the Kwagiulths, Haisla, Nuxalk, Heiltsuk, Tsimshian and Nisga'a. Local custom determines the choice of fish, whether or not a male oolichan is propped up on the "stinkbox" to oversee the process "to ensure fair play," what the ratio of male fish to female should be, whether or not to line the planked stinkboxes with cedar boughs, whether at a particular rivermouth a human hand may come into contact with rotting oolichan, how long to let the fish rot, how long to boil the mash, and whether to strain or not to strain and how thoroughly. Old Andy Siwallace at Bella Coola insisted that grease must be cooked twice by no other method than red-hot rocks taken from a fire or the taste would be ruined, and the whole thing would be shot anyway unless it's scooped up at precisely the right time, when the sound of the boiling grease reaches just the right "tune."

Oolichan grease provided a rich and necessary dietary supplement with all sorts of reputed curative powers, but it was also a condiment to liven up a steady winter diet of dried salmon and dried berry cakes and dried deer meat. It was the unlikely currency of precolonial trading empires and the main item of transport along elaborate networks of trading trails known as grease trails that extended from the coast far into the Interior. These were the trails followed by Alexander Mackenzie in 1793, when he earned the distinction of being the first white man to traverse this continent north of Mexico. He finally came upon the Pacific Ocean when he stumbled out of the bush near Bella Coola.

Oolichan grease is valued and rated according to individual taste and preference, the way different kinds of wine are valued in European culture. There are entire villages on this coast that maintain they can discern from the colour or the consistency or the flavour or the smell whether a particular serving of grease has come from the Kitlope or the Kildala or the Nass, and some oldtimers will say they can narrow it down to the family that made it. Varieties of grease are at least as numerous as the variant spellings applied to the Chinook-jargon word for the fish, which include oolichan, eulachon, hoolakan, hoolikan, oloachen, ollachan, oulachon, oulacon, ulchen, ulichan and uthlecan. Oolichan is often pronounced "hooligan," and it is also widely known as "candlefish," from its reputed ability to be stood on end and burned, with a wick like a candle, because it's so oily. On the lower Fraser, the Sto:lo people called them swavie, and they nicknamed them chucka, which means "old woman." In the early days of the maritime fur trade, ships' captains called them "shrow," and the grease from the fish was called "shrow tow," words that appear to have been derived from the Haida words for oolichan and oolichan grease, a product the Haida obtained by trade every spring, in massive quantities, from their mainland neighbours, the Nisga'a. Central Coast Natives sometimes called oolichan the "salvation fish," for the fact that the oolichan's arrival after a long, cold winter provided the year's first great flourish of fresh marine flesh, certain salvation if the winter had been particularly rough. Their arrival was a sure sign that winter was truly gone, that it was not the end of the world and that the cycle of the seasons could begin again. Salvation fish became "saviour fish" in some Central Coast communities, which was pleasing to the first Methodist missionaries until it became apparent that the oolichan's ascent from the sea, triggered partly by river temperature and partly by the tide (which is itself determined by the phases of the moon), tended to coincide with Easter. Easter Sunday always falls on the first Sunday after the paschal full moon, which is the first full moon after March 21, so the arrival of the oolichan often meant deserted church pews on the holiest day of the liturgical calendar, because everybody was away "making grease."

Howard White, who first came upon the substance in Bella Coola in 1976 at forty-eight dollars a gallon, wrote:

> ... *it smelled like the cracks*
> *between the deck planks of an old fish barge*
> *if you can imagine spreading that*
> *on your bread – quite enough to hurl*
> *the European palate toward the nearest*
> *toilet bowl ...*

As a consequence, there wasn't much of a non-aboriginal market for the fish, and there had been little scientific interest in it, and not much was known about its life history or the role oolichan played in marine ecosystems. So when things began to go haywire among the various populations of Osmeridae, specifically among oolichan populations, all DFO's biologists could turn to was a body of scientific literature you could fit in a desk drawer. The generally held wisdom about oolichans was that they probably returned to their natal streams to spawn, but not necessarily; that they tended to spawn at two or three years of age, mainly (but not always) in rivers that were formed from glacier-fed creeks along the mainland coast; and that they seemed to die after spawning, the way salmon do, but not necessarily all of them. Morley Farwell, the DFO management biologist who was in charge of the Fraser River oolichan fishery in the 1980s, used to joke that his decisions about oolichan openings consisted of looking out the window of his New Westminster offices in late March to see if there were lots of seagulls around.

Except for the Nass River – which gets its name from the Tlingit word for "food depot," after the great oolichan harvests near the river's mouth – oolichan runs coast-wide appear to have begun a fairly rapid descent about 1985, after a period of localized declines. These things went largely unnoticed by DFO officials, and those who had their suspicions were unwilling to attempt a guess at the extent of the declines, partly because fisheries' records were either nonexistent or based almost solely on hunches, guesses and rumour. On the Fraser River, commercial catches dropped from 329,000 pounds annually in the early 1960s to less than 100,000 pounds through the 1970s and about 50,000 pounds in the 1980s. DFO scientists conceded that they didn't know how much these declines reflected shifts in market demand or reduced catch effort, but the fishermen on the river were insisting that there were just way fewer oolichans around and the seals and the sea lions had begun to fight them for what was left. Upriver, Sto:lo fishermen were complaining that oolichans that used to run beyond Agassiz were no longer making it even two-thirds that far, to Mission (in the 1940s, fisheries scientists were sure that the short stretch of river from Mission up to Deroche was the main spawning area for the fish). Chawathil elder Bill Pat Charlie remembered joining in the annual fishery, when Sto:lo families scooped huge buckets of fresh oolichan from behind a sandbar below the old Saint Mary's residential school, "but then they just stopped coming" some time around the mid-1980s. "Used to be that only thunder and lightning would scare them away, but then they didn't come so far. They just started dying away."

Even as far downriver as the Katzie village in Pitt Meadows, something was changing, and the changes were particularly ominous because it was at that very spot in the river, just off what is now the foot of Bonson Road where the reserve is, that oolichans first appeared in this world, in the first few years after human beings were placed on the earth. According to Katzie traditions, the oolichan came from the dowry box brought to earth by the sky-born wife of Swaneset, who is sort of a Katzie version of Moses. In Old Pierre's account of the first oolichan, which he related to the anthropologist Diamond Jenness in 1936:

> The people gathered at the river to witness the opening of the box, which was divided by a partition into two parts. Swaneset's wife opened one part first. Instantly a cloud of feathers flew up into the air and changed to sea-gulls, which soared up and down the Fraser River just as they do today. The woman then turned homeward, saying to her husband, "I will open the other half tomorrow."
>
> At daybreak she opened the other half of the box and emptied its contents into the river. Forthwith immense shoals of eulachon crowded the water from bank to bank. She waited until the sun rose, then ordered the people to rake the fish into their canoes.

"For one month only each year will these fish appear," she said. "Gather them diligently ..."

As late as the 1960s, as many as eighty Katzie people were busy at oolichan time, fishing from boats and working in dock crews, picking nets and packing fish in boxes for the local markets. Even as recently as 1990, as many as a dozen Katzie people were busy every spring for the two or three weeks that the oolichans ran in the river, and at twelve oolichans to a pound and $1.50 a pound, it meant reasonable wages in the long months before the sockeye runs. Back then, the oolichans were still running thick and heavy, and the sky was filled with seagulls. Then everything started to change.

On a spring day in 1995 at Katzie, Jimmy Adams, Mark Petrunia's upriver test-fishery colleague, stood on the reserve's rickety dock and pointed to the sea lions gathering in the river just behind a log boom. "See? When I go out to do one of these test sets, they're waiting for me, the bastards. When I go downriver, they follow me. They follow me all the way down. They go right through the net. They bite right through the net. They won't leave me alone."

Beginning in about 1990, the annual Fraser River catch had fallen to 20,000 pounds, less than a fifteenth of the 1960s catch. Then in 1994, everybody's nets were coming up empty. The Musqueam fishermen staged a protest and called for a fishing closure. Alarm bells started to go off at DFO, and for the first time in history, the Fraser River oolichan fishery was shut down in-season.

Meanwhile, on the Columbia River, an even more dramatic event was occurring. In 1994, hardly any oolichan were caught at all in the Columbia or its tributaries. The total catch was ninety-five percent below average, almost a total loss. But in the nearby Wynoochee, the river was thick with oolichan, and nobody had ever seen them spawn there before.

On the Central Coast that year, the unimaginable happened. In late March, Nimpkish fisherman Stephen Beans and his family headed out in their seine boat, the *Ocean Predator,* for the season's fishing and grease-making up Knight Inlet. But day after day went by and there was no sign of oolichan anywhere. The days turned into weeks. Families from Alert Bay and other Kwagiulth communities waited at their Knight Inlet fishing camps, but no oolichan came home. For Beans, it was the first time anything like it had happened in the thirty-five years he had been fishing. Runs had been dropping drastically in the Kingcome River for four or five years, but none of the old people could remember anything quite like this.

The Klinaklini River, which takes its name from the Kwakwala term meaning "lots of grease," was barren.

The oolichan were gone.

"It was a total failure," Beans said. "Up here, we depend quite a lot on the oolichans. When they come, we stop everything we're doing for it. Up Knight Inlet, you'll have maybe half a dozen to a dozen families, maybe fifty to eighty people. All over this part of the coast, people depend on us to supply them. So it was really hard, because it's really a necessity, and you can't put a dollar figure on it. We had a hard time coming home and telling people 'No.'"

There was a lot of harsh talk about Interfor's logging practices in the Klinaklini Valley. Farther north, on the Kitimat River, the Eurocan pulp mill was an obvious contributor to the declines up there. Pacific white-sided dolphins had been moving into Knight Inlet by the hundreds, and they'd never been seen there before. There was a new pollock trawl fishery in Johnstone Strait, and nobody at DFO knew what its incidental catch of oolichan might have been, but DFO's own surveys showed that in the shrimp-trawl fisheries, oolichans and other nontarget fish were showing up in nets. In 1991, a DFO survey showed that seventy percent of the shrimp-trawl catch was nontarget species, primarily oolichans and dogfish that ended up thrown back and wasted, and a 1992 survey concluded that only ten percent of the shrimpers' overall catch was actually shrimp.

At the Pacific Biological Station, research scientist Doug Hay was trying to add it all up, and by the spring of 1995, none of it was making all that much sense. No single culprit could be to blame, Hay reckoned, and it didn't make sense that a whole range of culprits could conspire to gang up on oolichans throughout the coast, all at different times. What seemed to make more sense was that something was happening in the ocean, something as subtle as changes in ocean temperature during the summer months while the coast's oolichan populations – many, if not most, of them, anyway – were in the midst of their migrations, somewhere near the edge of the continental shelf, say, off the west coast of Vancouver Island. But Hay said: "If you're asking me what's going on, the answer is 'I don't know,' and I don't think anybody does."

The smart thing to do seemed to be to establish some greater certainty about the oolichans' life histories: Where, exactly, do they spawn in the Fraser River, for instance? How long does it take the egg to grow to larval stage, get washed out to saltwater and start migrating seaward? Where do they go? How long do they live? How does something so small, something that seems to get washed out to sea so quickly, remember its natal river?

Do they always come back to their natal rivers? How many of them die after spawning? Can they spawn twice?

To begin to find answers to these questions, the fisheries research vessel *W. E. Ricker* was sent out off Vancouver Island's west coast to look for migrating oolichan. For several weeks in 1995, the *Reviser* was dragging a trawl net – with tiny, tiny mesh – at seventeen different sites up and down the Fraser River, fishing for oolichan larvae. Mark Petrunia, Jimmy Adams and Harold Wolf were out with the seals and sea lions, conducting test sets at their spots in the Fraser. And up at the head of Knight Inlet, biologist Mike Berry, whose childhood was spent hanging around the edges of Haisla oolichan camps and snorkelling down the Kitimat River for lost lures to sell back to steelhead fishermen, was busy trying to come to grips with the tragedy on the Klinaklini.

Berry was working for the Tanakteuk band, which holds ancestral villages at the head of Knight Inlet, so when he began his research in 1995, he knew it was serious business. Oolichans mean everything to the Tanakteuk. So Berry threw himself into the work, assembled everything he'd ever done on oolichans, reviewed aerial photographs of the Klinaklini River to assess potential logging damage to the spawning grounds, set up a system to analyze the flow regime in the river and check it against rainfall records, filled jar after jar with various specimens, assembled counts of the white-sided dolphins that started showing up in the inlet about four years ago, set up transacts on the Klinaklini and nearby rivers, and settled down into camp with all the Kwagiulths who had arrived in hope that the oolichan would come back.

The days went by and no oolichan showed. Everybody's mood was grim. People from Nimpkish and Campbell River and Alert Bay sat around in their camps with nothing much to do, while seventy-two-year-old Charlie Matilpy sat at the mouth of the Klinaklini and sang mournful songs in Kwakwala, asking the oolichan to come home.

On Good Friday, there were 214 Pacific white-sided dolphins in Knight Inlet. On Saturday, the dolphins turned down the inlet and disappeared somewhere around the Broughton Archipelago.

On Easter Sunday morning, the oolichan came home.

"It was unbelievable," Berry remembered. "It was like gangbusters. The sun was shining; the people were so incredibly happy. Everybody was on cloud nine. It was beautiful."

Over at the Kingcome River, where hardly any fish had been seen in four years, it was the same thing. On the nearby Franklin River, never a big oolichan river, "it was absolutely chockablock plugged," Berry said. A count of eight thousand square metres of river bottom turned up a hundred fish per square metre, which adds up to 800,000 fish. On the Columbia River, catches were way up over 1994. The Nass fishery was tremendous, as always. On the other northern rivers, abundance seemed to be holding, at least, and on the Fraser River, there were big changes: logbooks were made mandatory for the commercial fishermen; they had to report the catches on a weekly basis; and the commercial openings for Mark Petrunia and his fellow oolichan gillnetters were cut back from six days a week to three, a plan that Petrunia would fairly shout about if you asked him his opinion. He said it was a completely bonehead deal.

But if you asked him how he did in 1995, Petrunia would tell you he figured he'd caught about five thousand pounds in half the time it took to catch thirty-five hundred pounds the year before. DFO management biologist Marilyn Joyce reported that everybody's catches were up in the Fraser, and Cheam band fisherman Isaac Alex saw oolichans jumping in the river, way beyond Mission, just past the Rosedale Bridge, near Agassiz.

"And if it wasn't for the goddamned seals and the goddamned sea lions, I'd have caught a lot more," Petrunia said.

Out with Petrunia on his gillnet boat, the day's test fishery took longer than usual. The run was nearly over, and it took two sets to get the hundred-fish minimum the fisheries scientists wanted. There were fewer seals around, and hardly any sea lions, so less than one quarter of the fish Petrunia caught came up half-eaten. When we got back to his dock in Annacis Channel, just as he was tying off the *Escorial II*, Petrunia said: "I make grease too, you know. First time, this year. Want to try some?"

I'd had grease before. The first time, it was just a little bit on the side of a plate of smoked seal meat, barbecued salmon and salad at a Nisga'a get-together in Prince Rupert, eight years before. There had been a huge bowl of it on the serving table, and I took just the tiniest bit to see what it was like. It was only a taste. It was indescribable, true enough, but after a moment or two it didn't seem anything near as horrible as I'd been led to expect, so I went back for more. But by then it was all gone, and the sides of the bowl had been scraped clean, and all around the hall the people were eating silently and smiling. It was like being in church.

In Howard White's poem "Oolachon Grease," the degree to which white people recoil from the substance is supposed to be a measure of something important, and it is

... how far
Indian is from White how far
learning is from knowing how
far we are from this ragged place
we've taken from them ...

Barry Manuck, an old friend, a gillnetter, skipper of the *Panther*, dropped by Petrunia's place for a chat. The three of us sat in the kitchen, and in the living room, Mark's wife, Mary, and their kids, Matthew, Willy, Chrissy and Samantha, were watching something on television. So there we were, three white guys sitting at the kitchen table, and between us sat a huge glass jar full of an extremely primitive form of oolichan grease Petrunia had cooked up in a steel pot on a Coleman stove beside his shed on the dyke.

After waiting to see who'd go first, Petrunia opened the jar and helped himself to a spoonful.

"It's good. See?"

Then it was my turn. It was a bit startling at first, but certainly tame compared to the real stuff as I remembered it. It was actually pretty good. A lot like sockeye belly oil. Tasty.

Then it was Manuck's turn.

"You know, it's not bad," Manuck said.

... and however far you are from loving that
is how far you are
from arriving

Or so the poem goes.

"I think I could have this with, I don't know, rice, maybe," Manuck said.

Petrunia said he thought that was a good idea. He took another heaping spoonful and passed the jar around again.

"See?" he said. "Excellent."

DON GAYTON (1946–)

In his essay "Fossicking on the Border," Don Gayton speaks of a special way of relating to landscape: "fossicking, a kind of relaxed, omnivorous exploration that embraces all tangible and intangible aspects of the landscape ... a brief escape into the noneconomic, lyrical, perhaps even non-rational dimension, that some of us never do, and none of us can do for very long." Along with his friend, Peter Taylor, Gayton searches for margins or borders — the places where histories, natural landscapes and personal identities may intersect, the ways natural landscapes define human community. The essay is included in *Landscapes of the Interior: A Re-exploration of Nature and the Human Spirit,* which won the prestigious National Outdoor Book Award for 1997. Gayton's writing on the environment has appeared in numerous magazines in Canada and the United States, including *Harrowsmith, Equinox* and *Canadian Geographic*. An earlier book, *The Wheatgrass Mechanism: Science and Imagination in the Western Canadian Landscape* (1990), grew out of fifteen years experience and work on the Canadian prairies, and won the Saskatchewan Writers' Guild Non-Fiction Award. In all his writing Gayton seeks to locate points of contact between the scientific, the poetic and spiritual — and increasingly he has sought to define an ecological view which honours the imagination and science as equal and necessary partners. Trained as a scientist, Gayton has had a varied career — from community developer in Latin America and hired man on an Okanagan cattle ranch, to agricultural extension agent on Saskatchewan Indian reserves and steelyard worker. Gayton lives in Nelson, B.C., where he is employed as an ecologist with a non-profit extension society.

FOSSICKING ON THE BORDER

IT WAS INEVITABLE that a re-exploration would draw me to the ambiguities of the border. Politics, once laid crudely and arbitrarily across a latitude, split a single region into two different identities. Then in the subtle, ongoing confusion of culture and landscape, those differences ultimately become real.

Peter, my friend from Vancouver, came with me on the first border foray. He was studying the journals of members of the original U.S./Canadian Boundary Survey party, and we had met through a mutual friend. He and I were close enough in age to be contemporaries, and I was willing to violate my rule of solitary re-exploration because I sensed a kindred spirit.

We started out on the Salmo River, on the Canadian side. The Salmo starts near Nelson and flows southward uninterrupted almost to the border, where it joins the much larger Pend Oreille River on its northward loop into Canada. We agreed that the Salmo had no real connection with the border, but it was on the way and we thought it might be good fishing water. Besides, there was a roadless stretch of the Salmo called Shenango Canyon that I wanted to reconnoiter. Locales with place names like Shenango call out to me, and we were not pressed for time.

The Salmo did turn out to be good water. It had a bottom of rounded, watermelon-sized rocks with bigger boulders here and there, boulders that harboured interesting backeddies and riffles and logjams. This was September, and if you picked a wide spot and took your time, you could wade from one side of the river to the other, following whims and possibilities. Peter and I did that, splitting up in a gentlemanly, fly-fishing sort of way, each vying for the poorest-looking spot to start fishing in. After ten minutes I realized we were in world-class water indeed, doctor/lawyer water. In fact, I found a shiny surgeon's hemostat lying on the bottom, confirming the presence of doctors. Ordinary mortals like Peter and I would not remove hooks with tools of surgical steel.

I fished my way downstream and got close enough to the mouth of Shenango Canyon to have a look. It was not a major canyon, but there was a visible break in the angle of the water surface as it ratcheted downward at the entrance. The boulders in the water got bigger, and the hillsides swept up more steeply, with bare rock outcrops visible. Shenango's forest was a cornucopia of species: looking only casually, I saw cedar, Douglas fir, hemlock, aspen, cottonwood, ponderosa, lodgepole and white pine, plus larch and yew. I marked it as a place to come back to.

The fish were not biting, so we drove on down to Nelway, a tiny village at the border crossing. Peter wanted to walk a stretch of the actual border, but neither of us had any idea how the authorities — or even remote sensing devices — might react to two middle-aged men on foot, with backpacks. We decided to follow the Pend Oreille for a while and then try to reach the border at a more isolated spot. As we drove, we compared notes on isolated border crossings we knew: Nighthawk, Yahk, Rykerts, Chopaka and so on. Peter knew far more of these places than I did.

The Pend Oreille River is shackled by three dams along this stretch: Boundary Dam just as it crosses from Washington into British Columbia, the Sevenmile Dam, midway along the Canadian loop, and the Waneta Dam as the river joins the Columbia on its way back into Washington. We detoured onto a steep trail that took us right down to the reservoir created by Sevenmile, and then scrambled on foot back upstream along steep, lifeless shore and slack water. On undammed rivers, water levels vary predictably by season and by year, a kind of variation plant life understands and copes with. Water levels on dammed rivers vary unpredictably within seasons based on electrical need, so all of these shackled rivers — the Columbia, the Kootenay, the Pend Oreille — have lifeless bands of foreshore that are beyond the powers of plants to colonize. Scrambling further, we could just make out Boundary Dam in the distance. Boundary is owned outright by the power utility of the City of Seattle, and much of the power from the two Canadian dams is sold to large urban areas in the U.S. I speculated aloud to Peter how satisfying it might be to bring some of the good people of Seattle out here, one at a time, so they could know the actual price the river pays for them to run their Cuisinarts and cappuccino machines.

The clear, sluggish water in dam reservoirs does favour fish raptors, such as ospreys and eagles, and we did catch a glimpse of an eagle overhead. It had a branch in its mouth about the length and thickness of a broom handle.

Getting back on the single-track logging road that clung to the Mountainside above the river, I was reminded how steep the Kootenay (and Kutenai, on the American side) country really is. I was glad of Peter's four-wheel drive, and found myself hugging my elbows to my sides, an unconscious effort to ease our passage along the narrow road. The CB radio chatter in these mountains is full of cryptic announcements like "Gold Creek, 13, unloaded," or "Teepee, 25, loaded," which gives log truck drivers a very necessary and very precise sense of just when and where they will meet oncoming trucks.

Part of my adjustment to the landscape of the mountains has meant coming to terms with this steepness, and what it meant for my sense of distance, my psyche and my sense of belonging. Steepness has to be assimilated here, in all its manifestations: the abbreviation of sunrises and sunsets; the buildup of calf muscles; the overcoming of acrophobia. The potent duality of mountain and valley must also be assimilated. Life is mostly carried on between four hundred and eight hundred metres in the bottoms of these steep, confused valleys, but the landscape only becomes clear and obvious from the tops of the ridges, at fifteen-hundred metres and upward. Valley orientation, whether north-south or east-west, becomes biologically important: the east-west valleys capture more sunlight, but north-south valleys are corridors for the movement of weather, species and large rivers. The valley orientations often bear no relation to the older bearings of the mountains. Just when I think I have a grasp of the lay of a particular Kootenay landscape, an anomalous valley or ridgeline cuts transversely through my understanding.

Continuing westward along the Pend Oreille toward the Columbia, we came upon an abandoned orchard, and Peter, an avid birder, stopped the car and pulled out his field glasses virtually in a single motion. He was pleased to describe for me a bright, canary-like western tanager, which I finally located with the glasses. A little way further on, he pointed out a brilliant blue lazuli bunting.

A friend who lived in this valley as a child, before the dams, the relocations and the flooding, told me the Pend Oreille valley was once known for its curative properties. Hot summer sun would heat up the pines and firs high up on the rocky, south-facing slopes, and in the evening, cool air would flood down those same slopes, carrying the forest's aromatic essences down into the valley below, where they acted as a balm to congested lungs and spirits. As a contemporary visitor, I could certainly visualize the original valley as restorative, whether I believed in the medical value of forest aromatics or not.

The advancing day drew us forward, into itself. I was able to try out some very frivolous and scandalous ideas on Peter, ideas that had been bottled up for some time, and needed to see the light of day. We took a short side hike to see a waterfall, and spent some time speculating on fates in a tiny graveyard. I proposed a term for our activities: fossicking, a kind of relaxed, omnivorous exploration that embraces all tangible and intangible aspects of the landscape. To fossick was originally an Australian word for random, overland gold prospecting, an activity sufficiently distant and obscure that I felt confident about modifying the term for my own ends. Like any number of other outdoor pursuits — and fly fishing is a prime example — our fossicking provided a purposeful guise for the simple enjoyment of nature. This trip had had absolutely no prospect of economic gain attached. It was a brief escape into the noneconomic, lyrical, perhaps even nonrational dimension, that some of us never do, and none of us can do for very long. It was, in a word, frivolous, but I freely acknowledge a personal tendency to be very serious about frivolity.

While we stopped for lunch, I leafed through the elegantly bound 1866 journals of the Englishman John Keast Lord, which Peter had brought along. Lord was a member of the U.S./Canadian Boundary Survey, and his claustrophobic impression of this part of the Kootenays is evident in this passage:

> … impassable barriers of mountains, so closely piled and wooded
> that the valleys between them were little else than rocky gorges,
> devoid of grass or other food for pack animals.

He is much kinder to the Colville valley, in northeastern Washington:

> … The Colville valley is, roughly speaking, about thirty miles
> long, the hills on one side being densely studded with pine trees,
> and the other quite clear of timber, but thickly clothed up to
> their rounded summits with the bunchgrass.

Lord was here referring to a key geographical dynamic of the valleys of the Kootenays: the relative dryness of the east sides of north-south valleys, like the Colville, and of the north sides of east-west-trending valleys, like the one in which Nelson resides.

Lord was a veterinarian by trade, and showed an earnest, methodical interest in mammals, insects and aquatic life in his journals. He described both the tanager and the bunting, confirming the two species as long-term residents of the Kootenays. He also described the delightful little horned toad as occurring on the Canadian side of the valleys of the Columbia, Kootenay and Flathead rivers.

One of the benefits of middle age is the ability to support several obsessions at once and, because reptiles are one of mine, I knew that there have been no confirmed sightings of the horned toad in southern British Columbia in contemporary times. Some curious phenomenon, some unknown natural or human-caused event, has extirpated them since Lord's time. I filed that bit of information away for further investigation. Reptiles, which loomed so large in our ancient mythologies, have become incidental curiosities in modern life. The obscure ecology of the horned toad at the north-

ern edge of its range could actually turn out to be a powerful, even symbolic illustration of the dynamics of nature itself. We have found great
social and personal analogies in the laws of physics over the last few decades — words like entropy, fusion, meltdown and so on have become household terms. Perhaps we are now entering an age where the laws of biology,
ecology, and the horned toad will take on social relevance.

I closed Lord's book carefully and put it back in Peter's knapsack. A third
language, a third discipline, would have to be added to my re-exploration
work, along with science and spirituality: lore. Lore — the oral and written observations of nature and the human experience of the region, both
contemporary and historical — has its own language and its own discipline, and helps make a region what it is. Nature does not invest certain
landscapes with a sense of romance, or foreboding, or freedom: we do that.
We can actually quantify the value we vest in a landscape from which a large
body of water can be seen: realtors tell me that an ocean or lake view will add
twenty percent to the value of a lot. The totally artificial observations, distinc-
tions and stories we humans invest in nature become, paradoxically, important.

Still in search of an isolated stretch of border, we crossed the Pend Oreille
at the Sevenmile Dam, on to the narrow sliver of land between the river's
Canadian loop and the 49th parallel. Prospects looked good as we headed
southward on an isolated logging road, switchbacking along hillsides clothed
in second-growth cedar. Finally we glimpsed the razor-sharp cutline through
the trees on a distant mountainside.

We continued on the logging road as far south as we could, and then
struck out on foot, stumbling through the dense cedar on a thirty-degree
slope. The border in this forested part of the world has its own manner of
optical illusion. The cutline is of course always glimpsed on the hillside
opposite to the one you are on, and it is nearly impossible to project the
exact location of that cutline on to your side of the valley. Based on our
glimpse of the border on the far hillside, we could be anywhere from five
minutes to an hour away from it. Fortunately, after fifteen minutes of sidehill scrambling, a bright green strip appeared ahead, contrasting strongly
with the muted greys and browns of the cedars around us. Immediately I
started looking for laser beams and trip wires. A rancher friend who lives
near an isolated part of the border told me he once crossed it briefly on
horseback to retrieve an errant bull. Having coffee in town the next day,
one of the local RCMP asked the rancher how he had made out with that
Angus bull. Border country is full of these kinds of stories.

Finally we emerged into the sunlight and Douglas maple of the ten-metre-wide strip, and chose adjoining stumps to sit on. I was nervous, but Peter was happy. He described how the survey party would have dealt with this drainage; one crew would work its way laboriously to the new ridge, while another crew stayed on this one, still in sight of the last surveyed ridge behind them. When the lead crew reached the top of the new ridge, they would set up their instruments. In these dense forests, younger party members probably climbed trees to provide the first sightlines. They would establish a bearing, and then work back and forth until 49 degrees, 0 minutes and 0 seconds was found. Then the whole operation would advance by one ridge.

The survey party used Fort Colville, near the present-day Washington community of Kettle Falls, as a wintering camp and provisioning point. The fort was located near a traditional aboriginal fishing area, a series of rapids on the Columbia that were well known by everyone in the Interior as a place to meet, rest, gather information and food. Today the Fort and the rapids are underwater, a victim of the Grand Coulee dam.

The border was not always the visceral reality on the landscape that it is now. Wallace Stegner, in his book *Wolf Willow,* described life in an isolated town on the Saskatchewan-Montana border in the early part of the century. People moved unhindered across the border, and few of them knew, or cared, exactly where it was. That all changed, Stegner says, when Canada sent troops to Europe at the beginning of World War I, and the United States stayed neutral. The border became even more precisely defined in the 1920s when the U.S. went dry, Canada stayed wet, and crossborder bootlegging became a growth industry.

Borders always have a kind of uncertainty and tension, and I find the same qualities in my relationship to them. The tension multiplied as I crossed and recrossed the border during the Vietnam War. Borders are geographically precise, but mentally ambiguous. When I was young I dreamed of unknown and faraway places in Canada: now I dream occasionally of remembered landscapes in the U.S. As a student of border differences in accent, language and outlook, I frequently get lost in the phenomenon of observer proximity. Like the physicist and the elusive atom, the act of observation changes the observed.

My first few weeks actually resident in Canada were spent in Edmonton, Alberta, in the wintertime. I was daunted by the bitter cold and the darkness, and promptly moved further south. To this day I still have ambivalent feelings about those vast northern stretches across the tops of the provinces and into the Territories; they may be the next frontier for me. Landscapes that inspire fear also attract.

There is a curious development inversion that takes place around the border in this part of the world. Often the Canadian side is populated and developed, while the adjacent American side is hinterland. That is part of the weird alchemy of borders: the least desirable land and climate on one side of a border may be the most sought after on the other.

Peter and I finally left our stumps on the border strip, rejoined the logging road and followed the Pend Oreille out to its junction with the Columbia. This great regional confluence was celebrated with another dam, the Waneta. When we hit pavement, we knew our border fossick was over, and started reluctantly for home.

A week later I went back to Shenango Canyon alone, to let go the last shards of inhibition between myself and the landscape, to drop the borders. Shenango. I rolled it on my tongue, over and over. If I lived in, came from, this Shenango would I be different? Would the watermelon rocks have influenced me? Do we dwellers of the Ktunaxa, which we separately corrupt as either Kutenai or Kootenay, have more in common with each other than with our urban compatriots in Seattle or Vancouver? The sense of place is truly an elective affinity: you can choose to let it influence you, or you can choose not to. It comes down to a question of borders.

I had my pole with me on the second trip as well, mainly to provide some rational excuse for wading hip-deep down river. Occasionally I would take a cast, but mainly I let the fly just drift ahead of me. I wore old tennis shoes whose soles were worn thin, so my feet could sense the surfaces and textures of the slippery watermelon rocks. I worked my way down beyond the point I had reached last time, to where I felt the river channel narrow. In the still pools, the clear water magnified the river bed. I wanted suddenly, passionately, to learn every inch of the river's Shenango reach.

Most of nature is no longer wilderness, but this was, albeit a very small piece. The theoreticians tell me that wilderness as a place is shortly to become extinct, and that rather than devoting my energies to preserving the last remaining shreds of it, I must find and appreciate the individual qualities that make up wilderness in the rest of nature, even if it is an irrigation ditch or a vacant lot. Wildness, they call it, the individual mechanisms and species and essences that together make a wilderness. God, as they say, is found in the details. We residents of the Western Interior possess a kind of arrogance based on lifetimes of inhabiting huge tracts of natural and seminatural space, and often find urban preoccupations with a single tree or tiny plot of ground downright silly. But just as arrogance and humility can both be valuable human emotions, so are wilderness and wildness, I tell myself. I see the validity of what the theoreticians are saying but, from the perspective of hip-deep in the Salmo as it passes through Shenango Canyon, it will be tough. I will honestly try to drop my fondness for wilderness and come to love wildness, too, but I must be let down easy.

A large whaleback of dense, grainy basement rock broke the water surface ahead of me, and I moved closer to marvel at it. Its surface was full of unexpected curves, channels and cuppings. Like a Henry Moore sculpture, the black rock stood muscular and sexual, with an ambiguity about whether its origin was worked or natural. River water sluiced over parts of the whaleback, and was held still in others. I searched the nearby shore until I found a round, marble-sized rock, and put it gently into the bottom of one of the circular depressions that had water running over it. Sure enough, the small rock began to rotate slowly in the force of the current. This whaleback could easily grace a public square in a large city, I thought. Adults could see it as an evocative sculpture and graceful fountain, while children could appreciate the small geological nonsense machine contained in it.

Before I went any further, I put my wallet and fishing licence inside a plastic bag I had brought for fish, and tied it snugly. Everything else could get wet, I decided. I was going to make a day of it. Norman MacLean was right: in the end all things become one, and a river runs through it. The water moved around my legs with authority now, questioning any movement that was not directly downstream. I advanced slowly, forward foot sliding, toe pointed, following the surface of each rounded rock down to tricky, unknown footholds at the bottom. It was a kind of flyfisher's ballet, taking small leaps of faith and striving for grace in the separate medium of the waters of Shenango.

ERNIE CREY (1949–)

In the late 1980s, journalist Suzanne Fournier was working on a series of stories for the *Vancouver Province* about aboriginal children. One of the people she interviewed was Ernie Crey, who was then vice-president of an urban organization called United Native Nations. He told Fournier about the extraordinary number of aboriginal adolescents being moved about among foster homes and about adults trying to recover their birth families and identities. For three hundred years in Canada, he pointed out, aboriginal children were removed from their families and given over to various church agencies, principally residential schools; then in the 1960s, government welfare agencies took responsibility and they were sent out for adoption throughout North America, many never seeing their families again. Most memorably, Crey told Fournier about his own Sto:lo family that had been split apart by his father's death and the children placed in non-native foster homes. "The story of aboriginal children has never been told," he said, and with that challenge before them, Crey and Fournier set about to record "what it has meant to grow up aboriginal since the advent of widespread European settlement in North America."

The book they compiled, *Stolen From Our Embrace* (1997), through interviews and historical research, tells the story of residential schools and welfare agencies, of alcohol and sexual abuse, and of methods of aboriginal healing. Crey's own experience, the opening chapter reprinted here, is one of the most compelling in the book. As president of the United Native Nations, Ernie Crey has been a tireless activist on social issues, calling for better housing, more aboriginal foster homes, sexual abuse prevention and cultural competency for non-native social workers. He is currently an executive director of the fisheries programme for the Sto:lo Nation which numbers eight thousand people in twenty-five communities along the Fraser River. These were the First Nations people that Simon Fraser encountered on the last segment of his journey down the river.

from STOLEN FROM OUR EMBRACE
THE PERPETUAL STRANGER
Four Generations in My Sto:lo Family

THE SHOCK of my ritual submersion in the Fraser River took my breath away. Waist-high in the water, I waded upstream against the swift glacial current, speaking my prayers of gratitude to the river for allowing me to cleanse in its embrace. I submerged four times, facing upstream. From my mouth burst forth the wailing sounds the Sto:lo call "quinning," the moaning infant sounds that for me represented my rebirth, a spiritual and cultural reconnection to my homeland. In my state of intense psychic distress, the icy waters no longer startled my skin.

As I plunged, I began to sing in a voice I didn't know existed. I was astonished until I understood that Sto:lo healer Gwendolyn Point hadn't been speaking metaphorically when she told me I was weary from carrying around an ancient spirit. He hadn't meant me any harm, she said; he had felt the need to watch over me until my own spirit revived. I began to cry like a "baby," as we Sto:lo call a new initiate into the longhouse. I wanted the old spirit I'd carried to know he could depart. I was in good hands. I let the river begin to wash away the burdens I'd carried my whole life, the blackness of despair and grief at the losses my family had endured.

After many years away, I had come home to Sto:lo territory to regain the wellspring of cultural knowledge and strength that had guided our ancestors since time immemorial. Gwendolyn and my other Sto:lo spiritual teachers did not view my loneliness, alienation and burnout as an individual crisis but as a sign that I was finally in touch with my longing to come home. I was honoured to receive their guidance. I knew the spiritual work they gave me would be arduous, though never beyond what I could endure.

As a child, I was forcibly removed from Sto:lo culture by social welfare authorities. Our family life was shattered after seven of my eight siblings and I were split apart into separate foster homes. We were never again to reunite as a family. My grandparents were proud, independent people who had lived through the deliberate dismantling of Sto:lo culture by priests who probed and pried into every corner of our lives. I had seen my father's spirit dimmed by the residential school where his culture was choked out of him, so that all his life he held his Halq'emeylem language and spiritual knowledge in check, depriving us, his children, of our most precious birthright.

Since my earliest days of adulthood, I'd preoccupied myself with political organizations, working for justice for aboriginal people. Burying myself in my work like many First Nations leaders, I sought to escape from
my own pain. I tried conventional psychotherapy, which could not heal
the aching cultural and emotional void inside me but did help to control
my distress. My beautiful, bright children gave me joy, though my work
kept me away from home for long hours. When I could no longer stand
the suffering in aboriginal communities, I got angry. Non-native politicians got blistering broadsides from me about the welfare officials who
were still abducting aboriginal children, including my own nieces and nephews, about the appalling living conditions on and off reserve, about the
deaths and unsolved murders of aboriginal women and men, including
my own brother.

It was not until I returned home to live and work among the Sto:lo in
the summer of 1992 that a different kind of cultural and spiritual commitment was demanded of me. I wanted to reclaim my birthright for myself
and my own children, but I could not cross that cultural boundary until I
relinquished my despair, laid down other people's burdens and opened
myself to renewal. I welcomed the icy embrace of the river that had sustained the Sto:lo — People of the River — for fifteen thousand years. It
was the river, and the salmon, that had brought me back to work with my
own Sto:lo Nation, as fisheries manager. We were not just another level of
government, brown bureaucrats administering welfare on reserve; we were
Sto:lo, working in every way to restore our nation's economic and spiritual
self-sufficiency. I was invited into the longhouse of my Sto:lo forebears.
After forty-three years, I had come home.

The Sto:lo are a large Coast Salish nation, now organized into twenty-five
communities of eight thousand people, whose traditional territory extended
from the ocean mouth of the Fraser River all along the valley to the Fraser
Canyon. Four generations of my Sto:lo family lived through the mael-
strom of social change that began in the late 1700s, when white people
first entered the lush coastal rainforests of Coast Salish territory. The Salish
were a trading nation, procuring ochre and obsidian from Oregon, moun-
tain-goat horn from the Nlaka'pamux and sage from the Secwepemc in
exchange for our bounteous wealth of cedar, shellfish and five species of
Pacific salmon. Traders from Asia brought curious coins and beads.

Our first clues to the European invasion were the whalers and traders
who came from Spain and England. They gave us iron tools and trinkets
along with an epidemic of disease. Our Upper Sto:lo tribes were deci-

mated; population numbers fell from a pre-contact population of more than 25,000 to an all-time low of 8,046 people in all the tribes of the Fraser River by 1925, the year my mother was born.

Just two generations earlier, my great-grandparents had lived amid a thriving aboriginal populace, at the peak of the Fraser River civilizations. I'm reminded of what geographer Cole Harris has to say about those times in his book *The Resettlement of British Columbia*: "The Fraser was a huge source of food, and in the canyon, where fishing sites were abundant, and excellent, it probably supported as concentrated and dense a non-agricultural population as anywhere in the world."

In the midst of relative material wealth and ease, Sto:lo society evolved into a complex structure with a highly sophisticated government that we are now reviving after a century of imposed external rule. It was a harmonious, richly layered life, although not the idyllic era free of strife that has been conjured up. The Salish could be when necessary an aggressive people who took slaves from other tribes and used them as they pleased. We had our own rigidly observed caste system of high- and low-born people. Internal transgressions were swiftly and harshly punished. But a universal tenet that we shared with other First Nations all over the Americas was the reverence for and protection of children and elders.

Our Sto:lo life was stolen away. Our children were removed by priests, social workers and police to residential schools, foster care and jail. My own family was at the eye of the hurricane, and we are only now beginning to regain our bearings. All over North America, the experiences of other First Nations families parallel my family's trials and triumphs.

We would be dishonest if we said white people brought us nothing but bad. Some brought precious gifts. Nor is all change negative. We have moved on, and we cannot return to some false conception of a long-gone paradise. Nor do we want to. We are fortunate that we still possess within our First Nations links to a profound spiritual and cultural healing, from which other communities can learn. This is my story, and the story of my Sto:lo family.

My father was Ernie Crey, a Sto:lo born in 1905 at Katz Landing near Hope. The defining moment of his life came when he entered St. Mary's Residential School, which was perched on a high bluff overlooking the Fraser River in the town that became known as Mission, British Columbia. Until then, he had been raised as a boy of respectable birth and reliable prospects, in both the Sto:lo community and the non-native world. St. Mary's, founded in 1863, was the pride of the Catholic Oblate order that had established a "mission" to the Indians in the Fraser Valley. From their dormitory windows, Sto:lo children like my father would grieve for parents and home, pining for the life on the river they had left behind.

The school was such a powerfully negative experience for my father that as a parent he used it as a kind of threat to discipline us. If I didn't behave, he told me, I would be sent to a school where children had to rise at 5:00 a.m., say prayers on their knees for hours and eat thin gruel three times a day. Porridge, porridge and more porridge was his abiding memory of the school's fare, particularly galling to Sto:lo who thrived on the Fraser River's rich salmon and sturgeon resources. In my father's day, berries and wild game such as deer, duck, grouse and pheasant were still plentiful throughout the valley. His mother would preserve all manner of natural foods for the winter, and it must have caused my father special grief to know what he could have been eating if he had been home with his family.

My father was a fluent Halq'emeylem speaker, and he remembered having his knuckles rapped with a wooden stick or getting whipped for speaking either his language or the Chinook or Nlaka'pamux languages, both of which he also spoke well as a child. He'd learned them while picking hops every year with his mother alongside aboriginal people from across B.C. and the northwestern U.S.

St. Mary's, like other Indian residential schools, was designed to strip aboriginal peoples of our culture. My father was at the school to grow up to be a little white man and to enter the white world. Children were warned not to listen to their parents and grandparents when they returned home for holidays. Some of the priests' words, enforced by the rod, must have stayed with my father. He refused to pass on his rich heritage in aboriginal languages to his children. He told us it was important to learn to read and write in English to get by in the world. We older children picked up the language anyway, because it was spoken all around us. But today, as an adult, I regret that I know too little of the Halq'emeylem language to pass on to my children.

My father had been raised in a loving, nurturing Sto:lo family where he knew first-hand the benefits of traditional parenting, and he was under no illusions when he came out of residential school that the treatment he and others had received was the way to raise children to be good parents. But like most residential school survivors, my father did not survive the direct assault on his self-esteem levelled by the priests and nuns who ran St. Mary's with an iron hand. As a fisherman, trapper and hunter, my father was proud to pass on to us these integral aspects of Sto:lo life. But the teachings he might have passed on about the heart and soul of Sto:lo life were withheld, as though his tongue was frozen. Some Sto:lo who went to St. Mary's said the priests stuck pins in the tongues of children who spoke their Indian language. If that, or any of the widespread sexual abuse now publicly disclosed from every era of the school's existence, happened to my father, he never spoke of it. The emotional, physical and cultural abuse of course was universal; my father escaped none of it.

The Church and federal Indian agents had begun to stamp out many practices from my grandparents' time: social interactions built around the potlatch, and the ceremonial/theological complex that included the winter dance ceremonial, the sxwo:ywxey dance, the first salmon ceremony and the series of teachings provided by our deity figures, Xexa:ls, the four powerful transformer siblings who were the three sons and one daughter of Black Bear and Red-Headed Woodpecker. Xexa:ls travelled among the people to tell us how to live. The Xwelitem, non-native newcomers in our territory, neither understood nor respected our traditions. They saw that the large gatherings throughout Salish territory took adults away from their employment in the fishery and the hops fields, which depended on their labour, and also took children away from their forced indoctrination at residential schools.

The colonial governments in Canada had begun to exercise control over aboriginal people long before the days of my grandparents. As early as 1830, the British passed laws designed to "protect" or "civilize" Indian people, laws that herded aboriginal people in eastern Canada onto artificial "reserves" of land. Then there was the Civilization Act of 1857, and by the time of Confederation in 1867, the Constitution Act gave the federal Parliament full legislative jurisdiction over "Indians and Land reserved for the Indians." Amendments to the Indian Act in successive years only served to tighten the grip of the government on our lands, our resources, our children: our very souls. All across Canada, traditional sacred and ceremonial practices were rendered criminal offences by white law. In Coast Salish territory, a legal ban against our spiritual practices, known to the Sto:lo as the anti-potlatch law, was imposed in 1884 and not lifted until 1951, when my father was forty-six and I was just two years old.

I can remember as a child standing with my father on the bank of the Fraser River near Hope, watching my sister take part in the canoe races for Indian women. He turned to me and said sadly that this was one of the few ways that Indian people were still permitted by law to congregate; political meetings were prohibited. The Catholic parish priest was a frequent visitor to our home, making sure we and other Sto:lo met his standard of good Christian homes, free of the contaminating Indian language and spiritual practice.

These European religious influences had been utterly alien to my family just one generation before. My father's mother, Marnie Pierre, was born in 1874 at Yale, B.C. She married Walter Crey, a European who had emigrated from Leipzig, Germany, and set up a dry goods store in Hope. Grandma Marnie was raised in the traditional Sto:lo manner. Until I was six, she would come to visit regularly, bringing food, small gifts and candy and speaking Halq'emeylem to me and my older brother. No English was heard during her visits.

My mother, Minnie Charlie, was born in 1925 on the Soowahlie reserve to Susan George of Squiala and George Batt, a man of mixed blood heritage. Minnie didn't have to endure the residential school experience but she spent some of her childhood in a hospital recuperating from tuberculosis. She did not leave the hospital until she was a young teenager. She met my father at a social gathering. They soon married, and my oldest brother, Gordon, was born when Minnie was nineteen. Her second baby, Dwayne, died when he was a few days old. I arrived in 1949, followed by Frances in 1952. I was five when the doctor arrived in the very early morning to take away the tiny body of our newest brother, David, who was just a few weeks old. Jane, Louisa, Bruce and Alice were born over the next four years.

Both happiness and terror colour my earliest memories. We lived in a tiny shack at the foot of Hope mountain, because my father was employed off the reserve in hard rock mining or logging in the area. Around the time I turned six, both of my parents began drinking alcohol to excess. My father's work buddies would come over and fall to hard drinking and scrapping. During one fight in our home, a number of men pinned my father to the floor. I remember grabbing a huge wine jug, one of the gallon-size jugs that liquor came in in those days, and hitting one of the men as hard as I could on the back of the head.

Just before I started school, we moved into the town of Hope. Despite the hard weekend drinking, my father always held down a job. In the summers, my mother would take Gordon and me to the hops fields. It was backbreaking labour for the adults, who picked hops all day in the hot sun, but it was great fun for us. We played with friends we hadn't seen all year, jumping into the hops sacks and playing hide-and-seek among the rows of vines and behind the pickers' shacks. We'd join the adults at coffee break or lunch hour. In the evenings, we'd sit around and listen to the women talk to each other in Halq'emeylem. We lived in little tarpaper shacks put up for us on the edge of the fields by the white farmers.

My maternal grandfather was known as a quiet conservative who cut firewood for the paddlewheelers that still made their way up the Fraser River to Yale. The dry goods store owned by my father's father was the Hope Trading Company, the town's largest. Walter Crey had been on the local school board, and he was head of the merchants' association and a member of the Conservative Party. Well-educated in European schools, my paternal grandfather was also an accomplished pianist. My father had received a secure foundation in life in a home that brought together my grandfather's prosperity and European ways with my grandmother's Sto:lo cultural teachings. A generation later, it must have pained my father to see incipient instability and dysfunction in his own family. He prevailed upon my mother and announced they would both change their ways. Both of my parents quit drinking when I was about seven.

My childhood became much more stable and content. My father settled in to share with us some of his cultural knowledge. He would take my sister Frances and me wood-cutting and fishing for salmon in the Coquihalla River. Daddy was a patient man, ready to teach us all he knew. He possessed extensive botanical knowledge. In those days we didn't see a doctor; instead, my father would go into the woods and pick a plant. He had different kinds of teas that would cure headaches, stomach aches, cramps and other kinds of sickness. I can remember once when I was nine chopping kindling and having the axe strike deep into my left index finger. The wound was bandaged but did not heal. My father took me out in the woods near our home and picked a wide-leaved green plant from the forest floor. Its leaves had white stripes on each side. He grasped one of the leaves at the tip and neatly peeled it open along the white stripes, then wrapped it on my finger. He told me my wound would be healed in a day and a half, and it was.

At bedtime, my father sang traditional Halq'emeylem lullabies. He possessed all the songs meant to accompany traditional Sto:lo activities. When fishing, he had songs to will the salmon into the net and songs to the Sto:lo creators who put salmon into the Fraser River. He told how Xexa:ls had come up the river putting parts of the deer in different reaches of the river to create the five species of Fraser River salmon. Xexa:ls taught people how to live right, how to catch the fish he had put in the river and how to prepare and cook it. My father told me that the first spring salmon of the season had to be shared and its bones put back in the river. This special time with my father, almost a full five years for me, was a time of great security for our family. We children had a loving respect for our dad. I especially treasure the fact that I was able to know the man he really was.

But while my home life was happy, my school days were miserable. I attended a public school where I was made aware daily of the gap between my family's standard of living and that of my non-Indian classmates. The town of Hope was a working-class white community of loggers and miners mixed in with a few civil servants, social workers and police officers. At school I concentrated on surviving with some of my dignity intact; actually learning anything was secondary.

At first I was bright and eager to learn, but my initial openness was not reciprocated by either the teachers or the other students. My relationship with teachers was combative. They expected me to do poorly academically. I received little encouragement or help. Neither the teachers nor the white parents were comfortable having me or the few older non-status Indian kids in the school. They made it plain they thought we should be on the reserve or in residential school. To them, Indians firmly occupied the lowest rung of the social ladder.

I learned not to expect smiles from teachers. I'd stick my hand up to answer a question, but I knew I wouldn't be called on. Teachers frequently showed their resentment at having me in the room by not including me in the lessons or in the social interaction between children in the classroom. I could expect to be treated curtly and summarily, without warmth or respect. The teachers appeared to share the view of Indians held by the priests and nuns in the residential school of my father's era, though in the public school those views were disguised under a thin veneer of civilized disinterest.

There were exceptions. I recall a teacher at Coquihalla Elementary School, a young man who seemed to make no distinction between me and the other children. Marvin Cope, who is now a retired principal, went out of his way to encourage me. He'd draw my attention to aboriginal role models in the fields of entertainment and athletics. He'd describe Will Rogers, the Indian journalist with his own radio program who almost ran for president of the United States, and American athlete Jim Thorpe. I was taken aback that a teacher would introduce into the classroom for my benefit alone this gallery of famous Indian people I knew nothing about. He made me feel that I, too, could be a high achiever. My improved self-esteem was reflected in the high marks I got in Marvin Cope's class.

And then my happy family life began to unwind. The death of my paternal grandfather stripped from my father whatever social status he had in the white community. From that point on, to the townspeople of Hope, my father would always be a half-breed married to an Indian woman. Our family's economic fortunes went into considerable decline. By the time the fifth of my siblings was born, my father's health had deteriorated from a lifetime of hard physical labour. His spine had been broken during his time as a faller in the woods. Fortunately the accident had left his spinal cord intact, but he suffered intense back pain from then on. He also had a bad heart. Finally he was no longer able to work at all, and our family was forced to go on social assistance. One day, my brother Gordon and I returned from a fishing camp, walking the twenty miles from Seabird Island to Hope. As each step drew me nearer to home, my sense of foreboding grew until we reached our house. An ambulance bearing my father's body had just left. My mother wept silently, surrounded by frightened, sobbing children. It was the summer of 1961, and my father's death set in motion a string of events that would ultimately lead to the disintegration of my family.

Nothing in my mother's sheltered upbringing in a tuberculosis hospital — while recuperating from T.B., she had received very little formal education — had equipped her for life as a self-supporting single parent of six. My father had been her best and only lifelong friend, and his loss was devastating to her. She had a few people she could look to, including her beloved aunt, Rose Charlie of Cheam. But well before my father died, Rose had married Ed Sparrow, the patriarch of Musqueam, and had left the Cheam reserve to establish a new life for herself there. As the eldest child in the family, my mother would have been too proud and independent to appeal to her younger siblings for help. Without my father around, life in a white community became all the more confusing and threatening. My mother began drinking again. We all felt the tension. I can remember trying to bar the door to keep her from going out to get drunk. I started to act out in the community, stealing candy bars and soft drinks from the local stores, skipping school and, with my friends, making a general nuisance of myself.

A few months after my father's death, an RCMP cruiser pulled up in front of our home. I was taken to the local police station and placed in a cell that would be my home for the next week. No social worker or lawyer or courtworker visited me. I found out later that my brother Gordon had tried to visit and bring me food but was turned away. At the end of the week, I was brought before a judge. A number of people talked to the judge about me in a manner I couldn't understand. Gordon sat at the back of the courtroom. Finally, the judge told me that I was to be sent to someplace called Brannan Lake Industrial School on Vancouver Island. I was not allowed any contact with Gordon. I was led out of the courtroom and placed in the cell again. I was twelve years old.

I would not see Gordon or my mother for another four years. By that time, my younger sisters, my brother Bruce and baby Alice would all have been taken away. My family would never again live in the same home or even be in the same room together.

My mother had been judged by social workers, teachers and police officers as an inadequate parent well before the day I was asked to rise and stand in front of that judge. There was no one in the courtroom to represent my mother or me. Hiring a lawyer would have been unthinkable for my mother. The outcome of events was predetermined by legal, economic and social forces that Sto:lo families, including my own, had no chance of influencing or controlling.

It was 1961, the beginning of what became known as the "Sixties' Scoop." For the first time in Canada, provincial social workers were exercising the jurisdiction given to them by the federal government to go into Indian homes on and off reserves and make judgements about what constituted proper care, according to non-native, middle-class values. Their mandate was "child protection," which in practice meant the investigation of perceived neglect or abuse, then the apprehension of children and their placement in non-native foster homes. Poverty was the only reason many children were apprehended from otherwise caring aboriginal homes. For status Indians like my mother, there were none of the social services a white family in crisis might have received. For her, there were no homemakers, no preventive family counselling services, no funded daycare facilities. There was no respite at all from the day-to-day drudgery faced by an uneducated, widowed mother of six trying to survive on welfare.

My eldest two sisters, Frances and Jane, were placed in the care of an elderly fundamentalist Christian couple on Fairfield Island, near the town of Chilliwack. My brother Bruce and sister Louisa were fostered by a Christian family in Chilliwack, as was my sister Alice. They grew up within miles of each other but had no knowledge their siblings were so close by. Visits home were forbidden. Frances and Jane especially missed Gordon, the stable older brother who had looked after us all and tried desperately as a young teenager to keep the family together.

On my arrival at Brannan Lake I was "processed" in an office and then taken to an area of the institution where new inmates were showered, shorn and locked up. Each kid was given a pig-shave. My clothes were taken away to be replaced by a steel-blue institutional shirt and pants. Late in the evening of my first day, I was startled out of a fretful sleep by screams and the clanging of keys against the bars of the cell just a few feet from me. I couldn't make out exactly what was happening, but I found out in the morning that the kid in the cell next to mine had attempted suicide by slicing open his wrists with the metal top of an Old Dutch Cleanser container. I was to discover that self-mutilation and suicide attempts were common occurrences in that place.

Kids were forced to do hard physical labour at a nearby gravel pit, as well as more mundane chores such as sweeping and waxing floors. But the main "activity" at Brannan Lake was fighting. I was beaten up my first day in "intake," but after that I decided to establish my place in the pecking order by picking two fights in the most public areas of the institution. A guard broke up the first scrap I got into with a sharp blow to the back of my neck, and my opponent and I were thrown into the lock-up for several days. I swiftly learned that bullies were tolerated by the workers at Brannan Lake, so it was up to me to drop the most notorious bully or be left with the black eyes and welts most of the younger kids displayed. Officials used the violent hierarchy among boys to keep order. Rewards for the enforcers among the older boys included passes out of the school and small privileges such as cigarettes. The older boys also could count on school officials turning a blind eye when those boys preyed on smaller, younger boys for sexual favours.

Sexual abuse at Brannan Lake was common. Certain members of the staff preyed at will on all of us. To get a day trip out of the institution, a boy would have to be a "bum-boy" for certain male supervisors. Many of the older boys were street-hardened youth from big cities, used to trading sexual favours for money or privileges, and the staff willingly exploited them. It seemed as though there was no one safe to complain to.

As a relatively innocent twelve-year-old coming into this hellhole, I was deeply shocked and frequently terrorized. For stealing a few chocolate bars, I'd been thrown in with boys who had committed rape and murder and wouldn't think twice about doing it again. The reform school philosophy of hard knocks, of vigorous contact sports and tough discipline, didn't work at Brannan Lake. Tough kids left more hardened. It was what I imagined residential school had been like from what my father had said.

Three months later, a social worker came to take me away from Brannan Lake. I desperately wanted to go home. I missed my mother and my brothers and sisters. But no one would answer my questions about my family, and I was told the ministry had other plans for me.

I arrived confused and afraid at my first foster home. It was a large German family who already had three other native foster children. In my presence, the woman of the house openly displayed her dislike of Indians. Aboriginal women were called "smoked meat" or "brown stuff." To me, coming from a well-regarded social stratum on both the white and aboriginal sides of my family, my foster mom seemed very common and coarse. It was mystifying to me how she could regard my people as scum without knowing anything about us. It's one thing to face racism at school, but to live with it in the face of a "mom" every day was crushing to my self-esteem. I had to learn to harden myself and block out any longing for comfort or nurturing.

As an older native foster child, I was swiftly put to work. The three younger native children weren't worked as hard, but they were treated just as rudely. None of us was shown affection. I was sent to school in ill-fitting secondhand clothes, especially humiliating since I already stood out as one of the few Indian kids there. It was clear to me that although this woman had been lionized in her home community as a Mother Theresa to Indian kids, she was in the foster care business for the money. By this time, the early 1960s, the B.C. child welfare branch was taking aboriginal children into its care so quickly and in such huge numbers that anyone who was willing to take Indian children was deemed suitable. We were warehoused in homes that were by no stretch of the imagination suitable for any child, let alone a traumatized, culturally dislocated, grieving aboriginal child.

At fourteen, I was moved to another foster home in Chilliwack with a pleasant, middle-class family. The father valued achievement above all and soon made it clear that I was a disappointment to him, long before I'd been provided with enough stability to prove myself academically or in any other way. Pam Koczapska, the mother of the family, was a teacher and a well-respected woman in the Sto:lo community. I really came to love her, but she was unable to defend me when the father decided I had to go. Later, as an adult, he and I reconciled; I always remained close with Pam, but at the time the experience was very hurtful.

By then, I knew the basic lie of the foster "home," with its foster "mother" and "father" who supposedly loved me as their own child. If I made the most minor error, or a character trait of mine was judged wanting, I'd be out on my ear. I'd been cocky and defiant in my first foster home, hardened by their openly racist dislike of Indians in general and me in particular. But this second family had more power to hurt me, because I had come to care for them. After that, I was determined not to get close to anyone. I told the social workers I didn't want any more foster "homes." I told them just to give me a bed to sleep in.

But I continued to bounce around in non-native foster care. I was in the heart of Sto:lo territory, surrounded by villages in which my aunts, uncles and cousins lived, but I was the perpetual stranger. A palpable grief and longing seemed to dog my footsteps. I desperately wanted my own family back, but the social workers told me there was no one at home who wanted me. I tried to hide my loneliness and grief in long-distance running, running miles through villages like Rosedale, Tzeachten, Soowahlie and Cheam, my mother's home community. Powerful emotions welled up in me, but I felt helpless to stop in those Sto:lo homes. I'd run back, drained and exhausted, to the only sense of belonging I felt, however tenuous: my borrowed corner of the next white foster family's life.

Growing up as a government ward made me very cynical about the collaboration between the government and the evangelistic Christians who were "saving" Indian kids from their own families. Again I felt echoes of my father's residential school experience. We were kept from our families to hasten our assimilation into the white world. We were told our culture was inferior and doomed to extinction. My last foster family was an aged German-Canadian couple who practised relentless evangelism. I escaped as often as I could to my lonely upstairs room. I ended up in several different high schools but still managed to maintain a B average. Counsellors knew I was bright and could do better. But I was continually dogged by anxiety, worrying about my siblings and my mother. I was afraid I wouldn't be there to stop her from winding up dead in a ditch somewhere, from drinking.

Meanwhile, as I would later learn, my mother was frantically trying to find out what had happened to her children. She wrote letters to each of us individually. She and my brother Gordon, the only child left in her home, desperately searched for us. Gordon would take the bus to Fraser Valley communities, one by one, looking for Indian children, asking teachers and shopkeepers and visiting playgrounds to search for a sign of his brothers and sisters. He covered every street of Abbotsford on foot, because he believed at one point that we were in foster homes there.

None of Gordon's sleuthing met with success, although social workers could have helped him at any time. Our files were not sealed as they would have been if any of us had been adopted. But we were Indian kids in care. The social services ministry's ostensible goal to reunite families apparently applied only to white children. Social workers accepted letters my mother addressed to us, but these were placed in thick government files. None of those letters ever reached me or my siblings in our white foster homes.

The first time I saw those letters was many, many years later. I had dropped into a Fraser Valley social services office in my quest to reestablish my federal Indian status. (After my father's death, my mother had married a white man, which robbed her and her children of Indian status. Under Bill C-3 1, introduced in 1985, I knew I was entitled to get it back.) A sympathetic social worker in the office offered to show me my file from my days as a child in care. There were the letters my mother had sent me. They'd obviously been opened. In them, my mother poured out her fears and concerns for me and tried to reassure me that she still loved me, that I should never think she did not. She told me how much she missed me and thought of me. And in one letter, she had an ingenious plan. The social workers would not tell her exactly where I was, but she proposed that I meet her one Saturday at a tiny park in Abbotsford. My mother had died by this time, and I couldn't help but wonder how many times she had driven by that park, looking for me.

When I was fifteen, still in foster care, I figured out how to get a bus to Hope to see my mom and brother. By then I knew that all of the younger children had been taken away. When I stepped off the bus, there was Gordon. He was working as a janitor in the Greyhound depot. We hugged each other and tried to catch up on the past three years. Gordon told me that our mother had been searching for me and my siblings. We walked home after Gordon finished work and there was my mother. She was overcome with emotion, crying and laughing at the same time. She asked me questions about where I had been and exclaimed over my growth and the change in my appearance. She had gained control over her drinking; there seemed to be no reason why I couldn't remain in that cozy old log home with her. But I knew the police would come and get me if I did, and that would make it harder for her. I didn't tell her about my misery at Brannan Lake or in the foster homes; there was no point in hurting her any further.

I saw Gordon four or five more times while I was still a foster child. The thirty-two-mile distance between me and my brother and mother was a greater distance then, especially to people without money, than it is today. Gordon was especially dear to me. We'd been constant companions as children, and he'd saved my life three times. But the years we spent apart, in vastly different circumstances, divided us and eroded our special bond. Perhaps I resented that he had escaped foster care and had our beloved mom all to himself.

In the early 1970s, Gordon died in mysterious circumstances after a night of drinking. His body was dumped on the front lawn of my aunt's house. The police report said he had died of head injuries and exposure. True to form, the RCMP had little interest in the death of a young Indian male. Over the years, the circumstances of his death continued to plague me. When I had saved enough money, I tried to hire a prominent Kamloops lawyer, who later became a judge. I told him I believed Gordon had died of the severe head injuries someone had inflicted. The man gave a contemptuous laugh and told me no lawyer would bother looking into why a drunken Indian had died two years earlier. To my regret, I believed him.

Throughout my time in foster care, I beseeched social workers for news of my siblings. They responded with platitudes that my sisters and brothers were happy in good homes, far away. Based on my own experience, I viewed those statements as bald-faced lies. In fact, as it turned out, all my brothers and sisters lived within miles of me. One day Pam Koczapska called to tell me there were two little Indian girls named Frances and Jane attending the Chilliwack elementary school where she taught. I was sure they were my sisters. A strange but infinitely precious meeting was arranged.

The two little girls were dropped off at a prearranged spot at a playground. We were given an hour and told not to exchange information about where we lived. They were delighted to see me, even if they had no clear memory of what I looked like. Jane, nine and shy, left all the talking to Frances, who was a year older. She was full of questions. All I could tell them was that all my mother's children except Gordon were gone and that my mother still loved them.

My former foster mom kept tabs on my sisters, and I was able to visit them later at a chicken farm in the Fraser Valley. She also found my brother Bruce, who was with my sister Louisa in a white Christian fundamentalist family. I went to visit them. The family sat me down in the living room and paraded out a nice young Indian boy, who was told to play the piano for me. Over the next eight years, until Bruce got out of care, I visited him and Louisa several times, but their foster parents were careful never to leave us alone. I didn't know what they were enduring until Bruce was an adult.

I had made no secret of my unhappiness in my current foster home, and finally a social worker took me to meet Frank, an engaging and handsome young man in his mid-thirties. Frank took me for a drive in his car and bought me an ice cream cone. He invited me to come and live in the group home where he worked, where he promised I'd have lots of freedom and few chores to do. He took me to see the home. There were five teenaged boys living there, most of them non-native. I decided to move in. Shortly afterwards, Frank moved in too. He'd split up with his wife, and he appeared to have persuaded his superiors the group home experiment would work best with a resident supervisor.

I soon saw Frank's true motive for living with teenaged boys. He openly pursued sexual relationships with them. "Watch out, Ernie, you're next for the blow job from Frank," was the joke. I'd hear boys tiptoeing down the hall to join Frank on the couch in the recreation room where he slept. He had a big collection of kiddie porn, which he left lying around. In one of the magazines, we found a picture of a boy we all knew, a child still in the care of the province of B.C., whom Frank had taken on a trip to San Francisco.

Frank was a skilled, intelligent pedophile, very exploitative. Boys weren't forced into sex, they were seduced. As foster children, they were starved for love, and very vulnerable. There was even competition to see who could win Frank's favours. I liked Frank. I had thought he was the first person to show a genuine interest in me, but it was only due to his sexual obsession. I experienced an enormous betrayal of trust, and I felt objectified. Frank even brought another social worker into the home to share the boys' sexual favours.

Looking back, I am angry and amazed that these two pedophiles could have preyed so openly on children in care in a government-financed group home. Mike, the young man who had been photographed for the porn magazine, bragged that Frank had arranged for him to have sex with two supervisors in the region. It seemed like a conspiracy to me. I made it my goal to develop a strategy to get out of there.

I was allowed to get a summer job on a Canadian Pacific railway gang. The next summer, I got my file as a government ward transferred to Kamloops and got a job as a bellhop in a hotel. I lived with a kind, elderly hotel janitor and his wife. I was earning real money. At the end of that summer, I called Frank and told him I didn't want to come back, but he said he wanted to meet with me in person. I realized he was afraid I'd expose his pedophilia, but I made it clear to him when we met that I only wanted to get on with my own life.

I started to attend high school in Kamloops, but only after Frank had convinced the principal that I was a bright, independent kid who deserved a chance. I did well, and the principal became fond of pointing me out as a model Indian foster child, something any kid could be if they'd just pull themselves up by their bootstraps. After I built up a rapport with a Kamloops social worker I trusted, I disclosed Frank's rampant pedophilia to her. No one ever contacted me. But years later, when I was the head of a provincial aboriginal organization, the same Kamloops social worker told me privately that police reports from the other boys as well as my disclosure to her had prompted an investigation. In 1984, Frank's fellow pedophile was convicted in provincial court on six counts involving four males aged thirteen to seventeen, some of whom were in his care. The offences included buggery, fellatio, fondling and masturbation. He was sentenced to four years in jail. Frank died in a mysterious accident, believed to be suicide. From time to time, I still come across some of the boys I knew from Frank's group home. One is a cocaine addict I've seen on Vancouver's downtown streets. I lost touch with Mike, the kiddie porn model, after he became a hustler and attempted suicide several times.

In 1969, the province of B.C. declared the age of majority to be nineteen. In June of that year, at the age of twenty, I was officially free of the Department of Social Welfare. The government was no longer my parent. But it wasn't for another decade, after my brothers and sisters were old enough to legally seek each other out, that I learned about the appalling treatment they had received at the hands of their foster parents. We began hesitantly, painfully talking as adults.

I did not suffer as severely as my siblings, escaping the worst of the physical and sexual abuse they endured. But my experiences in foster care left me just as scarred. I was fearful and guarded and could not trust people, something that has deeply affected my adult relationships.

I remember my first encounter with aboriginal politics: hearing the magnificent Shuswap orator George Manuel, president of the National Indian Brotherhood, speak at the Kamloops hotel where I was working. I was spellbound. He helped me to see the links between my own family's pain and the paternalism of a federal government that persisted in regarding all Indians as children and our children as their property. Manuel first spoke out loud for me what I instinctively knew, that as First Nations we had to wrest back control of our children if we were ever to return to being self-governing. When an opportunity came to work for the B.C. Association of Non-Status Indians, I leaped at the chance. I travelled all over the province to report on off-reserve living conditions. I found families living alongside railway tracks in abandoned shacks, squatting on Crown land and inhabiting the worst fleabag hotels. Non-status aboriginal people had been shut out of employment in ranching, mining and logging communities that openly loathed them. Nor were these disinherited families welcome back on the reserve. I realized the majority of aboriginal children were growing up off reserve, in mother-led families, without supports of any kind. They were the poorest of the poor in Canada and nobody gave a damn what happened to them, not the federal government, not the province and certainly not their beleaguered elected chiefs back home.

Later, I worked for the Company of Young Canadians in an isolated west coast reserve, until the toll of suicides, alcoholism, poverty and unending human despair wore down even my boundless optimism. A physical and emotional breakdown taught me to use my resources more wisely. It also made me realize how lonely I was, that I had to let someone pierce my guard and open myself to the possibility of reciprocal love.

With my first wife, Bonnie, a schoolteacher, I moved to my next post as a social worker in the Shuswap village of Alkali Lake. At that time it was called "Alcohol Lake," a booze-soaked reserve of relentless misery. As two of the few sober people with a car, we were called upon every weekend to ferry the bloodied, drunken and beaten to the nearest emergency ward forty miles away. Once, an injured woman died, briefly, in our back seat. Roused back to life in the hospital, she described an out-of-body experience where she'd floated up in the air and watched us frantically racing towards help, with her lifeless form in the back of the car. That image, together with the sight of the hungry little faces of neglected children clustered around our back porch, has stayed in my mind to define the kind of social work I was able to do in that era, before the people of Alkali Lake, through their own heroic efforts, vanquished alcoholism and led First Nations all over North America on the path towards sobriety. I was honoured to return to Alkali Lake in the early 1990s for a powwow and community celebration, and delighted to see healthy, vibrant young girls with jingle dresses and braids flying in traditional dance, and young boys sporting coyote masks and elaborate feather bustles. A whole room full of healthy elders performed a slow honour dance. I could see that young adults affected by fetal alcohol syndrome were being well taken care of within their own village. The elders had their own memories: they teased me about the much slimmer young social worker who'd blown off steam by tearing around the dry Cariboo hills on a big motorbike. To me, the journey of Alkali Lake, begun when a little girl named Ivy Chelsea refused to go home with a drunken mother, exemplifies the resolve and redemption of which our communities are capable.

My marriage to my first wife broke up in 1974. Although we had shared many profound experiences, including the birth of our son, Saul, I could not cast off my fear of abandonment. I tried to control her every move. I could not accept that anyone could love me and stay committed to me, because no one ever had.

When I remarried in 1977, and my second wife, Lorraine, and I subsequently had four children, I had to learn how to become a good parent. I had to be continually shown how to be a loving father, and constantly reminded to share the responsibilities of household chores and childcare. I loved my children so fiercely that I feared everything would be taken away from me: I was hypervigilant about their safety and wanted their happiness so badly that it must have been quite oppressive. Still, despite my parental lapses, my children have all grown up to be independent, healthy beings.

My very public struggle to change the situation in which aboriginal families find themselves ironically came at a terrible cost to my own family life. After years of intense political activity as the vice-president and then acting president of the United Native Nations, including the failed battle to enshrine off-reserve aboriginal rights in the Canadian constitution, I felt drained and empty. I was appalled by the cynicism and financial wrongdoing of some urban First Nations politicians I saw around me. Then, after only a brief vacation with my family, I leaped with both feet into the fire of my first long hot summer as fisheries manager for the Sto:lo Nation. It was to cost me my second marriage, but it would lead ultimately to the cultural healing that would be my salvation.

During my years in urban aboriginal politics, I tried to keep an eye out for my siblings in the city. Over the years, I established the closest relationship with Bruce, while he in turn kept in touch with our sisters. The whole sad tale of my siblings' childhoods became known to me. In the good Christian home in which Bruce grew up, he and Louisa were kept in the basement on Christmas Day while the foster family gathered upstairs for turkey dinner. Both Bruce and Louisa were subjected to bizarre, cruel punishments: they were locked in the closet, threatened with a large hunting knife when grades were poor, and had their heads stuck in the toilet bowl while it was flushed repeatedly. My brother and sister were told constantly that they were the spawn of the devil. Like most of the aboriginal children who grew up in care, they will battle self-esteem issues all their lives. Bruce, whose early job opportunities were compromised by an alcohol addiction, has now been sober for twelve years.

My sister Louisa is a strong woman, but in her early years as a mother, she was unable to cope on her own with two small children, and one of her children was apprehended. Her daughter stayed with her. My wife and I asked the ministry to place Louisa's small son, Jason, in our home until my sister was on her feet. Bruce, too, asked the ministry to be involved in planning for Jason's care. But on the eve of proposed changes to child welfare regulations, Jason was abruptly removed from the foster family and given up for adoption to a non-Indian family. His adoption was arranged with all the stealth and secrecy the B.C. Ministry of Social Services could muster, as if the minister of the day took special pleasure in thwarting the wishes of the Indian politician who had been such a thorn in his side. Louisa soon got on top of her alcohol problem and stayed steadily employed while Jason grew up hundreds of miles away in a white family. With support, Louisa could have parented Jason, but he was already gone, lost to Louisa as she had been lost to my mother. Within a few years, however, as soon as he was old enough to choose, Jason came home to Louisa and his extended family — with the support of his adoptive parents.

Frances and Jane had fared no better in their foster homes. Their fundamentalist Christian foster parents exerted strict "discipline" through whippings, psychological terror and heavy farm labour. The girls were told if they didn't submit to discipline they'd burn in hell along with all the other pagan Indians. As adults, my sisters told me with tears flowing down their faces about their foster father's favoured punishment. For any imagined infraction, he'd march the girls in the middle of the night down to the poultry barns to shovel out chicken shit until dawn. Both Frances and Jane carried deep shame throughout their lives about being Indian and a lot of anger towards white adults. After Frances began drinking heavily as a young mother, her baby daughter, Roberta, was apprehended by social workers, again without any notification of family members. The loss of a second generation of Crey children was well underway. It seemed like nothing could ever repair the abandonment and grief Frances felt, and her guilt for failing Roberta. In the late 1980s, she died of a heroin overdose.

As an adult, Jane told me of being sexually abused by her foster parents' son, who was never charged and is now a Christian missionary in Africa. In her late teens, Jane gave birth to a son who was adopted by the same parents and continues to live there. It hurts me to see my nieces and nephews repeat our history as foster kids in white, ultra-Christian homes. Jane now spends most of her time on Vancouver's meanest streets, on a methadone-maintenance program but receiving no psychiatric care or counselling to help her cope with the immense losses in her life.

My mother continued to drink after all her children were taken from her, and she later gave birth to two more children, Sally and Donald, both of whom wound up in the care of an aboriginal foster family. Both were abused. Donald, who suffers from minor intellectual impairments, is friendly and outgoing, though he will require assistance all his life. After Sally became drug-addicted herself, her two children were placed in the care of the new Sto:lo agency, Xolhmi:lh Child and Family Services. Our devastation about Sally's future was complete when she learned last year she is infected with AIDS.

The troubles my siblings and I have suffered can only truly be understood in a cultural context, not just as a series of traumatic life events but as a deep spiritual estrangement from the complex of Sto:lo beliefs. As Sto:lo, we believe that our ancestors continue to play a role in our daily lives. In our society, when you are ill or feeling discomfort, you are described as being "Indian sick," which means that spiritual forces are at work in your life. In order to understand these forces, you must return to spiritual teachers. The elders believe the voices and spirits that non-native medical experts might diagnose as a profound mental illness are in fact an expression of the cultural estrangement so many of us have suffered.

I had been able to survive by channelling my personal grief into anger and action, but in the autumn of 1993, everything seemed to come crashing down on me. I was consumed by an overwhelming feeling of fatigue and depression. Solace began only when I visited Sto:lo spiritual leader Gwendolyn Point. After examining me quietly, with her eyes closed and her hands moving over my body for several minutes, Gwendolyn told me a very old spirit had settled on me and was there to protect me. She told me this was a good thing. She advised me to hang cedar branches throughout our home. Undesirable influences would be caught in the boughs.

I was advised to embark on a course of spiritual healing, including immersions in cold water. The Sto:lo Nation's knowledgeable anthropologist, Gordon Mohs, arranged for me to go to the Nooksack reserve, accompanied by Yakweakwioose Chief Frank Malloway, a spiritual leader known as Siyemchess. I was frightened about making the excursion, since I had had little direct experience with our cultural practice. But the two elders parked in front of a giant colour television in a small reserve bungalow turned out to be anything but frightening. Elders of the Indian Shaker church, they spoke with me quietly, then began to pray and move their hands over my body to sense where the sickness lay. After several minutes, my eyes began to stream and my chest to heave, and a clear mucus poured out of my nose. My long-confined pain and tension, like a band of blackness tightly wrapped around my chest, began to collapse and break up like ice floes in spring. I coughed and expelled mucus until I felt drained of all the negativity I'd carried around.

After my immersion in the glacial tributary of the Fraser River and the Nooksack men's workover, I felt a renewed optimism and a fresh wellspring of will to carry me through the work ahead, both in the aboriginal fishery and in my own spiritual development. My wife, Lorraine, agreed to undergo a similar experience with another Sto:lo spiritual leader, since, as my partner, she had absorbed unconsciously some of the blackness I carried with me. For a time our family life improved. But the demands of my job continued to put strains on our marriage, and in the spring of 1994 Lorraine and I separated. I am still closely involved in the lives of my children. Naomi, Karrmen and Aaron all have worked with the Sto:lo Nation at a sacred Sto:lo heritage site known as the Xa:ytem Longhouse Interpretive Centre. Aaron, now sixteen, works for the Sto:lo environmental youth corps and lives with me part of the year in my new home on the Soowahlie reserve, close to the banks of the Fraser River.

Through the Sto:lo spiritual practices, I know that the spirits of my parents, my grandparents and my ancestors are alive in this world. I call the spirits of my ancestors forth to invite them to a traditional Sto:lo burning to honour the dead, and I feel their presence with me, at the burning and in the smokehouse. When I walk in the ways my ancestors walked for tens of thousands of years, the pain of the last few decades seems to fall away. My parents, grandparents and ancestors walk beside me, concerned and involved in all the events of my life. This is not theoretical, but very real: it allows me the intimacy and unconditional love that was missing from the years I was culturally and spiritually separated from them. I've come to realize that they never left my side, even in my lonely days as a child kept away from anyone who knew me. I was blinded to their love.

For any Sto:lo or other aboriginal person who grows up in boarding schools, foster care, hospitals or jail, the traditional ways can heal. I feel this is the great hope for aboriginal children who have been devastated by their life experiences. By entering the belief system of their own First Nation, they can resume a spiritual relationship with their parents and grandparents that can comfort them and heal the emotional void they feel.

Despite a century of government interference, today the longhouse traditions of winter dances are flourishing among the Sto:lo. With my children, I go throughout the year to longhouses at Sumas for the dances that fill the long rainy winter months as they have since time immemorial. All important Sto:lo occasions, such as naming ceremonies and memorial services, are consecrated in the big house. Inside the huge cedar longhouse, smoke rises from two gigantic, constantly fed bonfires to smoke-holes fifty feet in the air. Drums rhythmically pound for dancers who are in a trance-like state. The Sto:lo dances are like no others. They are not a public First Nation ritual to be captured on videotape or performed for tourists. Neither the Syúwél winter dances nor the masked Sxwó:yxwey ceremonies have ever been photographed or filmed. My children know, as Sto:lo children have known for hundreds of generations before them, that the spiritual state of new dancers is so intense that young ones must stay well clear of them. There are always huge dinners served after a night's dancing, but what is really fed is the soul. My children know that the longhouse tradition is at the heart of their identity as Sto:lo. They may live contemporary lives in a suburban neighbourhood, but they are above all Sto:lo. They know that the door to the longhouse is always open to them.

In so many ways, the history of my family is the history of aboriginal children in Canada. We have lived through the worst of times: epidemics of disease brought by the first white traders; the black-robed Oblates who trekked into our territory and teamed up with the government to bring us residential schools; the cycle of disintegration that exposed us to all the ills of the modern world. I intend to make sure my family and my people will be around to experience the best of times, too, as First Nations all across North America work to restore and redefine our communities, economically, spiritually and culturally. What happened to me, to my family, to my community and to my First Nation has fuelled my work as an activist seeking economic justice, social cohesion and political power for all aboriginal people.

MAURICE GIBBONS (1931 –)

During the summer of 1994, people came from many parts of the world to the west coast of Vancouver Island to demonstrate against the clearcut logging of one of the world's few remaining stands of ancient temperate rainforest. Protests had been occurring intermittently on a small scale for several years, but reached fever pitch in 1993 when the NDP government announced its decision to allow MacMillan Bloedel to log sixty-two percent of Clayoquot Sound. In spite of a court injunction to keep the logging road open, a crowd of people massed at the Kennedy River Bridge (more than twelve thousand during the summer) and approximately nine hundred of those chose to be arrested rather than abandon the blockade. This represented one of the largest civil disobedience actions in Canada's history; as Ronald Hatch has stated in *Clayoquot and Dissent*, the protestors "chose to break a small law ... in order to stop a large injustice." The protest at Clayoquot had far-reaching effects in changing both public opinion on environmental issues and government legislation on logging practices.

The people who protested came literally from all walks of life and they included Dr. Maurice Gibbons, a retired university professor, and his wife, Margot. Gibbons was born in Peterborough, Ontario, but grew up in Vancouver, B.C. He holds degrees in English Literature from UBC and the University of Washington, with a Doctorate in Education from Harvard. He taught for several years at Simon Fraser University where his special field, in which he is widely published, was self-directed learning. He lives in retirement on Bowen Island where he is a writer, exhibiting sculptor and consultant. Gibbons was arrested at the Kennedy River Bridge on August 9, 1994 and received a fine of $1,250. His wife was also arrested and fined the same amount. The essay below (which has been abridged) first appeared in *Clayoquot and Dissent*, a collection of essays by six authors on the events of 1994.

THE CLAYOQUOT PAPERS

THESE PIECES ABOUT THE PROTEST at Clayoquot Sound and the struggle to stop the mismanagement and misuse of our forests began as items in my journal written during the unfolding events of my involvement, arrest and trial. I am proud to be a part of that protest, but the honour for its successful impact on logging policies and practices in British Columbia must go to the young people who organized it, managed it and manned the front lines for months in relative anonymity and at considerable risk to themselves and their futures. Their dedication, sacrifice, vision and competence assures me that there is a new generation coming that may yet save the planet from our plundering.

ON THE LINE AT CLAYOQUOT

On August 9, 1994, my wife, Margot, and I were arrested at the Kennedy River Bridge in Clayoquot Sound for refusing to obey a court injunction against obstructing logging operations of the MacMillan Bloedel employees in the area. We are not activists; we have never been arrested before; we were deeply shaken by the experience.

People ask, "Why did you do it?" Our answer is that we believe that the forests and other resources of B.C. belong to all of us, and that we have both a fight and a responsibility to speak and act when we think they are being misused. We think that falling any more of the old-growth rainforests on Vancouver Island is misuse, especially if the timber is clearcut and then shipped abroad as whole logs rather than as products we make from them. We feel that we need to take action for ourselves, for our grandchildren and for their children. We want them to know that we did not sit idly by while their treasure, their inheritance that we hold in trust, was destroyed. When the government announced that two-thirds of Clayoquot Sound would be logged, our journey to Kennedy River Bridge began.

We phoned the Sound Majority in Victoria offering to help, and on Saturday, August 7th, we received a call back from Friends of Clayoquot Sound asking us to be at The Bridge on Monday for a special rally. We packed up, caught an early Sunday ferry to Nanaimo and drove to the Peace Camp, a scattering of tents and tarps perfectly situated in "The Black Hole," a mountainside sheared to stumps and burned to embers. A vegetarian dinner for three hundred residents was underway. The young leaders were organizing a circle meeting to discuss strategy and training sessions in civil disobedience for newcomers. As an educator, I was impressed by the participation of the children and youths in the camp, and the respect shown for their contributions.

That night we stayed at Tur na nog, a bed and breakfast in Tofino run by Sile Simpson, who, it turns out, had been arrested three times in Clayoquot and was currently confined to her house rather than a cell only because of her children. We talked into the night with a drop-in group of Sile's friends and had to be prodded out of bed at 3:30 a.m. to drive back to the camp. We arrived just in time to join a cavalcade of cars, trucks and buses carrying over one thousand people as it turned off the highway onto a dusty logging road heading for the Bridge. After several kilometers, marshalls told us to pull over, park and walk. As the crowd gathered in the breaking dawn, the drums and singing began. Nothing had really happened yet, but I felt my heart thumping.

The crowd assembled as a noisy mob until someone held up a hand. Soon there was a forest of hands and suddenly, complete silence. This was the first sign of discipline, order and strategy that characterized the protesters throughout this amazing day. Signs and speeches reminded us all that this was a peaceful, orderly, drug-and-alcohol-free protest. With feelings running high and talk of blowing up the bridge among the most passionate, control was a challenging task. One of our three guides, Tzeporah Berman, stood on top of a van with a microphone, welcomed us and set the scene. "If the loggers are coming, they will be here between 5:45 and 6:00. You have until then to decide if you will be arrested today. If this is the day, simply stay on the road." Margot turned to me and said, "If we are going to make a stand, it has to be today. With so many people, this is the day that will count." I agreed and we walked onto the road.

As people waited, a chant started behind us, "If we all stay on the road, they can't arrest us all!" and soon everyone was chanting to the beat of the drums. Then we were instructed to sit. People with arm ribbons came to take our names and addresses. Others followed to write the phone numbers of lawyers on the palms of our hands. We were urged to get buddies who would look after our cars and track us through the arrest process from outside the jail. I found Sam Meisle who did all of those things for us and almost immediately brought us sandwiches, "For jail." Others came by and asked, "Are you all right?" or "Do you need anything?" Several stopped to touch us or hug us and say, "We're so glad to have you here." Suddenly in the hubbub a hand went up and in seconds a thousand people were silent again.

Margot whispered to me, "It's nearly 7:30. They're not coming." William Thomas, told us on the PA, "We respect all beings and we do not engage in violence, no matter how badly we are provoked. The company man will read the injunction and ask us to disperse. Then the RCMP will announce that you will be arrested if you don't move, and finally, they will carry or walk you to the buses. If you feel threatened at any time, hold up one finger and one of us will be there immediately."

Then the helicopters from TV stations arrived and circled the blockade, giving the scene an *Apocalypse Now* atmosphere. Teams of newspaper, radio and TV people appeared everywhere, shooting and interviewing. One American TV announcer stood beside us and spoke into his camera, "In this summer of discontent, dozens of people have been arrested …" Cries of protest interrupted him. "Not dozens — hundreds!" He stalked off, snarling, "Screw these jerks." We never saw him again. Someone had just yelled, "It's nine o'clock and no trees are falling in Clayoquot Sound!" when Valerie Langer announced, "We have just learned that the loggers are on their way." A cheer went up. They had chosen to give us this confrontation. We never figured out why, unless they hoped — as the rumour went — to show us up as an unruly mob. The protest would have fizzled without them; and when the crummies finally went through, there were no loggers in them. The company was not even trying to get its men to their workplace.

We began reaching out to each other and introducing ourselves — a secretary, two teachers, another professor, a corporate accountant, a nurse, a mother with two kids, a grad-school student, a mechanic, a pediatrician. Our conversation stopped in mid-sentence as a MacMillan Bloedel pick-up truck rolled into sight with a scowling man standing like Patton behind the cab. Police cars, buses and huge logging trucks with their piggybacked bunks pulled up to the blockade perimeter and loomed behind him. While he read the court injunction against our protest, another employee walked among us with a video camera, scowling and holding the lens up to our faces as if to say, "We've got you now!" People began leaving the road for the perimeter as the RCMP announced that we would be placed under arrest if we did not move. For a moment it seemed that only a few of us would be left, but when the dust settled, more than three hundred people remained on the road.

A logger made a speech, asking us to let him go to work. A handful of loggers' wives walked up the road among us, wearing the yellow ribbons of Share, their support organization. They joked and laughed nervously, not knowing quite what to do. Neither did we. Our struggle was with

MacMillan Bloedel and the NDP, not them; our opposition is to clearcutting the last of our irreplaceable old-growth, not to logging.

The RCMP began arresting people and carrying them to the buses. You could walk or go limply passive and be carried. A chant started up and grew to thunder, "The whole world is watching … Shame!" In the cacophony of helicopters, drums, chanting, cameras and urgent loudspeaker announcements about our rights, the tension grew. Margot and I tightened our grip on each other. The police came closer and closer. In front of us, they tried to grab a young, mentally handicapped boy from his mother and he began screaming. Other children, calm up to this point, began to cry. Support people closed in followed by cameras. Margot said, "I won't go if we can't go together." Three officers came to us. I said, "Help us both up and we'll walk," and they did. As we left, I turned and called out, "It was an honour to be here with you on this day," and I meant it.

There were so many of us that the recreation hall in Ucluelet had to be pressed into service as a jail. When we walked in at about 10:00 a.m. the first bus-load stood and cheered, as we all did for the next bus and the bus after that. When everyone was assembled we held hands in a circle around other circles, sang our songs and ended, with very 60's warmth, in a mass hug. The RCMP charged us, photographed us and required us to sign guarantees that we would not block the road again. Around 6:30 p.m. we were released until our court date in Victoria on August 12th. Although swamped by the largest protest arrest in Canadian history, the police remained courteous and professional. As someone said about this very civil disobedience, "Only in Canada." When we left, Sam was waiting with our car. That night the Clayoquot protest was the lead story across the country without a window being broken or a shot fired.

THE JOURNEY: ENCOUNTERS WITH TREES

My journey to Clayoquot began long before the summer of 1993. Trees — the forests, the wilderness — were an important part of my life and a shaping influence upon me from my earliest years. The same must be true for most British Columbians. When the call came to protest our disappearing old-growth rainforests, it seemed natural, almost required, for me to go. These episodes in my story tell why.

• • •

As a child I seemed always to be in the trees. They were my refuge and playground. We climbed high up vine maples to kick out and ride the tops down again. Fresh from a Johnny Weismuller Tarzan movie, we took turns sitting in the big tree holding a swing-rope, gathering the courage to launch out into that long dizzying swoop to our wind-shattered tree fort in the branches opposite. We watched in awe as our classmates, Albert and Pee Wee, climbed to the tops of tall cedar trees, dropped their homemade bombs, blew out foot-square chunks of pavement, and when the sirens wailed, slid down spread-eagled on the outside of the branches with amazing speed and scurried into the woods. I would sit for hours unseen as high up as I could climb into the raftered green of the huge maple tree in our backyard, sitting quietly, feeling the wind moving in the branches I clung to, commanding my cutter in full sail around the Horn in pursuit of wily buccaneers; or watching the real war games unfolding before me on English Bay. The trees held me as often as anyone in my family ever did.

Vancouver was a city on the edge of wildness. You could walk up any street on the North Shore, pass the last house and step onto a trail into wilderness that could wind all the way to the Arctic Circle. I grew up on that edge, moving easily from the city to the woods and back. Like living in trees, living among them was a powerful experience. Whenever a crisis arose, I turned instinctively to a quiet place in the forest. If the family centre wouldn't hold, if professional opponents conspired to do me in, if someone I loved was dying, I went to where the pavement ends and passed into the reflective solitude of a wilderness grove to think the problem through. In that great calm I could hear my voice, encounter my feelings and find a pathway forward. The night my brother was shot down in Europe I walked into the woods. As dawn broke in the clearing where I sat, sunlight fell on a moss covered nurse-log thick with the seedlings and saplings of new growth. "Cedar tree falling among shoots," I wrote of my first metaphysical thought; even in death there is life. With this understanding, in this eternal place, my healing began.

In the woods I feel a presence I cannot define, a "force that through the green fuse drives the flower," an aesthetic intelligence organizing this profusion of life in perfect disarray, a power much greater than mine, than ours, flowing through this ever unfolding landscape with only one imperative — to create life. When I go to one of my wild places and become quiet, reflective, it is this presence that I feel, and a primal connection with it. All gods were born in such places. Our metaphors are rooted in, and arise from, nature. Surely, sanity is a wild place where we renew ourselves, our nature; and madness is an urban place of concrete and straight lines, where we see only ourselves looking back at us everywhere, masters of a lifeless universe. We need a world with two hemispheres as certainly as our brains do: one wild and natural, the other ordered and structured. Our hope is the holographic merging of wild and ordered minds in people determined to ensure both a wild and ordered future.

Few wild places create a greater sense of awe than groves of the huge ancient trees in the temperate rainforests of Vancouver Island, such as those in Clayoquot Sound. In these sacred places, the grandest trees are as much as fifteen hundred years old and spiral up as high as three hundred feet. Such forests — standing long before Captains Cook or Vancouver, long before Columbus, before the crusades, even before Charlemagne — are our ancient monuments, our cathedrals: the oldest, largest living things in our land. Once taken down, they are gone forever. What little is left is disappearing fast. Will we defend and preserve our old-growth rainforests for their spiritual, aesthetic and recreational values, as well as their environmental necessity and great commercial value, or will we once again find ourselves saying, "Gone! How did we ever let that happen?"

• • •

My childhood solitudes were shattered in my fifteenth summer when I found myself on the way to a remote logging camp in Holberg Inlet on the northwest coast of Vancouver Island, hired on as a whistle punk, a kind of signalman. Logging gave the boy a chance to become a man, taught me how to work and over the span of six years put me through school and university.

The first morning at Holberg float camp, when four-hundred-and-fifty men assembled on the wharf, everyone was mustered into a crew except me; I was forced on one crew boss — "Charlie, you take this kid!" — by his boss. For ten days no one at that site said anything to me, a lethal summer wonder, except the barest descriptions of my job, and I didn't know what to do about it. I had never seen anything so dramatic as our workplace. From the hillside we were logging we looked straight down a valley crowded with trees as far as we could see. On the hillside across from us you could hear fallers yell and watch the slow swish of those huge trees to the ground. Nearby, a highrigger was climbing a huge fir tree, trimming the branches as he went, topping it to be our next spar tree, then sitting on the top, one-hundred-and-twenty feet up, to have lunch and talk to the men below. Some logs we pulled into the pile swayed and surged forward like battering rams, ploughing and smashing everything ahead of them. Some were ten feet or more thick; the biggest enough to be a truckload by themselves.

It took twelve work days to earn enough to go home, and I couldn't wait to leave. On the twelfth day we were setting up at the new spar tree. The enormous mainline and haulback blocks were hung but needed to be threaded with pencil-thin strawline that would haul the heavy yarding cables through them and out for several hundred yards in a wide clothesline loop back to the yarding machine. Chokers hung from a steel plate that was pulled out to the bush by the haulback, and pulled back by the mainline, dragging logs into a pile around the spar tree. The hooker asked, "Who's goin' up to thread the f___ing blocks?" Everyone kept silent until I heard myself say, "I will." They sat me in a loop of chain on a thin line, handed me the strawline I was to thread through the blocks, and suddenly I was hurtling up the tree. Strawline is light to lift, but holding a hundred feet of it can tax even a strong person. I quickly spun the loose end around the line that was carrying me and clamped it with my hands, but as I did so I raced past the blocks toward the top of the tree. I tried to yell but no noise came out. I waved, but no one was looking up. I saw myself flying off into space, but two feet from the small block at the top of the tree, they stopped and then slowly lowered me in bumps to the big blocks. I put the loose end of the strawline I was carrying through the mainline block, hooked it onto my chain seat and then let go of the slack I was holding. As they lowered me down, the straw line was pulled through the blocks.

When I landed, no one said a word, but something was different. Perhaps I was supposed to be scared but not successful. We worked hard that day hauling out lines, getting ready to log, and when I walked toward the crummy at quitting time, I was so tired I didn't think I could scramble over the tailgate into a seat. Suddenly the hooker melted out of the woods beside me and, lifting me up by the back of my pants said, loud enough for the others to hear, "You're going to be okay, kid." They were the sweetest words I ever heard, and as vivid in my mind now as they were then. The twelve-day deadline completely forgotten, I worked all summer with the fifteen men on our crew. I was proud to be one of them, to feel that I knew how to do a man's work and to know that I had earned my pay. But I cannot forget the image of that once lush valley as we topped the hill on my last trip to camp before going home: as far as the eye could see, there was not a tree left standing.

• • •

No other experience better prepared me for environmental radicalization than what happened to our summer camp on Porpoise Bay, the body of water that makes a peninsula of the land from Sechelt to Earl's Cove on the Sunshine Coast. As a struggling young husband and father, I was delighted to find that the forestry branch would occasionally, for a small fee, issue special use permits for plots of land in some of its reserves. A forester gave us a tour of the plots available and we selected one on a beautiful little bay in the wilds about eight miles up Porpoise Bay from Tillicum Fish Camp. For each of the next five summers my wife, two children and I paddled our canoe to this treasured retreat and set up camp.

The sand and pebbles of our beach stretched about two hundred yards between two arms of rock that came together another two hundred yards behind the beach making a delta-like triangle of land divided by a small stream that emptied into the bay. We cleared a camp space beside the stream in the thick cover of cedars, fir, hemlock, yew and alder. From our drift-wood table we looked up Salmon Inlet to the peaks of the Tantalus mountains. The forest and ocean teemed with birds and animals. At night we often swam wrapped in the purple glow of the phosphorescent waters, then lay by the fire looking up at a sky crowded with stars and went to sleep waiting for the next meteorite to streak across the heavens. It remains a special place for all of us, and at its heart was the magical stream pouring from its cool mossy canyon and winding among the trees. If camp became a spiritual experience, our creek was at the heart of it. Years later I described it as:

A perfect disorder of waters
Spilling over stones;
Pure spirit moving in music
Under cedar boughs
To the waiting sea.

At the end of our fifth season we stopped in to discuss our permit fee for the next year with the forester. He warned us that loggers would be taking out a dozen trees about a quarter of a mile up the creekbed on our property. I stopped the logger foreman on the road and was assured that the logs would be removed with minimum damage to the site. The next year we made our first trip early to clear a space for the cabin we planned to build. As we paddled around the first arm of rock, and camp came into view, we stopped in grim and silent disbelief. Every tree on either side of our lot and right to the beach was gone; only stumps remained. A derelict yarding machine the size of a bus was dug in across the stream bed and surrounded by rusting cables. The logs coming down the canyon and across the landing had ploughed out everything to the raw rock and deposited it in a wall of broken tree trunks, boulders and other debris fifty feet deep about a hundred feet back from shore. The stream, now diverted, fanned out across the property removing a wide swath of soil and depositing tons of rock and gravel from upstream. Camp as we knew it was gone and in its place an ugly, devastated war zone. My wife and daughter cried. My daughter remembers it as one of the worst traumas and shaping experiences of her youth.

I tried to continue with our cabin plans. Late one afternoon, while I was cutting and burning, I heard a motor coming into the bay. The logger, holding his launch off the rocks with a pike pole, called out, "Sorry about the mess. My fallers got a bit out of control." He was taking his men home from work and I could see their faces laughing at me through the portholes as I stood amongst that wreckage with a double-bitted axe in my hands, furious and helpless. We complained to the forester. The logger, we were told later, was fined $50 per stump, but allowed to keep the logs. This experience became my metaphor for logging and the land. The industry has never given me a reason to change it. Last week a logger said into TV cameras, "If there is one tree left and it will put food on the table for my wife and kids, I'll cut it down." I wonder if a fisherman said the same thing about the last fish the year before they shut down our totally decimated eastern fishery? We never went back to Porpoise Bay.

• • •

In 1969, during my first class as a university professor, my students began my education in environmental issues. With a brand new doctorate in hand and filled to the very top with knowledge, I began the lecture reading from my erudite notes. They gave me a half-hour's grace and then someone said, "Maurice, what the hell are you talking about?" I put my notes aside and we began a conversation that continued through most of the course. As one young woman said, "It's hard to get excited about philosophies of education when the threat of nuclear war has convinced many of us that we likely won't live to be thirty."

I focussed quickly on the first key question in my course, "What is the most important thing to teach?" The issues that they raised surprised me. In the two decades that separated us the world and our youth had changed dramatically. Among more familiar topics, they listed such items as, nuclear holocaust, the establishment and power, global conflicts, space, technology, information and the new media, and race and gender equality. But the key issue for them was the environment.

"We are destroying our planet," they said, "and we have to do something about it." As a start, we listed all the environmental crises we could think of and soon filled every blackboard in the classroom with such items as pollution, extinct and endangered species, resource depletion, desertification, deforestation, overpopulation, urbanization, starvation and disease. The list seemed endless. What astounded the students most was that they could not find any reference to these issues in the official school curriculum or assigned textbooks. Students could spend twelve years in school and never address the state of their own planet. I was caught in no-man's-land too. I had followed Rachel Carson's heroic battle with pesticide companies and their scientists over *Silent Spring*, but I was basically un-educated about the environment and began scrambling to catch up.

We came next to the second question, "What is the best way to teach the topic you choose?" After lengthy discussion we decided that experience was more important than information and drama was more important than drill. Someone noticed that many students in the class had special performance skills, another suggested, "Let's do a production," and every-one agreed. They named their one hour call-to-action "Earthrise" after the image of the planet, seen from the Apollo spacecraft, rising blue and glow-ing from behind a desolate grey moonscape. Using film and slides, the students contrasted that stunning view of earth with the uglier close-up realities of pollution, population and environmental disaster. Two dancers began in love and joy, but that turned to anguish at the sights they saw, and ended in robotic, automated isolation. After a series of brief vignettes of human indifference to planetary degradation, the actors faced a decision between taking action or facing an atomic explosion that filled all the screens in the room. "Earthrise or earthfall?" they asked; "It depends on you."

Working with these students was an education; they taught me well. Five years later, asking myself the first curriculum question, I decided that the most important things to teach next were their environmental ideals. In partnership with an elementary school principal and friend, the late Andy Neuman, I launched World Citizens for a Global Generation, which promoted programmes designed to teach students to be responsible citi-zens of planet earth, loving members in the family of humankind, respon-sible stewards of the environment, practitioners of the peaceful resolution of conflict and organizers determined to plan the future rather than let it happen by chance, for better or for worse. The main principle is that re-sponsible citizens take informed action. Students choose their issues, study them from all sides and then decide what action they will take. Some of the Clayoquot participants could be graduates of a World Citizen's programme. I would be very proud if some were. Democracies survive only as long as there are people determined to preserve them; natural environments endure only as long as there are people prepared to nurture and defend them.

• • •

During a holiday with the family on Saltspring Island, when I was about forty years old, I stumbled upon a new career which changed my relationship to trees and timber completely. With a reputation as a kid who was "bright enough but no good with his hands," I was unprepared for what happened when I went to the beach to supervise my small children at play in the water, picked up a piece of driftwood, unclasped my pocketknife and absentmindedly began to whittle. The cedar released a pungent perfume as I cut; the grain patterns changed as each shaving curled and fell away. Soon I noticed the shape of a woman's body emerging and began consciously to complete the vision that I saw. As an acknowledged klutz, I was surprised at the quality of what I had done, and when I set it up on the deck table, so were others.

Afterwards, I started reading books on carving and sculpture, purchased a few carving tools and then began collecting carvable woods. Many different people became my informal teachers over the years, including a pair of Makonde carvers in Dar es Salaam, Tanzania, a furniture carver in Chiang Mai, Thailand, a master carver in Mas, Bali, and a craftsman from Sydney, Australia. The ebony, which was so plentiful in East Africa when I was there in 1972, was logged out for fast profit; the teak of Thailand, once thought inexhaustible, has almost all been shipped abroad as logs; the many beautiful eucalyptus timbers I carved for an exhibition in Australia were rare then and only recently became regulated; and the Balinese are now reduced to carving woods they would have thought beneath them, perhaps unholy, to carve before. As the demand for wood increases, availability decreases, and the value skyrockets, placing even greater pressure on disappearing timber resources everywhere.

No wood sculptor in British Columbia can carve without being influenced by the work of West Coast Native artists, their spiritual relationship with trees and their peoples' history of utilization of all that the red cedar can provide. Like the carvers of totems and masks, I draw my imagery from nature, from the shapes of bark, snags, roots and rot. One of my early exhibitions was a series of kings, studies in power, all derived from forest images: one king was tormented by the roots of his own treachery, another rotted from corruption, a third was hollow as a burnt-out snag in his emptiness and a fourth was wise with forest light shining through him.

Carving, for me, is a meditation fed by journal sketches of observations and sculptural ideas. The mind struggles until a vision forms, and with it, the desire to see that vision made real. Then with the right wood and sharpened tools, the rough shaping begins. As the image appears, the vision shifts; the piece takes on a life of its own. Concentrating with greater and greater intensity, slipping deeper into total absorption, the cutter in my hand appearing to move on its own, I seem to become one with the wood, out of myself, beyond the shop, the house and even time. As native carvers were reported to do, I ask the spirit of the wood to let me in, to share its power with me. The next piece is never certain in art. I can only hope that the wood will.

Artists put themselves into the timber and try to shape the spirit of it as beautifully as possible. With such devotion to wood and such intensity of interaction with it, I am especially distressed that we still allow whole logs and cants — logs trimmed square to class them as lumber — to be shipped abroad unworked, and with them, the jobs and increased value that making products from them will provide. One of our oldest, most beautiful woods, yellow cedar, is rare and only grows in the Pacific Northwest. This incredible close-grained ancient timber, which fills any workshop with its incense and comes up in carving like ivory, is so highly regarded by some countries it is sliced into the thinnest veneer and used to finish other products. We are, to those countries, their East Africa, their Thailand. It's one tragedy to lose such magnificent old-growth, a second tragedy to see it sold cheap, one-time only, for quick profit. And a third to see all the special industries, skilled jobs and long-term profits go with them. The spirits of such trees as our yellow cedars are mute; we must speak for them ...

IT MAY BE LAW, BUT IS IT JUSTICE?

After our arrest, the Clayoquot experience shifted location from the woods to the courtroom. What began as a confrontation with a logging company removing old-growth rainforest ended up as a confrontation with the Supreme Court of British Columbia over our violation of its injunction. That confrontation became critical when we were informed that the charge against us had been raised from civil to criminal contempt. If we were found guilty we faced fines, jail, community service and the possibility of a criminal record. With a criminal record we would be unable to travel to most countries, and that meant that Margot and I would be unable to visit our office in the United States or to keep business engagements abroad, including several already arranged for the coming year. Discussions with other protesters at our arraignment in court and with lawyers who were volunteering their services increased our concern. No promising line of defense was emerging. When Judge Bouck's horrendous sentences for the first group of protesters were announced — forty-five days in jail and fines up to $1500 — our concern turned to panic. We began looking for a lawyer.

When we explained our situation and our reasons, the first lawyer we consulted said, "You don't seem to understand; the business of the court is law, not justice. There is only one issue here; whether or not you disobeyed a court injunction — a law — against interfering with MacMillan Bloedel's logging operations in Clayoquot Sound. The police and the company both have you on videotape, and you were both on the evening news. If you were there-and you were-you are guilty of civil contempt; if you flagrantly attracted public attention to your acts — and you did — it's criminal contempt."

We were beginning to feel hopeless. "What can we do?" we asked. "Your defence," he replied, "is either to attack the law itself, or plead guilty and get off with the lightest sentence possible. Challenging the law would cost a great deal of money, and the result would still be in doubt. I think we should argue for a light sentence, take as little of the court's time as possible and get this over with." What would that mean? "First we will plead guilty and present as many character references as possible to show that you are otherwise upstanding citizens. Then we will claim that you were confused and didn't realize what you were doing, that you never intended to show contempt for the law. You will take the stand and apologize to the court for your contemptuous acts and promise that you will never do such a thing again. It is really the only plea that will help you."

But what about the reason we were there, the preservation of the old-growth forests in Clayoquot Sound? "That is your motive," the lawyer told us; "the reason you went to Kennedy River Bridge. The court is only interested in your intent, what your acts were implicitly intended to ac-complish. Because you flagrantly attracted attention to your contempt for the law, you must be punished to preserve order and prevent chaos. The trees, the environment, the fights of native people, logging practices like clearcutting, shipping unworked logs abroad may all be important issues, but the court will say that they have nothing to do with these charges and this case." Although our consultant did not end up defending us, he proved to be absolutely right about the court's point of view.

Margot and I pleaded guilty — we were, according to the court — and although we neither apologized nor assured the court we would not do such things again, we could say truthfully that we did not act to show contempt for the court. I must admit, however, that, as we experienced the court in action against us, our contempt for its proceedings steadily deepened. We are not lawyers, we cannot argue the law; but as thoughtful citizens, we can argue whether or not we felt unjustly treated.

My first concern was that the court seemed grimly determined to make criminals out of people who were not criminals at all, for deeds that are difficult to characterize as crimes. These people — mostly young people representing many walks of life, most if not all, without any previous record of trouble with the law — went to Clayoquot at their own expense and endured considerable discomfort living on the land, some of them for several summers, for the single purpose of drawing public attention to the massive logging of old-growth rainforests in Clayoquot Sound. Their camp was run in an orderly way and their protest was conducted according to rigorous rules. No intimidation or attack was ever conducted against any person associated with the logging operations; no property was ever damaged or destroyed as part of the protest; no damage to the environment was allowed or any mess or litter left behind. We stayed overnight at the bridge and the next morning where one thousand people had been milling the day before, we could find no trace, not even a cigarette butt. While logging was delayed on a number of occasions, it was never halted, and when anyone was arrested they went with the police without resisting. Above all, not one protester was there for personal gain; no one stood to profit from his or her actions in any way. The outcome they sought was a benefit for the province at large and for future generations.

These are the strangest criminals I have ever met, committing a crime so strange it is difficult to distinguish from an act of citizenship or public service. The government's subsequent attention to Clayoquot and logging proves that the protesters had an important point to make. Why did the authorities not establish a dialogue rather than criminalize worthy young people for attempting to contribute?

Faced with criminalizing non-criminals, the court understandably practised law in a cave, focussed on its own arcane ground without any reference to the world outside or to the critical issues involved. The legal options open to the defendants were severely limited. Applications for a jury trial and requests to call expert witnesses were routinely denied. All arguments based on the peoples' rights protected by the Canadian constitution, all arguments based on precedents in law and in protest, and all arguments based on local and global forest and environmental issues were denied, along with all appeals lodged in a higher B.C. court. It is difficult to feel justice at work in a court of such foregone conclusions. The only issue the court would consider was the insult to its injunction, proven with an interesting update on the Star Chamber, namely, "We turn on the VCR: if your face appears, you are guilty; if it doesn't, you are innocent." The protest was about forestry issues of vital concern to the people of this province, but the charge was interpreted so that no forestry issue was ever considered. By restricting all debate to injunction law, the court effectively disarmed the protesters of their strong and most appropriate defense, eliminated all the significant issues and trivialized proceedings that continued for nearly a year. As a result, the courts spent hundreds of hours and millions of dollars without clarifying a single issue in the debate, except, "Don't infuriate a Supreme Court judge who has signed an injunction." Law in a cave, far from the world.

What made our situation worse was the feeling that the RCMP, MacMillan Bloedel and the Supreme Court considered it their case against us. Of course, it was the Supreme Court's injunction granted to M&B to be enacted by the RCMP, so they were the front-line triumvirate. Despite their protests to the contrary, the government and the Attorney General's office also appeared to be on the team determined to silence us. I have always believed that the law is scrupulously even-handed and dedicated to protecting the rights of the people in action against those with power and in positions of privilege. It seems that we are the people, but we were on a very steep playing field against very powerful and privileged opponents. There was never a single opportunity for us to prevail; none of us did; and we saw no effort by the courts to ensure that we ever had a glimmer of hope. There is an obscenity in so much power massed to crush citizens with so little. Democracy shudders.

Even if we grant the court its focus on injunction law, we can still argue that we were driven to act by a situation of imminent peril. It seems to me that there are situations where it is essential to violate an injunction, or at least where one can act without obedience to the law as one's first consideration. The following are extreme examples but, as analogies, show the possibility of exception. If the court issued an injunction to keep us at least two hundred yards away from a sex offender living in our community, and we violated it to stop him from forcing a young girl into his van, we would, I assume, be praised, not punished by the court. Similarly, if the public were forbidden by injunction from entering a property, but ignored it to save the children inside the house when a fire broke out, they would at least be pardoned on the grounds of imminent peril. This is exactly our case. We did not go to Clayoquot Sound with any thought about violating a court injunction, but rather because of our perception that irreplaceable old-growth is in imminent peril of destruction. Studies conducted before and since the protest confirm that the peril is real.

If we wait for police, the young girl will be gone; if we wait for firefighters, the children will be burned alive; and if we wait for legislation or an election, the old-growth in Clayoquot will be cut and shipped. Surely the issue is not, can the court prove we were naughty, but can we prove that we responded to a situation of imminent peril: the loss of threatened, irreplaceable, very valuable old-growth rainforests.

I am also convinced that these judges had no right to try us, that all decisions against us should be reversed and that the court should issue a public apology, on the grounds that accusers cannot fairly judge those they accuse because they have a predisposition to find them guilty. It is not justice when the accuser — the Supreme Court — sits in judgement of those they have accused: the Clayoquot protesters. The fair judge is not predisposed to find a defendant guilty, but weighs, like justice herself, innocence or guilt evenly in the balance and is blind to any circumstance or condition that might unfairly tip the scales. The accuser has already declared his prejudice, making him fit to prosecute guilt, but clearly unfit to fairly judge it. But that is only the beginning. These men were not accusing us of violating just any law; they were accusing us of violating a law they created themselves. They had not only a predisposition but a necessity to find the protesters guilty. They had to find us guilty to preserve their power by injunction. Think of it. Someone makes a rule, accuses you of breaking it and then is appointed to judge whether you are innocent or guilty of breaking the rule he has made and accused you of breaking. Not only that, but only by finding you guilty can your judge maintain the authority of the rules he makes. And he is angry at what you have done. If that makes you think of kangaroos, too, you won't be surprised by the final score: Supreme Court judges: 630 (at last count); Clayoquot protesters: 0.

Even the injunction law we were tried under seems shaky to me. Judge J.A. Middleton of Ontario said that, "Government by injunction is a thing abhorrent to the Law of England and of this Province." He was referring to the fact that by issuing an injunction, a judge is making law where none existed before. Laws normally emanate from legislation passed by elected representatives of the people, not by individual, politically-appointed judges. But there was no law regulating logging, only a forestry code, and no officers of the law to enforce these regulations or laws, if any existed, since foresters can hardly be expected both to work with loggers and to police them. Despite the evidence that logging companies exceeded allowable cuts, for instance, no charges were laid by foresters. Surely, "exceeding allowable cuts" is a technical way of saying stealing our trees. If anyone gets caught exceeding the allowable shopping they have paid for, they get arrested, and they don't get to keep the goods. Logging companies seriously exceed the allowable cut — apparently they are on a self-monitoring honour system — are caught, but never charged, and get to keep the stolen trees. So technically, the only law of the forests was made by the judge who signed an injunction against the protests. That judge, apparently, made no effort to study the forestry situation or to seek arguments from the protesters, but simply heard the complaint from the company and signed.

Surely it is time to take this power to make temporary legislation away from judges in cases of public dispute. They do not represent the people or follow a democratic decision-making process. Let us instead assign legislation by injunction to a legislative committee responsible to the province and its citizens. This shabby, so-called law that had to be defended at all costs is an outrage to any thoughtful person and should be an embarrassment to the judiciary. Only royalty and tyrants have the power to make arbitrary law and then stomp on the people who will not obey it. My lord, the judge, does not quite qualify.

After we had been sentenced, we returned to court in support of two colleagues from the University of British Columbia whose cases were to be heard. During the proceedings, Jessica Michalofsky's name was called. She rose and said something close to the following: "My Lord, I cannot afford a lawyer so I will defend myself." She was tall, self-assured, simply dressed and had her hair cut short. "I plead guilty to criminal contempt. I went to Clayoquot to preserve the old-growth forest. I did not go to show contempt for the law, but I'm not sorry I went either, and I cannot promise that I will never do such a thing again." The judge asked how he should sentence her. She replied, "I am a student at college and cannot afford a fine; I live in too remote a place for electronic monitoring so I will have to take a jail sentence. I would like to begin it right away because I have a job treeplanting that begins in three weeks." My wife and I were impressed by her quiet strength and clarity. The judge was in a quandary; this was no criminal, and he, like us, would be proud to have her as a daughter. "Can't you suggest any alternatives?" he asked with concern, but she couldn't and was sentenced to six days in jail with nine months probation added to deter her from further "criminal" activity.

When the country begins to devour its strong and dedicated young people, it is in great need of deep reflection, a rededication of purpose and some dramatic changes in process. Fortunately, young people like Jessica can take great pride in the significant changes their protest has already wrought in forestry practice in this province since August, 1993: a new and tougher forestry code, much stiffer fines against companies that violate logging regulations, a prohibition against exporting whole logs, increased payments from companies for logging our trees and the Vancouver Island Core Report extending the amount of protected old-growth forest. It is easy to see these developments as admissions that the protesters were right all along, and that their action drew attention to an outrage in our forests. Outrage happens and we should be both reassured and grateful that Jessica Michalofsky, and many people like her, are ready to stand up and be counted whenever it does. Jessica's trial for C-Day was on the fiftieth anniversary of D-Day.

BILL RICHARDSON (1955–)

Writer, CBC broadcaster and winner of the Stephen Leacock Award for Humour for the immensely popular book of sketches, *Bachelor Brothers' Bed and Breakfast* (1993), Bill Richardson has become a Canadian celebrity for his whimsical and wise insights into the human heart. He refers to himself as both "a victim of the muse" and "Canada's self-appointed Poet Laureate." His published works include: *Canada Customs* (1988), *Queen of All the Dustballs* (which records Friday-night laundry rituals and little-known facts about how cats stay busy when left at home alone) (1992), *Come Into My Parlour: Cautionary Verses and Instructive Tales for the New Millennium* (1994), and *Scorned and Beloved: Dead of Winter Meetings With Canadian Eccentrics* (1997). "The Forest Primeval" is the concluding essay from this last volume and in many ways sums up Richardson's desire to recognize the marginal, the eccentric and the outcast. The essay begins by mentioning someone named Clara from an earlier narrative. This unknown woman is a person whose face the speaker puzzles over in a 1928 graduation photo of the Marvel School of Cosmetology, which he found in a Vancouver antique store. At the extreme edge of the photo, and turned away from the other graduates, Clara has the look of someone who does not belong, someone who longs to escape. She travels through time and space to "The Forest Primeval" and brushes past a Lillian Alling, who sets out in 1927 to walk from New York City to Siberia. All that is known for certain "is that one day she set out walking"; then the woman disappears from history and other Canadian eccentrics begin to appear on stage — Glenn Gould hunched over his piano, Emily Carr telling her own story from *The Book of Small* and, finally, David Curnick, a teacher, writer, homosexual and lover of Robin Hood — and the "only murder victim" the author has known. Curnick's life, and death, remain as mysterious, as unknown, and miraculous as any of the other characters who populate the forest primeval. The author ends with an image from one of Emily Carr's most profound paintings — "Scorned As Timber, Beloved of the Sky" — in which the spindly, unwanted trees left behind by loggers' saws become symbols of uncompromising, "purposeful selfhood. Which is loneliness. Which is happiness. Which is communion with the sky." Bill Richardson was born in Winnipeg, but has lived in Vancouver for many years. He is currently host of "Richardson's Roundup" on CBC Radio One.

THE FOREST PRIMEVAL

This is the forest primeval; but where are the hearts...

— Longfellow, "Evangeline"

CLARA WAS NOT ALONE. In 1928, Lillian Alling — pronounced "ailing" — was likewise walking. One foot in front of the other, for 5,000 miles. Walking, walking, never balking, merrily on she rolled.

"Lillian Alling, steadfast, unfailing, where does your garden grow?" That was what the lonely telegraph linesmen demanded of her as she hiked past their cabins, through the dense British Columbia forest, as fixed on the north as any compass.

"Siberia" was her answer.

"Where are you off to, miss?" asked the police when they stopped her from travelling in the deep-snow country of the Bulkley Valley, alone in the dead of winter.

"Siberia! Let me go. Let me go. I am going to Siberia."

At the New York Public Library, they had been no less incredulous when she told them her plan.

"You want to walk where?"

The librarian was certain she had misheard, or had not been able to make out the request through the young woman's Eastern European accent. Was she Russian? Polish?

"Siberia," answered Lillian, a little too loudly. "Siberia," she whispered, and she carried every available map to the long, varnished table in the hushed reference room. She spread them out. She took out her pencil and notebook. She began to plot her route.

She left New York in the spring of 1927. What was she leaving behind? The throbbing metropolis. Her job as a maid. The usual disappointments. She never said why she turned her back on the bustle and the promise of the city, never said why she had come there in the first place. Adventure, let's suppose. Rumour. Because it was there.

"Siberia" was the answer she gave to anyone who asked as she walked west. Through Chicago, St. Paul, up to Winnipeg, and west across the prairies. Thirty miles a day she walked, in her simple brown skirt and shirt, her sensible boots. If she sang "Val-da-ree, Val-da-rah" as she walked with her knapsack on her back, no one thought to write it down. "Siberia" was Lillian Alling's constant refrain as she walked, through the foothills, over the mountains, all the way to Vancouver. Then she veered north, bearing straight for the Bering Strait. She followed the Cariboo Wagon Road, walked through Ashcroft, Hundred Mile House, 150 Mile House, Quesnel, Prince George, New Hazelton, and Hazelton. She was a thousand miles south of Dawson when she joined up with the telegraph line. Imagine the surprise of the linesmen who heard "Siberia" when she turned up at their cabin doors, thin, ragged and on fire with determination. Of course she was mad. Why else would she do such a thing? She had to be stopped, she had to be reported, at least. The police were summoned. Questions were asked.

"What do you eat?"

"Berries. Bark."

"Why do you carry that iron bar?"

"Protection."

"Against animals?"

"Against men."

"Where are you going, miss?"

"Siberia."

They took her in. For her own good, they said, they sent her back to Vancouver. She spent a couple of months in jail, serving a sentence for vagrancy. On her release, she got a kitchen job in a restaurant. Spring came, and she put on her walking boots. By mid-July 1928, she was back in Smithers. This time, she would not be deterred.

Lillian Alling followed the line, and the telegraph messages scuttled above her. Telegraph Creek, Sheslay, Nahlin, Nakina, Pike River, Atlin, Carcross, Whitehorse, Fort Selkirk. When she reached Dawson, early in October, she was wearing a different style of men's shoe on each foot. She wintered there. She got a job, slinging hash. She bought a boat and fixed it up. She waited for the thaw. Sometimes, during the twenty-two-hour nights, the northern lights would sing, and Lillian would join in the chorus. Siberia. Siberia.

In the spring of 1929, she launched her skiff and set off up the Yukon River. She was sixteen hundred miles from the Bering Sea. And that is where her story peters out. There were rumours that she was seen pushing a two-wheeled cart, somewhere near Teller, Alaska. There were rumours that she was apprehended by authorities on the other side. Nothing is known for sure, though. Some say she was homesick, inhabited by a desperate longing for her family, country, language. Some say she was driven half-mad by a love that went wrong. She offered no explanation other than Siberia. When all is said and done, the only certainty is that one day she set out walking.

For a while she had a dog, Bruno. One of the linesmen gave him to her as a guardian and gift. He was a pack dog, and she loved him, but he drank from a poisoned stream and died. It broke her heart. She had him skinned and tanned, and when last she was seen, she was carrying Bruno — who was beyond cure but nonetheless cured — with her, schlepping his pelt on her back. Lillian Alling, what was she trailing, what did she have to show? Her tattered skirt streaked with sweat and dirt and the corpse of a dog in tow. She dragged him behind her, just as St. Simeon Salus had done with his no-name dog, wandering and babbling along the streets of Emesa, sixteen hundred years before. God's dear fools. Salus and his children. All his sons, and all his daughters, all their funny little ways. Look what I found, Ma! He followed me home. Can I keep him?

July 1, 1997. Just a few hours ago, and for the last time, the Union Jack was lowered in Hong Kong. Never one to shrink from jumping on a band-wagon, I, too, have reverted to china. As recently as last year, it would have been paper plates, disposable forks and a plastic tumbler of cheap champagne. Not today, though. Not any more. I have acquired standards to which I cleave. I have an image to uphold. Middle-aged. Stodgy. Conservative. Establishment. I have worked hard for this, and I have no intention of throwing it away. Do without china? Unthinkable. Why, if someone should saunter through this meadow and see me eating my Canada Day/St. Simeon Salus picnic from something ersatz like, say, Chinette, I don't know what I'd do. Word would get out. I know it would. There'd be no point in going on.

What a varied array of delicacies I've assembled on my grandmother's Blue Mikado. What a colourful assortment of comestibles! Hummus. Dolmades. Roasted peppers: red, yellow and orange. A fragrant bread laced with olives and sun-dried tomatoes. Smoked trout. Roasted chicken (free-range) with a tasty little pepper and garlic condiment on the side. A runny Brie (French). A good Fumé Blanc (Californian). Some lemon sorbet, insulated against the warmth of the day with an ice-pack. However did privilege get such a bad name when it's this much fun? My grin is so wide you can see my gums. Which I note is "smug" spelled backwards. Which may or may not be significant. I read less into such coincidences than was once the case.

I am not absolutely alone. My shaggy old dog is with me. She lies beside me, doing her celebrated impersonation of a bath mat. She is not so very long for this world, and I have promised her that she will be spared the postmortem indignities foisted on their animals by Lillian and Simeon. She gave no outward sign of gladness at this news, though I am confident that in her heart she rejoiced. There are some cows who graze nearby, safely contained in their pasture by an electrified fence. They call to mind Emily Carr, who wrote in *The Book of Small* of how she would sing to the denizens of the cow-yard.

"When Small began to sing the old cow's nose-line shot from straight down to straight out, her chin rose into the air, her jaws rolled. The harder Small sang, the harder the cow chewed and the faster she twiddled her ears around as if stirring the song into the food to be rechewed in the cud along with her breakfast."

How grand it would have been to have had Emily here today. It would be grander still had Glenn Gould been able to come along for the ride. They were both dog fanciers, and Glenn was also known to serenade cows. He turned his back on sold-out concert halls, would not perform for an adoring and paying public, but would happily croon to a select audience on the hoof. There's a photograph of him doing just that in Peter F. Ostwald's book, *Glenn Gould: The Ecstasy and Tragedy of Genius*. It's a fuzzy-edged shot snapped by the soprano Roxolana Roslak. Glenn is perched on a rock, in a field. He wears his overcoat and familiar peaked cap while he vocalizes for some appreciative bovine fans. This was on Manitoulin Island, a place that exerted an Edenic tug on Gould. He fantasized that one day he would buy a farm there and establish a retirement home for beasts who were past their prime.

In fact, my cows — I hold them now in proprietary regard — have been getting the Gould treatment this afternoon. I have brought along a tape-deck and the soundtrack to *Thirty-two Short Films About Glenn Gould*. It contains his performances of music by Strauss, Beethoven, Sibelius, Hindemith, Prokofiev, Schoenberg, as well as several selections by J. S. Bach. Now and again you can hear his guttural, trademark "dum-dum-dumming" rumbling through. I am obliged to say that the cattle have not been visibly stirred by his lowing. Nor do they seem responsive to the quintessentially sixties sound of "Downtown." Its inclusion on an otherwise classical album is a tribute to Glenn's fondness for Petula Clark.

Downtown. Manitoulin Island. For Gould, they both held Utopian possibilities. Me, I'm a downtown kind of boy. Mine is not a voice fit for crying in the wilderness. Even to so pastoral a place as this — this meadow on the forest edge, only half an hour from the city — I bring along the trappings of urbanity. I find my peace in concrete and crowds, in fumes and noise. Not for me the forest primeval. Though I admire it in the abstract, and appreciate the important role it plays in the maintenance of the biosphere, and value it as a symbol, there is little that makes me as nervous as a thick tangle of trees. It has ever been thus. As a little child, I would listen to the story of Hansel and Gretel and squirm when they left the safety of their home, when they turned their backs on comfort and civilization and entered that dark and pathless wood. *Don't do it! So much that's bad can happen in there! You don't know what you're up against! Bears, bogs, badgers, witches! You'll get lost! Fools! Fools!* This was what I'd want to shout, to warn them, even though I knew perfectly well it would all work out fine, just fine, in the end. Similarly, the many legends of Robin Hood, and his merry men in Sherwood, made me feel more agitated than elated, and all because of the setting. I could see that it was an expedient environment for a bunch of well-intentioned outlaws, but I couldn't help but wish that they had found some other, more citified place for their redistribution-of-resources initiative. I would have been so much more comfortable, so much more willing to absorb their socialist message, had they robbed from the rich and given to the poor in Chelsea, say. Or Soho. Even downtown Nottingham would have done.

Despite this deep-rooted aversion, I experienced a twinge of sadness when I read in *The New York Times,* on April 8, 1994, an article with the headline "SHADES OF ROBIN! FOREST MAY BE SOLD." The story had to do with the hue and cry that erupted over the then Conservative government's plan to privatize the management of England's woodlands and heaths, including Sherwood Forest. Not that there was much left to manage in Sherwood. Most of the oak, birch and yew that gave shelter to Robin and company was gone. Where there was any vegetation at all, it tended to be clusters of Mediterranean pine that had been imported after the Great War. By and large, the land had been given over to settlement and industry. It made me glum to think of all the gullible and disappointed pilgrims who must surely visit Nottinghamshire every year, only to have their mind's-eye vision of this brooding, mythic shadowland dashed beyond repair. It made me glum because it reminded me of David Curnick, who will always be linked in my mind with Robin Hood, and who died on January 31, 1994. He was — is — the only murder victim I've ever known.

I cannot say I knew him well. We were peripheral to each other's lives. We met through friends of friends, would intersect at parties and on the street. For a couple of years we lived a few blocks apart and we'd bump into each other fairly regularly. These meetings always took place by chance, never by design, but they happened often enough that our acquaintance-ship became more than nodding. David was on the short side, about five feet, six inches, and puckish, the kind of person about whom you'd be tempted to use the phrase "elfin twinkle." He was bright and friendly. He had a keen sense of humour. He was articulate. By the time I met him he was in his mid-forties and had had a varied career. He'd been active as a film-maker, had written and/or produced several low-budget features. I'd never seen these, and was under the impression that they had either been held up for years in post-production limbo, or had had only a very limited release. As well, he'd done some work with the National Film Board. It wasn't lucrative, and he kept body and soul together with a half-time job teaching English at Gladstone Secondary School on Vancouver's east side. He had been there for years, and was well known throughout the school for his unconventional approach to classroom management and for the musical extravaganzas he staged every year. These were elaborate, choreo-graphed mime shows, which featured students lip-synching along with popular tunes.

David had much to recommend him, but he always made me edgy. Wary, sort of. When we had our occasional collisions, he would throw me off balance with the way he could steer the chat away from the bland pleasant-ries that are usual in such encounters into a voluble disquisition about what was new and vital in his ongoing research into the life and times of Robin Hood. There was an inevitability about the conversational drift that I found both engaging and dispiriting. With David, it was Robin Hood this, Robin Hood that, Robin Hood round the Maypole. He just loved, loved, loved Robin Hood. Ever since his childhood days in England, ever since he first saw the 1950s television series starring Richard Greene, Robin had been his governing passion. It grew with him. It followed him to Canada. He became an avid collector of films and videos and books and articles and visual representations of the Sherwood legends. It spilled over into his every undertaking. While it was lovely to see someone in whom a childhood enthusiasm had not withered, and while this youthful sprightli-ness inhabiting a middle-aged man presented a charming incongruity, I sniffed a depressing air of hopelessness about his obsession. He was always laying plans, big plans, which had Robin Hood paving David Curnick's path to the glory and recognition he had been denied, and somehow those plans never came to fruition. Of smoke there was plenty, but there was never a sign of flame in the forest.

Whenever I saw him, he would bring me up to date on the Robin Hood documentary he wanted to make but which was caught in a state of perpetual delay. He would give me the latest news about a book he planned to write. He had been talking about the damn thing for years. It was a project on a grand scale, the "definitive" examination of screen treatments of the Robin legend. It was a good idea, and as a filmmaker and self-made Sherwood Forest authority, he was ideally positioned to bring it off. To his credit, he did more than merely talk about it. He sent query letters to many publishers and received several encouraging expressions of interest. He travelled to England and interviewed some of the actors, directors and producers who had been involved with film and television presentations of the Sherwood legends. He met and maintained a friendly correspondence with Alan Wheatley, Nickolas Grace, Sidney Cole, Paul Eddington and Patricia Driscoll, among others. In 1985, he visited Bristol and landed a walk-on role as a peasant in one of the episodes of *Robin of Sherwood.*

He prepared, and prepared and prepared, but never got around to doing. He was like someone who winds and winds a jack-in-the-box that refuses to pop. David was not oblivious to the tragi-comic aspects of his quixotic tilting. There's a current of irony in the annual report he sent to his various correspondents and confederates, and in which he summarized his progress to date on the book that never was.

"August, 1990. How time flies. Eight years since I contacted most of you and told you of my plans. You'd think I was writing some kind of Decline and Fall."

"August 1991. It seemed that ten whole weeks of summer would provide me with so much time to work on 'the book.' Alas, I was wrong."

"May 1992. Well, I have to reluctantly admit that this is the 10th anniversary of my pronouncement that a book on Robin Hood in film and on television was happening. I carry on, each year inexorably moving towards … what?"

Looking back from this temporal vantage point — the feast day of St. Simeon Salus, 1997 — I see how there was something dear about all this fudging and delaying and hoping. Something sweet. But at the time, I'm afraid I dismissed David as a bit of a flake, as one of those would-be writers who was more talk than typing; who bag on endlessly about how they long to string words together but never get down to the hard slog of it.

Of course, when I heard David had been murdered, I was jolted by stupid guilt. *I once thought badly of him, and now he is dead.* As if there were some causal connection. As if fondness would have made a difference. I had not seen him for some time. He had moved from the neighbourhood, and it had been a year at least since I had spoken to or of him. At such a remove I responded to the news of his violent passing with more shock than grief. I didn't know him well enough to mourn. But of course I was curious. Murder victims are never people one knows. How could this have happened to David? He was not innocuous, exactly, but he hardly seemed a candidate for harm. How on earth? However on earth?

When I began my winter's wandering, when I undertook to write about Canadian eccentrics, I determined that Rumour would be the pillar of fire I would follow to narrative's promised land. My methodology, such as it was, was passive and reactive. I would make it known, as best I could, that I was looking for stories. I would wait for word to come. Then, I would follow up on proffered leads. In this regard, David Curnick is an aberrant inclusion in the gallery. No one mentioned his name to me. No one spoke of his qualities or nominated him for inclusion. He surfaced in my own meditations early on, and I determined that he would find a place here. In some ways, for me, he came to personify the pleasures and perils of a life abstracted from the centre. Two poles exerted their influence on his compass: the scorned and the beloved.

We admire people who give rein to their passions and obsessions, who fly in the face of convention, who have easy access to an id unmediated by a prissy, stultifying ego. We need them. You could say they have a societal utility. They shake up the old order. They remind us that our familiar priorities, whether personal or political, are arbitrary; the product of unthinking convention, and nothing more. We cherish these outsized characters because they amplify qualities we each of us possess in some small measure. And we love them because they give us stories. When all is said and done, it is stories that keep us buoyant.

On the other hand, we are suspicious of such psychic spaciousness. It makes us uneasy. It can be messy and inconvenient. We like to know that there are mavericks and rule-breakers among us, but we want them at a tidy remove. We want them across the block and down the street. We are fearful of the contact that leads to contagion. All that "in your face" passion and volubility quickly wears thin. It's like a hot wind, pleasant and novel for a short while, but shrivelling and unnerving in the long run.

I knew him only slightly, but David Curnick stirred in me a strong reaction. He muddied my waters with both fascination and aversion. The more I thought about his eccentricities — his Robin Hood obsession especially — the more I wanted to learn about his story. His fanciful life. His brutal end. I would not have been able to venture into such hard territory had I not had the co-operation of three men who knew him well and whose friendship he valued. I am indebted to Graham Peat, who was the executor of his estate, and who kindly gave me access to his files and papers; to

Dennis Pilon, who was one of David's students and who is now completing his doctoral work in political science at York University; and to Larry Killick, who was a long-time colleague at Gladstone Secondary School.

Larry, like most of the teachers at Gladstone, knew about David's all-embracing fondness for Robin Hood. David left full-time teaching in 1984, in favour of a half-time position, with the intention of devoting himself to the famous book. As well, he wanted to focus his attentions on a music business he had run for some years, a disc-jockey service, called Robin Hood Mobile Sound. The students were likewise apprised of his passion for all things Sherwood. Anyone who had Mr. C. as an English teacher soon learned that all his roads led to Nottinghamshire. He found ways of working the stories and films — especially the Richard Greene series — into his lesson plans. He justified their inclusion, when he was required to, by saying that folklore and mythology were part of the curriculum, and that the Robin stories were central to Anglo-Saxon traditions. The screen presentations, he said, enriched his students' vocabularies and were wonderful examples of tightly written narrative. And yes, there were quizzes.

Larry, like most of the teachers at Gladstone, knew that David was gay. He was discreet, but not secretive about his sexuality. He had written letters to the editor in support of gay causes. Some of his films had homoerotic themes. He belonged to an educators' gay and lesbian advocacy group. From all reports, he did not share this aspect of his life with his students, at least not in a direct way. Some may have drawn their own conclusions. Dennis Pilon recalls that there was a distinct campiness to his choice of classroom decorations, and his annual lip-synch extravaganzas held certain clues, particular drag-show references, for those who chose to find them. David had dallied with drag, had done a turn or two on stage in a club called BJ's. It was a lark, nothing more. It never became a lifestyle.

Larry was one of only a very few teachers at Gladstone who knew that David had once run a gay dating service called — no surprise here — Sherwood Forest Personal Introductions. That was in the mid-seventies. He may have matched a few true loves, but his interest was mostly in getting dates for himself. When he sold the business, he placed a running personal advertisement in a now-defunct sex-trade rag called *Star*. When that paper floundered, he transferred his allegiance to a weekly called *Buy & Sell*. He developed a niche-marketing strategy, and composed an ad that was a friendly, non-threatening come-on directed towards bisexual men, or to nominally straight fellows who might be in the mood for some experimentation. He used the usual catch phrases. First-timers welcome. Don't be shy. Give it a try. Call the Hotline. That was what he called it. The

Hotline.

"David," remembers Dennis Pilon, "was a fan of all things British, a true Anglophile. It wasn't just Robin Hood. He loved such comedy series as *Yes, Minister,* and the *Carry On* movies. He was also very keen on espionage, especially the James Bond books and films. When he set up his Hotline, he actually installed a red telephone. Over the twenty years that he ran this service he met an astonishing number of men. More than anyone would have thought possible. Some would come over once, some more often.

"David never felt he was very good at presenting himself as an attractive commodity on the meat market, so he looked for other ways to meet sex partners. Like many people who spend years longing and never achieving, he got very fixed ideas about what he found attractive. He never got into that dialectic of sex when your whole sense of attraction changes, when you discover that your partners don't have to be muscled, or hairless, or whatever. He became set in his ways. He liked big guys, muscular guys, Italianate guys. He liked them to be sort of menacing, but not very much so. He liked the illusion of rough trade but was certainly not into getting hurt or pushed around. He was severe with anyone who got out of place, and he developed a remarkable set of skills for knowing who might be trouble."

Dennis and Graham Peat and David were part of a group of friends who would meet every Sunday for brunch. Often, David would regale them with stories of the "studs" he had met over the phone and whom he subsequently entertained in his home. These tales were received with a mixture of fascination and horror. Both Dennis and Graham warned David, as did Larry Killick in whom he also confided some of his adventures, that he was treading on thin ice. He was almost fifty. He was not a paragon of athleticism. He was putting himself in harm's way. David countered that he had taken the risks into account and that he took precautions to safeguard his person. He set an alarm when his visitors arrived, so that it would go off when they left unless he disarmed it. He kept a baseball bat under his bed.

He was lucky. Once or twice he had to eject a gentleman caller who was drunk and disorderly. Otherwise, there were no problems. There were plenty of guys who wanted what he offered, and for twenty years he enjoyed an active no-fuss, no-muss, no-obligations sex life. Little wonder he felt confident. He even began covertly videotaping his encounters, concealing a camera with a wide-angle lens in a stereo stand. His brunch buddies didn't mince words when they learned of this development. They told him such a tactic was both foolish and reprehensible. Many of the men he was meeting were insecure about their sexuality. Confidence, for them, was paramount. He was betraying a trust, and he was risking terrible consequences if he should be caught. David heard these concerns, but persisted. He had no intention of ever showing the tapes he made, and he further rationalized his actions by citing reasons of security. What if he were to be robbed? The videos could help identify the thief.

"POLICE THINK VICTIM KNEW HIS MURDERER"

That was the headline in the *Province* on February 2, 1994. And the police, it turned out, were right in their surmise. His name was Darin Young. David didn't know him well, but they had met on at least three occasions. They saw each other on the night of the murder, when Darin stabbed David repeatedly, in his own home, with one of his own kitchen knives, and they had seen each other earlier in that same week. Some six or seven years had elapsed between their second meeting and their first. They got together through the Hotline. Graham Peat remembers that David told him about that first meeting. He remembers that his friend was concerned. There was something about Darin that wasn't quite right. For one thing, he seemed rather young, even though he claimed to be nineteen. David was always, by every account, scrupulous about meeting only with callers who were of legal age. He activated his trouble-sensing radar, and his instincts proved spot-on. The boy called him again, not long after their first encounter. He'd changed his story. Now he claimed to be under age. He threatened to go to the police and lay charges of molestation unless they could agree on a cash settlement. David declined to play along. Darin never followed through. He disappeared.

When he resurfaced, some years later, he was fresh out of jail. He had served time for several misdemeanours, including violent misconduct. There was no longer any question of his majority. He was older, twenty-six, and his appearance was radically different.

"TATTOOED MAN SOUGHT IN SLAYING"

That was the headline in The *Province* on February 11, 1994. Why did Darin seek David out after so troubled a parting? Had he held him in his head the whole time of his incarceration? Or did he just happen on the ad again when he was flipping through the personals section of *Buy & Sell*, and call him up for old time's sake? On such arcane points as these, no one is clear. All that is sure is that they had a reunion. David, who was always sharing of such information, told his brunch companions that Darin was back on the scene, told them that he was now tattooed from stem to stern. They warned him against having any further contact. They told him the young man was surely disturbed, that he was bound to be trouble. "But he's terribly exciting" was David's answer.

Dennis Pilon says that David would engage in fantasy play with his Hotline friends. He would construct scenarios and have his friends act them out. He would ask them to pose for him, flex their muscles, encourage them to come at him in a threatening, but not too threatening, way. When Darin Young dropped by for the last time, on January 31, 1994, he went along with the prescribed scenario until it came time to turn on his host with mock menace. Then, he abandoned any pretense of play acting.

He left the apartment with David's wallet and chequebook. By the time the neighbours came to investigate the alarm, it was too late. "It's a terrible thing to happen at your own front door," one condo owner told a reporter, and she was surely right. The papers reported that David was stabbed more than a hundred times. And all the while, the video camera was taking it in. An unblinking eye. A terrible record. His final film.

David had been right all along about the utility of such evidence. In the end, he helped capture his own killer. The police released images from the tape to the papers. Darin's picture — his long hair, his muscled chest, his many tattoos — was published all over the country. He turned himself in in Kelowna, pleaded guilty, and was once again confined. Dennis and Graham attended the sentencing.

"David," said Dennis, "was my oldest friend, one of my best friends, and I miss him all the time. When I went to that sentencing though, all I could think was that there were two victims. Two tragedies. There was David, of course. And there was Darin. Here was someone who came from a background of terrible abuse, who was in and out of foster homes, who had sustained a head injury, who never really stood a chance, who held tremendous anger, and who, on top of everything else, got stuck with this uncertainty about his own sexuality in a society that hates gay people. And now where is he? In jail. And what kind of help will he get there? And in ten years when he's out, what's going to happen?"

What one wants, of course, is closure. What one wants is what one can't have, and that is the answer to the variations on the question: why? Why would anyone stab someone a hundred times? Why would David have willingly put himself in so vulnerable a situation with so dangerous a predator? Fatalism? Thrill seeking? Or was it just misplaced trust? A bad call? That's not so unlikely. Many of us can look back on an encounter that made perfect sense in the moment, and been appalled that it ever took place; shuddered at the prospect of what might have been.

It would not have been out of character for David to have met Darin with the hope of some kind of reconciliation in mind. Each of his friends told me, independently, that David was pathologically reluctant to let go of people who had passed through his orbit, to release them, or allow them to slip from his grasp and life. He knew that he could alienate people. He was always doing battle with some imagined foe, and he was argumentative and controlling by nature. He would fight with his friends, would give or take offence. There would be a sundering, a cooling off and then a *rapprochement.* He would make overtures of friendship that were pleading, toadying almost. It was a familiar pattern. It happened time and again. He couldn't bear the weight of contempt. He wanted nothing more than acceptance. He wanted everyone to be his friend. He wanted to belong. He wanted to be part of a band of merry men.

Why did he love Robin Hood and the boys of Sherwood so much? Pick your reason. Because they were anti-authoritarian, and David felt he had been squashed by people who were in power. Because they stood up for the little guy. Because they looked great in tights. Mostly, all his friends agree, it was because they were naughty and got away with it.

David Curnick was a man who was lucky in his friends. They cared for him, watched out for him. They speak well of his accomplishments as both an artist and a teacher. They would like to see his films get wider attention. They were pleased when his family established a scholarship in his name. They want to see his memory and the several truths of his life preserved. They loved him for who and what he was. They loved him for his passion. For his naughtiness.

David was an adoring fan of Brenda Lee, Connie Francis and Petula Clark. I imagine he might have enjoyed this little outing; would have enjoyed spending an afternoon here on the edge of these brooding woods — thicker than Sherwood — with Petula reprising yet again her hit of 1964. "Downtown," she sings, and it sounds like a good idea. This picnic is done. The country is another year older. St. Simeon Salus Day is withering on the vine. Even the cattle have taken a powder. I've always wanted to be able to say I wrote till the cows came home. Now I can.

Let's call it a day. It's time. The forest primeval is no longer content to hold back its shadows. It's sending them out in our direction. Look, look. Now they come. You can hear their steady jackboot tread. Their merciless advance. I shiver and do what I always do in moments of psychic distress. I close my eyes and think of Kipling ("The Way Through the Woods"):

They shut the road through the woods
Seventy years ago.
Weather and rain have undone it again,

And now you would never know
There was once a road through the woods
Before they planted the trees.

Seventy years ago. Nineteen twenty-seven. The year Lillian Alling began her walking. The year Letitia Reed made her big decision, sat down at her desk and wrote, "To Whom It May Concern, I am interested to know more about the courses offered by the Marvel School of Cosmetology. I enclose a stamped, self-addressed envelope for your reply." Nineteen twenty-seven. The year Marius Barbeau, who would later write down the story of Alexis Le Trotteur, recommended that Emily Carr's paintings be considered as part of an exhibition of West Coast art at the National Gallery of Canada. Nineteen twenty-seven was the year the Gallery director, Eric Brown, went to Victoria to visit Emily and see her work. He was overwhelmed — as millions of us have been since — by their energy and heft and vibrancy. He was charmed by the round little woman who had seen the forest in so particular and striking a way, and who lived with her dogs and her monkey called Woo, and was funny and quick and odd, and embittered. At his request, she composed an autobiographical sketch. In 1927 she wrote:

"When I sent to an exhibition they dishonoured my work in every way, putting it behind things, under shelves, or on the ceiling. My friends begged me to go back to my old way of painting, but [as] I had tasted the joys of a bigger way it would have been impossible had I wanted to, which I did not. When ever I could afford it I went up north among the Indians and the woods and forgot all about everything in the joy of those lonely wonderful places, I decided to make as good a representative collection of those old villages and wonderful totem poles as I could, for the love of the people, and the love of the places, and the love of the art, whether anybody liked them or not I did not care a bean.

"I painted them to please myself in my own way ..."

The joys of a bigger life. Emily Carr achieved greatness before anyone had ever heard of her, but I don't suppose she could have known or imagined, as she wrote those anxious and defensive words, that her greatness was about to lead to fame. She was on the cusp of success. She would go to the east, and step into the warm light of approbation. She would feel the seductive tug of the centre. But she knew who she was, and where she belonged. She would never relinquish her claim on the margins. She would always be, in every way, eccentric.

In 1935, as though to renew those joyous, big-life vows, she painted

Scorned as Timber, Beloved of the Sky. A tall and spindly fir is all that remains in a harvested forest. It was not worth the bother of cutting, not worth dulling the saw. There was no paper in it, no lumber. They passed it over. They left it where it stood, whole and uncompromised, paying the price of purposeful selfhood. Which is loneliness. Which is happiness. Which is communion with the sky. Scorned and beloved.

The breathless hours like phantoms stole away.

There's nothing left to do but pack away our feast. See? We've devoured so much, and so much still remains. It will always be like this. We need never fear famine. We need never know want. We can eat till we are bursting and our hunger will always be intact. We will always know the joy of wanting more. Praise the holy hunger in this blessed, blessed land. Praise as well the ending of this odd and lucky road. Amen, good friends, and thanks for coming. For look, now. Look. We are home.

PERMISSIONS

Excerpts from *A Pour of Rain* by Helen Meilleur reprinted by permission of the author. *A Pour of Rain* was originally published by Sono Nis Press (Victoria, BC, 1980).

"Spark of Death" reprinted from *The Silent Call* by Hubert Evans with the permission of Elizabeth Bakewell and the author's estate. *The Silent Call* was published by Dodd, Mead and Company (New York, 1930).

Excerpts from *The Curve of Time* by M. Wylie Blanchet reprinted by permission of the publisher, Whitecap Books (Vancouver, BC).

Excerpts from *This is My Own* by Muriel Kitigawa reprinted by permission of the publisher, Talon Books (Burnaby, BC).

"Let Them Eat Sawdust" from *Measure of the Year* by Roderick Haig-Brown. Reprinted by permission of the publisher, Douglas & McIntyre (Vancouver, BC).

"Encounter with an Archangel," from *The Rejection of Politics and Other Essays*, and "Playing to the People," by George Woodcock, reprinted with the permission of Ingeborg Woodcock and the author's estate. *The Rejection of Politics and Other Essays* was originally published by New Press.

"The Pilgrimage" from *Silence is my Homeland* by Gilean Douglas reprinted with the permission of the estate of Gilean Douglas. *Silence is my Homeland* was originally published by Thomas Nelson & Sons (Don Mills, ON, 1976).

"Interview with Arthur Erickson" (1964) by Arthur Erickson and an anonymous interviewer reprinted with the permission of the author.

"My Very Good Dear Friends" from *The Only Good Indian: Essays by Canadian Indians* by Chief Dan George reprinted with the permission of Leonard George, in trust for the George family. *The Only Good Indian* was originally published by New Press.

Excerpt from *Fire in the Raven's Nest* by Norman Newton reprinted with the permission of the author. *Fire in the Raven's Nest* was originally published by New Press (1973).

Excerpts from "Maps of Dreams" and "To Quarry in Winter" from *Maps and Dreams* by Hugh Brody. Reprinted by permission of the publisher, Douglas & McIntyre (Vancouver, BC, 1981 and 1988).

BLANCHET, M. WYLIE. *The Curve of Time* (1961). Vancouver: Whitecap Books, 1990.

BOLTON, H. E. *Fray Juan Crespi: Missionary Explorer on the Pacific Coast 1769-1774* (1927). New York: AMS Press, 1971.

BOWERING, GEORGE. *Burning Water*. Don Mills, ON: General Publishing, 1980.

BRODY, HUGH. *Living Arctic: Hunters and Trappers of the Canadian North*. London: Faber, 1987.
— *Maps and Dreams*. Vancouver: Douglas and McIntyre, 1981.
— *Means of Escape: A Set of Stories*. Vancouver: Douglas and McIntyre, 1991.

CARR, EMILY. *Book of Small* (1942). Toronto: Clarke, Irwin, 1966.
— *Growing Pains* (1946). Toronto: Clarke, Irwin, 1966.
— *Hundreds and Thousands*. Toronto: Clarke, Irwin, 1966.
— *Klee Wyck* (1941). Toronto: Clarke, Irwin, 1967.

CHONG, DENISE. *The Concubine's Children*. Toronto: Viking, 1994.

COOK, JAMES. *A Voyage to the Pacific Ocean ... 1776-80*. London: W. and A. Straham, 1784.

CREY, ERNIE and Suzanne Fournier. *Stolen From our Embrace: The Abduction of First Nations Children and the Restoration of Aboriginal Communities*. Vancouver: Douglas and McIntyre, 1997.

CZAJKOWSKI, CHRIS. *Cabin at Singing River: Building a Home in the Wilderness*. Camden East, ON: Camden House, 1991.

DOUGLAS, GILEAN. *The Protected Place*. Sidney, BC: Gray's Publishing, 1979.
— *River for My Sidewalk*. Published under the pseudonym "Grant Madison." Toronto: J. M. Dent & Sons, 1953.
— *Silence is My Homeland*. Harrisburg, PA: Stackpole Books, 1978.

EVANS, HUBERT. *Mist on the River* (1954). Toronto: McClelland and Stewart, 1973.
— *The Silent Call*. New York: Dodd, Mead, 1930.

ERICKSON, ARTHUR. "Building Community." An interview by Jay Currie and

Michèle Denis. Vancouver: Two Chairs Publishers, 1999.

FISH, GORDON. *Dreams of Freedom.* Victoria: Provincial Archives Sound Heritage, c. 1982.

FRASER, SIMON. *Journals and Letters*, ed. W. K. Lamb. Toronto: Macmillan, 1960.

GAYTON, DON. *Landscapes of the Interior: A Re-exploration of Nature and the Human Spirit.* Gabriola Island, BC: New Society Publishers, 1996.

GEORGE, DAN. *My Heart Soars* (with drawings by H. Hirnschall). Toronto: Clarke, Irwin, 1974.
— *My Spirit Soars* (with drawings by H. Hirnschall). Surrey, BC: Hancock House, 1982.
— *You Call Me Chief* (with Hilda Mortimer). Toronto: Doubleday, 1981.
— "My Very Good Dear Friends …" from *The Only Good Indian: Essays by Canadian Indians.* ed. Waubegeship. Toronto: New Press, 1970.

GIBBONS, MAURICE. "The Clayoquot Papers" from *Clayquot and Dissent*, ed. Ronald Hatch. Vancouver: Ronsdale Press, 1994.

GLAVIN, TERRY. *Dead Reckoning: Confronting the Crisis in Pacific Fisheries.* Vancouver: Greystone Books, 1996.
— *A Death Feast in Dimlhamid.* Vancouver: New Star Books, 1990.
— *A Ghost in the Water.* Vancouver: New Star Books, 1994
— *A Voice Great Within Us* (with Charles Lillard). Vancouver: New Star Books, 1998.
— *This Ragged Place: Travels Across the Landscape.* Vancouver: New Star Books, 1996.

HAIG-BROWN, RODERICK. *Measure of the Year.* Toronto: Collins, 1950.
— *A Primer of Fly-Fishing.* New York: Morrow, 1964
— *A River Never Sleeps.* New York: Morrow, 1946.
— *Saltwater Summer.* Toronto: Collins, 1964.
— *Timber: A Novel of Pacific Coast Loggers.* New York: Morrow, 1942.

HUME, MARK. *River of the Angry Moon: Seasons on the Bella Coola.* Vancouver: Greystone Books, 1998.
— *The Run of the River.* Vancouver: New Star Books, 1992.

IGLAUER, EDITH. *Fishing with John.* Madeira Park, BC: Harbour, 1984.

JEWITT, JOHN. *The Adventures and Sufferings of John R. Jewitt.* Annotated and Illustrated by Hilary Stewart. Vancouver: Douglas and McIntyre, 1987. (Also published as *White Slaves of the Nootka.* Surrey, B.C.: Heritage House, 1987.)

KAIN, CONRAD. *Where the Clouds Can Go,* ed. with additional chapters by J. Monroe Thorington. (1935) New York: American Alpine Club, 1979.

KANE, PAUL. *Wanderings of an Artist Among the Indians of North America* (1859). Austin: University of Texas press, 1971.

KITIGAWA, MURIEL. *This Is My Own,* ed. Roy Miki. Vancouver: Talonbooks, 1984.

KOGAWA, JOY. *Obasan.* (1981) Markham, ON: Penguin, 1983.

MACKENZIE, ALEXANDER. *Voyages ... to the Frozen and Pacific Oceans in 1789 & 1793* (1801). Edmonton: Hurtig, 1971.

MEILLEUR, HELEN. *A Pour of Rain: Stories from a West Coast Fort.* Victoria: Sono Nis Press, 1980.

MILTON, VISCOUNT WILLIAM FITZWILLIAM AND WALTER B. CHEADLE. *North-West Passage by Land* (1866). Toronto: Coles, 1970.

MOIR, RITA. "Leave Taking" in *Event* 18, iii (Autumn 1989).

MOZINO, JOSÉ MARIANO. *Noticias de Nutka.* Seattle: University of Washington Press, 1970.

NEERING, ROSEMARY. *The Coast of British Columbia* (photographs by Bob Herger). Vancouver: Whitecap Books, 1989.
— *Down the Road: Journeys Through Small-Town British Columbia.* Vancouver: Whitecap Books, 1991.
— *In the Path of the Explorers* (with Steve Short). Vancouver: Whitecap Books, 1992.

NEWTON, NORMAN. *The Big Stuffed Hand of Friendship.* Toronto: McClelland and Stewart, 1969.
— *Fire in the Raven's Nest.* Toronto: New Press, 1973.

NICOL, ERIC. *The Clam Made a Face.* Toronto: New Press, 1972.
— *Still a Nicol.* Toronto: McGraw-Hill Ryerson, 1972.
— *Three Plays.* Vancouver: Talonbooks, 1975.

RABAN, JONATHAN. *Passage to Juneau: A Sea and its Meanings.* New York: Pantheon Books, 1999.

RICHARDSON, BILL. *Bachelor Brothers' Bed and Breakfast.* Vancouver: Douglas and McIntyre, 1993.
— *Canada Customs: Droll Recollections, Musings, and Quibbles.* Vancouver: Brighouse Publishers, 1988.
— *Scorned and Beloved: Dead of Winter Meetings with Canadian Eccentrics.* Toronto: Knopf. 1997.

ST. PIERRE, PAUL. *Boss of the Namko Drive: Story from the Cariboo.* Toronto: McGraw-Hill Ryerson, 1969.
— *Breaking Smith's Quarter Horse.* Toronto: Ryerson Press, 1967.
— *British Columbia: Our Land.* Saanichton, BC: Hancock House, 1977.
— *Chilcotin and Beyond.* Vancouver: Douglas and McIntyre, 1989.
— *Chilcotin Holiday.* Vancouver: Douglas and McIntyre, 1984.
— *Smith and Other Events: Stories of the Chilcotin.* Toronto: Doubleday, 1983.

STOUCK, DAVID and MYLER WILKINSON, ed. *West by Northwest: British Columbia Short Stories.* Victoria: Polestar, 1998.

THOMPSON, DAVID. *Travels in Western North America 1784-1812* (1916), ed. Victor G. Hopwood. Toronto: Macmillan, 1972.

VANCOUVER, GEORGE. *A Voyage of Discovery to the North Pacific Ocean, 1790-95* (1801), ed. W. Kaye Lamb. London: Haklyut Society, 1984.

WILSON, ETHEL. *Hetty Dorval* (1947). Toronto: McClelland and Stewart, 1990.

WOODCOCK, GEORGE. *Beyond the Blue Mountains: An Autobiography.* Markham,ON: Fitzhenry and Whiteside, 1987.
— *British Columbia: A History of the Province.* Vancouver: Douglas and McIntyre, 1990.
— *The Doukhobors* (with Ivan Avakumovic). London: Faber, 1968.
— *People of the Coast: The Indians of the Pacific Northwest.* Edmonton: Hurtig, 1977.
— *Ravens and Prophets* (1952). Victoria: Sono Nis Press, 1993.
— *The Rejection of Politics and Other Essays.* Toronto: New Press, 1972.

ABOUT THE EDITORS

DAVID STOUCK and MYLER WILKINSON collaborated on the highly praised *West by Northwest: British Columbia Short Stories*. David Stouck teaches in the Department of English at Simon Fraser University in Burnaby, BC. He lives in West Vancouver. Myler Wilkinson teaches Canadian Literature and Creative Writing at Selkirk College in Castlegar, BC. He lives in the West Kootenay region of BC.

BRIGHT LIGHTS FROM POLESTAR

Polestar takes pride in creating books that enrich our understanding of the world, and in introducing discriminating readers to exciting writers. These independent voices illuminate our history, stretch the imagination and engage our sympathies.

FICTION:

West by Northwest: British Columbia Short Stories
  edited by David Stouck and Myler Wilkinson
A brilliant collection of short fiction that celebrates the unique landscape and literary culture of BC. Includes stories by Bill Reid, Ethel Wilson, Emily Carr, Wayson Choy, George Bowering, Evelyn Lau, Shani Mootoo and others.
1-896095-41-0 • $18.95 CAN/$16.95 USA

Fresh Tracks: Writing the Western Landscape • edited by Pamela Banting
"A diverse gathering of over 40 writers, this is an entertaining and thoughtful exploration of how the western landscape influences all aspects of human life and creativity."   — *Quill and Quire*
1-896095-42-9 • $21.95 CDN/$18.95 USA

Pool-Hopping and Other Stories • by Anne Fleming
Shortlisted for the Governor-General's Award. Witty and engaging stories by a superb new writer. "Fleming's evenhanded, sharp-eyed and often hilarious narratives traverse the frenzied chaos of urban life with ease and precision."
— *The Georgia Straight*
1-896095-18-6 • $16.95 CAN/$13.95 USA

POETRY:

Beatrice Chancy • by George Elliott Clarke
This brilliant dramatic poem is the first literary work to treat the issue of Canadian slavery. "Clarke ... carries this story from our heads to our hearts to that gut feeling we all get when we have heard a devastating truth." — Nikki Giovanni
1-896095-94-1 • $16.95 CAN/$14.95 USA

I Knew Two Metis Women • by Gregory Scofield
Stunning in their range and honesty, these poems about Scofield's mother and aunt are a rich, multi-voice tribute to a generation of First Nations people.
0-896095-96-8 • $16.95 CAN/$14.95 USA

Inward to the Bones: Georgia O'Keeffe's Journey with Emily Carr
  by Kate Braid
In 1930, Emily Carr met Georgia O'Keeffe at an exhibition in New York. Inspired by this meeting, poet Kate Braid describes what might have happened afterwards.
1-896095-40-2 • $16.95 CAN/$13.95 USA